# 5.45-mm KALASHNIKOV ASSAULT RIFLE AK74, AKS74 AND AKS74U AND 5.45-mm LIGHT MACHINE GUN KALASHNIKOV RPK74 AND RPKS74

## MEDIUM LEVEL REPAIR MANUAL

### WITH RATE OF APPLICATION OF MATERIALS AND SPARE PARTS

ENGLISH TRANSLATION BY
MARTIN D. IVIE

ISBN: 978-0-9721-2094-4 (sc)
ISBN: 978-0-9721-2090-6 (e)

Lulu Publishing Services rev. date: 5/14/2015

MINISTRY OF DEFENSE USSR

# 5.45-mm KALASHNIKOV ASSAULT RIFLE AK74, AKS74 AND AKS74U AND 5.45-mm LIGHT MACHINE GUN KALASHNIKOV RPK74 AND RPKS74

## MEDIUM LEVEL REPAIR MANUAL

### WITH RATE OF APPLICATION OF MATERIALS AND SPARE PARTS

MOSCOW
MILITARY PUBLISHING HOUSE
1988

# MANUAL FOR MEDIUM LEVEL REPAIR

## 1. INTRODUCTION

This manual contains instructions for mid-level repairs of 5.45mm Kalashnikov assault rifle AK74 (6P20), 5.45-mm Kalashnikov assault rifle with a folding stock AKS74 (6P21), 5.45-mm Kalashnikov shortened assault rifle AKS74U (6P26), 5.45-mm Kalashnikov machine gun RPK74 (6P18), 5.45-mm machine gun Kalashnikov with a folding butt RPKS74 (6P19) and their modifications with night vision sights and is intended as basic repair documentation for the mobile repair units at the army and front levels in peacetime and in wartime.

In addition to this instruction for intermediate repairs, use the following documents:

General Guidelines on the repair of missiles and artillery (ch. 1* and 3**), Military Publishing, 1983 or General Guidelines on the standard repair of rocket, radio and artillery weapons (ch. 1* and 3**), Military Publishing, 1972;

Guide 5.45mm Kalashnikov (AK74, AKS74, AK74N, AKS74N) and 5.45 mm machine gun Kalashnikov (RPK74, RPKS74, RPK74N, RPKS74N) Military Publishing, 196;

Guide 5.45mm Kalashnikov shortened assault rifle AKS74U (AKS74UN2) Military Publishing, 1983.

This manual is used for the standard version of the 5.45-mm Kalashnikov assault rifle AK74 (6P20) with wooden (plastic) butt.

The assault rifle AKS74 (6P21) is different from the standard assault rifle AK74 with the presence of metallic folding stock.

The assault rifle AKS74U (6P26) is different from the standard assault rifle AK74 with short barrel, simplified sight, shortened stock, muzzle brake replaced with flash hider, and front sight block integral with the gas block.

---

* Hereinafter referred to as << General Guidelines>> (ch. 1).
** Same (ch. 3).

Machine guns RPK74 (6P18) and RPKS74 (6P19) differ from the assault rifle AK74 by the presence of a longer barrel, windage adjustable rear sight, bipod and a magazine capacity of 45 rounds.

Machine gun RPKS74 differs from machine gun RPK74 by the presence of a folding butt-stock.

Assault rifles AK74N1 (6P20N1) AKS74N1 (6P21N1, AKS74UN2 (6P26N2) and light machine guns RPK74N1 (6P18N1) RPKS74N1 (6P19N1) differ from conventional assault rifles and light machine guns in the presence of a mounting plate, which is used to attached a special night sight.

During the time of issue the assault rifles and light machine guns have not changed significantly.

Guidelines have been developed on the basis of the technical documentation for the assault rifles and light machine guns as of 01/01/1986.

This manual consists of 18 chapters and appendices.

The usage rates of spare parts and materials for the repair of assault rifles and light machine guns are given at the end of the Guide.

This manual has adopted the reference numbering of assembly units and parts according to the Guidelines for figures 1-5, 11, 13, 16-20, 46-50 and 65. In the figure captions to the other pictures, the sequence number and the name of the drawing assembly units and parts are denoted by their drawing symbols (numbers).

For repairing night sights refer to repair documentation for the sights. For sighting in night sights on rifles and light machine guns, refer to the operational documentation for these rifles and machine guns.*

The weapon is produced and repaired according to this Guide. All weapons for repair are subjected to a visual inspection, as specified in Section. 4.2, and are troubleshot according to the instructions of Sec. 6 -16. Checking a refurbished weapon is performed according to the instructions in Sect. 18.3.

Organizational and technical guidelines for the maintenance of weapons in military units and formations are given in Appendix 7.

Spare parts for routine maintenance are taken from the group SPTA {spare parts, tools and accessories}, as well as normal annual consumable materials for the operation of the weapon.

---

* In the future, assault rifles and machine guns are called <<weapon>>.

## 2. SAFETY INSTRUCTIONS

When you receive the weapon for repair, fault detection, disassembling, correcting problem, assembly, testing, test firing and issuance of repaired weapons; comply with the safety requirements laid down in the General Guidelines (ch. 1 and 3) and in parts of the weapon manual.

For the repair and testing of the weapon, when working on machine tools, conducting chemical processes (etching, phosphating, etc.), welding, or test firing; follow security, fire safety and industrial hygiene procedures specified in the General Guidelines (ch. 1), this Guide (Sect. 4.1) and other general documents.

## 3. INSTRUCTIONS FOR ORGANIZATION OF REPAIRS

Repaired weapons are to be in complete compliance with current rules of safety for new weapons.

Disassembly and assembly of weapons and checks of the weapons are learned according to private tutorials on the weapons and the General Guidelines, and by making regular use of tools produced by the SPTA staff, and the instruments and devices specified in Appendix 1.

In the absence of specific instructions in this manual for detection and elimination of common faults, typical actions for similar situations can be identified according to the instructions in the General Guidelines (ch. 1 and 3).

When repairing weapons one must be guided by a sequence of eliminating the causes of faults:

clean weapon and replace contaminated lubrication and greasing;

validate weapon is assembled correction and the operation of parts under the action of the springs;

remove (strip of, relieve of) at the edges any raised metal such as nicks, burrs and other metal spatter;

eliminate deformation from any thin-walled parts without heating;

check and ensure correct mating of parts by operating elements around mated parts;

restore worn parts and elements by setting additional gaskets, inserts and hard-facing;

replace worn-out and (or) unusable parts with parts from the SPTA or parts with repairs made by authorized personnel;

make categorical adjustments to (repair) parts to compensate for the wear limit of interfaces in the mechanisms (nodes).

In the absence of spare parts for the repair of weapons, reference can be made to the drawings, which are placed in Appendix 2.

Spring manufacturing can be performed according to the General Guidelines (ch. 1) and the drawings in Appendix 2 of this manual only in wartime.

Guidelines for acceptable replacement materials are given in Appendix 4.

In the manufacture of parts from drawings in Appendix 2, soften sharp edged corners and outer edges to the radius of 0.2 - 0.3 mm, and inner corners create a radius of 0.1 - 0.2 mm.

Stamps are made of carbon steel in accordance with GOST 1050-74 and GOST 1051-73; alloy per GOST 4543-71 is shown in the figures.

Types of electrodes used for arc welding and surfacing are in accordance with GOST 9467-75 and GOST 10051-75.

The drawings for manufacturing canvas bags and covers are found in Appendix 3.

Clarification, unlike newly manufactured parts and components, tools and other items in the process of repair are acceptable to be painted (tinted) instead of being phosphated as according to the General Guidelines (ch. 1).

Restoration of worn protective coatings on metal parts is performed according to the General Guidelines (ch. 1).

If the number on the bolt, bolt carrier, selector lever, top cover, gas tube, or a piece of the firing mechanism does not correspond to the weapon number marked on the receiver, gently strike out (score) the incorrect numbers and put the number of the weapon near the struck out number. In all cases, it is permitted to apply numbers using electro-etching.

This guide covers the repair of weapons with the use of spare parts from the repair kit of spare parts, as well as parts made in the repair agency, and, in time of war - from incomplete, written off (unfit) weapons.

This guide is designed for gunsmiths to use to repair of firearms.

Repairs are to be done on purpose made gunsmith benches with the air temperature of the working area not less than 16 °C.

# 4. FAULT DETECTION OF WEAPONS

## 4.1. Preparing for fault detection

Obtain a fresh caliber kit as specified in Appendix 1, and 30 training rounds.

Direct the barrel in a safe direction.

Remove the magazine and check whether it is loaded with combat or training rounds. Unload the magazine and surrender (turn in) the rounds.

Set the weapon's selector lever to ОД, take the bolt carrier back and observe the chamber of the barrel, there should not be cartridge or case present. If a cartridge or case is present try recharging {letting the bolt carrier go forward and pulling back again} to remove the cartridge from the chamber. If it is still not removed, then set the selector lever to the safe position, remove the receiver cover and the recoil mechanism from the weapon, set the selector lever to the ОД position and remove the bolt carrier with the bolt; in this case it is necessary to securely hold the weapon in hand and be sure to prevent the hammer from falling. If the cartridge (case) stays in the chamber of the barrel, use the ramrod inserted in the barrel from the muzzle to clear cartridge (case).

Clean the weapon and wipe the barrel bore dry.

## 4.2. External inspection

All of the parts must be on the weapon; there should not be looseness in the rivet and pin connections; chips, cracks and dents are unacceptable on wooden parts.

Missing parts and parts unfit for repair are to be replaced according to the instructions of Sec. 5; straighten bent parts without heating and check their function; clean and make flush raised metal nicks at the edges; restore protective coatings.

Weapons having a complex bend or crack in the receivers send for reclamation.

Weapons that require replacing the barrel, bipod, rear sight block, gas block, cleaning rod ring or front sight block send direct to reclamation.

## 4.3. List of technical items that it is recommended to check for weapon

| Tested Characteristic | Technical specifications | Location of information for troubleshooting |
|---|---|---|
| Bipod attachment | The bipod base should rotate freely on the barrel; when bipod is up the latch should hold it in the retracted position; a self-opening latch is not acceptable | Sec. 14.2 and 14.5 |
| Attachment of parts crimped, riveted and fastened with screws | Movement of the front sight block, the gas block, and/or the rear sight block on the barrel, and/or the trigger guard, barrel, fore-end, and/or pistol grip in relation to the receiver, is not acceptable | Sec. 7.7, 8.1, 8.3 and 8.15 |
| Lock assembly for the muzzle brake (flash hider) | The latch must firmly hold in place the barrel muzzle brake (flash suppressor) | Sec. 7.8 |
| Alignment of the muzzle brake (flash hider) to the bore axis | When upright barrel caliber gauge on alignment must enter freely into the barrel bore | Sec. 7.9 |
| Attachment of the upper handguard/gas tube assembly | Movement of the upper handguard on the gas tube is not permitted. Vertical movement of the rear end of the upper handguard/gas tube assembly at the lock, for weapons AK74, AKS74, RPK74 and RPKS74 not permitted; for weapon AKS74U longitudinal and transverse movement of no more than 0.5 mm is acceptable | Sec. 8.8 and 8.10 |
| Retention check for the gas tube latch when in the closed position | The latch shall be able to be rotated by hand but only with the strong resistance | Sec. 8.7 |
| Attachment of lower handguard | Horizontal and vertical rear end movement of the lower handguard of no more than 0.3 mm is acceptable | Sec. 8.14 |
| | Longitudinal travel of the lower handguard of no more than 0.5 mm is acceptable | Sec. 8.12 |
| Attachment of the receiver cover | The cover should not be able to be removed from the receiver without pressing the return spring guide protrusion | Sec. 8.5 and 8.4 |

| Tested Characteristic | Technical specifications | Location of information for troubleshooting |
|---|---|---|
| Attachment of the front sight post, the front sight base and checking their condition | Movement, screwing and unscrewing, of the front sight post with only the fingers is not acceptable | Sec. 6.1 |
| | Movement of the front sight base in the front sight block with hand pressure is unacceptable | Sec. 6.2 |
| | On the front sight base and front sight block should be score marks, which must be aligned | Sec. 6.5 |
| | Bent or nicked front sight posts are unacceptable | Sec. 6.3 and 6.4 |
| Function of rear sight | When raised by 25-30 mm (measured from the rear sight blade) and released the rear sight leaf should under the action of its spring pressure return to its starting position and the elevation slide be adjacent to at least one of the elevation indicator lines on the sight leaf | Sec. 6.8 |
| | Unrepaired side movement of the rear sight leaf (measured at the rear sight blade) of no more than 0.3 mm is acceptable | Sec. 6.6 |
| | When the elevation adjustment slide latch is pressed the slide should move smoothly along the sight leaf, when the latch is released the latch must securely hold the slide in the selected position | Sec. 6.10 and 6.11 |
| | The windage adjustment knob on the light machinegun sight should move freely in rotation and lock securely | Sec. 6.13 and 6.14 |
| | Movement play of the windage adjustable rear sight leaf along the screw of no more than 0.2 mm is acceptable | Sec. 6.12 |
| | Unrepaired side movement of the rear sight leaf for the AKS74U of no more than 0.2 mm is acceptable | Sec. 6.7 |

| Tested Characteristic | Technical specifications | Location of information for Troubleshooting |
|---|---|---|
| Attachment of buttstock | Wobble of the wooden (plastic) buttstock within the receiver is not acceptable | Sec. 11.7 |
| | Folding stock latches (rear and front) should be easily manipulated by hand and the stock moved easily into the firing (open) and transporting (folded) positions and held securely in place in these positions | Sec. 12.1, 12.2, 13.8, 13.9 and 13.11 |
| | Movement of the folding butt latched (rear and front) in the firing position of up to 4 mm is permitted, but not in the transporting position, when the stock is held securely by the hook in this position | Sec. 12.3, 12.4 and 13.10 |
| Condition of buttstock | Splits, dents and chips longer than 10 mm or deeper than 5 mm, delaminating veneer and turning (*stripped out*) screws are not acceptable | Sec. 11.1 and 11.2 |
| Function of the cleaning kit trapdoor in the buttstock | Pressed all the way in the trapdoor should return to its original position vigorously under the influence of its spring | Sec. 11.6 |
| Retention of the cleaning kit tube | When shaking the weapon without the cleaning kit spring, the cleaning kit tube shall not be displaced from the cleaning kit channel in the buttstock | Sec. 11.4 |
| Function of the magazine parts | The floor plate should fit firmly on the magazine body. The follower, when pressed all the way down must move vigorously back to its original position under the action of the spring | Sec. 15.1 and 15.2 |
| | When shaking the magazine with one cartridge loaded, the cartridge must not fall out | Sec. 15.3 |
| Attachment of magazine | The magazine must be attached to the weapon easily by hand and the latch must securely hold it against falling out | Sec.8.17 and 8.18 |

10

| Tested Characteristic | Technical specifications | Location of information for troubleshooting |
|---|---|---|
| Loading of cartridges in the chamber of the barrel. Removing the spent case from the chamber and ejecting it from the receiver | When moved to the rearmost position the bolt carrier with bolt should vigorously return to the forward position under the action of the return spring having sent a cartridge from the magazine into the chamber of the barrel. Working the bolt carrier, will empty the magazine. Chambering of cartridges should be without delay and/or jamming; verification is done with 5-10 reloads and the barrel in the vertical position. | Sec. 9.3 and 9.4 |
| | Case (cartridge) must be extracted from the chamber via the extractor, and at a meeting with ejector - vigorously ejected from the receiver | Sec. 9.6 |
| Mounting of the axis pins for the firing mechanism | Axis pins should not be able to be pushed out of the receiver by hand force | Sec. 10.11 |
| Function of the selector lever | The selector lever must be securely held in a fixed position and moved from one position to another by manual force with a noticeable resistance; overshooting the selector stop by the selector lever is not acceptable | Sec. 10.3 |
| | When you move the selector lever to the single fire (semi-automatic) position the selector must not overlap the tail of the disconnector; when you move the selector lever to the automatic fire position the selector should overlap the tail of the disconnector; when you move the selector lever to the safet position the selector should contact the rear rectangular protrusions on the trigger | Sec. 10.4 |
| Function of the auto-sear | When the bolt carrier is moved back the hammer must first engage the auto-sear, and then the disconnector | — |
| | The auto-sear trip should occur when the bolt carrier has not arrived in the full forward position by 3-6 mm | Sec. 10.8 |

11

| Tested Characteristic | Technical specifications | Location of information for Troubleshooting |
|---|---|---|
| Function of the hammer | The hammer must be securely held by the auto-sear and/or sear | Sec. 10.1 and 10.2 |
| | The hammer when released (sear and auto-sear), should vigorously go to the forward position and strike the firing pin | Sec. 10.6 |
| Function of the retarder | By pressing on the retarder it must rotate on the axis pin, and after the termination of pressing – it must return to its home position | Sec. 10.12 and 10.13 |
| Function of the trigger | When you push the bolt carrier forward and squeeze the trigger the hammer should fall | Sec. 10.6 |
| | Released trigger must return to its original position | Sec. 10.7 |
| | When the selector lever is set to the single fire position, the trigger pull for release should be 1.5-2.5 kps * | Sec. 10.5 |
| Function of the fire control group | When you set the selector lever to the safe position, being able to retract the bolt carrier and dropping of the hammer are not acceptable | — |
| | When you set the selector to the position single fire position and retract the bolt carrier the firing mechanism must become cocked; after returning the bolt carrier forward the firing mechanism should stay cocked. Verification is done by pulling and releasing the trigger. If you pull the trigger the hammer should drop. | |

* 1 kps≈9.8N {*kps= kilopond≈ 2.2lb force so this translates to 3.3-5.5lb pull*}

| Tested Characteristic | Technical specifications | Location of information for troubleshooting |
|---|---|---|
| Condition of the bore and chamber | When you set the selector lever to the automatic fire position and retract the bolt carrier the firing mechanism must become cocked on the auto-sear; after returning the bolt carrier forward while not pulling the trigger the firing mechanism should stay cocked and if done when the trigger is pulled the hammer should drop to the fired position.<br>Rounding of or breaks in rifling, entering caliber K-2 in the bore from the muzzle, rust, and dished or chipped chromium, as well as the outer surface of the metal ring around the muzzle not being convex are acceptable if they meet the requirements of a normal combat. Loose chromium, rust and case fragments in the chamber of the barrel, which cause tight extraction of spent cartridges are not acceptable | Sec. 7.1-7.5 |
| Chamber gauge K-5 | The bolt should not close on chamber gauge K-5. | Sec. 9.5 |
| Protrusion of firing pin | Should be 1.4-1.52 mm; the firing pin is to move in the channel of the bolt under its own weight. | Sec. 10.10 |
| The distance between the bottom face of the extractor and the bolt face | Should be 1.65-2 mm | Sec. 9.6 |
| The clearance between the cylinder of the gas block and the head of the gas piston | Should be no more than 0.2 mm in weapons AK74, AKS74, RPK74 and RPKS74 and in AKS74U - no more than 0.15 mm; and not less than 0.06 mm | Sec. 9.2 |
| Wobble of the gas piston in the bolt carrier | There must be no more than 6 mm in weapons AK74, AKS74, RPK74 and RPKS74 and 3mm for the AKS74U | The same |
| Condition of the bayonet knife | Bayonet shall be removable from its sheath with a noticeable resistance | Sec. 16.2 |
| | No visible cracks in the plastic parts and components are acceptable | Sec. 16.3-16.5 |

| Tested Characteristic | Technical specifications | Location of information for Troubleshooting |
|---|---|---|
| | Nicks on the blade are acceptable a maximum depth of 1 mm, blade length must be not less than 137 mm | Sec. 16.7 and 16.6 |
| Mounting bayonet knife on rifle | Bayonet latch must hold the knife on the rifle securely | Sec. 16.1 |
| Condition of accessories | Accessories must be intact | Sec. 17.1-17.4 |
| Corresponding numbers on the parts of weapon | Numbers on parts of the weapon must match the number of the weapon marked on the receiver | Sec. 3 |
| Mounting an optical sight | Optical sight must be easily mounted on the weapon and must be mounted securely on the weapon without any wobble | Sec. 6.15 and 6.16 |

## 5. REPLACEABLE CONSTITUENT PARTS OF THE WEAPONS

### 5.1. General information

This section provides instructions for replacing most of the major components of the weapons.

The procedure for replacing individual parts of weapons, which are considered repair components, is given in sec. 6-16.

In this section of the Guide, the word << new >> refers to a part or subassembly that is new, or second-hand-part that meets specifications or has not been previously on the repaired weapon.

Subsections are arranged in alphabetical order of Russian names of the item.

Appendix 5 List gives applicability and interchangeability of components of the weapons, usage of these parts for the repair of weapons; carrying out this, it is necessary to check all the relevant subsections as in some cases, when paired with new parts, worn parts fit and interchangeability do not work.

### 5.2. Replacing the recoil assembly and its parts

5.2.1. Remove (open) the top cover *14* (Fig. 1-3) from the receiver and remove the recoil assembly.

5.2.2. Disassemble the recoil assembly (Fig. 4), replace faulty pieces and assemble a new recoil assembly.

5.2.3. Check that the guide lug *1* of the recoil assembly slides freely into the groove in the rear trunnion of the receiver, if necessary; adjust the ledges of the lug.

5.2.4. Install the receiver cover on the weapon. Pull back on the bolt carrier all the way and push forward on the rear protrusion of the recoil spring guide, the recoil spring guide must move forward at least 5 mm. The weapon is assembled.

5.2.5. If movement of the recoil spring guide is less than 0.5 mm, file or hone off the lower rear of the protrusion of the return spring guide until there is free motion in the range of 0.5 to 0.9 mm.

5.2.6. Load a magazine with 10 training cartridges and insert it in the weapon.

5.2.7. Place the weapon on the bench barrel up and by pulling the bolt carrier back and releasing it, empty the magazine; any stoppages are unacceptable.

## 5.3. Replacing the muzzle brake, flash hider and retainer pin

5.3.1. Use a punch or a screwdriver to press in the retainer pin *33* (Fig. 1-3) and unscrew the muzzle brake (flash hider) *34* from the barrel.

5.3.2. To replace the retainer pin *33* or spring *29* drive out the retaining pin *28* for the retainer pin (spring), remove the retainer pin and the spring, replace the faulty pieces, reinstall the retainer pin and its spring into the weapon and reinstall the retaining pin.

5.3.3. Push in the retainer pin and release it, after the load is removed the retainer pin should vigorously return to its original position under the action of its spring. Screw the muzzle brake (flash hider) on the barrel as far as it will go, and then unscrew it to align the notch on it with retainer pin; the retainer pin must enter into the notch on the muzzle brake and securely hold the muzzle brake from screwing off or further on.

5.3.4. Re-flare the end of pin *28* and verify the retainer pin functions as specified in Sec. 5.3.3.

5.3.5. Using a punch press on the end of the retaining pin; the pin should not be displaced by hand pressure.

5.3.6. Check the vertical and horizontal movement of the muzzle brake (flash hider) on the weapon as specified in sec. 7.9.

## 5.4. Replacing the bolt and its parts

5.4.1. Perform a partial disassembly of the weapon.

5.4.2. Keep the bolt *2* (Fig. 5) in the bolt carrier *1* with the bolt's camming lug in the bolt carrier's camming groove and move the bolt all the way forward in the groove; the bolt head should extend beyond the end of the bolt carrier face by the charging handle not less than 0.5 mm and the rear face of the bolt carrier at the bolt stem channel should extend past the end of the bolt stem not less than 0.5 mm.

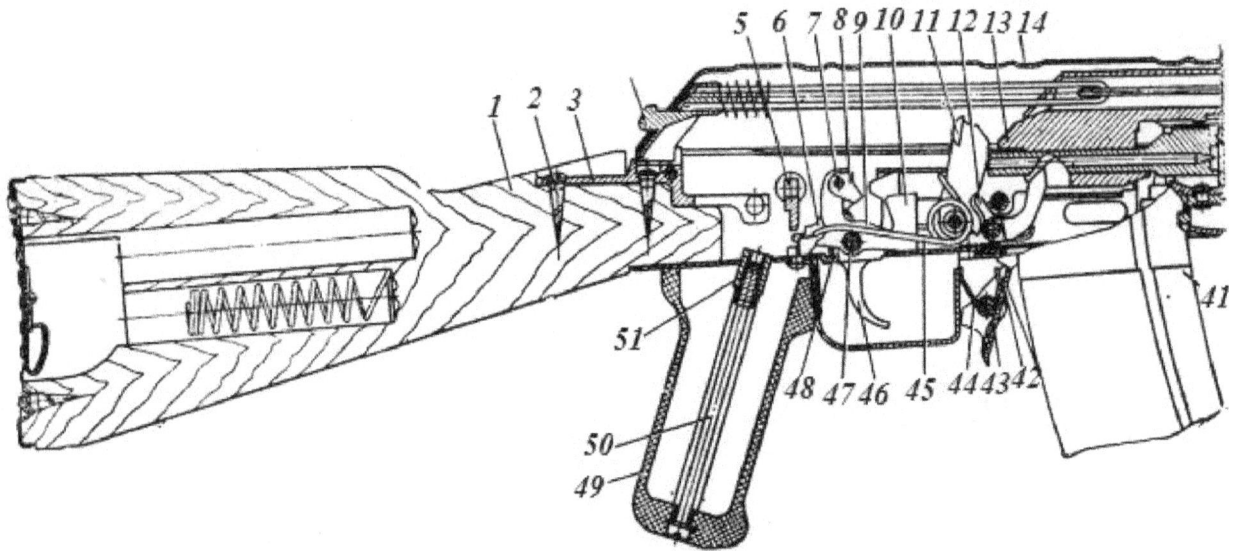

**Fig. 1.** 5.45-mm assault rifle

*1* - buttstock assembly 6P20.Sb 5 or 6P20.Sb 14;  *2* - buttstock screw 6P20.5-3;  *3* - receiver with barrel assembly 6P20.Sb 1;  *8* – retarder latch 6P20.0-7;  *9* – retarder 6P20.Sb 0-2 and retarder spring 6P20.0-28;  *10* – retarder base 6P20.0-4;  *11*- hammer cover 6P20.0-1;  *15* – rear sight leaf assembly 6P20.Sb 2;  *16* - rear sight leaf spring 6P20.0-23;  *17* – rear sight block and rear upper handguard 6P20.1 - 40;  *21* – upper handguard/gas tube assembly 6P20.Sb 1 - 2;  *22* – lower hand guard retainer latch 6P20.1-10V;  *28* - retaining pin for muzzle brake retainer 6P20.1-33;  *29* – muzzle device retainer spring 6P20.1-38;  *30* – front 6P20.1- 37;  *34* – muzzle brake 6P20.0-20;  *37*- lower handguard retainer 6P20.1-27;  *38* – lower handguard assembly 6P20.Sb 6 or 6P20.0 - 11;  *43*- magazine catch pin 6P20.1 - 13;  *44*–magazine catch spring 6P20.0 - 12;  *45* – hammer spring *50* - grip screw 6P20.0-19;  *51* - grip nut 6P20.0-16

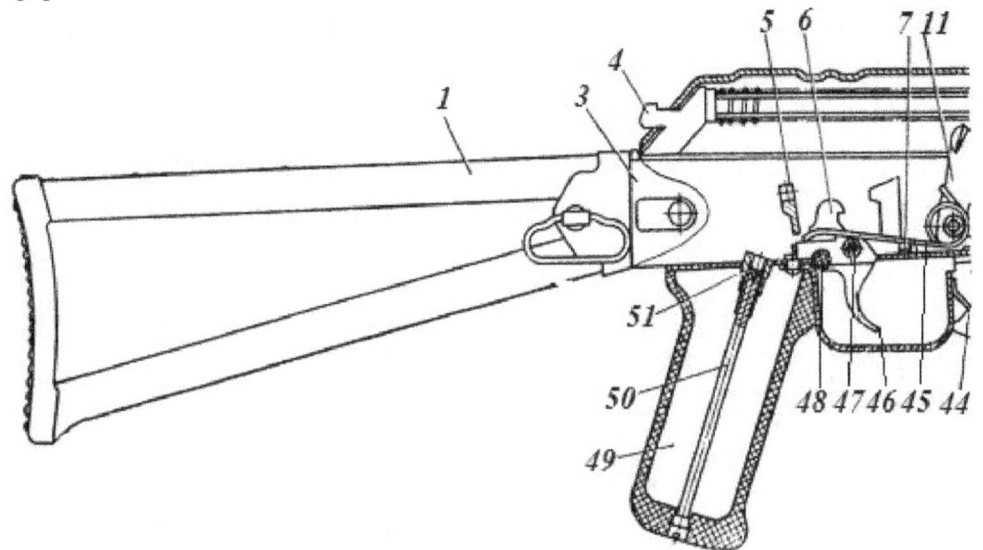

**Fig. 2.** 5.45-mm assault rifle

*1* - buttstock assembly 6P26.Sb 5;  *3* - receiver with barrel 6P26.Sb 1;  *4*– recoil assembly 6P26.Sb 4;  *5*- selector 6P20.Sb 1-3;  spring 6P20.0-6;  *13* – bolt carrier with bolt assembly 6P26S6 3;  *14* – receiver cover assembly 6P26.Sb 7;  *15* – rear sight 0 - 21;  *19* – upper handguard retainer spring 6P26.1 - 41;  *20* – upper hand guard 6P26.1- 40;  *21* – upper handguard/gas tube *28* – retaining pin muzzle device retainer 6P26.1 - 35;  *29* – flash hider retainer spring 6P26.1-38;  *30* - combination front pin 6P26.1-37;  *34* – flash hider 6P26.0-20;  *35* – gas block retaining pin 6P20.1-39;  *37*- lower handguard retainer 6P20.1 - 27;  6L20 or 6L23;  *42*- magazine catch 6P20.0 - 11;  *43* - magazine catch pin 6P20.1 -1 3;  *44* – magazine catch spring 6P20.0 - 12;  *49* – pistol grip 6P4.Sb 9;  *50* - grip screw 6P20.0-19;  *51* - grip nut 6P20.0-16

16

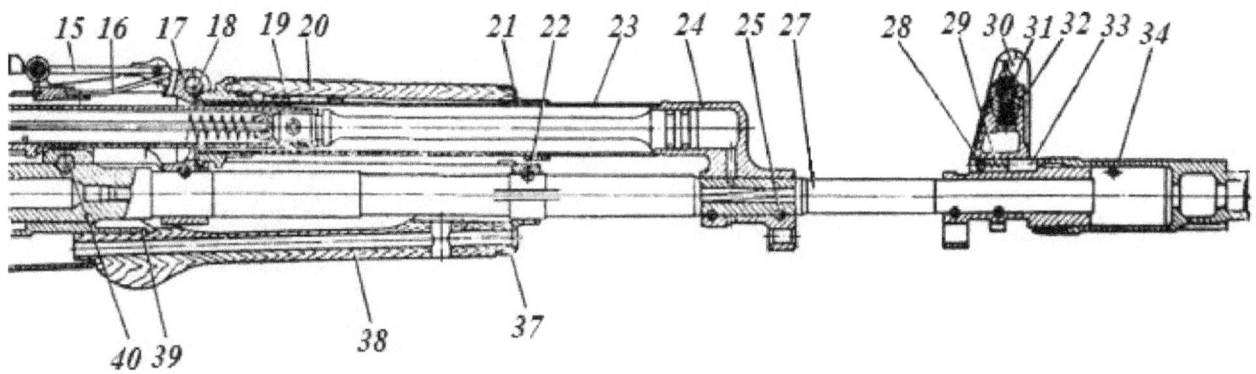

## Kalashnikov AK74 (6P20):

4– recoil assembly 6P20.Sb 4; 5- selector 6P20.Sb 1-3;6 - disconnector 6P20.0-9; 7– axis pin for retarder catch 6P20.0-17; 6P20.0 - 2; 12 - auto-sear 6P20.0 - 5 and spring 6P20.0 - 6; 13 – bolt carrier with bolt assembly 6P20S6 3; 14 - receiver mount for gas tube 6P20.Sb 1-8; 18 – gas tube latch 6P20.Sb 1-6; 19 – upper handguard retainer spring 6P20.1-41; 20 – 6P20.1-28; 23 – gas tube 6P20.Sb 1-12; 24 – gas block 6P20.1-54; 25 – gas block retaining pin 6P20.1-39; 27 – barrel sight block 6P20.1 - 30; 31 - front sight post 6P20.1 - 32; 32 – front sight base 6P20.1-31; 33 - muzzle brake retainer pin S6 9; 39 – lower handguard spring 6P20.6-4; 40 – barrel pin 6P20.1 - 52; 41 - magazine 6L20 or 6L23; 42 - magazine catch 6P20.0-3; 46-trigger 6P20.0-8; 47 –trigger axis pin 6P20.0-25; 48 – disconnector spring 6P20.0-10; 49- pistol grip 6P20.Sb 8;

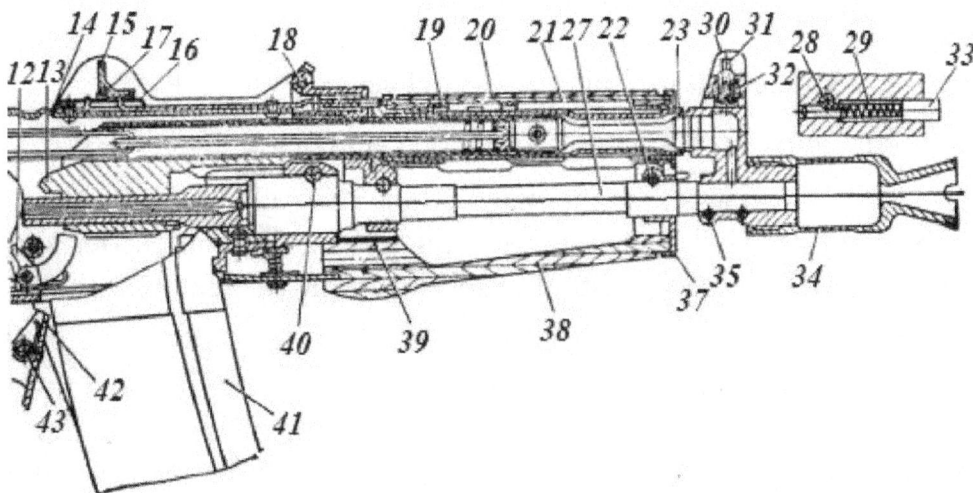

## Kalashnikov shortened (6P26):

6 - disconnector 6P20.0-9; 7 – trigger assembly spacer 6P26.0 - 39; 11 - hammer 6P20.0-2; 12 - auto-sear 6P20.0 - 5 and leaf 6P26.7-31; 16 - rear sight leaf spring 6P26.7 - 33; 17 - rear sight leaf axis pin 6P26.7-32; 18 – top cover axis pin 6P20. assembly 6P20.Sb 1-2; 22 – lower hand guard retainer latch 6P20.1-28; 23 – gas tube 6P26.Sb 1-13; 27 – barrel 6P26.1-10; sight/gas block 6P26.1 - 30; 31 – front sight post 6P26.1- 17; 32 – front sight base 6P26.1 - 31; 33 – flash hider retainer 38 – lower handguard assembly 6P26.Sb 6; 39 – lower handguard spring 6P20.6 - 4; 40–barrel pin 6P20.1-52; 41- magazine 45–hammer spring 6P20.0-3; 46 - trigger 6P20.0-8; 47 – trigger axis pin 6P20.0-25; 48 – disconnector spring 6P20.0-10;

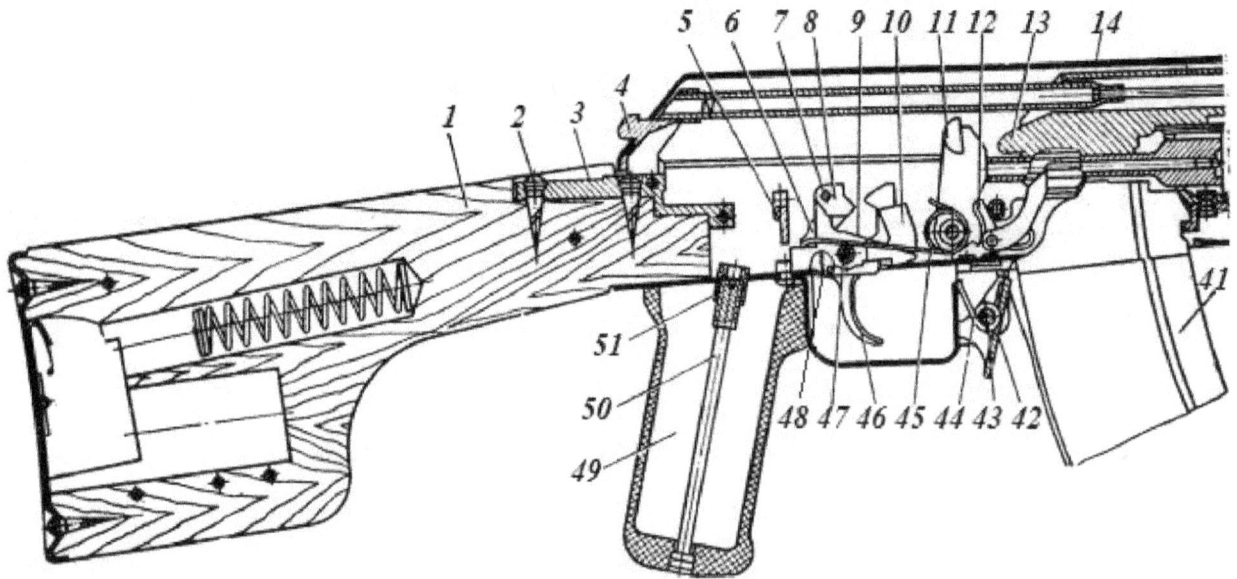

**Fig. 3.** 5.45-mm light machine gun

*1* - buttstock assembly 6P18.Sb 5; *2* - buttstock screw 6P20.5-3; *3* - receiver with barrel assembly 6P18.Sb 1; *4* – recoil ass-
*8* – retarder latch 6P20.0-7; *9* – retarder 6P20.Sb 0-2 and retarder spring 6P20.0-28; *10* – retarder base 6P20.0-4; *11* - hammer
cover 6p18.0-1; *15* – rear sight leaf assembly 6P18.Sb 2; *16* - rear sight leaf spring 6P20.0-23; *17* – rear sight block and rear
upper handguard 6P18.1 - 40; *21* – upper handguard/gas tube assembly 6P18.Sb 1 - 12; *22* – lower hand guard retainer latch
guide ring 6P18.1 - 44; *27* – barrel 6P18.1 - 10; *28* - retaining pin muzzle device retainer 6P20.1 - 39; *29* – muzzle device
*33* – flash hider retainer pin 6P18.1- 7; *34* – flash hider 6P18.1-61; *36* – bipod assembly 6P18S6 1-13; *37*- lower handguard
pin 6P18.1-15; *41* -magazine 6L18; *42* -magazine catch 6P20.0-11; *43* - magazine catch pin 6P20.1-13; *44* – magazine catch
disconnector spring 6P20.0-10; *49* - pistol grip 6P18.Sb 8; *50* - grip screw 6P20.0-19; *51* - grip nut 6P20.0-16

5.4.3. Insert the bolt carrier with the bolt in the receiver and check its movement.

The carrier with the bolt must move freely within the guide channels in the receiver.

5.4.4. Insert a magazine in the weapon, press the magazine to the right and left, check to see if there is clean movement of the bolt carrier and bolt; retract the bolt carrier and bolt, they must move over the magazine freely without rubbing on the magazine. Remove the magazine.

5.4.5. The bevel *A-B* (Fig. 6) on the left locking lug is such that rotation of the bolt at the top of the camming bevel of the feed ramp produces a gap between the chamber end of the barrel and the bolt face in the range 2 to 2.5 mm and contact of the bevel on the locking lug to camming bevel on the feed ramp has a width of not less than 1 mm.

Fit is determined by sooting the left locking lug and then checking the gap 2 - 2.5 mm using the gauge with ends of thickness 2 and 2.5 mm (Appendix 1, item 2.12), laid between the face of the chamber end of the barrel and the bolt face. When checking the gap thickness at 2.5 mm the bevel on the bolt must not touch the bevel on the feed ramp, and when checking the gap thickness at 2 mm width, they should touch as checked using

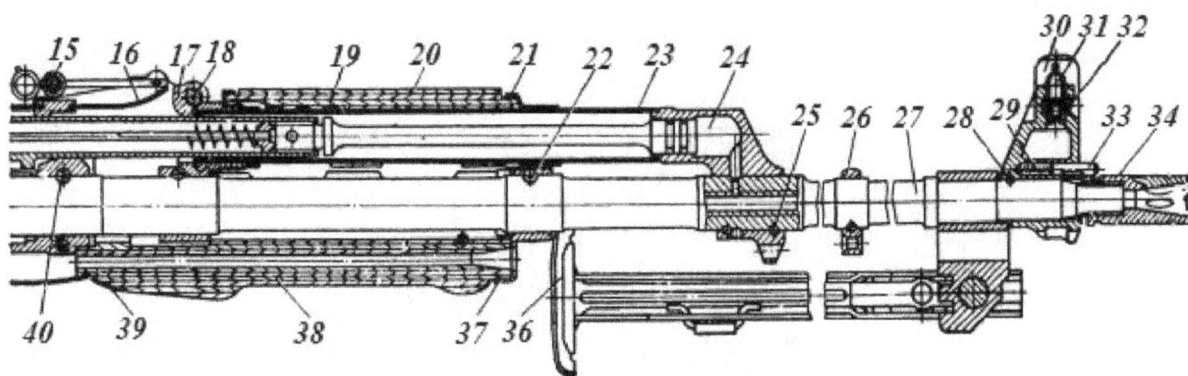

## Kalashnikov RPK74 (6P18):

embly 6P18.Sb 4; *5* - selector 6P20.Sb 1 - 3; *6* - disconnector 6P20.0 - 9; *7* – axis pin for retarder latch 6P20.0 - 17; 6P20.0 - 2; *12* - auto-sear 6P20.0-5 and spring 6P20.0 - 6; *13* – bolt carrier with bolt assembly 6P20S6 3; *14* – receiver mount for gas tube 6P18.1-21; *18* – gas tube latch 6P18.Sb 1 - 6; *19* – upper handguard retainer spring 6P18.1-41; *20* – 6P18.1-28; *23* – gas tube 6P18.Sb 1-2; *24* – gas block 6P18.1-29; *25* – gas block retaining pin 6P18.1-33; *26* – cleaning rod retainer spring 6P18.1-38; *30* - front sight block 6P18.1-30; *31*– front sight post 6P20.1-32; *32* – front sight base 6P20.1-31; retainer 6P20.1 - 27; *38* – lower handguard assembly 6P18.Sb 6; *39* – lower handguard ferrule 6P18.6 - 2; *40* – barrel spring 6P20.0 - 12; *45* – hammer spring 6P20.0 - 3; *46* - trigger 6P20.0 - 8; *47* – trigger axis pin 6P20.0 - 25; *48* –

soot (this check is made with the extractor removed).

5.4.6. Coat the surfaces of the right, ЕЖ3, and left lugs, ВГД, of the bolt (with soot) so as to check that their contact to the locking lugs of the receiver is not less than 60% of the surface area; the bolt should close on the head space gauge K-3 (Appendix 1, item 2.6) with a force of not more than 15 kg (closure is determined by the absence of a gap between the bolt carrier and the receiver/trunnion on the left side) and should not close on the head pace gauge K-4 (Appendix 1, item 2.7) with a force up to 30 kg.

5.4.7. Check for misalignment of the bolt. To do this, insert the head space gauge K-3. Close the bolt, inset the bore rod (Appendix 1, item 2.23), and instead of the muzzle brake (flash hider) screw the clamp mechanism (Appendix 1, item 2.24) on the muzzle of the barrel, and with the rod and clamp mechanism press the bolt against the receiver/trunnion locking lugs; in this case the bolt carrier should move by its own weight on the receiver guide rails.

5.4.8. If the bolt carrier does not move freely in the receiver, determine the cause and correct the skew, as described in sec. 5.4.6.

*For assault rifles AK74 and AKS74*

*For shortened assault rifle AKS74U*

*For light machine guns RPK74 and RPKS74*

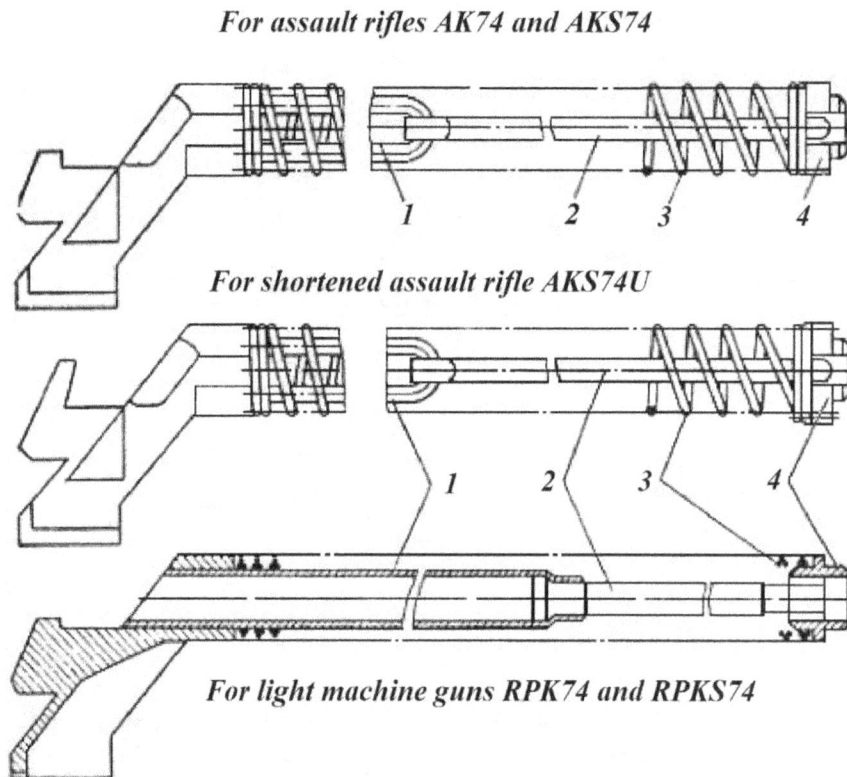

**Fig. 4.** Recoil mechanism assembly 6P20.Sb 4 for assault rifles AK74 and AKS-74. 6P26.Sb 4 for shortened assault rifle AKS74U and 6P18S6 4 for light machine guns RPK74 and RPKS74:

*1* - recoil spring guide 6P20.Sb 4-1, 6P26.Sb 4-1 and 6P18.Sb 4-1;
*2* – forward guide rod 6P20.4-5 and 6P18.4-5; *3* - recoil spring 6P30.4-3 and 6P18.4-3;
*4* – retainer 6P20.4-4, retainer rod type 6P18.4-4

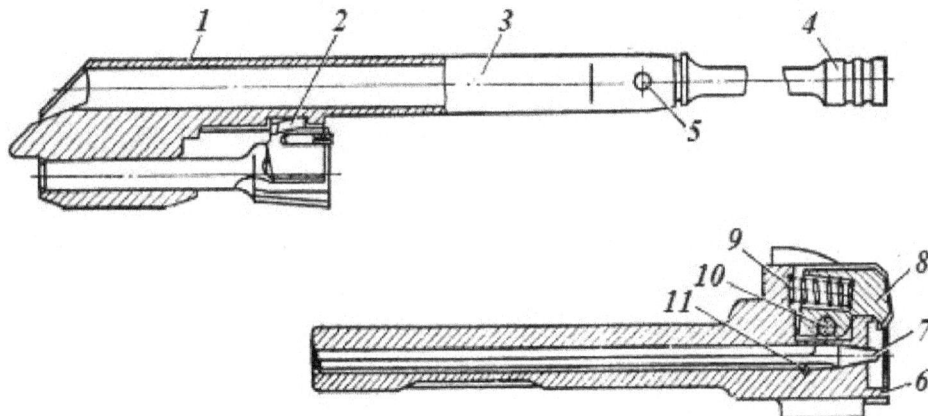

**Fig. 5.** Bolt carrier with bolt assembly 6P20.Sb 3 and 6P26.Sb 3:

*1* - bolt carrier assemblies 6P20.Sb 3-1 and 6P26.Sb 3-1; *2* - bolt assembly 6P20.Sb3-2;
*3* - bolt carriers 6P20.3-1 and 6P26.3-1: *4* – gas pistons 6P30.3-2 and 6P26.3-2; *5* – gas piston
pin 6P20.3-3; *6* – bolt body 6P20.3-4; *7* – firing pin 6P20.3-5; *8* - extractor
6P20.3-11; *9* – extractor spring 6P20.3-7; *10* - axis pin for extractor 6P20.3-10;
*11* – firing pin retaining pin 6P20.3-9

5.4.9. When adjustment is necessary for the bolt to pass between the bolt carrier guide rails and the bolt rails of the receiver, hone the sides of the bolt lugs.

5.4.10. Check (with soot), whether when the bolt is closed there is contact between the extractor *8* (Fig. 5) with the rear face of the chamber; contact is not acceptable.

5.4.11. Assemble the weapon.

5.4.12. To replace other parts of the bolt partially disassemble the weapon, remove and disassemble the bolt, replace the faulty pieces and re-assemble the bolt.

5.4.13. After replacing the firing pin *7* (Fig. 7):

5.4.13.1. Check movement of the firing pin in the bolt channel, when the bolt *6* is turned 180; the firing pin must move freely under the force of gravity.

5.4.13.2. Move the firing pin fully forward, the rear face of the firing pin must sink below the rear face of the tail section of the bolt.

5.4.13.3. Move the firing pin fully back to the rear of the bolt, the protrusion of the firing pin above the bottom plane of the bolt face recess should measure not more than 0.15 mm (dimension *A* fig. 7) or recess below not more than 0.1 mm; if the protrusion is more than 0.15 mm hone the firing pin on the surface *B* shown in fig. 7.

If there is more than 0.1 mm recess, use another firing pin.

5.4.13.4. Check firing pin protrusion using gauge K-1 (Appendix 1, item 2.4) push the firing pin fully forward and measure the protrusion of the firing pin above the bottom plane of the bolt face recess, the protrusion should be between 1.4 - 1.52 mm (measurement *Г* in Fig. 8); if the protrusion is more than 1.52 mm hone end of the firing pin on the surface *Д* on Fig. 8; when the protrusion is less than 1.4 mm,

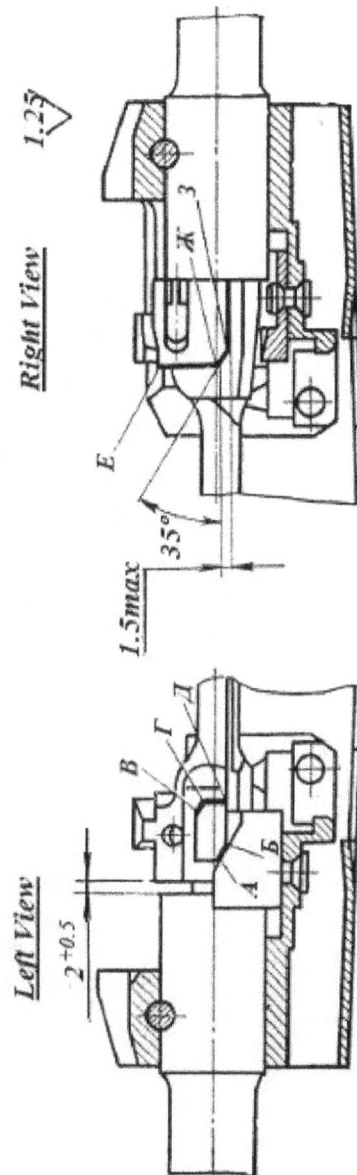

**Fig. 6.** Fit of the bullet guide and locking lugs to

use a hammer weighing 0.2 kg to slightly stretch the firing pin.

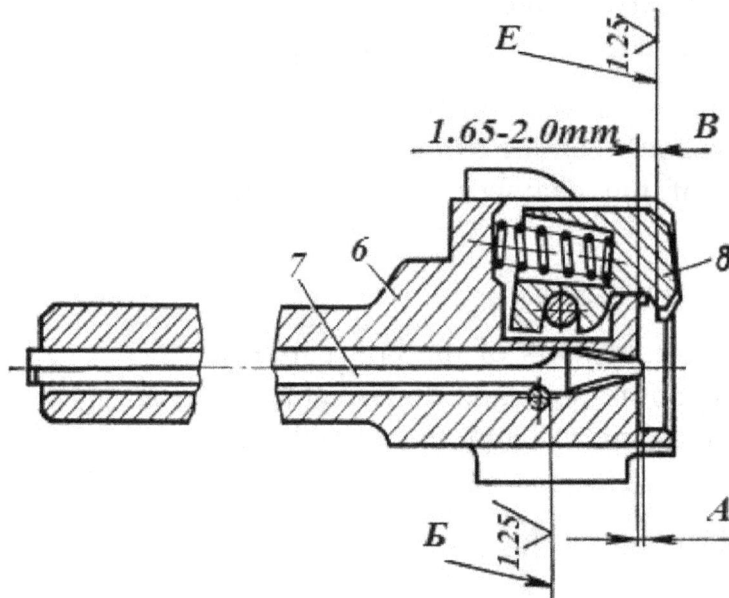

**Fig. 7.** Fit of the firing pin, bolt and extractor:

6 – bolt; 7 – firing pin; 8 - extractor

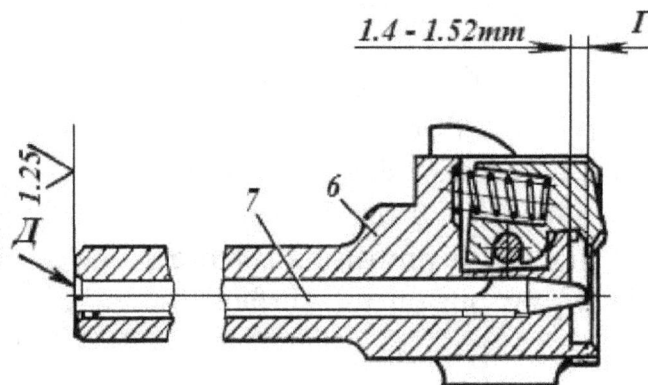

**Fig. 8.** Fit of the firing pin:

6 – bolt; 7 - firing pin

5.4.14. After replacing the extractor *8* (Fig. 5):

5.4.14.1. Press the extractor toward the center of the bolt; release the pressure and check that the extractor returns vigorously to its original position by the action of the extractor spring *9*.

5.4.14.2. Check using gauge K7 (Appendix 1, item 2.9), the distance from the bottom of the extractor hook to the bolt face, it should be 1.65 - 2 mm (dimension *B* in Fig. 7).

5.4.14.3. If the distance is less than 1.65 mm, install another extractor, or in an emergency hone the extractor hook on the surface *E* on Fig. 7; if the distance is 2 mm or more install another extractor.

5.4.14.4. Seat a training cartridge into the bolt face, under the toe of the extractor; it must be securely held by the extractor in the bolt and not fall out when the bolt is gently shook.

5.4.14.5. Insure that the extractor axis pin *10* (Fig. 5) does not extend outside of the bolt, if necessary hone it flush to the bolt.

5.4.14.6. With the weapon assembled and the bolt carrier with the bolt assembly at its most forward position, check that the bolt carrier touches the trunnion on the left; if it doesn't touch, hone the face of the extractor until it will.

5.4.14.7. Load 10 training cartridges in the magazine, insert it into the weapon and, using the action of the bolt carrier, unload the magazine; all training cartridges must be extracted from the chamber of the barrel and after hitting the ejector, vigorously ejected and expelled from the receiver.

5.4.15. After replacing the pin *11* (Fig. 5) to test the holding strength of it on the firing pin lightly strike the bolt with a wooden object and insure firing pin does not fall out of the bolt.

5.4.16. Assemble the weapon.

## 5.5. Replacing the magazine catch

5.5.1 Remove the magazine.

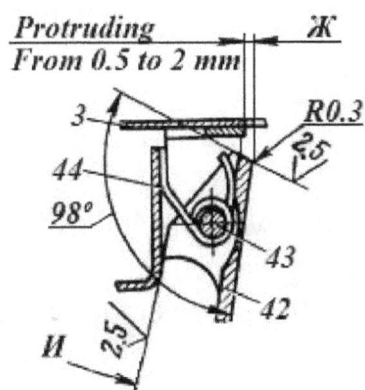

**Fig. 9.** Fit of the magazine catch:

*3* – receiver; *42* – magazine catch;
*43* – magazine catch axis pin; *44* – magazine catch spring

5.5.2. Remove the crimp from one end of the magazine catch axis pin *43* (Fig. 9), use a punch to knock out the magazine catch axis pin and separate the magazine catch *42* with the catch spring *44* from the receiver.

5.5.3. Install a new magazine catch with catch spring into the weapon with a temporary magazine catch axis pin (Appendix 1, item 2.1); if necessary, also install a new catch spring.

5.5.4. Press the tail of the magazine catch forward and let it go; the magazine catch upon release must vigorously to return to its original position and stop by the limiter (release) bracket [*on the trigger guard assembly*].

5.5.5. Check protrusion of the upper end of the magazine catch into the receiver (dimension Ж in Fig. 9), which should be 0.5 - 2 mm.

When the dimension Ж is less than 0.5 mm, hone the rear surface of the limiter projection on the magazine catch И, when the dimension Ж protrudes more than 2 mm stretch (pull, redistribute) the limiter projection without heating; insure that thickness of the limiter projection [*after stretching*] is not less than 1.2 mm.

5.5.6. Insert a magazine; the end of the magazine catch is to move toward the back stop plate of the magazine body *1* (see fig. 13) until it touches the magazine on the vertical plane of the rear wall of the body and magazine is held securely in the receiver.

5.5.7. Check movement of the magazine in relation to the magazine catch, not more than 0.5 mm is acceptable.

5.5.8. If the movement of the magazine is more than about 0.5 mm, install another magazine catch.

5.5.9. Check the installation and movement of all magazines [to *be issued with the weapon*], as described in sub-sec. 5.5.6 and 5.5.7.

5.5.10. Replace the temporary magazine catch axis pin with a standard magazine catch axis pin *43* (Fig. 9) and the flare its ends so that each end protrudes not less than 0.3 mm and the magazine catch axis pin is when pressure is applied on it with a drift. Cracks in the flared ends of the catch pin are acceptable, a piece broken out is not acceptable.

5.5.11. Check the operation of the magazine catch, as described in sub-sec. 5.5.4.

## 5.6. Replacing the receiver cover

5.6.1. Remove the receiver cover.

5.6.2. Choose a cover *14* (Fig. 1 and 3) appropriate for the weapon and fit on the receiver. If necessary, grind the front end of the receiver cover or wall cutout *аб* shelf for the receiver according to Fig. 10 so that it easily mounts on the receiver; longitudinal movement of the cover should be less than 0.5 mm.

Longitudinal movement is determined by the presence of a gap between the rear edge of the cover and the wall of the transverse groove for it in the rear trunnion when pressing the cover forward; the clearance is checked using a feeler gauge.

5.6.3. Check the clearance *K* (Fig. 10) between the cover and the receiver.

The gap may be up to 1 mm over the entire length of the cover on both sides.

5.6.4. Check that the button of the return spring guide *1* (Fig. 4) protrudes freely through the rear wall of the receiver cover.

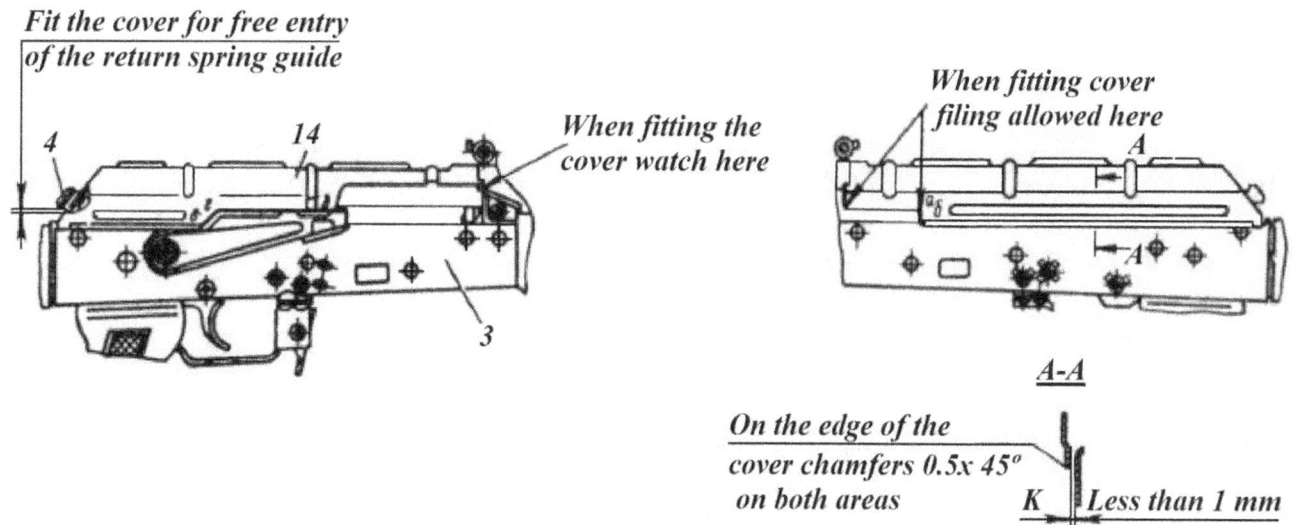

*Fit the cover for free entry of the return spring guide*

*When fitting the cover watch here*

*When fitting cover filing allowed here*

*A-A*

*On the edge of the cover chamfers 0.5x 45° on both areas*

*K* | *Less than 1 mm*

**Fig. 10.** Fit of the receiver cover for assault rifles AK74 and AKS74 and light machine guns RPK74 and RPKS74

*3* - receiver; *4* - return mechanism; *14* - receiver cover

5.6.5. If necessary file the wall so that the projecting button fits easily through the receiver cover; when the rear end of the cover is released it should not lift up out of the slot in the rear trunnion.

5.6.6. Put the selector lever in the safe position and check the contours at *вгд* of the selector lever and receiver cover as shown on fig. 10.

The contour of the selector lever must match the contour of the receiver cover.

A gap between the selector lever and the cover is permitted.

5.6.7. If the contours are not the same, file edge *вгд* of the receiver cover.

After fitting the cover, deburr the edges.

5.6.8. Check whether there is rubbing of the bolt carrier *13* (Fig. 1 and 3) on the receiver cover during movement.

Rubbing of the bolt carrier handle on the receiver cover is not acceptable. Check is carried out when the bolt carrier handle is moved up and down the cover.

5.6.9. If there is rubbing of the bolt carrier handle on edge of the cutout of the receiver cover, clean [*file*] the cover edge to eliminate the rubbing.

5.6.10. Check whether there is a longitudinal movement of the button end of the return spring guide with bolt carrier at the rearmost position; longitudinal movement must be at least 0.5 mm. If longitudinal movement is less than 0.5 mm, grind the heel of the guide to get free movement between 0.5 - 0.9 mm.

5.6.11. Assemble the weapon.

## 5.7. Replacing the receiver cover of the AKS74U

5.7.1. Perform a partial disassembly of the machine.

5.7.2. Remove using a punch the axis pin *18* (Fig. 2) of the receiver cover *14* and separate the receiver cover from the receiver, and remove the gas tube plunger pin *2* (Fig. 11) and its spring *1*.

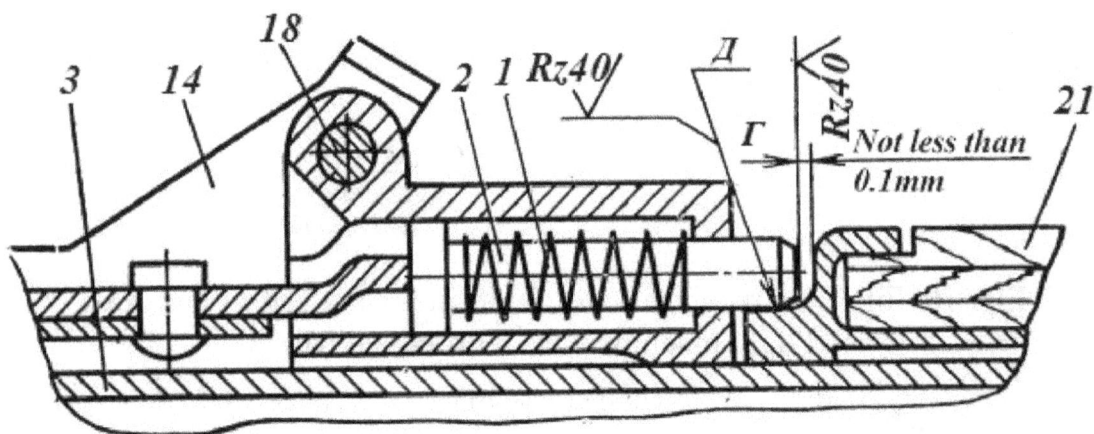

**Fig. 11.** Fit of the gas tube retainer assembly for AKS74U

*1* – gas tube retainer spring 6P26.1-22; *2* – gas tube retainer plunger 6P26.1-36; *3* - receiver 6P26.S6 1-1; *14* – receiver cover 6P26.S6 7; *18* – axis pin for cover 6P26. 0-21; *21* – gas tube with upper handguard assembly 6P26.S6 1-2

5.7.3. Select a new receiver cover, seat it firmly on the receiver and check that the gaps between it and the receiver are less than 1 mm. If necessary, adjust the receiver cover.

5.7.4. Install the gas tube retainer plunger *2* with its spring *1* in the receiver *3*.

5.7.5. With the help of a punch, press forward the retainer plunger and release, upon release it must vigorously to return to its original position by the force of the spring.

5.7.6. Install the receiver cover on the receiver block and secure it with the receiver cover axis pin or a metal rod with a diameter of 4 mm.

5.7.7. Close the receiver cover to check the clearance between the shelf of the rear trunnion and the rear face of the receiver cover (dimension *A* in Fig. 12), this gap should be not less than 0.1 mm.

5.7.8. If the gap is less than 0.1 mm, select another receiver cover. Adjustment of the rear edge of the receiver cover is acceptable.

5.7.9. With the cover closed on the receiver check the clearance between its front edge and front trunnion (dimension *Б* in Fig. 12), this gap should be no more than 1.2 mm.

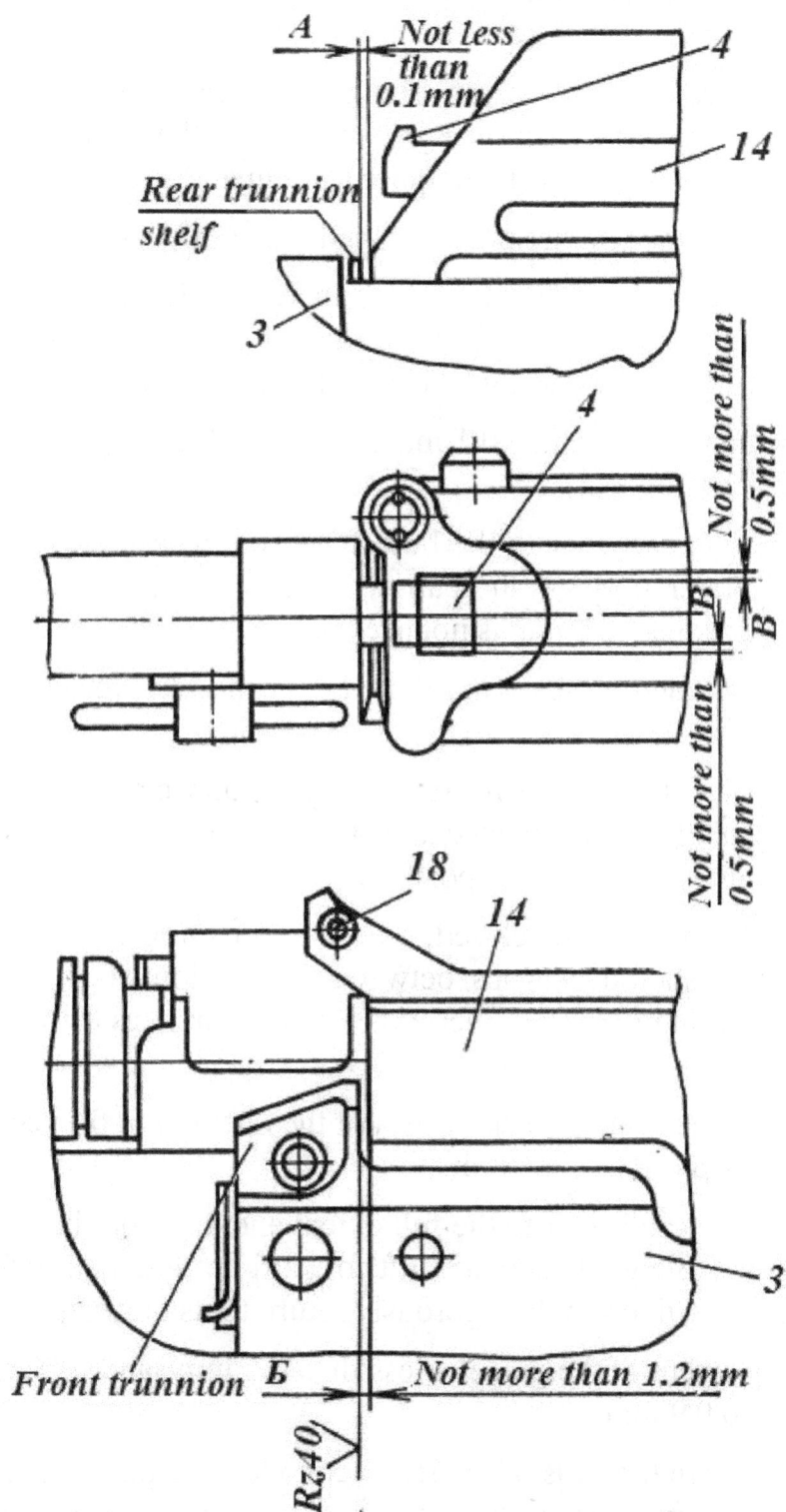

**Fig. 12**. Fit of the receiver cover for the AKS74U

*3* – receiver; *4* – recoil mechanism; *14* - receiver cover;
*18* - the axis pin of the cover

5.7.10. If the gap *Б* is more than 1.2 mm, select another receiver cover.

If there is no gap, sand the front edge of the receiver cover to obtain clearance for dimension $Б = 0.1 \ldots 0.3$ mm.

5.7.11. Open the cover of the receiver. The gas tube retainer plunger must be held in the open position by the effect of spring *1* (Fig. 11), the retainer plunger must not interfere with the removal of the gas tube/upper hand guard assembly.

5.7.12. To fit the gas tube retainer plunger, sand the gas tube on the plane $Д$ (Fig. 11).

5.7.13. Close the receiver cover; when done there should be a gap between the back surface of the rear upper hand guard bezel on the gas tube assembly, *21*, and the end of the retainer plunger (dimension $Г$ in Fig. 11) which should be not less than 0.1 mm.

5.7.14. When the gap $Г$ is less than 0.1 mm sand the front end of the retainer plunger to produce a gap of $Г = 0.15 \ldots 0.2$ mm.

5.7.15. Install the bolt carrier with the bolt. Close the receiver cover and pull the bolt carrier back, while pressing up on the carrier handle, check for rubbing of the carrier handle on the receiver cover, rubbing is not acceptable.

5.7.16. If the carrier handle rubs, sand the edge of the receiver cover to eliminate the rubbing.

5.7.17. Install the recoil mechanism *4* (see Fig. 2) and close the receiver cover; the protrusion on the rear of the recoil mechanism must enter the opening in the receiver cover and hold it securely in the closed position.

5.7.18. With the receiver cover closed, using the opening in the receiver cover rear wall as a guide, there should be gaps between the portion of the recoil spring guide protruding and the opening in the receiver cover with clearances (dimension $B$ in Fig. 12) of no more than 0.5 mm.

5.7.19. In the absence of gaps file the edges of the opening in the receiver cover in Fig. 12 until the clearances $B = 0.2 \ldots 0.4$ mm.

5.7.20. Pull the bolt carrier back to the full extent and press on the protruding button of the recoil spring guide, the guide should shift forward not less than 0.5 mm. Release the recoil spring guide, the guide should vigorously return to its original position.

5.7.21. When movement of the guide is less than 0.5 mm sand its rear end to achieve a displacement of 0.5 to 0.9 mm.

5.7.22. Crimp and flare the ends of the receiver cover axis pin. Using a punch press the end of the cover axis pin from each side, displacement of the cover axis pin by this pushing is not permitted.

Open and close the receiver cover, it must freely rotate on the cover axis pin.

5.7.23. Prepare the weapon for battle as indicated in the operation manual for the AKS74U.

## 5.8. Replacing the magazine and its parts

5.8.1. Remove the magazine from the weapon and insert a new magazine.

5.8.2. Check the connection of the magazine to the receiver.

Magazine must be securely held by the magazine catch *42* (Fig. 1-3) in the receiver, wobble of the magazine in the magazine catch no more than 0.5 mm is acceptable. Magazine should be easily removed from the receiver when the toe of the magazine catch is pressed forward.

If necessary, repair any identified faults as described in sec. 8.17.

5.8.3. Check whether the magazine rubs the auto-sear *12* (Fig. 1-3), following specification in sub-section 5.19.3.1.

5.8.4. Load 10 training cartridges in the magazine, insert in to the weapon and, using the bolt carrier, empty the magazine; any hang up is not acceptable.

5.8.5. Disassemble the magazine to replace any malfunctioning parts, remove the problem piece(s) and replace with new one(s).

After joining coils of the magazine spring *5* (fig. 13) to the metal locking tabs of the magazine follower *2* or the magazine lock plate *3*, shake the follower (lock plate) to be sure that the follower (lock plate) does not separate from the magazine spring.

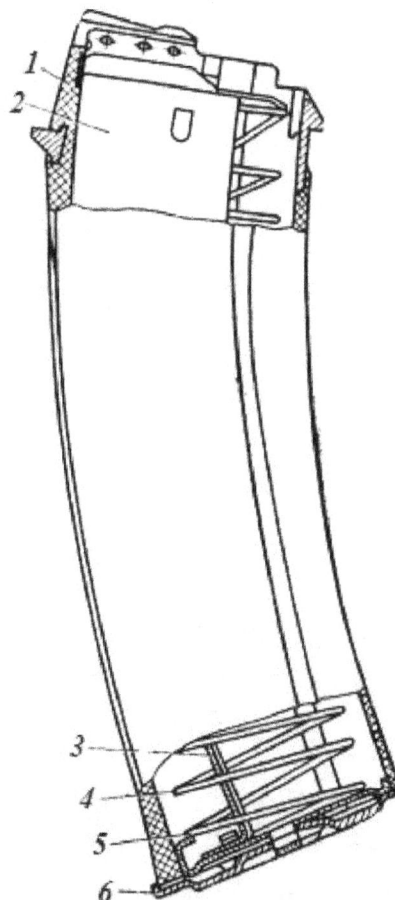

**Fig. 13** magazine 6L20 for assault rifle and 6L18 magazine for light machine guns:

*1* – magazine body 6L20.Sb 0-5 and 6L18.Sb 0-1; *2* - follower assembly 6L20.Sb 0-2; *3* – lock plate assembly 6L20.Sb 0-3, *4* – lock plate springs 6L20.Sb 0-4 and 6L18.Sb0-4; *5* – magazine springs 6L20.0-9 and 6L18.0-9; *6* – magazine floor plate 6L20.0-11

5.8.6. After replacing the lock plate and magazine floor plate, check the reliability of the locking of a magazine floor plate; without pressing the projection on the lock plate separation of the floor plate from the magazine body is not acceptable.

5.8.7. When replacing the follower, check the movement of the follower into the magazine body; the follower should move freely in the magazine body.

5.8.8. After replacing the follower, magazine spring or follower with magazine spring push the follower and magazine spring down (preload) in the feeder body using a rod until it stops and release it, after removing the load, the follower and the spring should vigorously to return to their original position.

Insert a training cartridge in the magazine and shake, falling out of the cartridge from the magazine is not acceptable; insert another cartridge in magazine and shake, falling out of the top cartridge is not acceptable. Load magazine with 30 (45) Training cartridges, the top cartridge should show spring tension on pressing; ability to load another cartridge above the specified number is not acceptable; Shake the magazine, falling out of the top cartridge is not acceptable.

5.8.9. Check the operation of the magazine as described in Sec. 5.8.4.

## 5.9. Replacing the front sight post and the front sight base

5.9.1. Unscrew the front sight post *31* (Fig. 1-3) using the key, which is available on the screwdriver supplied with accessories.

5.9.2. Screw the new front sight post into the front sight base *32* using the key. The installed front sight post should not be tilted and should unscrew and screw in using the key with a visible effort, front sight posts moveable with fingers only are not acceptable.

5.9.3. If necessary, replace the front sight base, unscrew the front sight post, and use a punch to knock the front sight base out of the front sight block *30*, press a new front sight base into the front sight block.

5.9.4. Pressing in the front sight base should not be able to be done by hand but require the use of a driver ($\approx 10$ kg).

5.9.5. If the front sight base can be shifted by hand pressure, use another front sight base or adjust the front sight base, as described in sec. 6.2.

5.9.6. Install the front sight post, as described in sub-sec. 5.9.2.

5.9.7. After replacing the front sight post or sight base, sight in as indicated in the operation manual for the weapon.

## 5.10. Replacing wooden buttstocks

5.10.1. Perform a partial dismantling of the weapon, unscrew the screws *2* (Fig. 14 and 15) and remove the buttstock *1*.

5.10.2. Fit the new butt on the receiver with a tight fit so that the top of the buttstock tang rests on the against the bottom plane of the rear trunnion *3*; contact area shall be not less than 75% buttstock tang. Sand the buttstock tang until the desired fit is achieved.

5.10.3. Check the clearances between the receiver and buttstock Fig. 14 and 15; these shall not be less than 0.3 mm.

If the gap is less than 0.3 mm work the ledge on the buttstock to obtain clearance in the range of 0.3 to 0.7 mm.

5.10.4. Bore and thread the holes for the screws as per Fig. 14 and 15 and secure with buttstock screws.

For synthetic stocks

Clearance of at least 0.3mm over the entire contour

A gap between the end of the butt stock and the back of the rear trunnion is not allowed

Insure the butt stock fits tightly in the receiver with some resistance, wobble is not allowed

o.d. Ø 3.5$^{+0.5}$

Clearance of at least 0.3mm over the entire contour

Gap around the perimeter of at least 0.3mm

R7.25

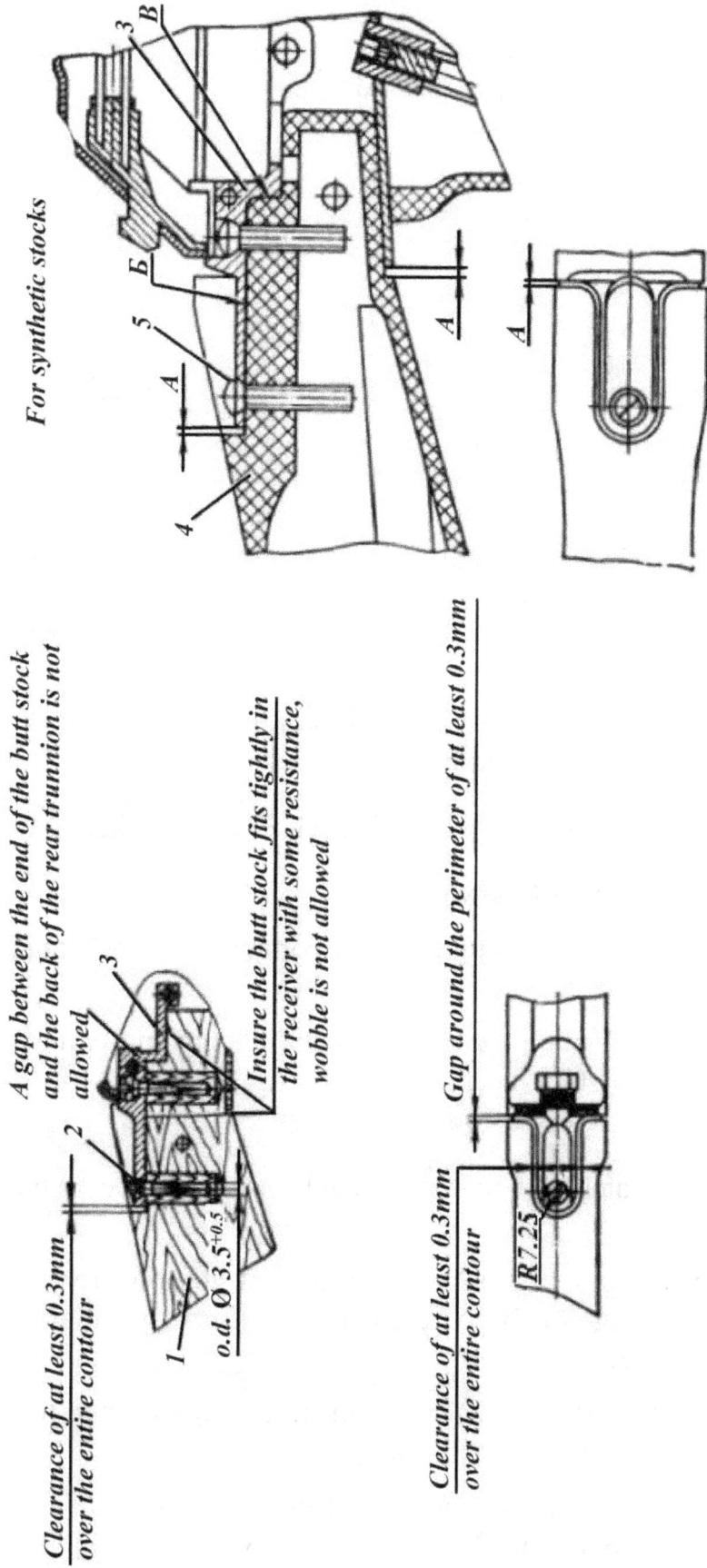

**Fig. 14.** Fit of stocks for assault rifle AK74 and machine gun RPK74:

1,4 – buttstock assembly; 2,5 – buttstock screws; 3 – rear trunnion
Fitting butt on planes Б and B; gaps around the perimeter A of at least 0.2 mm

5.10.5. Check for wobble of the buttstock in the receiver, wobble is not acceptable.

5.10.6. Assemble the weapon.

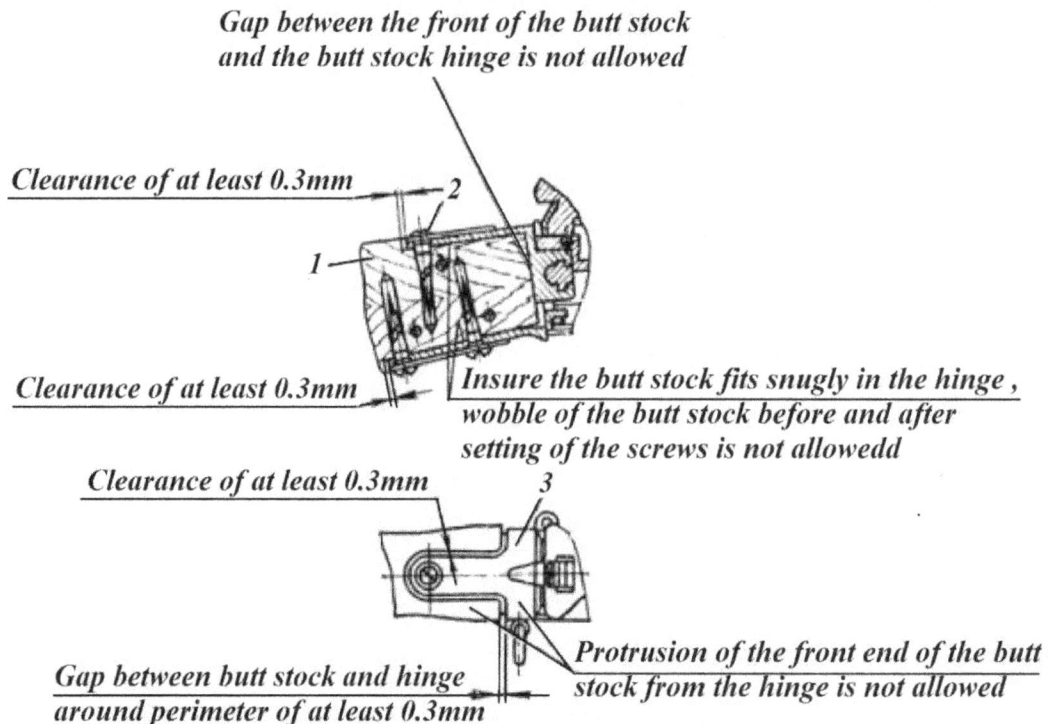

*Gap between the front of the butt stock*
*and the butt stock hinge is not allowed*

*Clearance of at least 0.3mm*

*Clearance of at least 0.3mm*

*Insure the butt stock fits snugly in the hinge ,*
*wobble of the butt stock before and after*
*setting of the screws is not allowedd*

*Clearance of at least 0.3mm*

*Gap between butt stock and hinge*
*around perimeter of at least 0.3mm*

*Protrusion of the front end of the butt*
*stock from the hinge is not allowed*

**Fig. 15**. Fit of the buttstock to machine gun RPKS74
*1* - buttstock assembly; *2* – buttstock screw 6P19.5-14; *3* - hinge

### 5.11. Replacing stocks for assault rifles AKS74, AKS74U and their parts

5.11.1. Perform a partial disassembly of the weapon.

5.11.2. Knock out axis pin *3* (Fig. 16) using a punch coming from the bottom of the stock and separate the stock *1*.

If necessary, push out the retainer pin *5* for the rear stock-latch *4* and remove the rear stock- latch and spring *6* for the rear stock-latch.

Replace any faulty pieces.

5.11.3. Reinstall the rear stock-latch with rear stock-latch spring and secure the retainer pin.

5.11.4. Press on the button of the rear stock-latch and let it go; after removal of the load the rear stock-latch should vigorously to return to its original position under the action of the rear stock-latch spring.

5.11.5. Install the stock and its axis pin, the axis is installed from the top down; once installed protrusion of the upper end of the shaft is not permitted.

5.11.6. Move the stock into the firing position and check side rocking of the stock in the rear stock-latch as described in Section. 12.3.

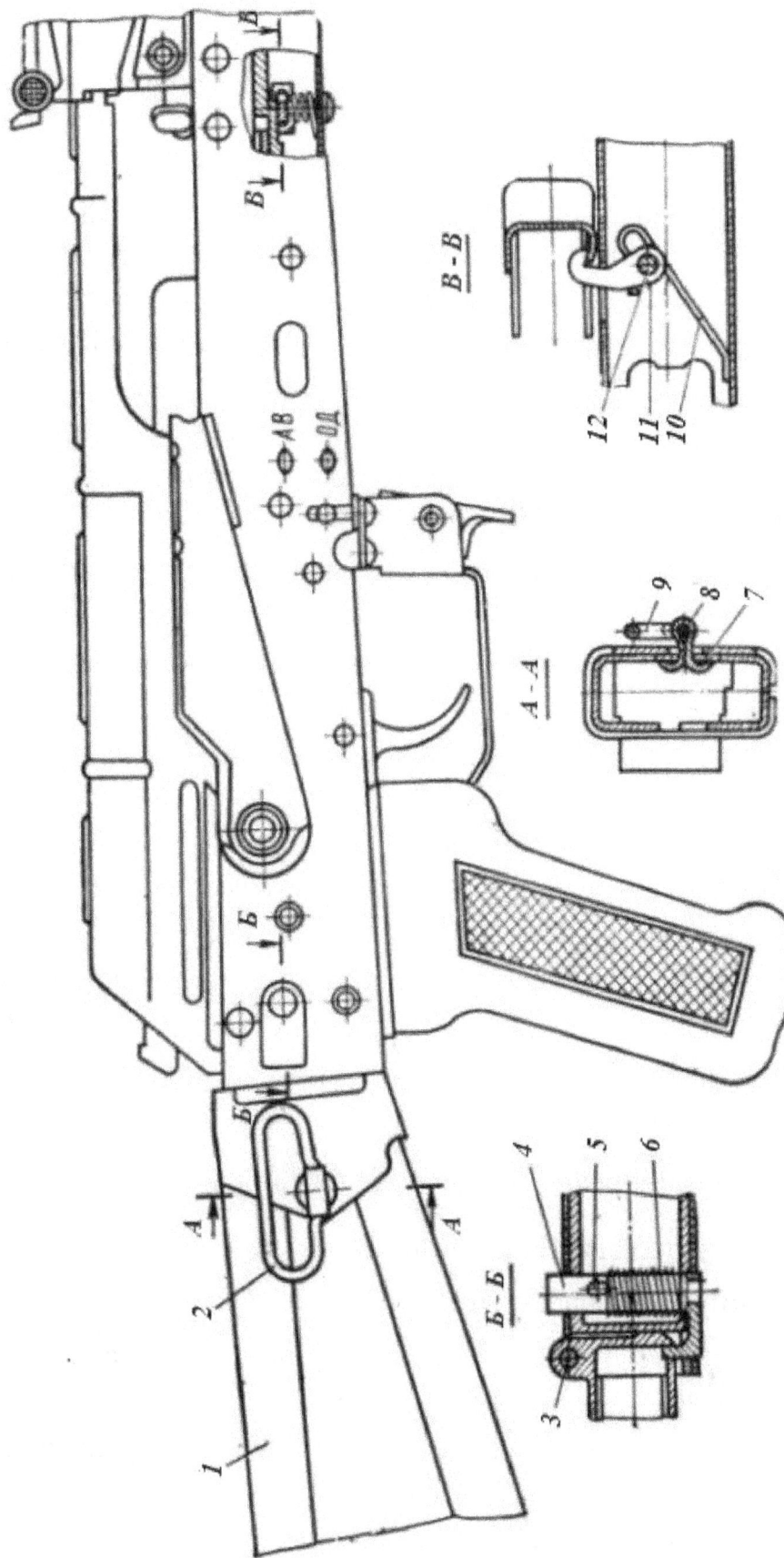

**Fig. 16.** Fit of stocks for assault rifles AKS74 and AKS74U:

*1* – stock assembly 6p21.Sb5 and 6P26.Sb 5; *2* – sling loop assembly 6P21.Sb 5-1; *3* – stock axis pin 6P21.0-41; *4* – rear stock latch 6P21.0-35; *5* – rear stock latch retainer pin 6P21.0-37; *6* – rear stock latch spring 6P21.0-36; *7* – washer 6P21.5-13; *8* – sling swivel hinge 6P21.5-6; *9*- sling loop 6P21.5-7; *10* – front stock latch spring 6P21.0-39; *11* - front stock latch hook 6P21.0-42; *12* - front stock latch axis pin 6P21.0-40

When unacceptable rocking is noted, fit the hook of the rear stock-latch as described in Section. 12.3.

5.11.7. Stake the upper end of the stock axis pin at two points, the diameter of each stake point is to be at least 1 mm.

5.11.8. Move the stock into the folded position; the forward stock-latch *11* should automatically drop behind of the flat on the stock and securely hold the stock in the folded position; wobble of the stock in the forward stock-latch is acceptable.

5.11.9. If the stock is not retained by forward stock-latch, straighten the flat on the stock or replace the bad forward stock-latch spring 10, as indicated in sub-sec. 5.11.10.

5.11.10. To replace the forward stock-latch and (or) the forward stock-latch spring, remove forward stock-latch axis pin *12*, replace faulty pieces, install the forward stock-latch with the forward stock-latch spring and secure with the forward stock-latch pin; use a forked tool (appendix 1, item 2.28) to bend the end of the forward stock-latch spring.

5.11.11. Press the hook of the forward stock-latch and let it go, forward stock-latch by a spring latch must vigorously to return to its original position upon release.

5.11.12. Move the stock to the opposite position, the stock must be securely held by the rear stock--latch.

5.11.13. To replace the sling swivel assembly on the stock, use a screwdriver to fold in the ends of the sling swivel hinge *8*, remove the washer *7* and pull out the sling swivel hinge with the sling loop.

Replace any faulty pieces.

Install a sling swivel hinge with a sling loop into the stock, put a washer on the ends of the sling swivel hinge and fold ends of the sling swivel hinge out, tightly pressed to the wall of the stock.

Try to wrest the sling swivel assembly out by hand; separation of the sling swivel assembly from the stock is not permitted.

## 5.12. Replacing the stock for machine gun RPKS74

5.12.1. Perform a partial disassembly of the machine gun.

5.12.2. With a drift, knock out the stock axis pin *16* (Fig. 17) and remove the stock.

5.12.3. If it is necessary to replace the stock latch hook *17*, knock out the hook axis pin and remove the hook and hook spring *13*.

5.12.4. If it is necessary to replace the stock latch *18* or stock latch spring *15*, knock out pin *19* and then remove them, replace the faulty pieces and reattach the stock.

5.12.5. Replace faulty hook, latch, spring, axis pins or mount pins and fit new one to the machine gun; after fitting these parts stake both ends of each axis and mount pin.

5.12.6. Attach the stock to the weapon and install the stock axis pin.

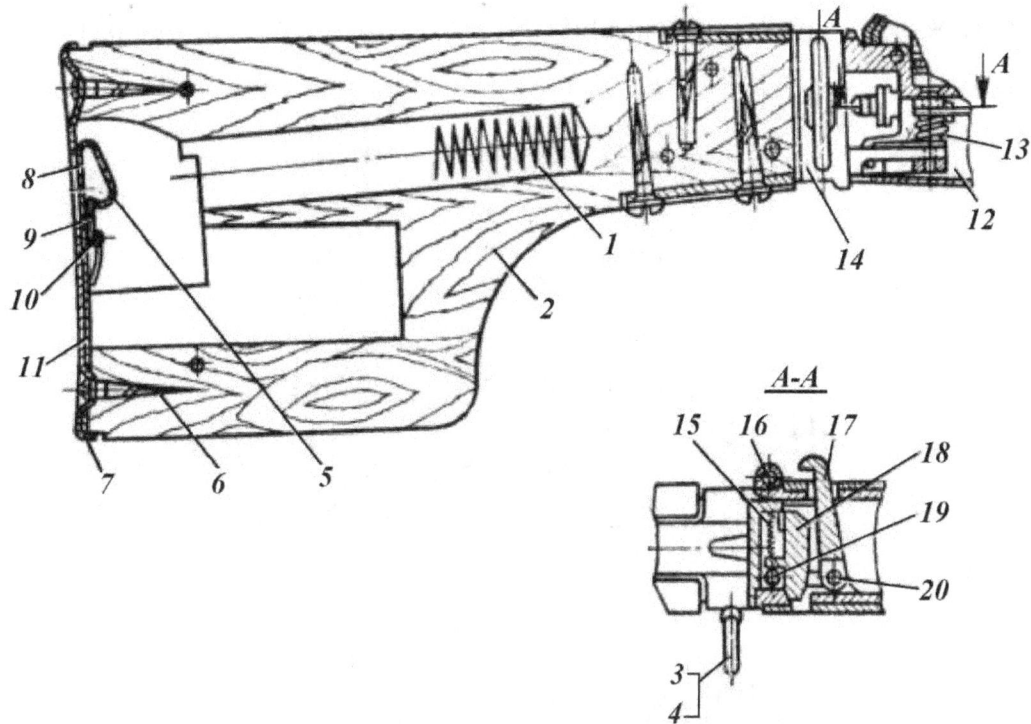

**Fig. 17.** Fit of stock assembly 6P19.Sb 5 RPKS74 for machine gun RPKS74:

*1* – cleaning kit case retainer spring 6P20.5-5; *2* - buttstock 6P19.5–1; *3* – sling loop 6P19.1–56; *4* - sling swivel assembly 6P19.Sb 1–10; *5* – cleaning kit trap door assembly 6P18.Sb 5-2; *6* – butt plate screw 6P20.5-3; *7* - butt plate 6P18.5-2; *8* trap door cover 6P20.5-8; *9* – trap door spring 6P20.5-10; *10* – trap door axis pin 6P20.5-11; *11* – trap door hinge 6P18.5-9; *12* - receiver 6P91.Sb 1 – 1; *13* - hook spring 6P19.0 – 27; *14* – stock hinge 6P19.1-51; *15* – stock latch spring 6P19.1-53; *16* – stock axis pin 6P19.1-55; *17* – hook 6P19.0-25; *18* – stock latch 6P19.1-52; *19* - pin 6P19.1-54; *20* - hook axis pin 6P19.0-26

5.12.7. Check movement of the stock when latched, it may be no more than 4 mm; if stock movement is more than 4 mm, eliminate movement as specified in Section 13.10.

5.12.8. Check the connection of the stock in the folded position, failure of the stock to be held by the hook is not acceptable; if the hook fails to hold the stock, eliminate failure as specified in Section 13.11.

5.12.9. After replacing the parts, install the stock and the axis pin and stake both ends of the axis pin.

5.12.10. To replace the sling swivel assembly *4* (see. Fig. 61) it is necessary to separate the wooden part of the stock from the hinge, squeeze the tabs of the sling swivel hinge, detach sling loop and hinge, replace the faulty pieces, reattach the sling swivel assembly to hinge as in Fig. 61 and reattach the wooden stock.

5.12.11. Assemble the machine gun.

## 5.13. Replacing the sight leaf assembly, sight blade and their parts

5.13.1. Remove from the weapon the sight leaf assembly *14* (Fig. 1, 3) and sight leaf spring *16*, replace the bad sight leaf and (or) sight leaf spring and install on the weapon.

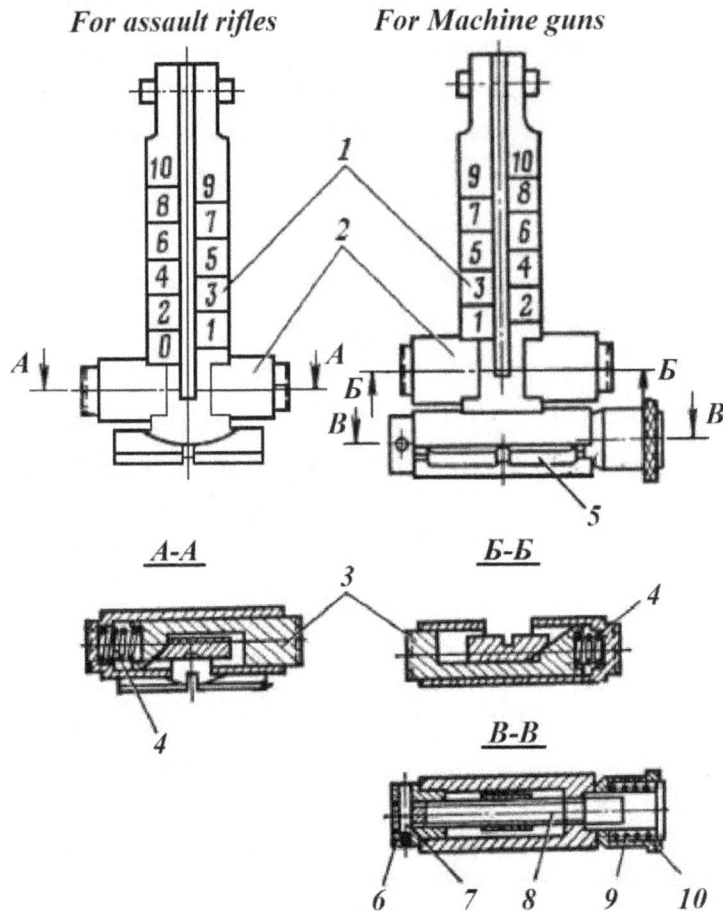

**Fig. 18.** Sight leaf assemblies 6P20.Sb 2 for assault rifles AK74 and AKS74 and sight leaf assemblies 6P18.Sb 2 for machine guns RPK74 and RPKS74:

*1* – sight leaf 6P20.2-1 and 6P18.2-1; *2* – elevation slide 6P20.2-2; *3* – elevation slide latch 6P20.2-3 *4* – elevation slide latch spring 6P20.2-4; *5* – rear sight blade 6P18.2-5; *6* - nut for windage adjustment screw 6P18.2-9; *7* - pin for windage adjustment nut 6P18.2-10; *8* - windage adjustment screw 6P18.2-7; *9* - windage adjustment tension spring 6P18.2-8; *10* - windage adjustment lock knob 6P18.2-6

5.13.2. Raise up the rear of the sight leaf 25 - 30 mm and let it go, upon release the sight leaf should vigorously return to its original position, and the elevation slide 2 (Fig. 18) must be adjacent to at least one of the elevation indicator lines on the sight leaf.

5.13.3. Check to see if there is any non-reparable skewing of the sight leaf, skewing may be no more than 0.3 mm.

Irregular skewing of the rear sight shall be removed, as indicated in sec. 6.6.

5.13.4. To replace the rear sight elevation slide *2* (Fig. 18), elevation slide latch *3* and (or) *4* elevation slide latch spring latch, separate the parts of the sight leaf assembly, press on the elevation slide latch and remove the elevation slide assembly and its parts from the rear sight leaf [*by sliding it forward off the end of the sight leaf*].

Replace unfit parts. Install an elevation slide latch spring and elevation slide latch in an elevation slide and slide the elevation slide assembly on sight leaf.

Install the sight leaf assembly on the assault rifle (machine gun).

5.13.5. Check the movement and secureness of the elevation slide assembly on sight leaf. While pressing the elevation slide latch, elevation slide assembly must move freely along the entire rear sight leaf. When released, movement of the elevation slide assembly is not acceptable and it must be securely held at each division on the sight leaf.

5.13.6. To replace sight blade *5* and (or) the screw *8* remove the sight leaf assembly from the machine gun, remove the elevation slide assembly, using a punch knock out the pin *7*, unscrew the nut *6*, remove the screw and sight blade from the rear sight and separate the screw from the sight blade.

Replace unfit parts.

5.13.7. Insert the sight blade into the slot in the rear sight, put the tension spring *9* on the screw, put the windage adjustment knob on the screw and over the spring *10*, screw the screw into the sight blade in the rear sight leaf, screw the nut *6* on the screw until it stops and install the pin *7*.

If there is no screw hole for the pin, use a drill bit of diameter of 1.5 mm to drill hole as per Fig. 32 and install the pin.

Check longitudinal movement (rocking) of the sight blade along the slit in the rear sight leaf, not more than 0.2 mm is acceptable.

Stake both ends of the pin.

Assemble the sight and install it on the machine gun.

5.13.8. To replace sight blade *15* (Fig. 2) and the spring *16* for the AKS74U rear sight knock out the axis pin *17* and remove the sight blade and the sight blade spring.

Replace unfit parts.

Install the sight blade and the sight blade spring into the receiver cover pillar and insert the axis pin.

5.13.9. Check the movement of the sight blade on the AKS74U.

The sight blade should be transferred from one position to the other and back using only thumb pressure and it should be held securely held by the spring at the extreme positions.

Side movement of the sight blade of no more than 0.2 mm is acceptable; displacement of the axis pin of the rear sight blade by hand pressure is not acceptable.

5.13.10. After replacing the complete rear sight leaf assembly, the rear sight leaf itself, the rear sight elevation assembly wholly or any part thereof, or the sight blade and (or) any part of the windage adjustment assembly on the machine gun, or the sight blade and (or) spring on the AKS74U, prepare the weapon for battle as indicated in the operation manual for the weapon.

## 5.14. Replacing the pistol grip

5.14.1. Perform a partial disassembly of the weapon.

5.14.2. Use a screwdriver to remove the grip screw *50* (Fig. 1-3) from the nut *51*.

5.14.3. If the end of the grip screw is flared too much and it will not unscrew using a screwdriver, then split (saw) the bad grip, screw the grip screw into the nut all the way, compress or grind off the flared portion of the diameter of the grip screw and unscrew it from the nut.

5.14.4. Install the new grip and nut on the weapon are new, screw the grip screw into the nut to a point with noticeable resistance.

5.14.5. Wobbling of the grip on the weapon, with the screw secured, is not permitted, local clearance between the grip and the receiver is acceptable of no more than 0.5 mm, protrusion of the head of the grip screw from the grip is not acceptable.

5.14.6. Flare the grip screw at the nut end using a triangular punch.

5.14.7. Assemble the weapon.

## 5.15. Replacing the handle of the bayonet-knife

5.15.1 The necessary materials and equipment.

Epoxide resin ED-16 GOST 10587-84.
Polyethylene polyamine TU 6-02-594-80.
Solvent GOST 18188-72 646.
Acetone technical GOST 2768-84.
Fume cupboard.
Thermostat controlled oven with heating temperature of 40-200°.
Technical scales with lifting capacity of weights up to 200 g.
Burette 25 - 50 ml.
Metal trays.
Cloth wipes.
Absorbent gauze.
Die M5.
Tap M5.

5.1512. Preparation of glue.

Resin is prepared in a small amount, since the time of the resin's suitability for use is no more than 40 minutes, therefore you must prepare it immediately before use.

In the metal tray weigh 5 g of epoxy resin ED-16, and flow into it from the burette $0.75$ cm$^3$ hardener (polyethylene polyamine). Mix the resin with the hardener to form a homogeneous mass of a light brown color.

If the resin is thick and poorly mixed with the hardener, then, before you pour in more hardener to the resin, preheat to a temperature of 40-60°C, then mix thoroughly or add to the mixture 5-20 parts by weight of acetone, and mix thoroughly.

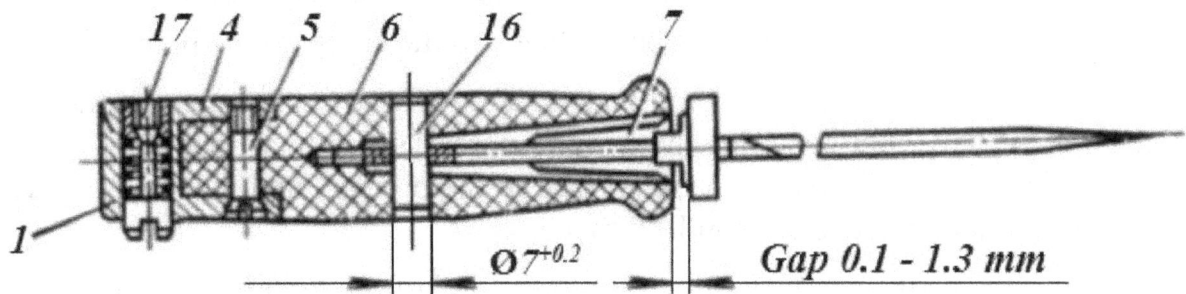

**Fig. 19.** Replacing the handle of the bayonet-knife:

*1–* latch spring 1-7, *4* -pommel 1-12, *5* - pommel screw 1-5, *6* - handle of bayonet-knife 1-11, *7 –* bayonet-knife assembly Sb 1, *16* - plug 1-9, *17 –* latch screw1-8

Sometimes due to moisture the polyethylene polyamine glue turns white. In this case, the polyethylene polyamine needs to be dried at a temperature of 100°C for 2 hours.

The remaining unused adhesive must be immediately removed from the mixing tray, as after curing the resin mass loses its ability to dissolve in any solvents. Adhesive residues need to be burnt, and then the tub cleaned to bright metal.

5.15.3. Preparation.

Heat bayonet 140-189°C in thermostat controlled oven to a temperature for 20-30 minutes, push plug *16* (Fig. 19) out of handle and remove the handle from the blade tang.

Unscrew screw *5* from the pommel *4*.

Remove glue residue [*on the tang*] with a wire brush and scraper.

Clean the threads on the screw with the die M5 and the screw hole in the pommel with the tap M5.

Check the operation of the latch. Press flush and then release the latch *17,* it must energetically return to its original position by the force of spring *1*.

Using the aperture in the blade tang, mark and drill a hole in the handle with a diameter of 7 mm in a position so that between the hilt and the end of the handle is a clearance of not more than 1.3 mm.

Attach the blade to the handle and secure with the plug; between the end of the handle and the hilt should be a gap of at least 0.1 mm, if there is no gap sand the [*hilt*] end of the handle to produce a gap of 0.1 - 0.3 mm.

Protrusion of the ends of the plug through the plane of the handle is not acceptable, inset is acceptable. If there is protrusion, sand the end flush with the side of the handle.

5.15.4. Bonding.

Blade tang, screw, plug, the pommel projection on the handle, the hole in the handle and the socket in the handle for the blade tang, carefully degrease. Degreasing is carried out using gauze soaked with solvent 646, followed by drying for 10 min.

Generously apply the glue using a wooden blade to the cavity in the pommel.

Attach the handle to the pommel and install screw after brushing glue on the threaded portion. Immediately after installing the pommel screw, stake at two points [*on the screw end*]. Remove excess adhesive from the surface of the pommel and the handle so that the glue does not protrude above the handle surface.

For a distance of 20-25 mm from the hilt to the end of the tang to the flat of the blade tang blade that goes in the handle, liberally apply adhesive, insert the blade into the handle so that the latch is positioned the sharp edge side of the blade, brush the plug with glue and insert it into the hole of the handle so that the ends do not protrude outside the handle.

Drive in the plug using a wooden screw clamp.

Use a wooden spatula and oiled cloth to remove excess adhesive from the surface of the hilt and handle - scrape after complete drying of the adhesive.

Dry bayonet assembled at room temperature for 24 hours (until adhesive is completely hardened).

Use a scrape on the outer surface to remove the excess glue.

5.15.5. Quality control.

Assembled and dried bayonet must meet the following requirements:

protrusion of the ends of the plugs outside the plane of the handle is not acceptable;

a gap should be between the hilt and the front end of the handle;

the blade should have a small amount of elastic lateral movement in the handle; if no such displacement exists the blade can easily fracture at the hilt;

press latch with thumb, and its spring should move without rubbing.

Check bayonet with scabbard putting on the weapon and if it turns out that the handle jams somewhere due to rubbing on the weapon, clean up the place on the handle that rubs with a fine file.

5.15.6. Storage of materials.

The resin and hardener should be stored in glass or aluminum hermetically closed container in a dry place at room temperature. Keep the resin from being exposed to light.

5.15.7. Safety measures.

The room for the assembly must have sufficient ventilation and lighting.

Preparation of glue should be done in a fume hood or in a well-ventilated area while wearing goggles. When working with glue and its components they must be prevented from contacting the skin. In case of contact of adhesive or its components on the skin you want wipe their traces off with gauze napkins, and then wash the skin with soap and water.

After the work is finished and before eating, use gauze napkins to wipe your hands with and wash them with warm soapy water.

## 5.16. Replacing bipod parts

5.16.1. Remove the crimp from one end of the axis pin *7* (Fig. 20) and drive out the axis pin. Separate the bipod leg assembly *1* and bipod spring *4*.

Attach a new leg and spring to the bipod base *6* and install the axis pin.

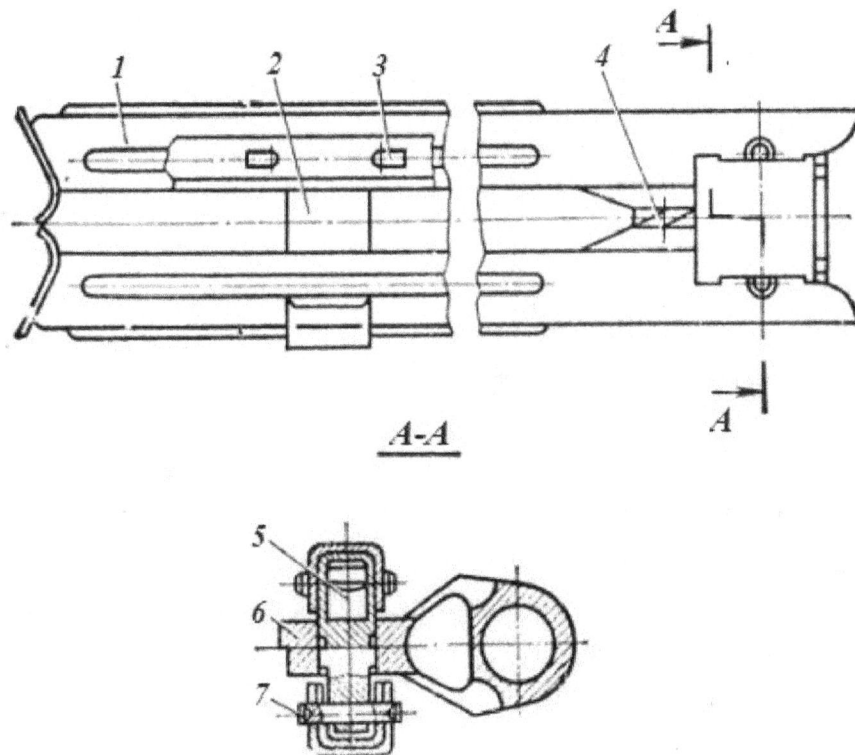

**Fig. 20** Bipod assembly 6P18.Sb 1-13 for machine guns:

*1* - leg assembly 6P18.Sb 1-14; *2* -  latch 6P18.9-7; *3* – latch axis pin 6P18.9-8; *4* - bipod spring 6P18.9-11; *5* - bipod axis pin 6P18.9-10; *6* - bipod base 6P18.1-65; *7* - magazine catch axis pin 6P20.0-13

5.16.2. Squeeze bipod legs together and release them, after releasing the bipod legs they must separate under the action of the spring and be held in the fighting and battle position.

5.16.3. Re-stake (re-crimp) the end of the axis pin, for a new axis pin crimp both ends; press on the end of the axis pin using a punch, displacement of the axis pin by force of hand is not acceptable.

Cracks at the ends of the axis pin are acceptable, a piece broken out is not acceptable.

*Preparation for mounting to the bipod leg*

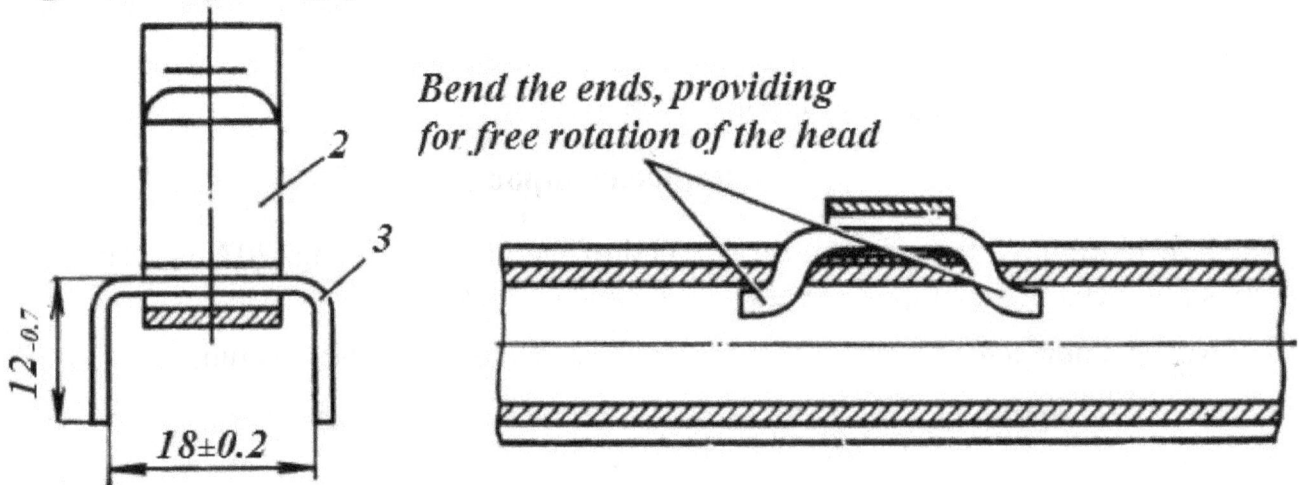

*Bend the ends, providing for free rotation of the head*

**Fig. 21**. Installation of the bipod latch:

*2* - Latch, *3* – latch axis pin

5.16.4. To replace the latch *2* is necessary to straighten the ends of the latch axis pin *3* and separate the latch from the axis pin.

Replace the bad axis pin with a new one in the latch and bend the ends of the axis pin down, as shown in Fig. 21.

Install the latch mounted on the axis pin in the bipod leg and bend the ends of the axis pin out, as shown in Fig. 21.

5.16.5. Install the bipod legs, bring them together, and fasten the latch; the latch must securely hold the bipod legs in the retracted position and when the machine gun is shaken the latch should not become unfastened.

Replacement of the bipod assembly is done during a major overhaul.

### 5.17. Replacing the gas tube/handguard assembly

5.17.1. Perform a partial disassembly of the weapon.

5.17.2. Select a new gas tube/hand guard assembly and install. If necessary, file the front end of the gas tube along the plane *E* (Fig. 22) so that freely drops into place, for

AKS74U it may be necessary to form a bevel on the upper half of the end of the gas tube as shown per the plane *B* in Fig. 22. After filing the front end of the gas tube, smooth any sharp edges along the contour the gas tube end.

5.17.3. File the tab on the rear end of the gas tube so that it fits into the slot in the rear sight block *17* and with an open gas tube lock *18* there is no longitudinal movement of the gas tube/handguard assembly. Contact of tab on the rear end of the gas tube to the

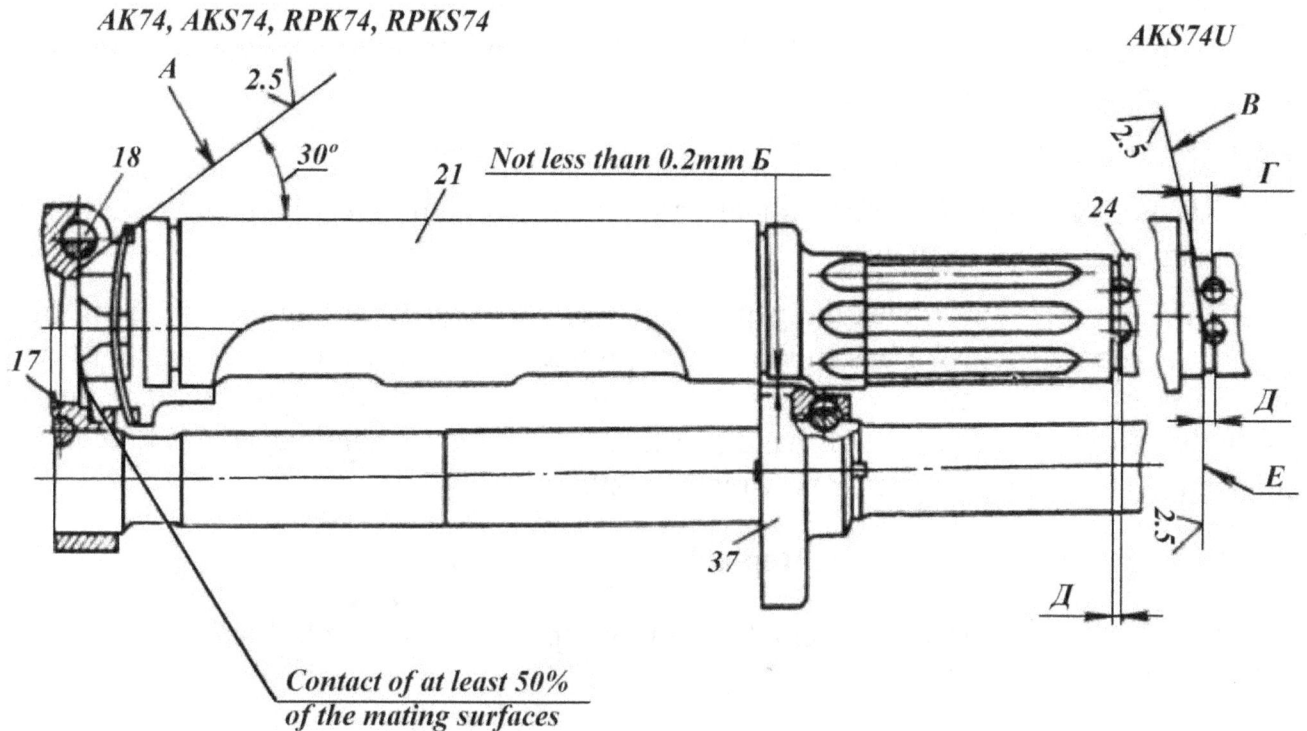

**AK74, AKS74, RPK74, RPKS74**

**AKS74U**

*A*  2.5  30°  21  Not less than 0.2mm Б  *B*  2.5  Г

18  24

17  Д

37  E

Д  2.5  Д

*Contact of at least 50% of the mating surfaces*

**Fig. 22.** Fit of the gas tube/handguard assembly:

*17* – rear sight block; *18* – gas tube lock; *21* gas tube/handguard assembly; *24* gas block; *27* lower handguard retainer

rear sight base should not be less than half of the contact surface, and the gaps Д and Г between the chamber flange of the gas block *24* and the front end of the gas tube should be for the lower half 0.2 - 1.2 mm and for the upper half of not more than 2 mm max for AKS74U. For AK74, AKS74, the gap Д = 0.1 ... 1.9 mm for RPK74, RPKS74 gap Д = 0.3 ... 1.2 mm.

5.17.4. Adjust the rear bevel on the gas tube to 30° by plane *A* and turn the gas tube lock so that the bar touches the bevel for a length of at least 3 mm and a width of not less than 1 mm, and that confirm when the gas tube lock has been locked there is no vertical movement of the rear of the gas tube/handguard assembly.

5.17.5. Check the clearances *K* and *Л* between the upper and lower handguards per Fig. 29. If the gaps are less than those in Fig. 29, then adjust the bottom plane of the upper handguard to achieve the dimensions in Fig. 29.

5.17.6. To replace the wooden upper handguard *20* (Fig. 1-3) need to turn it on the gas tube *23* and remove the upper handguard retainer spring *19*.

Install new wooden upper handguard with upper handguard retainer spring, it must take a noticeable effort to rotate the handguard onto the gas tube.

5.17.7. Check the gaps between the upper handguard retaining rings *1* and *2* (see. Fig. 29) and the edge of the ledge on the wooden handguard (dimensions *И* Fig. 29), which should not be less than 1 mm.

If a gap is less than 1 mm cut back the ledge on the wooden handguard to achieve clearance in the range of 1 to 1.2 mm.

5.17.8. Assemble the weapon.

5.17.9. For the AKS74U, longitudinal and transverse pitching of the handguard of not more than 0.5 mm is acceptable.

5.17.10. For AKS74U check the gap *Г* (Fig. 11) between the handguard retaining ring on the gas tube *21* and the gas tube retainer plunger *2*, as described in Sec. 5.7.13 and check to insure the plunger does not prevent removal of the gas tube/handguard assembly. Replacing the wood handguard with a plastic handguard 1-51 requires satisfaction of the specifications shown in Fig. 29.

## 5.18. Replacing the gas piston

5.18.1. Perform a partial disassembly of the weapon, remove the bolt carrier *3* (Fig. 5) and separate the bolt assembly *2*.

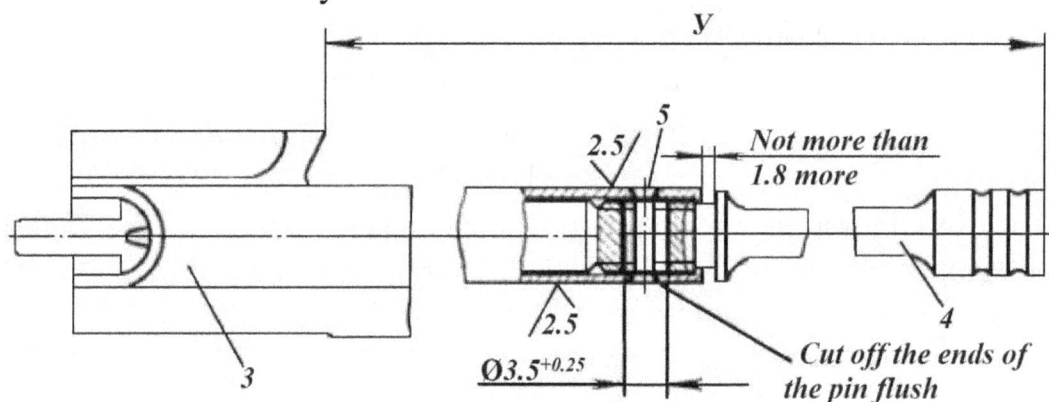

**Fig. 23.** Configuration of the gas piston in the bolt carrier:

*3* – bolt carrier; *4* – gas piston; *5* – gas piston pin

5.18.2. Un-crimp the end of the gas piston pin *5*, use a drill with diameter 3.5 mm ad drill out the pin end to a depth of 2-3 mm, then, using a punch knock the pinout and unscrew the gas piston 4 from the bolt carrier.

5.18.3. Select a new gas piston so that the gap between the inner walls of the gas block cylinder and the head of the gas piston is not more than 0.2 mm for AK74, AKS74, RPK74 and RPKS74 and 0.15 mm for the AKS74U, but less than 0.06 mm.

44

5.18.4. Screw the selected gas piston into the bolt carrier so that the dimension $Y$ (Fig. 23) is in the range of 294.8 to 295.2 mm, for AKS74U dimension $Y = 203 ... 203.3$ mm, when done movement of the gas piston in the bolt carrier of no more than 4 mm is acceptable (without pin installed), for the AKS74U - no more than 3 mm.

5.18.5. If there is not a pin hole in the gas piston, drill a hole in it to match the hole in the bolt carrier using a drill diameter of 3 mm, and then enlarge it to a diameter of 3.5-3.75 mm. [*Normally start the hole while in the carrier then remove to enlarge.*]

If a gas piston has a hole and it does not coincide with the hole in the bolt carrier, file it to an oval as per Fig. 24.

5.18.6. Assemble the bolt carrier with the gas piston, install the gas piston pin and check movement of the gas piston in the bolt carrier and dimensions, as described in sub-sec. 5.18.4.

5.18.7. Saw off the ends of the pin s, peen and smooth them as shown in Fig. 23.

5.18.8. Check the gas piston fit in the bolt carrier as described in sub-sec. 5.18.4.

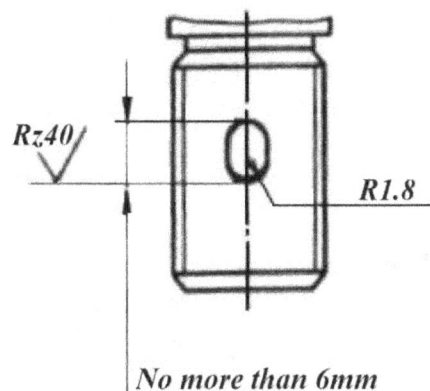

**Fig. 24.** Modification of the hole in the gas piston

5.18.9. Install the bolt carrier into the weapon and check that the gas piston end does not hit on the gas block (gas block/sight block combination).

5.18.10. Assemble the weapon.

Check function of the weapon shooting in automatic mode for 10 shots; interruption is not permitted.

### 5.19. Replacing parts of the firing mechanism

15.19.1. Perform a partial disassembly of the weapon and remove the parts of the trigger mechanism.

15.19.2. Replace unfit parts of the firing mechanism with new and install in the weapon.

15.19.3. After replacing the auto-sear *12* (Fig. 25):

15.19.3.1. Check (with magazine installed and with auto-sear pressed to the right) clearance between the lever of the auto-sear and the wall of the receiver *1*, and check clearance between the lever of the auto-sear and the wall of the installed magazine which should be at least 0.2 mm.

15.19.3.2. With a gap of less than 0.2 mm straighten the auto-sear lever or select another auto-sear; the end of the auto-sear lever should be coincident with the bolt carrier by at least 1 mm.

15.19.3.3. Push the auto-sear lever forward and release it; after releasing the load the auto-sear must energetically return back to its original position under the action of the spring until its sear arm locks in the hammer *11*; catching of the auto-sear on the receiver is not acceptable.

5.19.3.4. Catch the hammer on the auto-sear and check the distance from the upper edge of the receiver to the upper end of the auto-sear lever (dimension $\Gamma$ in Fig. 26), which should not be less than 3.9 mm.

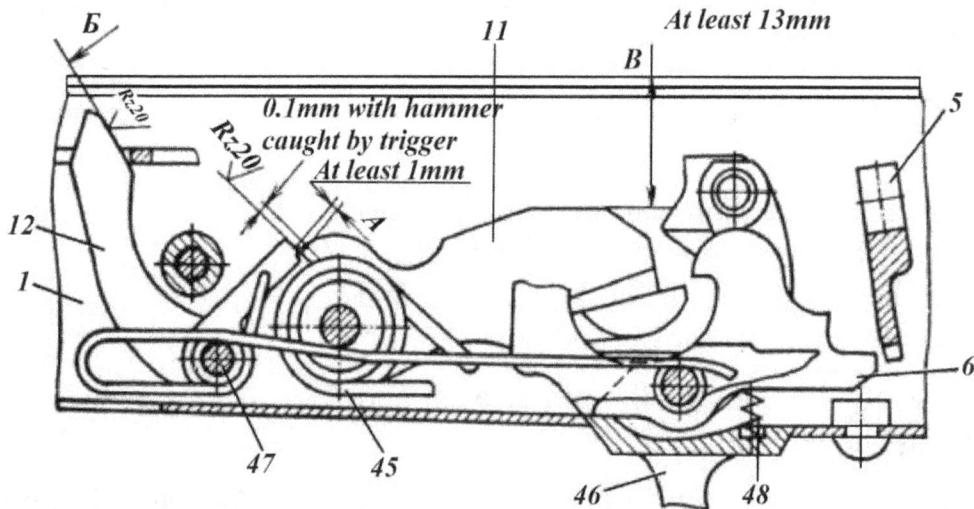

**Fig. 25.** Firing mechanism. Selector lever set on a single fire. Trigger not pressed, hammer hooked on auto-sear:
*1* – receiver; *5* – selector; *6* – disconnector; *11* – hammer; *12* – auto-sear with spring; *45* – mainspring; *46* – trigger; *47* – firing mechanism axis pin; *48* - disconnector spring

5.19.3.5. If dimension $\Gamma$ is less than 3.9 mm file the upper end of the auto-sear lever on the plane $Д$ in Fig. 26 to get the dimension $\Gamma = 3.9 ... 4.3$ mm.

5.19.3.6. Catch the hammer on the auto-sear to check the overlap of the auto-sear with the sear notch on the hammer (dimension *A* in Fig. 25); it shall not be less than 1 mm.

5.19.3.7. If the overlap is less than 1 mm work the sear edge of the auto-sear and (or) the sear notch on the hammer, as described in Sec. 10.8.1.

5.19.3.8. Check the hammer sear notch engagement with the auto-sear with the bolt carrier out of battery. Cock the hammer and move the bolt carrier out of battery.

Insert the 6 mm end of the gauge (Appendix 1, item 2.26) between the rear left face of the front trunnion and front left edge of the bolt carrier, bring the bolt carrier forward to clamp the gauge and squeeze the trigger, the hammer should not drop with the 6 mm end in place; release the trigger, remove the gauge, bring the carrier out of battery and place the 3 mm end between the trunnion and the bolt carrier, bring the bolt carrier forward to clamp the gauge, and squeeze the trigger, the hammer must drop with the 3 mm end of the gauge in place.

5.19.3.9. Check whether the auto-sear spring presses the auto-sear to the right side of the receiver.

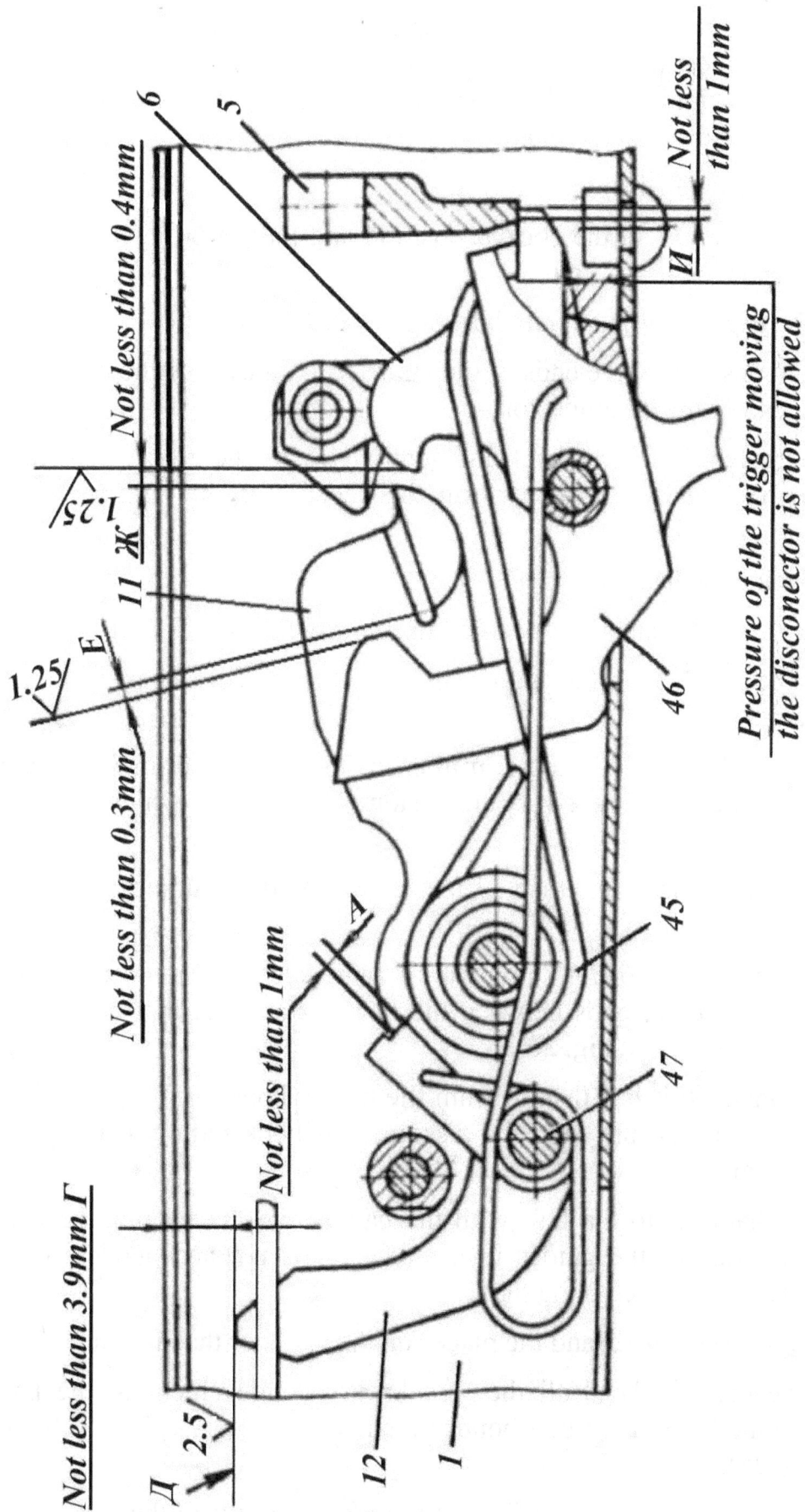

**Fig. 26.** Firing mechanism. Selector lever set on automatic fire. Trigger not pressed, hammer hooked on auto-sear:

*1 – receiver; 5 – selector; 6 – disconnector; 11 - hammer; 12 – auto-sear with spring; 45 – mainspring; 46 – trigger; 47 – firing mechanism axis pin; 48 – disconnector spring*

Not less than 3.9mm Г

Not less than 1mm

Not less than 0.3mm

Not less than 0.4mm

Not less than 1mm

*Pressure of the trigger moving the disconector is not allowed*

47

5.19.3.10. If the hammer falls when bolt carrier is more than 6 mm out of battery, file the auto-sear on the plane Б in Fig. 25; if the hammer does not fall when the bolt carrier is out of battery 3 mm, select another auto-sear. In wartime, surface welding the end of the leg of the auto-sear using a 50A electrode and treating use of the auto-sear in the weapon as a temporary measure is acceptable.

5.19.4. After replacing the mainspring *45* (Fig. 26):

5.19.4.1. Put the hammer *11* in the cocked position and pull the trigger, the hammer should energetically rotate on its axis pin.

5.19.4.2. Check the trigger pull; it should be 1.5-3.5 kg [*3.3-7.7 lb.*].

5.19.4.3. Check the position of the ends of the mainspring, they must lie on the trigger *46* and not touch the end of the disconnector *6*.

5.19.4.4. Pull the trigger all the way back and gently let it go, the trigger must return to its original position without hang-ups, perform the checks for the hammer with and without the auto-sear engaged.

5.19.5. After replacing the hammer *11* (Fig. 25):

5.19.5.1. Check descent hammers, as specified in sub-sec. 5.19.4.1.

5.19.5.2. Check the contact of the auto-sear *12* with the cocked the hammer, as described in sub-sec. 5.19.3.6.

5.19.5.4. Catch the hammer on the auto-sear to check the distance from the head of the hammer to the upper edge of the receiver (dimension *B* in Fig. 25) which should be at least 13 mm.

5.19.5.5. If the measurement is less than 13 mm, select another hammer and (or) auto-sear.

5.19.5.6. Set selector *5* (Fig. 26) for automatic fire and catch the hammer on the auto-sear to check whether there are gaps between the hammer and the disconnector *6* and trigger *46* (dimensions *E* and *Ж* in Fig. 26).

5.19.5.7. If the clearance E is less than 0.3 mm file trigger hook until gap *E* =0.3 ... 0.5 mm, If gap *Ж* is less than 0.4 mm sand the disconnector hook radius so the gap *Ж* is between 0.4 and 0.6 mm.

5.19.5.8. Press the hammer to the left, with the hammer to the left, the head of the hammer touching the edge of the guides in the receiver is not acceptable; conduct a similar test with the hammer offset to the right.

5.19.5.9. If the hammer touches, sand the places on the hammer that are touching.

5.19.5.10 Push the hammer head all the way back, the movement of the hammer should be stopped by the base of the bolt bounce retarder (for the AKS74U - the trigger assembly spacer, Fig. 28).

5.19.6. After replacing the axis pins *47* (Fig. 26) to press the ends of the axis pins using a punch; ejection of the axis pins out of the receiver is not acceptable, protrusion of the right ends of the axis pins beyond the plane of the receiver is not acceptable; push the left

ends of the axis pins, when this is done there must be clearance between ends of the axis pins and the selector lever 5.

5.19.7. After replacing selector lever 5:

5.19.7.1. Install the receiver cover 14 (Fig. 1-3) on the receiver of the weapon, for the AKS74U close it; sharply move the selector lever up all the way, the movement of the selector lever should be limited by the receiver cover; move the selector lever down, it should clearly be held at positions ПР, АВ and ОД and limited by the projection on the selector stop on the trigger guard assembly.

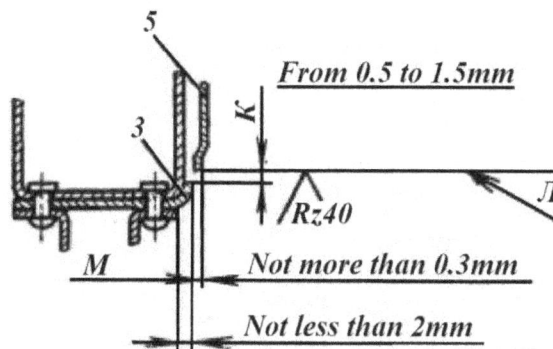

**Fig. 27.** Fit of the selector lever:
*3 - receiver, 5 – selector lever*

5.19.7.2. If the selector lever is not held in the preset intervals, then bend the arm toward the receiver.

5.19.7.3. Remove (open) the receiver cover and set the position of the selector lever to ОД; check the clearance between the selector lever and the tab on the selector stop of the trigger guard (dimension $K$ in Fig. 27); it should be in the range of 0.05 to 1.5 mm.

5.19.7.4. In the absence of gap $K$ sand the selector lever on the plane $Л$ in Fig. 27 to gain clearance $K = 0.05 ... 1.5$ mm.

5.19.7.5. Check selector lever overhang above the tab on the selector stop of the trigger guard (dimension $M$ in Fig. 27), it should be less than 0.3 mm.

5.19.7.6. If the overhang of the selector lever is more than 0.3 mm adjust the selector lever until the overhang is less than 0.3 mm.

5.19.7.7. Set selector lever to position ПР, in this position the selector should overlap the trigger 46 at least 2 millimeters (dimension $П$ in Fig. 28), and there should be a gap between the selector and the top edges of the back of the trigger 46 (Fig. 26) of at least 0.2 mm (dimension $H$ in Fig. 28).

5.19.7.8. If gap $H$ is smaller than 0.2 mm, file the edge of the selector 5 (Fig. 26) to obtain clearance $H= 0.2 ... 0.5$ mm.

5.19.7.9. Set selector lever to position АВ, in this position the selector should overlap the tail of the disconnector 6 at least 1 mm (dimension $И$ in Fig. 26), and between the disconnector and the cocked hammer 11 (the trigger squeezed and the hammer caught on the auto-sear) should be a gap of less than 0.4 mm (dimension $Ж$ in Fig. 26).

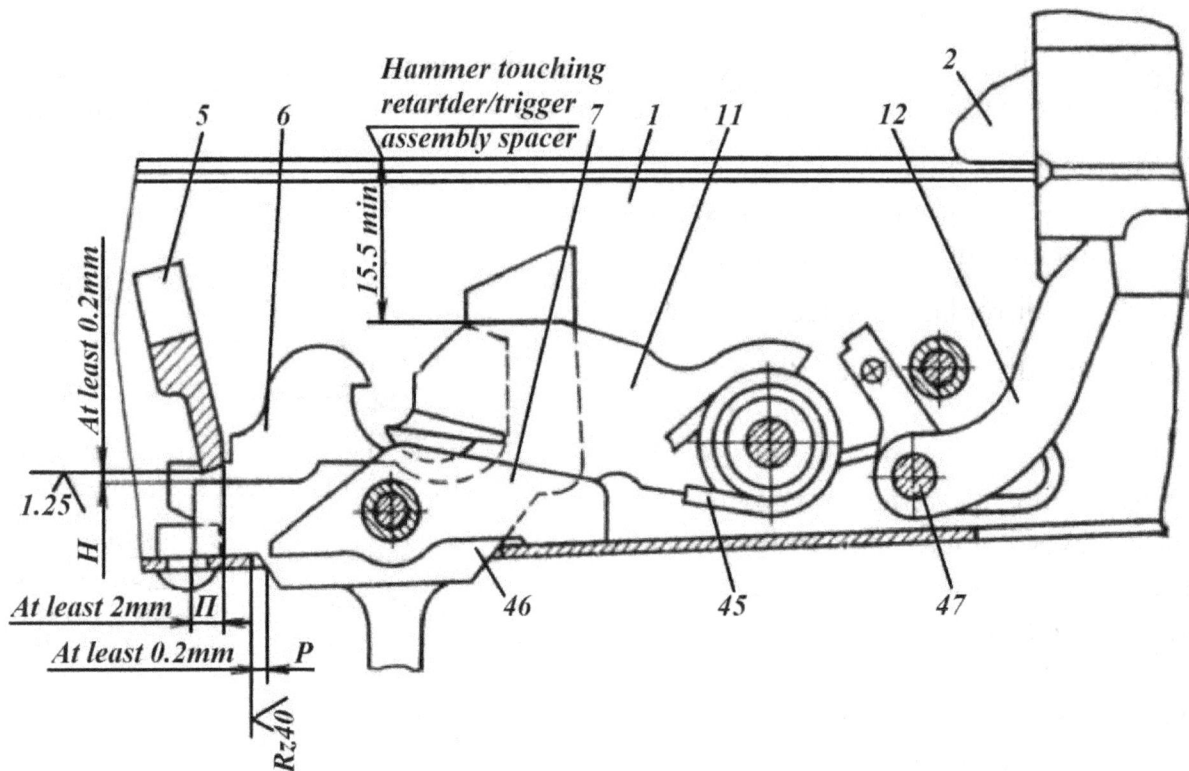

Labels on figure: Hammer touching retartder/trigger assembly spacer; 15.5 min; At least 0.2mm; 1.25; H; At least 2mm Π; At least 0.2mm; P; Rz40; 5; 6; 7; 1; 11; 12; 2; 46; 45; 47

**Fig. 28.** Firing mechanism. Selector lever is set to safe. The trigger is pulled all the way back:

*1* – receiver; *2* - bolt carrier with bolt; *5* – selector; *6* – disconnector; *7* - trigger assembly spacer; *11* – hammer; *12* – auto-sear with spring; *45* – mainspring; *46* – trigger; *47* – firing mechanism axis pin

5.19.8. When replacing the auto-sear spring *12* (Fig. 28), check installation of firing mechanism axis pin *47* as described in sub-sec. 5.19.6, and the auto-sear function as described in sub-sec. 5.19.3.3, and insure the loop of the auto-sear spring does not contact the body of a magazine installed in the receiver.

Check to insure the auto-sear is pressed to the right side of the receiver by the auto-sear spring.

5.19.9. After replacing the disconnector spring *48* (Fig. 25), release the hammer *11* from the cocked position, push the head of disconnector *6* back and release it, upon release the disconnector must vigorously return to its original position under the action of the spring.

5.19.10. After replacing the trigger *46* (Fig. 26):

5.19.10.1. Check the distance between hammer *11* and the trigger 46 (dimension *E*) as described in sub-sec. 5.19.5.6.

5.19.10.2. Check overlap of the sector *5* with the trigger (dimension *H*), as described in sub-sec. 5.19.7.9.

5.19.10.3. Check the clearance between the trigger wall and the edge of the opening in the receiver (dimension *Π* in Fig. 28) which should be less than 0.2 mm.

50

5.19.10.4. Check if when the trigger is released whether the rear sides of the trigger rub the bottom of the receiver. If necessary, sand the places that rub.

5.19.10.5. Check the overlap of the trigger with cocked hammer *11* with the selector lever set in position AB, and the trigger not pressed.

5.19.10.6. Check that for the AKS74U, with the trigger not pressed, whether the bolt carrier rubs on hook of the trigger.

5.19.11. After replacing the disconnector *6* (Fig. 26), check the distance between the cocked hammer *11* and the disconnector (dimension *Ж*), as described in sub-sec. 5.19.5.6; check the overlap of the selector *5* with the disconnector *6* (dimension *И*) as described in sub-sec. 5.19.7.9.

## 5.20. Replacing the lower handguard

5.20.1. Perform a partial disassembly of the weapon and remove the lower handguard *38* (Fig. 1-3).

520.2. Install a new lower handguard on weapon; the handguard should require some force to install.

5.20.3. If it takes too much force, adjust the attachment protrusion on the lower handguard until the handguard can be installed on the weapon with normal force.

5.20.4. Push the lower handguard retainer *37* on to the lower handguard until it stops and rotate the lower handguard retainer latch *22*.

If the latch does not lock into the lower handguard retainer groove, sand the front end of the lower handguard.

5.20.5. Check the horizontal and vertical movement of the rear end of the lower handguard; they may be no more than 0.3 mm. Unwanted movement of the lower handguard is eliminated as indicated in sec. 8.14.

5.20.6. Check the clearance between the shoulder on the front end of the handguard and the rear edge of the lower handguard retainer (dimension *H* in Fig. 29); it should be not less than 0.1 mm.

5.20.7. Clearances *К, Л, M* (Fig. 29) between the lower and upper handguards are: *К* - not less than 1 mm, *Л* - not less than 0.5 mm, and *M* - not less than 0.2 mm.

5.20.8. To ensure dimensions for *К, Л, M, H* adjust the appropriate places on the lower handguard.

5.20.9. Check the movement of the front end of the lower handguard; lateral and vertical movement of the front end and tightness in the longitudinal direction are not permitted; check that there is elastic longitudinal movement of the handguard on the weapon when the handguard retainer is latched, it may be not more than 0.5 mm.

When the movement of the lower handguard is inappropriate adjust as described in sec. 8.12.

5.20.10. Check that the cleaning rod holes in the lower handguard retainer and the lower handguard match. If the holes do not match, clear out the hole in the handguard so that the cleaning rod is easy to insert and remove; when clearing out holes it is allowed to have some break through between the bottom of the channel and the cleaning rod hole in the handguard at the front end of the handguard.

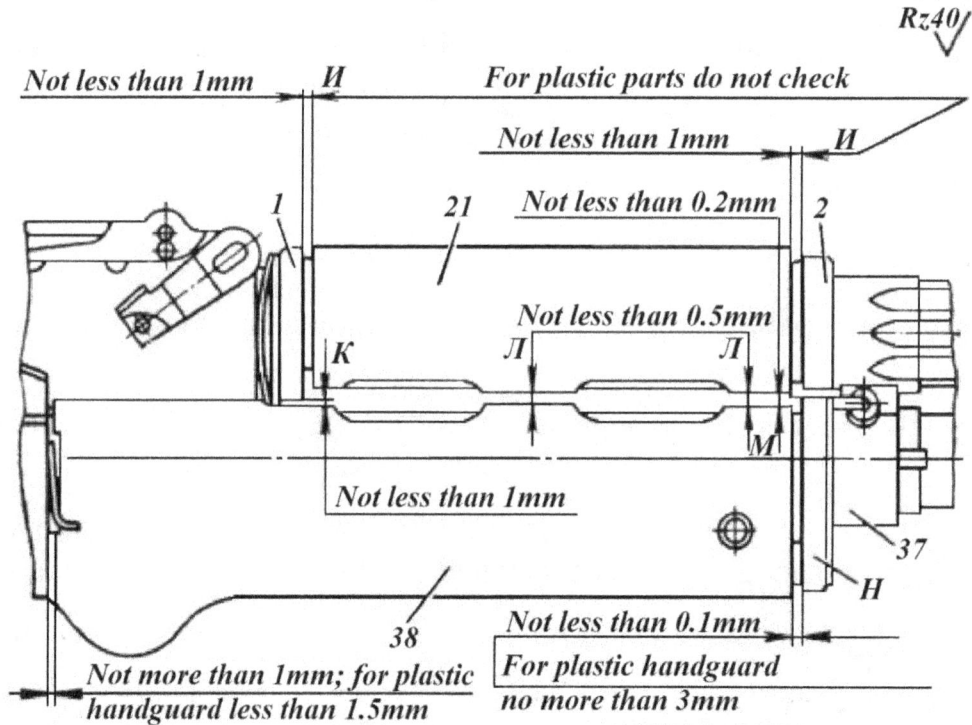

**Fig. 29.** Fit of the lower handguard to the upper handguard:

*1* - rear upper handguard retainer; *2* - front upper handguard retainer; *21* – gas tube/upper handguard assembly; *37* - lower handguard retainer; *38* – lower handguard

5.20.11. Assemble the weapon. Replacement with the plastic lower handguard, 6P20.Sb 9 (see Fig. 50) requires satisfying the requirements described in Fig. 29.

### 5.21. Replacing the lower handguard retainer lock

5.21.1. Perform a partial disassembly of the weapon. Remove the lower handguard

5.21.2. Compress (remove) with the help of pressure the flared end of the shaft of the lower handguard retainer lock *22* (Fig. 30).

5.21.3. Move lower handguard retainer *37* forward and knock out the handguard retainer lock.

5.21.4. Install a new lower handguard retainer lock in the lower handguard retainer, slide it back and rotate the flag of the lower handguard retainer lock back, the flag should be in a horizontal position, and the lower handguard retainer lock should securely fasten the lower handguard retainer on the barrel.

52

5.21.5. If turning the flag requires great effort, work on the groove in the barrel and the cylindrical part of the lock shaft so that the flag can be rotated easily by hand pressure.

5.21.6. Crimp and flare the end of the shaft of the lower handguard retainer lock, to meet the requirements shown in Fig. 30.

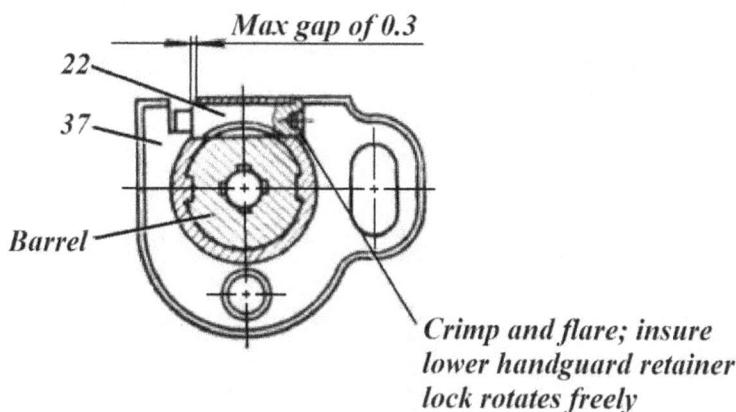

*Max gap of 0.3*

*22*

*37*

*Barrel*

*Crimp and flare; insure lower handguard retainer lock rotates freely*

**Fig. 30.** Configuration of the lower handguard retainer lock:

*22* - lower handguard retainer lock; *37* - lower handguard retainer

## 5.22. Replacing the gas tube lock

5.22.1. Perform a partial disassembly of the weapon.

5.22.2. Compress the flared end of the shaft of the lock *1* (Fig. 31) then use a punch to drive out the gas tube lock assembly *18* from rear sight block *17*.

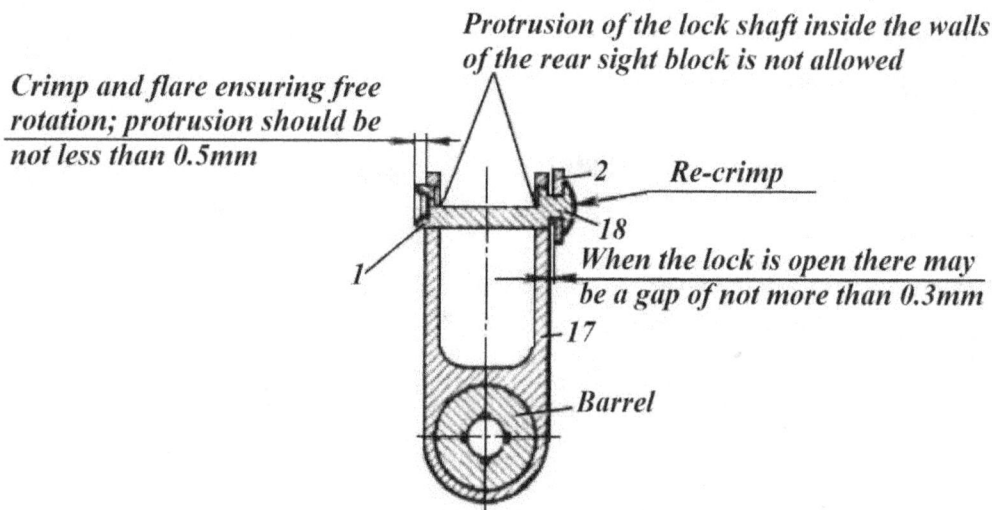

*Protrusion of the lock shaft inside the walls of the rear sight block is not allowed*

*Crimp and flare ensuring free rotation; protrusion should be not less than 0.5mm*

*2*   *Re-crimp*

*18*

*When the lock is open there may be a gap of not more than 0.3mm*

*1*

*17*

*Barrel*

**Fig. 31** Configuration of the gas tube lock:

*1* – lock shaft 6P20.1-36; *2* – lock arm 6P20.1-22; *17* – rear sight block assembly; *18* – gas tube lock assembly

5.22.3. Install new gas tube lock assembly in the rear sight block, inserting the shaft from the right side; crimp and flare the left end of the shaft, making sure to meet the requirements in Fig. 31.

5.22.4. Turn the arm of the lock, it must latch securely in the dimple on the rear sight block; if necessary, bend the lock arm.

5.22.5. If the inside edges of the lock shaft protrude inside the internal walls of the rear sight block, sand the protruding parts flush with the walls of the rear sight block.

5.22.6. Install gas tube assembly *21* (Fig. 22) and check its fastening cotter handguard.

5.22.7. If the check is closed with great effort, the process was raw bevel on the end of the receiver pad on the plane A from Fig. 22.

5.22.8. Assemble the weapon.

# 6. REPAIRING IRON SIGHTS

## 6.1. Iron sights

Moving front sight post *31* (Fig. 1-3), as well as being able to screw or unscrew it with only fingers of the hand is not allowed.

Replace the faulty front sight post as described in sec. 5.9.

## 6.2. Displacement of front sight base

Displacement of the front sight base *32* (Fig. 1-3) in the hole of the front side block *30* by using a punch with hand pressure only is not allowed.

Replace the front sight base, as described in sec. 5.9.

If necessary, make a new front sight base (Appendix 2, Fig. 99) using the base diameter (dimension *A*) equal to $Б\,^{+0.75}_{-0.04}$, where $Б$ - the actual diameter of the hole in the front sight block.

## 6.3. Nicks on the post of the front sight post, and the slots in rear sight leaf or rear sight blade

Clean up raised metal nicks on the edges of the front sight without changing the shape of the front sight post and the slit in the rear sight leaf or the rear sight blade.

## 6.4. Bent front sight, rear sight leaf

A bent front sight *31* (Fig. 1-3) must be replaced.

A bent rear sight leaf *1* (Fig. 18) can be straightened on a steel plate with a copper hammer; do not beat on the graduations and numbers.

## 6.5. Presence of several alignment marks on sight base or on the sight block

On front sight base *32* (Fig. 1-3) and the front sight block *30* there should be one scratch mark each, which should coincide with each other.

If the scratch marks do not coincide, move the sight base in the front sight block to make them coincide.

If there are a few scratch marks on the front sight base, turn the front sight base 180º, so that all the marks will be hid. [*Make a new mark on the sight base to coincide with the one on the front sight block.*]

If the front sight block has several scratch marks, sand the extra marks leaving one.

### 6.6. Side movement of the rear sight leaf

See the General Guidelines ch. 3.

Unrepairable side movement of rear sight leaf *15* (Fig. 1 and 3) (checked in all directions) is acceptable up to 0.3 mm.

If there is unacceptable movement of the front end rear sight leaf, then check the straightness of the rear sight leaf or squeeze the sight leaf lugs on the rear sight block closer together.

If there is jamming of the front end of the rear sight leaf in the eye slots of the rear sight block, then clean the lateral plane of the front end of the rear sight leaf.

If the above methods do not correct the unacceptable side movement, replace the rear sight leaf, as described in sec. 5.13.1.

### 6.7. Side movement of the rear sight blade AKS74U

Unrepairable side movement of rear sight blade *15* (Fig. 2) is acceptable up to 0.2 mm.

When unacceptable side movement exists, compress lobes of the sight housing, for which: drive out axis pin *17* and separate sight blade *15* and a spring *16* as a unit, put between the sight housing lobes a steel bar of 11.5 mm thickness and use a vise to compress the lobes until side movement of the blade is not more than 0.2 mm. Install in the weapon the spring and rear sight and secure with the axis pin; stake both ends of the axis pin.

### 6.8. No tension on the rear sight leaf

See the General Guidelines ch. 3.

Lift the end of the rear sight leaf 25-30 mm on an arc and release. The leaf should vigorously return to its starting position; for this the elevation slide should be set at division 4. Replace spring rear sight, as described in sub-sec. 5.13.1 - 5.13.3.

### 6.9. Sight blade for AKS74U does not hold in its positions

Sight blade *15* (Fig. 2) should with finger pressure move from one position to another and back and it should be securely held in the positions. If necessary, replace the sight blade spring *16*, as described in sub-sec. 5.13.8, 5.13.9.

## 6.10. Tight movement of elevation slide on rear sight leaf

See the General Guidelines ch. 3.

Replace the faulty pieces to produce results as described in sub-sec. 5.13.4.

## 6.11. Elevation slide is not retained at the divisions on the rear sight leaf

See the General Guidelines ch. 1.

Replace faulty elevation slide latch *3* (Fig. 18) and the elevation slide latch spring *4* to make the latch as described in sub-sec. 5.13.4.

## 6.12. Longitudinal movement (sliding) of the sight blade in the rear sight leaf for the machine gun

When pressed on the side with a finger, the rear sight blade *5* (Fig. 18) total amount of longitudinal movement (sliding) along the screw *8* may be up to 0.2 mm.

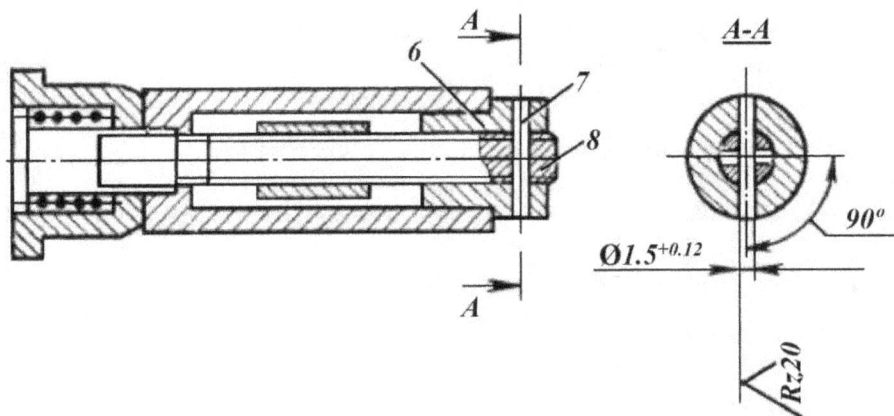

**Fig. 32** Installation of the pin in the windage adjustment nut for the machine gun:

*6* – nut; *7* – pin; *8* - screw

If longitudinal displacement is more than 0.2 mm, tighten nut *6* at least 45° to eliminate the longitudinal movement of the screw; drill a hole through the nut and screw with diameter of $1.5^{+0.12}$ mm and pin to fix the nut in place, as shown in Fig. 32. If it is impossible to tighten the nut enough, unscrew the nut 45° and add a steel washer/spacer ring between the nut flange and the edge of the windage adjustment channel of the rear sight leaf.

If the screw thread is worn out, replace the screw and (or) the entire windage adjustment mechanism as described in sub-sec. 5.13.6.

## 6.13. Sight blade moves tight in rear sight leaf for machine gun

See the General Guidelines ch. 3.

Assemble and disassemble sight to adjust and repair, as described in sub-sec. 5.13.6 and 5.13.7.

## 6.14. Windage adjustment lock-knob rotates freely on windage adjustment screw

Windage adjustment lock knob *10* (Fig. 18) on windage adjustment screw *8* when rotated with thumb must exhibit a noticeable resistance.

If the windage adjustment lock-knob free-wheels, replace the windage adjustment lock-knob spring *9*, as described in sub-sec. 5.13.6 and 5.13.7.

## 6.15. Optical sight is difficult to mount and dismount from the weapon

See the General Guidelines ch. 3.

## 6.16. Movement of optical sight

Movement of an optical sight mounted on the weapon is not allowed.

See the General Guidelines ch. 3.

## 7. REPAIRING THE BARREL
(Fig. 1-3)

## 7.1. Barrel wear in the grooves, rounding of corners of or broken rifling

See the General Guidelines ch. 3.

## 7.2. Chipped chrome in the chamber or the bore

See the General Guidelines ch. 3.

## 7.3. Bend in the barrel

See the General Guidelines ch. 3.

## 7.4. Dents in barrel

See the General Guidelines ch. 3.

## 7.5. Removal of the barrel

See the General Guidelines ch. 3.

For removing of the barrel with missing metal on the outer surface to send the product to a major overhaul.

## 7.6. Cracks in the barrel, the gas block, the rear sight block or front sight block

See the General Guidelines ch. 3.

## 7.7. Movement on the barrel of the gas block, the rear sight block or front sight block

See the General Guidelines ch. 3.

## 7.8. Retainer pin does not keep the muzzle brake on the assault rifle or flash hider on the AKS74U or machine gun screwed in place

See the General Guidelines ch. 3.

Replace retainer pin *33* and spring *29* to produce results, as described in sub-sec. 5.3.2.

## 7.9. Alignment of the muzzle brake or flash hider on the barrel of an assault rifle

7.9.1. Alignment of the muzzle brake or flash hider on the barrel of an assault rifle that causes rubbing on gauge K-8 (for parts with a cylindrical hole diameter of 6.3 mm) or K9 (for parts with a cylindrical hole diameter of 5.9 mm), for checking the alignment (Appendix 1, items 2.10, 2.11), or the appearance of traces of bullets residue due to deterioration of the alignment on the weapon from shooting, is not acceptable.

To check the muzzle brake (flash hider) alignment on an assault rifle you must:

unscrew the muzzle brake (flash hider) and clean the threads on the front sight block and the muzzle brake (flash hider)

screw the muzzle brake (flash hider) on the barrel until it stops, and then unscrew it (not more than one turn) until the retainer pin enters into the slot on the brake;

Put the assault rifle vertically with barrel up, press the muzzle brake (flash hider) with finger toward the front sight; force is applied to the front end of the muzzle brake (flash hider) perpendicular to the axis of the bore;

holding the muzzle brake (flash hider) in this position smoothly insert into the channel of the brake (flash hider) gauge K-8 (K-9) to check the alignment of the muzzle brake (flash hider); wherein the gauge must enter in the bore under the action of gravity; rubbing on the gauge of diameter of 6.3 mm (muzzle brake) and of diameter of 5.9 mm (flash hider) is not acceptable;

remove the gauge from the muzzle brake (flash hider), press the muzzle brake (flash hider) away from the front sight block and check the movement with the gauge as indicated; rubbing on the gauge is not acceptable;

remove the gauge from the muzzle brake (flash hider), press the muzzle brake (flash hider) to the left relative to the front sight block and check the movement with the gauge as indicated; rubbing on the gauge is not acceptable;

remove the gauge from the muzzle brake (flash hider), press the muzzle brake (flash hider) to the right relative to the front sight block and check the movement with the gauge as indicated; rubbing on the gauge is not acceptable. Remove the gauge.

7.9.2. Cause of the problem.

Deterioration of the interfacing areas of the muzzle brake (flash hider) and the front sight block.

When there is unacceptable movement of the muzzle brake (flash hider) compress it using device 6И17.Sb 2 (Appendix 1, item 2.21).

Secure the mandrel (Appendix 1, item 2.13) in a vise; remove the muzzle brake (flash hider) from the weapon and screw it onto the mandrel until it stops.

Place onto the muzzle brake (flash hider) the crimping roller device 6 И 17.Sb 2 and mount the device so that the bottom groove of the arcs of the device cover the ledge on the mandrel (Fig. 33) and screw both torque bars in until they stop with the aid of steel rods with a diameter of 6-8 mm, lubricate the rollers with rifle lubricant.

Turn the device on the muzzle brake (flash hider) in a clockwise direction, gradually screwing in the torque bars.

Next unscrew each capstan 1-1.5 turn, un-crimp the device, then remove the muzzle brake (flash hider) and check the muzzle brake (flash hider) movement on the assault rifle according to 7.9.1; the muzzle brake (flash hider) should be able to be screwed on by hand force (it is acceptable to assist turning with a steel rod of diameter of 6-8 mm) and have an acceptable level of movement, which is checked with gauges K-8 and K-9 for the absence of rubbing on the cylindrical part of the gauge with diameter 6.6 mm (for muzzle brake) and diameter 6.1 mm (flash hider).

If the movement is still unacceptable, repeat the procedure setting the device on the top groove of the sector.

If the muzzle brake (flash hider) screws on with great effort, then lap the threads of the brake with application of paste GOI.

To achieve the complete elimination of movement of the muzzle brake (flash hider) by increasing the effort it takes to screw them on the font sight block is not recommended.

After the elimination of unacceptable muzzle brake or flash hider movement assemble the assault rifle and verify its fitness as indicated in the manual for the assault rifle.

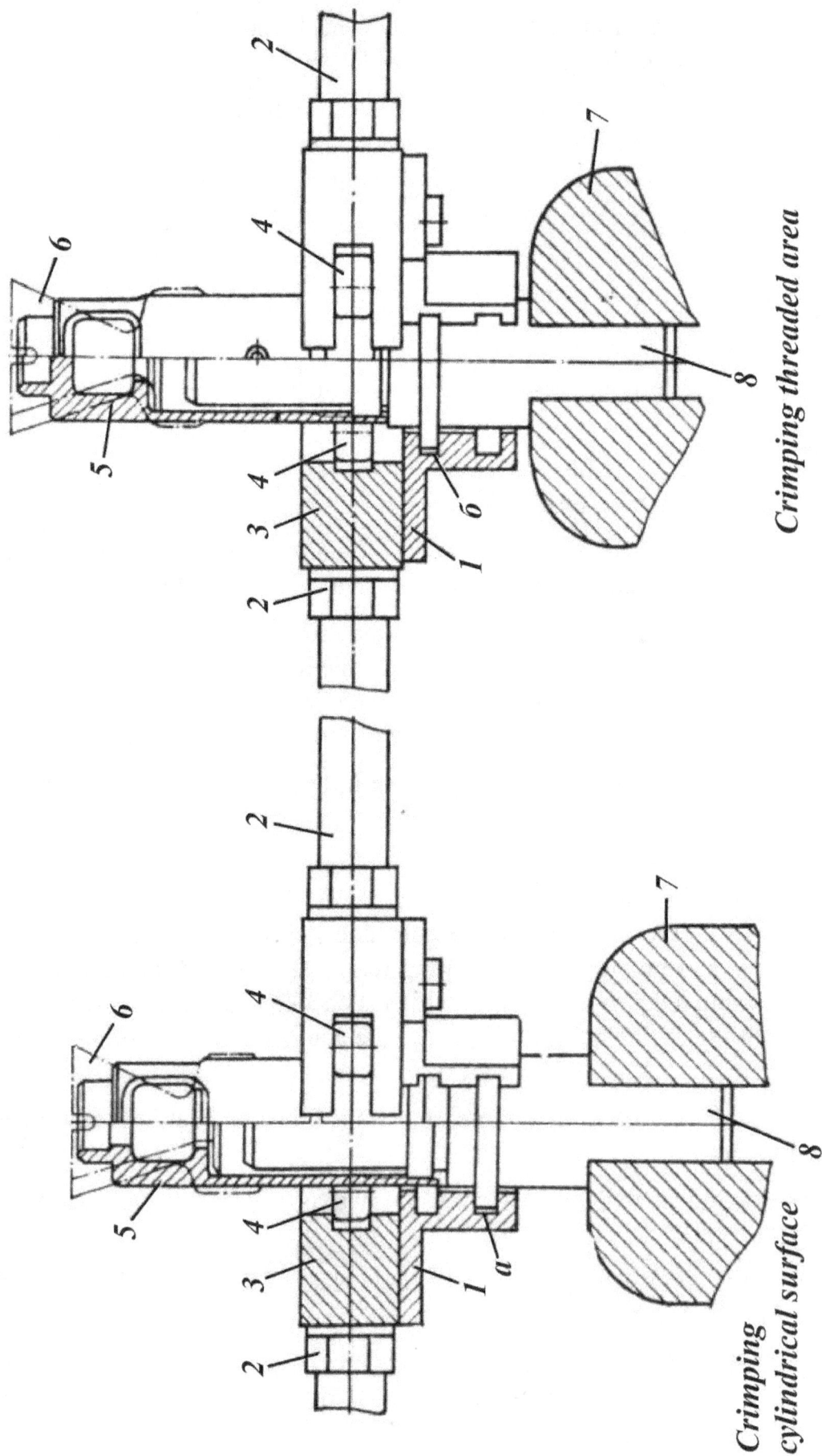

**Fig. 33.** Roll crimping of the muzzle brake and flash hider:

*1* – arc; *2* – torque bar; *3* – tool body; *4* – roller; *5* – muzzle brake; *6* – flash hider; *7* – vise; *8* – mandrel; *a* – bottom groove; *б* – top groove

*Crimping threaded area*

*Crimping cylindrical surface*

# 8. REPAIRING THE RECEIVER

## 8.1. Movement of barrel, rails, front trunnion or rear trunnion

See the General Guidelines ch. 3.

When these parts are moving, send in the weapon for a major overhaul.

## 8.2. Movement of the buttstock

See the General Guidelines ch. 3 and sec. 11.7 of this manual.

## 8.3. Movement of the trigger guard

Movement of the trigger guard in conjunction with the receiver is not acceptable, squeezing grease around the rivets is allowed.

If movement persists, disassemble the trigger mechanism and remove the selector from the receiver, tighten the loose rivets, install the selector and assemble the trigger mechanism.

After eliminating trigger guard movement, check retention of the selector lever by the selector stop, as described in sec. 10.3.

## 8.4. Difficulty removing and installing the receiver cover

When the heel of the return spring guide projection *1* (Fig. 4) is pressed by thumb it should move freely along the slot receiver.

Installing the receiver cover must be done by pressing forward and down on the back of the receiver cover by hand.

When there is difficulty removing or installing the receiver cover, straighten it on a mandrel (Appendix 1, item 2.14), and clean and make flush any raised metal on the edges with a file.

Rectify any bent parts of the recoil spring guide mechanism.

## 8.5. The receiver cover falls off

The receiver cover *14* (Fig. 1-3), should not separate from the receiver without pressing the heel protrusion of the recoil spring guide *1* (Fig. 4).

If the receiver cover falls off, replace unfit recoil spring *3*, recoil spring guide *1* and rod *2*.

For broken guides on the heel of the recoil spring guide assembly *1,* sand them down 1-1.5 mm, weld up using an electrode E50-W and machine according to Fig. 34.

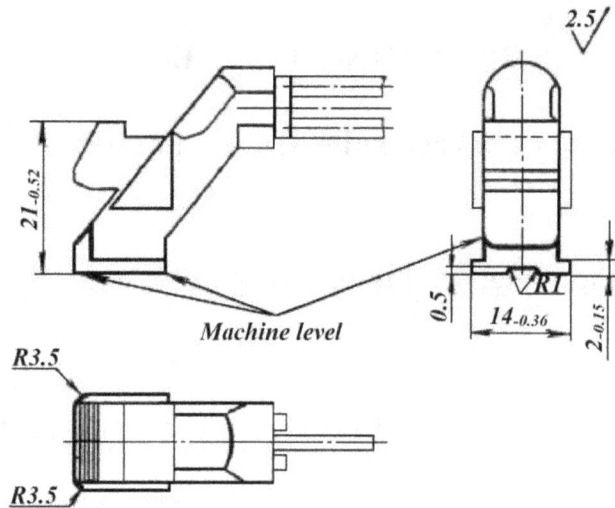

**Fig. 34.** Modification of the heel of the projection on the recoil spring guide assembly after resurfacing

## 8.6. Cracks in the receiver cover

If there is a crack in the receiver cover *14* (Figs. 1-3), drill a hole in the end of the crack with a diameter of 1.5-2 mm to allow use of the receiver cover without welding.

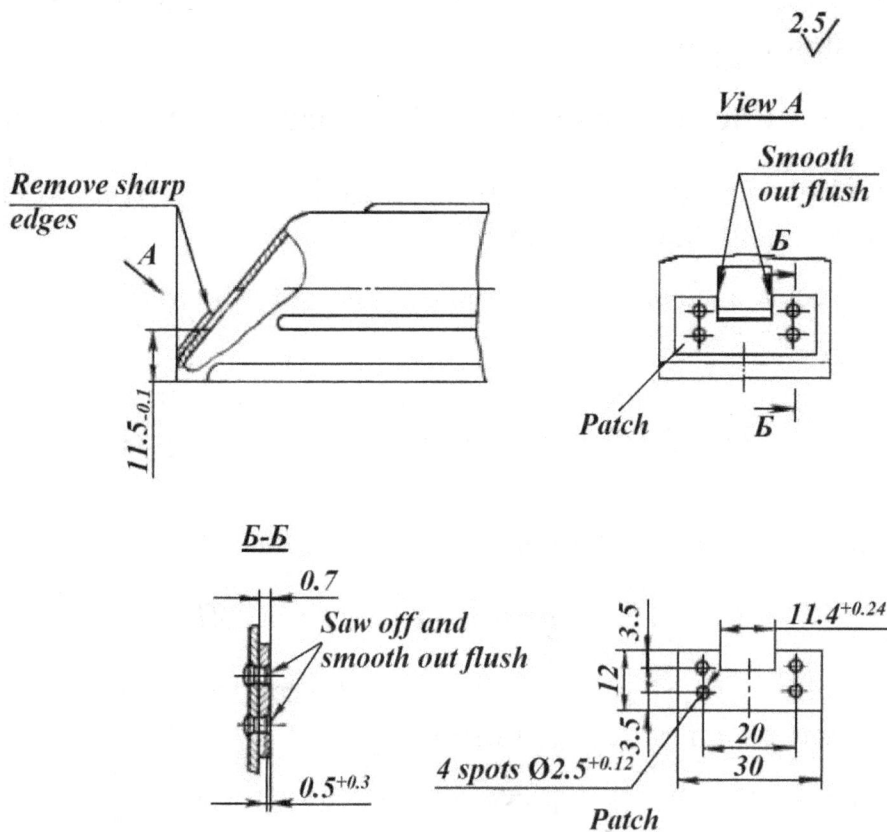

**Fig. 35.** Construction of a patch on the receiver cover
Material: Steel 35

If it is impossible to remedy the problem in this way replace the receiver cover, as indicated in sec. 5.6 and 5.7.

If there is a crack in the opening for the heel of the recoil spring guide, put a patch with thickness of 0.7 mm on the outside of the receiver cover using four rivets as shown in Fig. 35.

### 8.7. Gas tube latch is not retained in the closed position

Gas tube latch *18* (Fig. 1-3) shall be securely held in the recess in the rear sight block *17* when rotated by hand or using the cleaning kit case; self-rotation when shooting is not allowed.

When bending the arm of the gas tube latch put the arm of the gas tube latch vertically and bend arm against the rear sight block. To tighten the arm of the gas tube latch, re-crimp the head of the gas tube latch shaft with the gas tube latch supported on the mandrel (Appendix 1, item 2.17) to eliminate movement. If necessary, replace the gas tube latch arm with the shaft as described in sec. 5.22.

### 8.8. Movement of the upper handguard on the gas tube

Longitudinal and transverse movement of the upper handguard *20* (Fig. 1-3) on the gas tube *23* is not allowed.

If the upper handguard moves, crimp the handguard retainer ring sections of the gas tube assembly or replace the upper handguard retainer spring *19*.

### 8.9. Longitudinal cracks in the gas tube

Longitudinal cracks in the front end of gas tube *23* (Fig. 1-3) are not acceptable. Cracks in the middle of the gas tube are acceptable.

When there are unacceptable cracks replace the upper handguard/gas tube assembly *21*, as described sec. 5.17.

### 8.10. Movement of the upper handguard/gas tube assembly on the receiver with barrel assembly

Vertical movement of the rear end of the upper handguard/gas tube assembly *21* (Fig. 1-3) when the gas tube latch *18* is locked is not allowed.

Movement of the front end is not checked.

If there is movement, straighten cylindrical channel of the gas tube *23* from the rear using the conical mandrel (Appendix 1 item 2.16).

If necessary, resurface the worn bevel on the rear end of the gas tube with a layer of metal using electrode E38-2, work and adjust the gas tube assembly as per Fig.36 so that it will sit in place without movement as per Fig. 22.

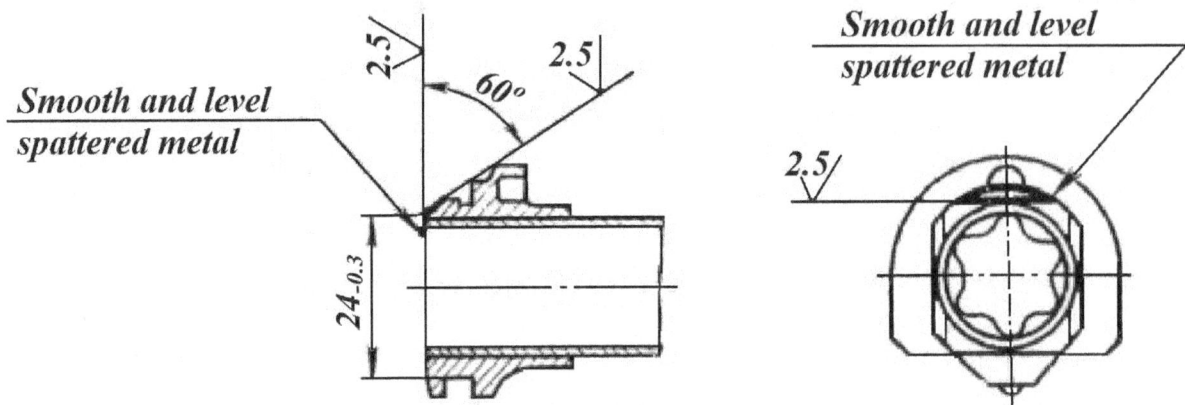

**Fig. 36.** Modification of the bevel of the gas tube after resurfacing

### 8.11. Difficulty removing and installing the upper handguard/gas tube assembly

When you turn the gas tube latch *19* (Fig. 1-3) up, the upper handguard/gas tube assembly should be removable by force of hand from the receiver with barrel assembly.

If the frontend of the gas tube *23* is bent, straighten it on a mandrel (Appendix 1, item 2.15).

### 8.12. Longitudinal movement of the lower handguard

Longitudinal movement of the lower handguard *38* (Fig. 1-3) when fixed to the receiver with barrel assembly may be no more than 0.5 mm.

If the longitudinal movement of the lower handguard is more than 0.5 mm, prepare putty using adhesive SFZh-309; apply a coat of it on the front end of the lower handguard; after the putty is dry fit the lower handguard in a place so that there is no movement.

If necessary, replace the lower handguard, as described in sec. 5.20.

### 8.13. Difficulty removing and installing the lower handguard

Removing from and installing on the lower handguard *38* (Fig. 1-3) to the receiver with the barrel assembly must be easily done by hand.

If a large effort is required, straighten any bent side of the lower handguard retainer *37*; straighten a bent arm on the lower handguard retainer lock *22*.

If necessary, replace the lower handguard retainer, as described in sec. 5.21.

### 8.14. Horizontal and vertical movement of the rear end of the lower handguard

Horizontal and vertical movement of the rear end of the lower handguard *38* (Fig. 1-3) of no more than 0.3 mm is acceptable.

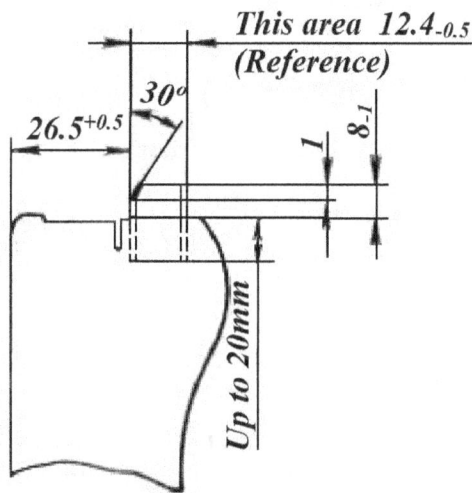

**Fig. 37.** Restoration of the tang of the lower handguard for assault rifle

When the tang is worn, cut slots to a depth of 20 mm and a thickness of 1.5-2mm install insets and adjust

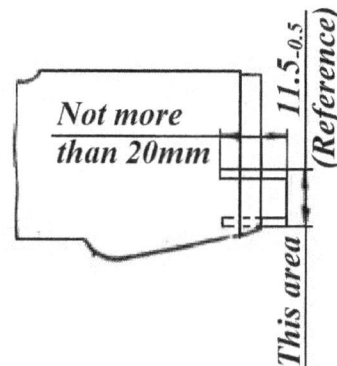

**Fig. 38.** Restoration of the tang of the lower handguard for machine gun

When the tang is worn, cut slots to a depth of 20 mm and a thickness of 1.5-2mm install insets and adjust

When movement is unacceptable, remove the lower handguard spring, prepare for installing the lower handguard (forearm) inserts, and install the inserts as shown in Fig. 37 and 38.

If necessary, replace the lower handguard, as described in sec. 5.20.

### 8.15. Movement of the pistolgrip on the receiver

Movement of the pistol grip *49* (Fig. 1-3) on the receiver is not acceptable.

If the grip is moving, screw the connecting screw *50* and the way in and stake and flare its end.

### 8.16. Broken pistol grip

Replace the pistol grip *49* (Fig. 1-3), as described in sec. 5.14.

### 8.17. Magazine falls out of the receiver

The magazine must easily be inserted into the receiver and the magazine catch *42* (Fig. 1-3) by force of the spring *44* should snap into place under the magazine lug without pressing by hand and it should hold the magazine from falling out.

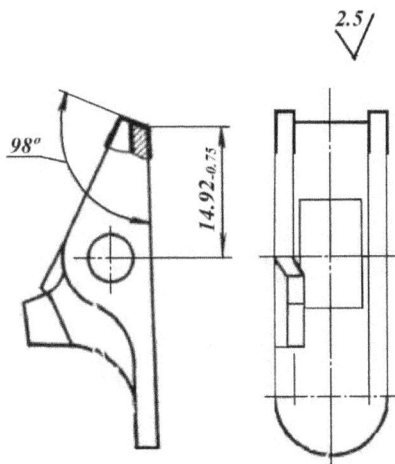

**Fig. 39.** Modification of the magazine catch after surfacing

Metal deposition on the side surface to be smoothed out flush

The magazine should only be able to be removed from the receiver when the magazine catch is pressed forward.

If the magazine falls out, replace the bad magazine catch spring *44*, as described in sec. 5.5.

When beveling the upper edge of the magazine catch, bevel the edge of the magazine catch at an angle of 98° as per Fig. 39.

After beveling the catch, install it on the receiver using the temporary axis pin (Appendix 1, item 2.1) and check the protrusion of the upper end of the catch out from the rear wall of the magazine opening in the receiver (dimension Ж in Fig. 9); if the protrusion is less than 0.5 mm, file the magazine catch stop on plane И.

After fitting the catch, check the vertical movement of the magazine in the receiver. To do this, pull the magazine all the way up against the selector stop plate and use the lower edge of the receiver to make a scribe mark on the magazine, then pull the magazine all the way down and apply a second scribe mark (the difference in the marks on the magazine is caused by the catch). Vertical movement of the magazine determined by the distance between the marks must not be more than 0.5 mm.

If the vertical movement of the magazine does not exceed 0.5 mm, install the magazine catch axis pin on the receiver, crimp and flare the ends of the axis pin and check the feeding of training ammunition from the magazine into the chamber.

If the vertical movement of the magazine is more than 0.5 mm, replace the magazine catch as described in sec. 5.5.

If the vertical movement of the magazine is more than 0.5 mm (in wartime), grind off the upper end of the latch 1-1.5 mm as shown in Fig.39 and repair the latch, as described in sec. 5.5.

It is acceptable to stretch the top front edge of the magazine catch and then adjust the magazine catch, providing the final vertical movement of the magazine on the magazine catch is not more than 0.5 mm.

### 8.18. Vertical movement of the magazine on the magazine catch

Vertical movement of the magazine on the magazine catch *42* (Fig. 1-3) is acceptable, if it takes place when there is normal load of ammunition.

When magazine movement is unacceptable replace the magazine catch, as specified in sec. 5.5.

# 9. REPAIR OF THE BOLT CARRIER WITH THE BOLT

## 9.1. Tight movement of the bolt carrier with the bolt

See the General Guidelines ch. 3.

Nick on the friction surfaces, smooth with a file.

Bend in the receiver cover *14* (Fig. 1-3) straighten on mandrel (Appendix 1, item 2.14). Bend in the gas tube *23;* straighten on mandrel (Appendix 1, item. 2.15).

Rubbing of the bolt carrier handle on the receiver cover, file the contact are on the receiver cover.

## 9.2. The bolt carrier with bolt does not move to the rearmost position

See the General Guidelines ch. 3.

When there is diametrical clearance of more than 0.2 mm for AK74, AKS74, RPK74, RPKS74 and 0.15 mm for the AKS74U of the gas piston *4* (Fig. 23), replace as described in sec. 5.18.

If after replacing the gas piston the bolt carrier with the bolt will not completely go to the rear position when the weapon is fired, send the weapon for major overhaul.

When movement of the gas piston is more than 6 mm for the AK74, AKS74, RPK74, RPKS74 and 4 mm for the AKS74U, eliminate it by selecting and installing a gas piston pin *5* with an increased pin diameter.

If chromium chips, traces of rust or corrosion exist in the chamber causing tight extraction of cartridges, send the weapon for a major overhaul.

## 9.3. If the bolt carrier with the bolt does not move completely to the forward position

See the General Guidelines ch. 3.

Se the fault causes and remedies in sec. 9.1.

Further, issue can be caused if there is deterioration of or a kink in the recoil spring *3* (Fig. 4).

Replace the defective spring as specified in sec. 5.2.

## 9.4. Failure to load the next cartridge in the chamber of the barrel

See the General Guidelines ch. 3.

Further, issue can happen if the vertical movement of the magazine on the magazine catch *42* Fig. 1-3) is more than 0.5 mm replace latch as described in Sect. 5.5.

## 9.5. Transverse rupture of shell case

If the Field No-Go gauge K-5 (Appendix 1, item 2.8) chambers (defined by the presence of no gap between the front wall of the bolt carrier and the receiver on the left), replace the bolt, as described in sec. 5.4.

## 9.6. Failure of spent cartridges to extract or eject

See the General Guidelines ch. 3.

If the extractor *8* (Fig. 5) allows the 2 mm no-go side of gauge K-7 to pass under the hook of the extractor; replace the extractor, as described in sec. 5.4.

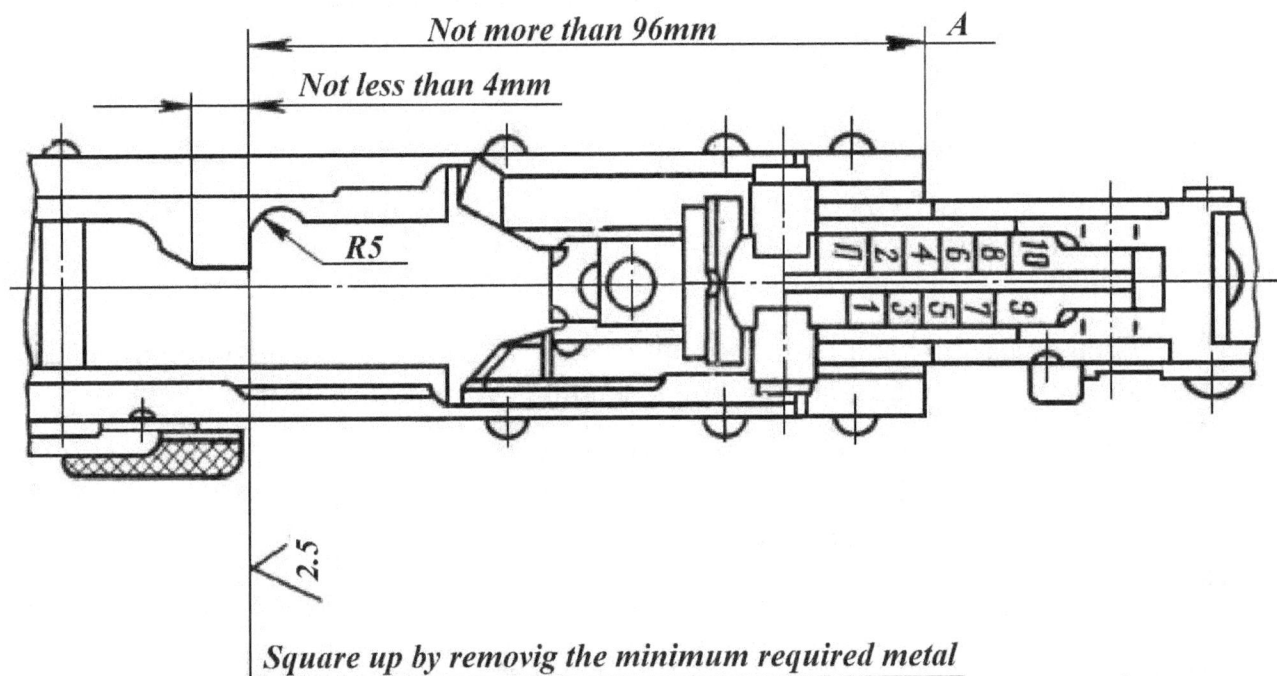

**Fig. 40.** Squaring up of the ejector in receiver

If there are nicks and rounding on the ejector smooth it out and square it up, and check it per Fig.40; if dimension *A* is more than 96 mm send the weapon for a major overhaul.

## 10. REPAIR OF THE FIRING MECHANISM

### 10.1. Hammer does not stay cocked

See the General Guidelines ch. 3.

If the single sear surface of the hammer *11* (Fig. 1-3) becomes rounded, square it on plane *Б* in Figure 41; if rounding occurs on the trigger sear hook, square it on plane *B* in Fig. 42.

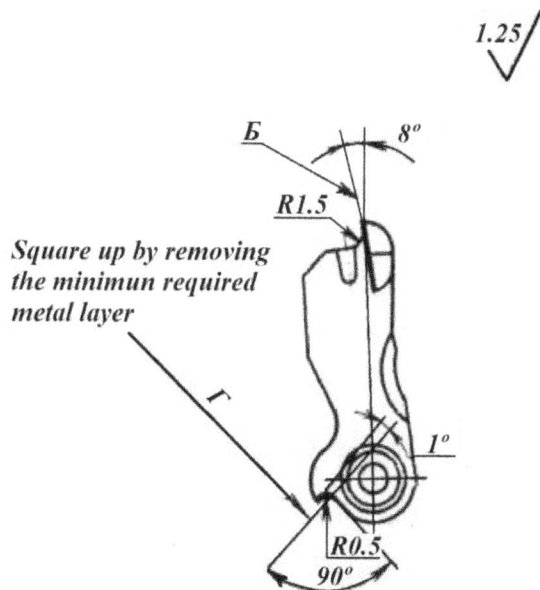

**Fig. 41** Modification of the single sear surface and the auto-sear surface on the hammer

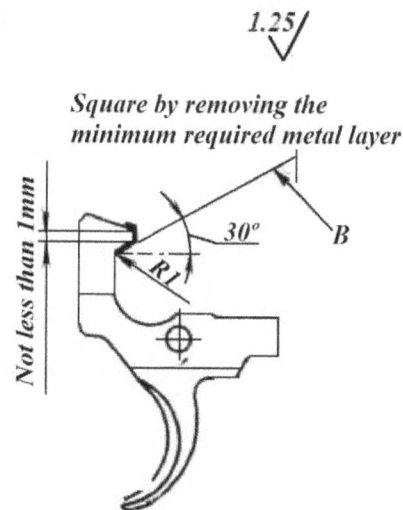

**Fig. 42** Modification of the trigger sear hook

Bad disconnector spring *48* (Fig. 1-3) is to be replaced as specified in sec. 5.19.9.

## 10.2. Interference of the hammer by disconnector or auto-sear

Partially disassemble weapon. Put the hammer *11* (Fig. 26) in the cocked position and set selector lever *5* for automatic fire.

Push the hammer head all the way back and abruptly let it go, interference with the hammer by the disconnector *6* is not allowed.

Pull the trigger *46*, the hammer should be caught on the auto-sear. Without releasing the trigger, press the hammer head all the way back and abruptly let it go, interference with the hammer by the auto-sear *12* is not allowed.

Cause of the problem.

10.2.1. Hammer will not cock on the auto-sear.

See sec. 10.1.

10.2.2. Rounding of the surface of the auto-sear hook on the hammer and the sear arm face of the auto-sear.

Modify the auto-sear hook on the hammer on plane *Г* as per Fig. 41 and the auto-sear as per Fig. 43.

10.2.3. Deterioration of or a kink in auto-sear spring.

Replace the bad auto-sear spring, *12* (Fig. 26), as specified in sub-sec. 5.19.8.

**Square up by removing the
minimum required metal layer**

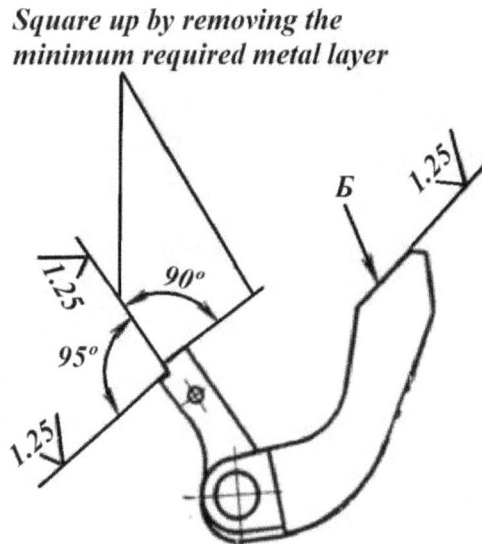

**Fig. 43.** Modification of the auto-sear

## 10.3. The selector lever does not hold in the position it is set to

See the General Guidelines ch. 3.

Overshoot of the selector lever *5* (Fig. 26) past the trigger stop of the trigger guard assembly is not allowed; if there is overshoot of the selector lever, straighten it.

Replace bad selector as described in sec. 5.19.7.

## 10.4. Hammer is not held in cocked position by the selector

Put the hammer *11* (Fig. 28) cocked in the firing position, set the selector lever *5* to safe position and pull the trigger *46*; release of the hammer is not allowed.

If the hammer releases, replace the selector, as described in sec. 5.19.7.

## 10.5. Tight or weak release of the hammer

With the selector lever *5* (Fig. 1-3) set on single fire, release of the hammer *11* must occur when the trigger *46* is pulled by a force between 1.5-2.5 kg.

If the hammer release is tight, polish any places the trigger is rubbing on the edge of the trigger opening in the receiver.

If the release is weak, replace the mainspring *45* as described in sec. 5.19.4.

## 10.6. Hammer does not release when cocked

Release of the hammer *11* (Fig. 1-3) from being cocked should occur when the trigger *46* is pressed after pushing the bolt carrier with the bolt *13* all the way forward. Catching of the hammer on the recoil spring is not acceptable.

If there is deterioration of or a kink in the mainspring *45*, replace it as described in sec. 5.19.4.

If the guide *1* (Fig. 4) or the rod *2* of the recoil spring assembly is bent, straighten it.

## 10.7. The trigger does not return to its original position

See the General Guidelines ch. 3.

If there is deterioration of or a kink in the mainspring *45* (Fig. 1-3), replace it as described in sec. 5.19.4.

## 10.8. Failure to fire automatically with the selector lever set at automatic fire

With the bolt carrier with bolt *13* (Fig. 1-3) moved back, the trigger *46* squeezed and the selector lever *5* set at automatic fire, the hammer *11* must engage the auto-sear and should not engage the disconnector *6* thus cocking the hammer on the auto-sear, and when the bolt carrier is moved to within 3-6 mm of the extreme forward position, the hammer must come out of engagement with the auto-sear *12* and strongly hit the firing pin.

Cause of the problem.

10.8.1. Worn or rounding of the auto-sear hook on the hammer or the auto-sear, causing the hammer to be retained by the auto-sear.

Polish the auto-sear hook on the hammer plane *Б* in Fig. 41 or the sear surface on the auto-sear (Fig. 43), reassemble and make sure the auto-sear hook on the hammer engages the auto-sear on a length of not less than 1 mm (dimension *A* in Fig. 25 and 26).

In addition, check the strength of retention of the hammer on the auto-sear by pressing the hammer back and sharply releasing it; failure of the hammer to be retained by the auto-sear is not acceptable.

If the failure of the hammer to stay engaged by the auto-sear cannot be eliminated, replace the hammer or auto-sear as specified in sec. 5.19.5 and 5.19.3.

10.8.2. Bending of the release lever on the auto-sear causing friction of lever on the wall of the receiver and magazine.

Straighten the release lever on the auto-sear *12* (Fig. 1-3), reinstall it and check the clearances between the auto-sear and the wall between the receiver and the auto-sear and the magazine, they must be not less than 0.2 mm.

10.8.3. Deterioration of or a kink in the auto-sear spring.

Replace auto-sear spring *12*, as described in sec. 5.19.8.

10.8.4. Worn or crushed end of the release lever of the auto-sear.

Replace the auto-sear as described in sec. 5.19.3.

After installing the new auto-sear, engagement of the end of the release lever of the auto-sear with the auto-sear trip extension on the bolt carrier should no longer be prevented.

### 10.9. Spontaneous firing of automatic or double shots at with the selector lever set to single fire

When the bolt carrier with the bolt *13* (Fig. 1-3) is moved back, the trigger *46* is squeezed, and selector lever *5* is set to single fire, the hammer 11 should engage the hook of the disconnector *6* and be held until the trigger is released.

Cause of the problem.

10.9.1. Rounding or wearing of the cocking sear surface of the hammer or on the disconnector.

Remove the disconnector and the hammer; modify the cocking sear surface of the hammer on plane *Б* as per (Fig. 41) or the disconnector as per Fig. 44.

After modification of the disconnector, the ability to set the selector lever 5 (Fig. 1-3) on single fire must be ensured.

10.9.2. Deterioration of or a kink in the disconnector spring.

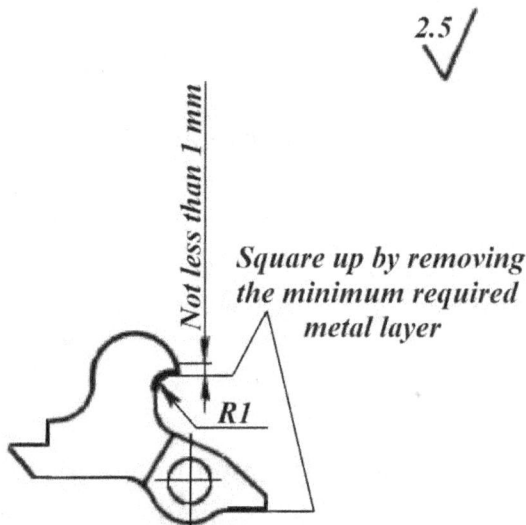

**Fig. 44.** Modifying the disconnector

Push downward (on the tail) on the disconnector *6* and release quickly, the disconnector must energetically return to its original position under the action of the disconnector spring *48*.

Replace the disconnector spring, as described in sec. 5.19.9.

10.9.3. Bending of the tab on the selector.

Replace the selector, as described in sec. 5.19.7.

### 10.10. Misfires

Check the protrusion of the firing pin *7* (Fig. 8).

Press on the firing pin so that its rear end is flush with the rear end of the bolt *6*, and check the protrusion of the firing pin from the bottom of the cup of the bolt using gauge K-1 (Appendix 1, item 2.4).

If the protrusion of the firing pin is less than 1.4 mm or the firing pin is broke, replace the firing pin, as described in sec. 5.4.13.

If the firing pin tip is damaged, smooth the firing pin tip removing the minimum required metal layer as per Fig. 45.

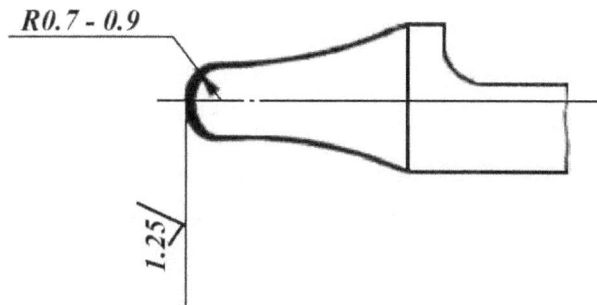

**Fig. 45.** Smoothing the firing pin tip

If there is deterioration of the mainspring *45* (Fig. 1-3), replace it as described in sec. 5.19.4.

### 10.11. Ejection of axis pins for the firing mechanism

Ejection of the axis pins for the firing mechanism *47* (Fig. 1-3) done by force of hand is not allowed.

If there is a kink in auto-sear spring *12*, replace the auto-sear spring, as described in sec. 5.19.8.

### 10.12. Bolt bounce retarder does not energetically return to the forward position

When the bolt bounce retarder *9* (Fig. 1 and 3) is pressed all the way back, it must rotate freely on its axis. Upon releasing it, it must actively return under the action of the bolt bounce retarder spring *9* to the forward position. While doing this it is allowed for the base of the retarder to touch the main spring if it does it without jamming.

If there is deterioration of or a kink in the bolt bounce retarder spring, replace it.

### 10.13. Jamming of the latch of the bolt bounce retarder

The bolt bounce retarder latch *8* (Fig. 1 and 3) should rotate freely on the axis pin *7*. If the latch jams, replace the axis pin.

When installing the axis pin, stake it so as to ensure free rotation of the latch; when installed, the axis pin is allowed longitudinal of movement of no more than 0.3 mm.

# 11. REPAIR OF WOODEN BUTTSTOCK, WOODEN UPPER HANDGUARD, LOWER HANDGUARDS AND PISTOL GRIP. PECULIARITIES OF REPAIR OF PLASTIC PARTS

General troubleshooting of wooden parts is done according to the General Guidelines (ch. 3).

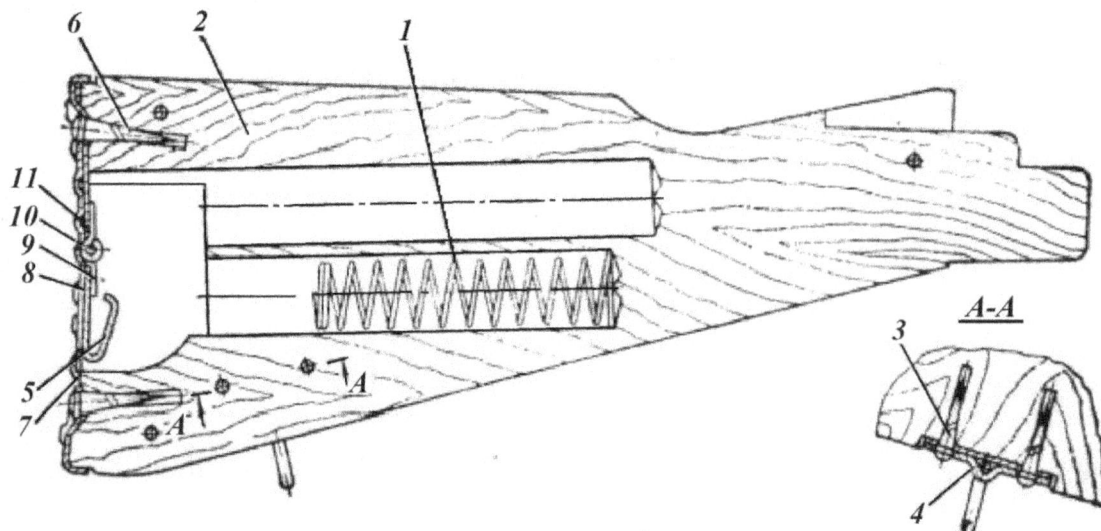

**Fig. 46.** Buttock assembly 6P20.Sb 5 for assault rifle AK74:

*1* – cleaning kit case retainer spring 6P20.5-5; *2* - buttstock 6P20.5-1; *3* sling swivel assembly screw 6P20.5-4; *4* – sling swivel assembly 6P20.Sb 5-1; *5* – cleaning kit trapdoor assembly 6P20.Sb 5-2; *6* – butt plate screw 6P20.5-3; *7* - butt plate 6P20.5-16; *8* - trapdoor cover 6P20.5-8; *9* trapdoor cover spring 6P20.5-10; *10* – trapdoor cover axis pin 6P20.5- 11; *11* – trapdoor cover hinge 6P20.5-9

Plates produce all wooden parts of the birch plywood board or birch bar. Processing inserts and fillings to produce flush with the main surface.

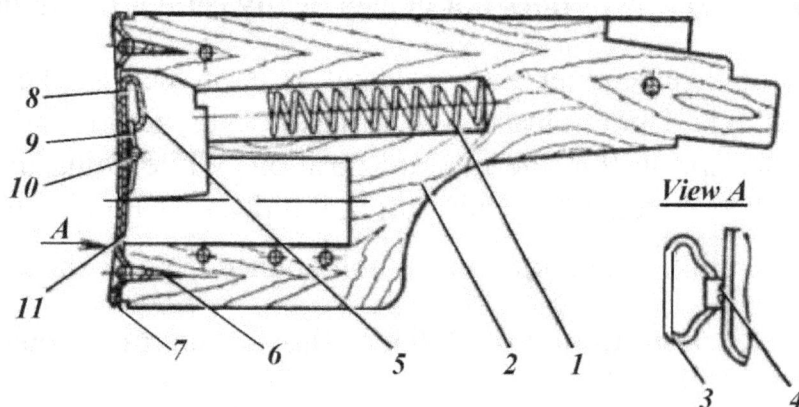

**Fig. 47.** Butt assembly 6P18.Sb 5 to the gun RPK74

*1* - cleaning kit case retainer spring 6P20.5-5; *2* - buttstock 6P18.5-1; *3* sling swivel assembly screw 6P20.5-4; *4* - sling swivel assembly 6P18.Sb 5-3; *5* - cleaning kit trapdoor cover assembly 6P18.Sb 5-2; *6* - butt plate screw 6P20.5-3; *7* – butt plate 6P18.5-2; *8* - trapdoor cover 6P20.5-8; *9* – trapdoor cover spring 6P20.5-10; *10* - trapdoor cover axis pin 6P20.5-11; *11* – trapdoor cover hinge 6P18.5-9

Configurations of buttstocks are shown in Fig. 46, 47, plastic buttstock – in Fig. 48 machine gun buttstock for RPKS74 - Fig. 17, the lower handguards - in Fig. 49, 50 and the upper handguards – in Fig. 1-3.

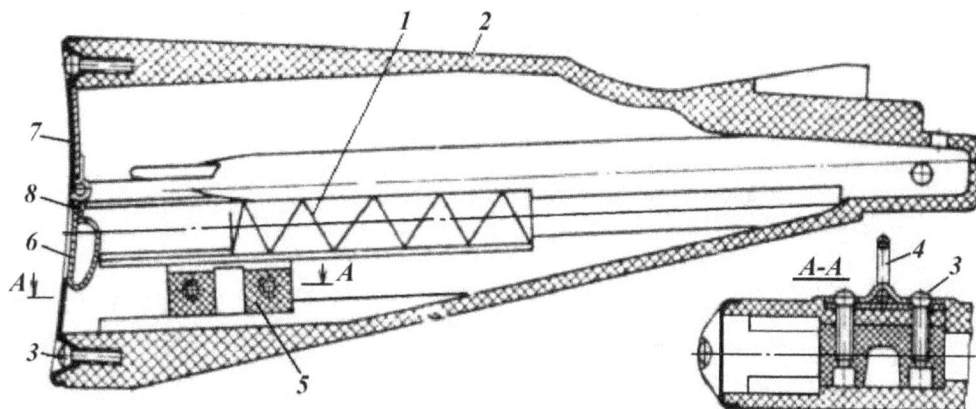

**Fig. 48.** Buttock assembly plastic 6P20.Sb 14 for assault rifle AK74:
*1* – cleaning kit case retainer spring 6P20.5-5; *2* - buttstock 6P20.14-1; *3* buttstock screw 6P20.14-5; *4* – sling swivel assembly 6P20.Sb 5-1; *5* – buttstock insert 6P20.14-4; *6* – cleaning kit trapdoor cover assembly 6P20.Sb 14-2; *7* - butt plate 6P20.14-2; *8* - trapdoor cover spring 6P20.5-8

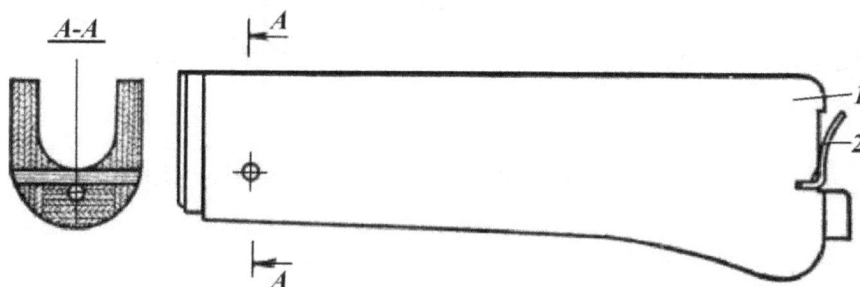

**Fig. 49.** handguard assembly 6P20.Sb 6 to AK74 machine and AKS74:
*1* - lower handguard 6P20.6-1; *2* - - lower handguard spring 6P20.6-4

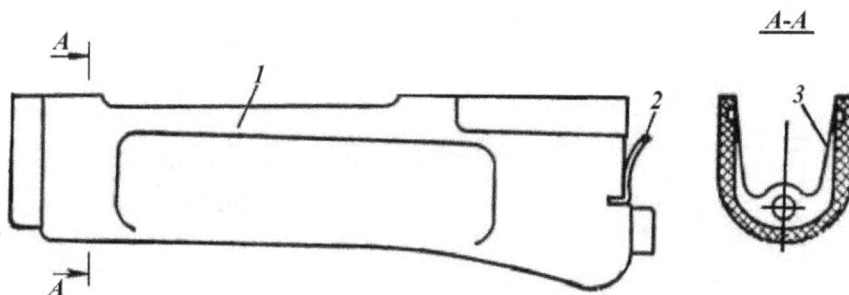

**Fig. 50.** Plastic handguard assembly 6P20.Sb 9 to the assault rifle AK74 and AKS74:
*1* - - lower handguard 6P20.Sb 9-1; *2* - - lower handguard spring 6P20.6-4; *3* - - lower handguard shield 6P20.9-3

### 11.1. Dents and chips on the surfaces of wooden parts

Dents and chips with length (diameter) of not more than 20 mm and a depth of no more than 5 mm, patch using putty made with adhesive SFZh-309; after drying of putty in the indented space, sand flush; it is allowed to put a patch in any place.

Dents and nicks length of more than 10 mm and a depth of more than 5 mm, patch using multiple applications of the adhesive with treatment to construct the patch as per Fig. 51; it is allowed to use a patch in any place. Insure the patch is flush with the surface of the component.

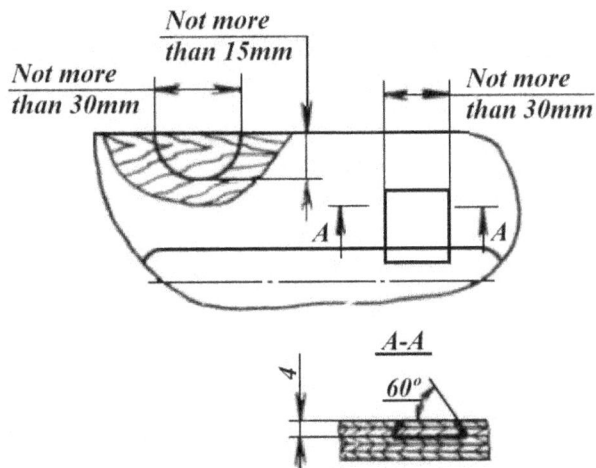

**Fig. 51.** Construction of patches for the wooden parts

## 11.2. Stratification of the veneer

If the veneer stratifies anywhere milled channel shown in Fig. 49, stick it back together with adhesive SFZh-309.

## 11.3. Movement of the butt plate or of the sling swivel

See the General Guidelines ch. 3.

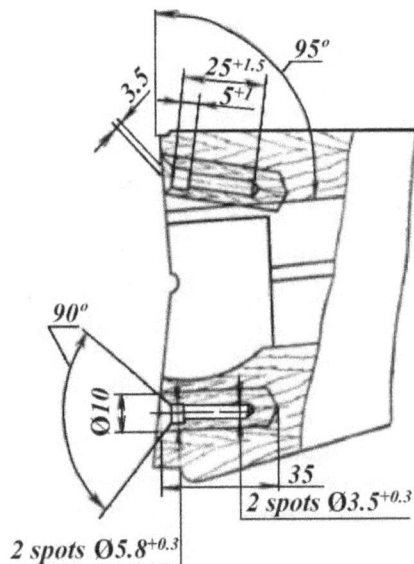

**Fig. 52.** Installation of plugs in the holes for the screws for the butt plate

If a screw for the butt plate or sling swivel is stripped out, drill the hole for screw to a diameter of 10 mm Fig. 52 and (or) 53, install a plug using adhesive SFZh-309, sand the ends of the plug flush, then reinstall the screw into the plug through the butt plate or sling attachment.

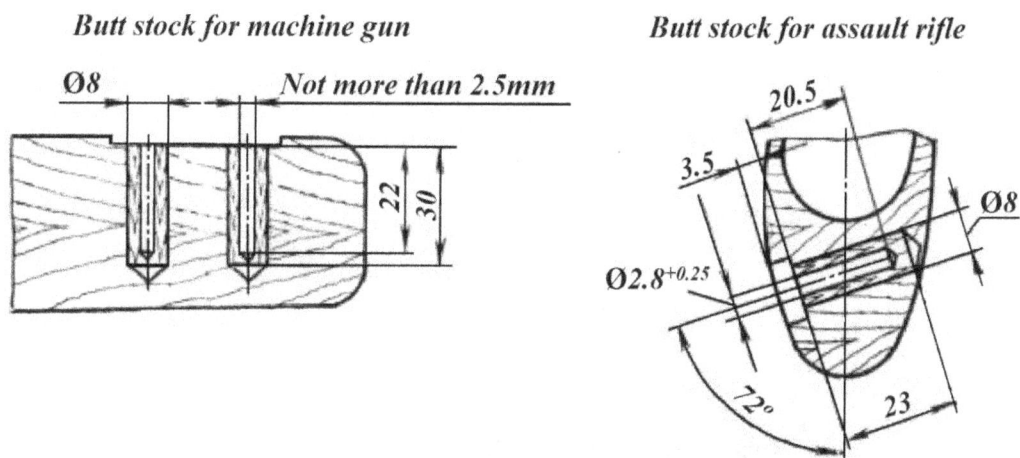

*Butt stock for machine gun*

*Butt stock for assault rifle*

**Fig. 53.** Installation of plugs in the holes for the screws for the sling swivel

### 11.4. Spring for the cleaning kit case not held in place with the butt

The spring for the cleaning kit case *1* (Fig. 46) should remain in the chamber in the buttstock and not fall out of it while vigorously shaking the weapon (without the case in the buttstock).

If the front coil of the cleaning kit case spring is bent or compressed, insert the spring in the chamber in the buttstock and check whether the spring is held in the hole.

### 11.5. The cleaning kit case with tools inside will not eject from the chamber in the buttstock

The cleaning kit case with tools inside should be easily removed from the chamber in the buttstock and easily go into it. When the thumb is pressed on the trapdoor cover *8* (Fig. 46), the cleaning kit case must be expelled far enough by spring *1* from the chamber in the buttstock so that it can be freely removed by hand.

Cause of the problem.

11.5.1. Chipped wood in the chamber in the buttstock.

Smooth out the chamber in the buttstock.

11.5.2. Deterioration of or a kink in the cleaning kit case spring.

Replace the cleaning kit case spring.

11.5.3. Trapdoor cover presses the case all the way into the chamber of the buttstock.

Apply putty to the top wall of the cleaning kit chamber in the buttock as per Fig. 54 using a mixture of adhesive SFZh-309 and sawdust (one part adhesive to one part of sawdust by volume) and dry for 5-6 hours.

After drying, smooth the area that was plastered so that there is no rubbing of the cleaning kit case on the chamber of the buttstock.

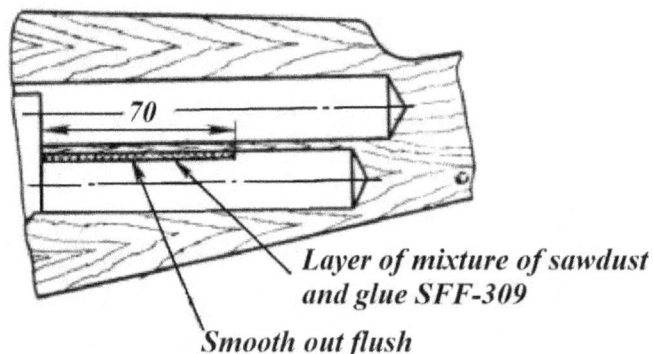

*Layer of mixture of sawdust
and glue SFF-309*

*Smooth out flush*

**Fig. 54.** Reworking the buttstock cleaning kit chamber

## 11.6. Trapdoor cover is held in the open position

When pressed all the way in and then released the trapdoor cover *8* (Fig. 46) under the action of the trapdoor cover spring *9* must energetically return to its original position.

If there is deterioration of or a kink in the trapdoor cover spring, replace it.

## 11.7. Movement of the buttstock in relation to the receiver or the buttstock hinge

Movement of the buttstock in relation to the receiver or the buttstock hinge is not allowed.

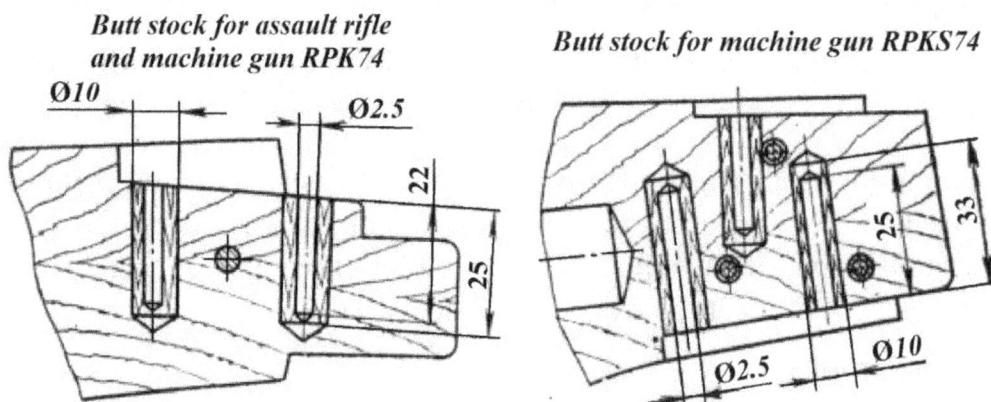

**Fig. 55.** Installation of plugs in the holes for the screws for the buttstock

Movement of the plastic buttstock is to be eliminated, as specified in sub-sec. 11.12.2.

Cause of the problem.

11.7.1. Wearing of the screw holes in the buttstock.

Drill out the hole in the buttstock for a 10 mm plug, make a wooden plug of diameter 10 mm and a length of 30 mm, secure it in the hole with adhesive and make the plug flush as per Fig. 55.

Use the hole in the rear trunnion to align and drill a hole for the screw and fasten the buttstock by screwing the screw into the plug.

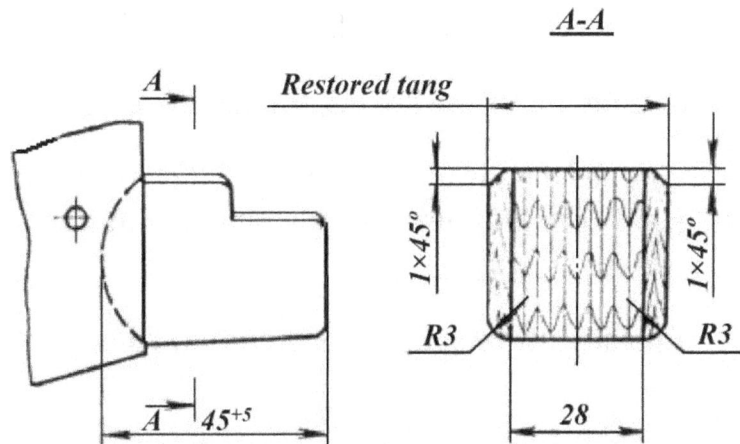

**Fig. 56.** Restoration of the tang of the buttstocks for assault rifle AK74 and machine gun RPK74

11.7.2. Deterioration of the buttstock tang.

Plane the sides of the buttstock tang as per Fig. 56 or 57 so it is 28 mm in width. Install shims on both sides and square them up.

Fit the buttstock as specified in sec. 5.10.

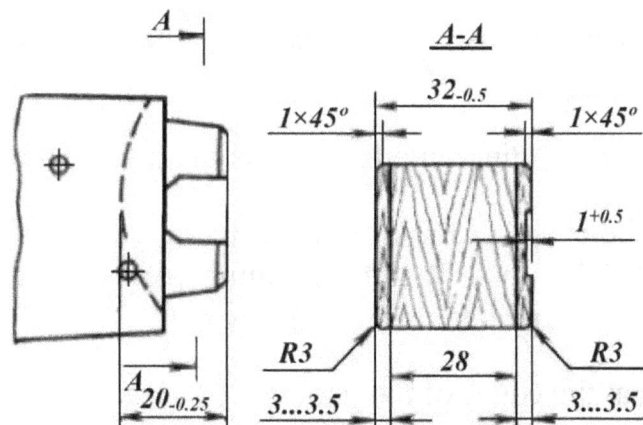

**Fig. 57.** Restoration of the tang of the buttstock for machine gun RPK74

### 11.8. Broken buttstock

If the buttstock cannot be repaired using the methods provided for in the General Guidelines ch. 3 and mentioned above in this section, replace the buttstock as specified in sec. 5.10.

### 11.9. Falling out from the pistol grip of the bushing for the grip screw

Reinstall the bushing for the grip screw using SFZh-309 adhesive or epoxy adhesive.

## 11.10. Gouge in the plastic parts buttstock, lower handguard or upper handguard

Sharp edges are to be knocked off, cleaned and smoothed with emery cloth.

## 11.11. Falling out of the spring for the lower handguard

Falling out of the spring for the lower handguard *2* (Fig. 49) is not permitted. If falling out of the lower handguard spring occurs, using a punch with a spherical end deepen the dimple in the lower handguard spring.

## 11.12. Repair of plastic buttstock, lower handguard or upper handguard

General instructions.

Repair of plastic parts made of polyamide brand PA6-211 GOST 17648-83-DS, produced with the use of an adhesive based on epoxy resin ED-16 GOST 10587-84 (for preparation see sec. 5.15.2) or glue on the basis of formic acid GOST 1706-78.

Prepare surfaces of the parts to be bonded by wiping (cleaning) with solvent 646 GOST 18188-72, and then let stand in the air to dry out the solvent.

After applying the adhesive, to cure the adhesive connection takes not less than 20 hours, and then it can be subjected to machining.

11.12.1. Possible defects in plastic buttstock, lower handguard or upper handguard and their solutions:

11.12.1.1. Chipping of the thin-walled ribs without opening the inner cavity of the part.

Chipped places on the crests of the ribs, work to an angle 30-60º, and blunt the sharp edges to a radius of 0.3-0.8 mm. If the remaining parts of the damaged edges are of length less than 10 mm, then reduce their height by half.

11.12.1.2. Chipping at the edges of the part.

If there are chips having a depth up to 5 mm, clean the sharp edges. Chips up to a depth of 15 mm restore with putty made of 1 part adhesive and 3 parts fine sawdust. At the built up place use a wooden block to remove excess putty. Degrease the damaged area. Apply a layer of putty on the damaged area. Dry the applied layer of putty and make flush with the surface of the part without damaging the ribs.

Chips with a depth of greater than 15 mm restore using inserts from plastic materials of dark color.

Set a wooden mandrel in place for use during the installation of the insert. Justify the edges of the damaged area by cutting them to an angle of 90º. Install an insert in the area with gaps between the insert and the part being repaired not more than 0.3 mm. Set the repaired item with the insert on the wooden mandrel and fasten them to the stationary mandrel using a clamp, thread, nails, etc. Clean the area being worked on and fill in the joints between the part and the insert with adhesive.

After the adhesive dries smooth any raised edges of the insert flush with the base of the work piece surface without damaging any ribs.

11.12.1.3. Cracks in the upper handguard and the lower handguard.

Drill a hole of diameter of 2-3.5 mm at the end of the crack. Cut at an angle of 90° to the surface the crack to a depth of 2/3 the thickness of the wall of the part, degrease the area being worked on and fill it with adhesive. After drying, do not remove the protruding part of the adhesive seam.

11.12.1.4. Holes.

For holes with a diameter of 20 mm, justify the edges. To fill a hole, machine a stepped shape plastic plug and to drive it through the hole so that the gap between the shoulder on the plug and the piece being repaired is less than 0.3 mm.

Degrease the modified area of the part and the plug. Liberally coat them with glue and install the plug in the part. Secure the plug in the part. After the glue has dried chamfer the plug.

11.12.1.5. Tangential breaks.

Tangential breaks that do not open into the internal cavity plug with putty as is done with chips at the edges of parts. Buttstocks with tangential breaks opening into the internal cavity having a cross direction with respect to the part cannot be repaired. Tangential breaks opening into the internal cavity and directed along the length of the buttstock of up to 4 mm plug with putty as is done with chips at the edges of parts.

11.12.1.6. Stripping out of the thread in the buttstock.

If the buttstock has a screw hole with stripped threads, degrease the bad hole and fill it with glue or putty. After drying of the glue or putty (about 20 h), re-drill the hole to a diameter of $4.5^{+0.3}$ mm, attach the buttstock to the receiver and secure it with screws. It is permitted in wartime to place the adhesive (mastic) on the screw.

11.12.2. Elimination of movement of the stock in the receiver.

Deterioration of the mounting area of the buttstock causing movement of the buttstock in the receiver is not allowed.

If there is movement, remove the buttstock from the receiver and determine where the worn (eroded) areas are on the buttstock. Use a file on the eroded areas to remove the surface layer of 0.2-0.3 mm. Degrease the modified areas and liberally coat them with glue (1.5-2.5 mm). After the glue is dry, fit the buttstock to the receiver so that the buttstock, before screwing in the screws, has no movement. Secure the buttstock with the screws.

# 12. REPAIR OF THE FOLDING BUTTSTOCK FOR THE ASSUALT RIFLE
(Fig. 16)

## 12.1. The butt is not retained in the folded position

Buttstock *1* must be securely held by the front stock latch *11* in the folded position. The self-locking front stock latch should catch the buttstock upon the approach to the extreme folded position. Movement of the buttstock in the front stock latch is allowed.

If the front stock latch does not hold the buttstock in the folded position, replace worn (broken) front latch spring *10* and (or) straighten the wall of the butt plate as described in sub-sec. 5.11.10 and 5.11.9.

## 12.2. The buttstock is not retained in the open position

Buttstock *1* must be securely held by rear stock latch *4* in the open position. The self-locking latch should catch the buttstock at the approach to the extreme open position.

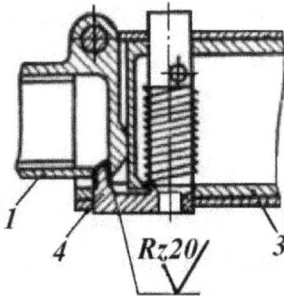

**Fig. 58.** Fit of the rear stock latch for assault rifles AKS74 and AKS74U:

*1* – buttstock; *3* – receiver; *4* – rear stock latch

If the rear stock latch does not hold the buttstock in the open position, check the fit of the rear stock latch as per Fig. 58; if there is deterioration of or a kink in the front stock latch spring *6,* replace it as specified in sub-sec. 5.11.1-5.11.7.

## 12.3. Movement of buttstock

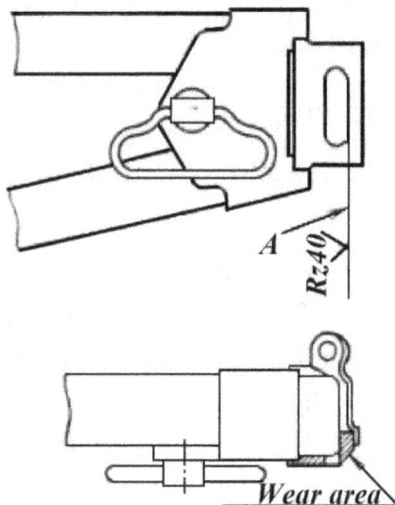

**Fig. 59.** Areas of deterioration of the stock latch window of the buttstock

Movement of buttstock *1* on the front stock latch *11* is allowed.

Movement of buttstock on the rear stock latch *4* is of no more than 4 mm on the at the back of the butt plate is allowed.

When there is unacceptable movement of the buttstock on the rear stock latch (Fig. 58) while hooked in the buttstock latch window (Fig. 59), file plane A of the window to adjust the movement of the buttstock on the stock latch so that it is not more than 2 mm. In wartime, sand the lock hook on the stock latch 1-1.5 mm, then re-surface it using a 50A electrode welder and rework it according to Fig. 60 so that the latch fits into the buttstock as per Fig.58.

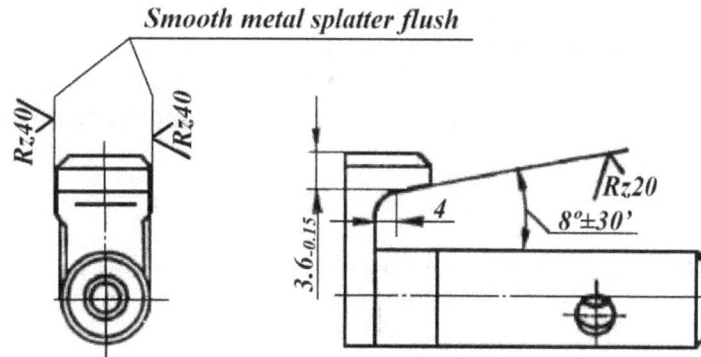

**Fig. 60.** Reworking the hook for the rear stock latch for assault rifles AKS74 and AKS74U after surfacing

## 12.4. Vertical movement of the buttstock

Total vertical movement of the buttstock in firing position, as measured at the butt plate of the buttstock is allowed to be no more than 4 mm.

If there is vertical movement of the buttstock that is more than 4mm replace stock axis pin *3*, as indicated in the sub-sec. 5.11.1, 5.11.2, 5.11.5, 5.11.7.

If with installation of a new axis pin unacceptable vertical movement of the buttstock persists, make a new buttstock axis pin (Appendix 2, fig. 117) without the section with diameter $4_{-0.2}$ mm.

## 12.5. Bent buttstock

Straighten out the stock so that the deviation of the rear end of the butt from the longitudinal axis of the weapon to the right is no more than 5 mm or to the left is no more than 3 mm.

If there are the cracks, make internal linings of steel type 35-50 with thickness 1.5-2 mm and weld them using electrode E42. Grind metal splatter flush.

# 13. REPAIR OF THE FOLDING BUTTSTOCK FOR LIGHT MACHINE GUN
(Fig. 17)

## 13.1. Dents and chips on surfaces of the buttstock

See sec. 11.1.

## 13.2. Stratification of the veneer on the surfaces of the buttstock

See sec. 11.2.

## 13.3. Movement of the butt plate on the buttstock

See the General Guidelines, ch. 3 and sec. 11.3.

## 13.4. Cleaning kit spring not held in place in the buttstock

See sec. 11.4.

## 13.5. Cleaning kit case with tools cannot be ejected from the chamber in the buttstock

See sec. 11.5.

## 13.6. Trapdoor for the cleaning kit chamber is held in the closed position

See sec. 11.6.

## 13.7. Movement of the buttstock in relation to the buttstock hinge

See sec. 11.7.

## 13.8. Difficulty transferring buttstock from the firing position to stowed position

When the stock latch, *18*, is taken off, transferring positions of the buttstock should take place without considerable effort.

The stock latch should be able to be taken off by pressing on it by hand.

When there is tightening up of the latch hole in the buttstock hinge and nicks on the locking part of the stock latch, clean up the edges of any raised metal from nicks.

## 13.9. The butt is not retained in the fighting (open) position

In the fighting position the buttstock must be securely held by the stock latch *18*.

If there is deterioration of or a kink in the latch spring 15, replace the bad spring as specified in sec. 5.12.

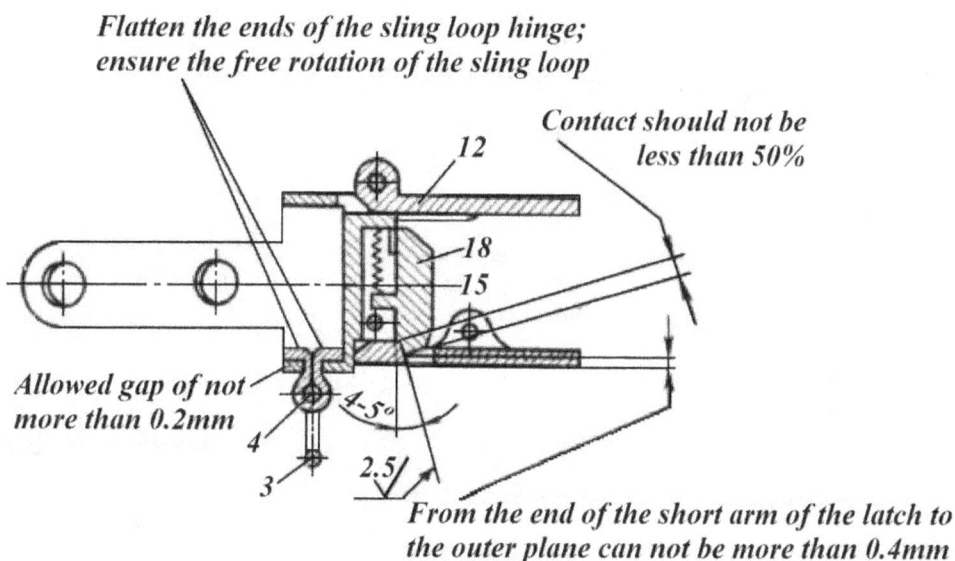

*Flatten the ends of the sling loop hinge;
ensure the free rotation of the sling loop*

*Contact should not be less than 50%*

12

18
15

*Allowed gap of not more than 0.2mm*

4-5°

4

3

2.5

*From the end of the short arm of the latch to
the outer plane can not be more than 0.4mm*

**Fig. 61.** Fitting the stock latch and restoration of the sling swivel for machine gun RPKS74:

*3* – sling loop and sling swivel hinge; *4* - sling swivel assembly; *12* – receiver; *15* - stock latch spring; *18* – stock latch

If the stock latch is worn, replace it, ensuring the requirements Fig. 61 are met.

In wartime, grind down the worn part of the stock latch 1-1.5 mm and re-surface with a metal layer using electrode E50-3, then process according to Fig. 62. Install the latch in the buttstock as per Fig. 61.

### 13.10. Movement of the buttstock on the stock latch in the firing position

Movement of the buttstock on the stock latch 18 (Fig. 17) butt when in the firing position, measured at the butt plate is allowed up to 4 mm provided weapon meets the cause of the problem and how to resolve them, see sec. 13.9.

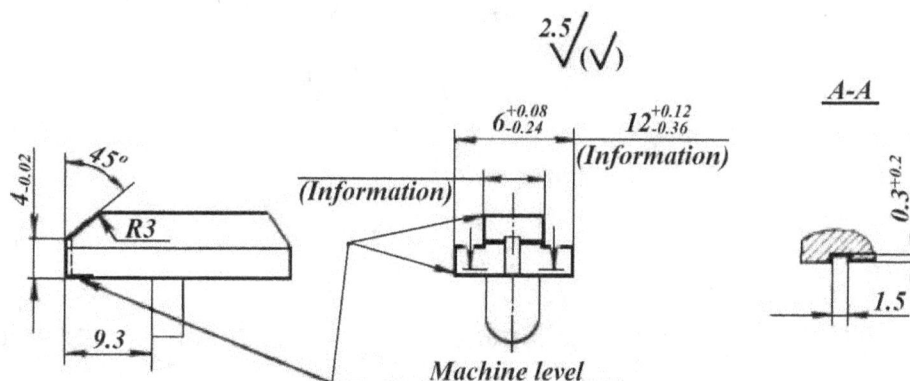

**Fig. 62.** Machining of stock latch for the machine gun RPKS74 after re-surfacing

## 13.11. The buttstock is not retained in the stowed (folded) position

In the stowed position, the buttstock must be securely held by the stock hook *17*. Movement of the buttstock is allowed, but is subject to the condition that it stays held hook.

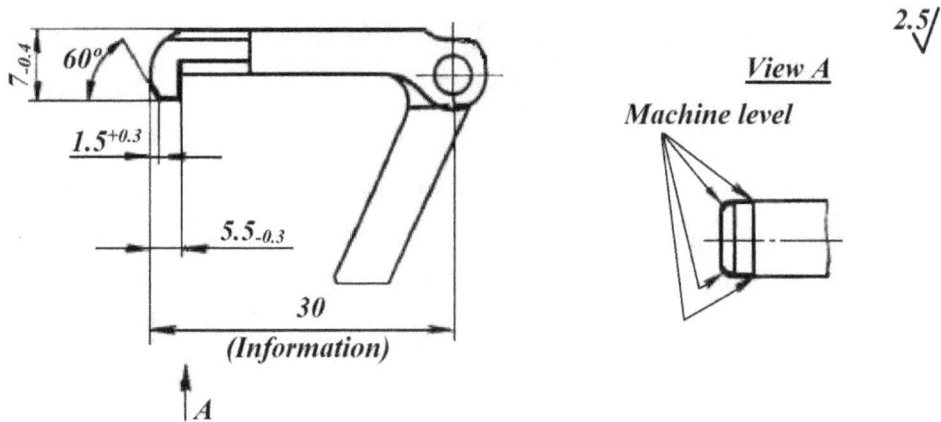

**Fig. 63.** Machining of latch hook tooth for machine gun RPKS74, after re-surfacing

If there is deterioration of or a kink in the stock hook spring *13*, replace it as described in sec. 5.12.

If the toe of the tooth on the hook is worn sand off 1-1.5 mm, re-surface with a layer of metal using electrode E50-3 and machine as per Fig. 63 or 64, so that it will hold the buttstock in place without movement of the buttstock on the hook.

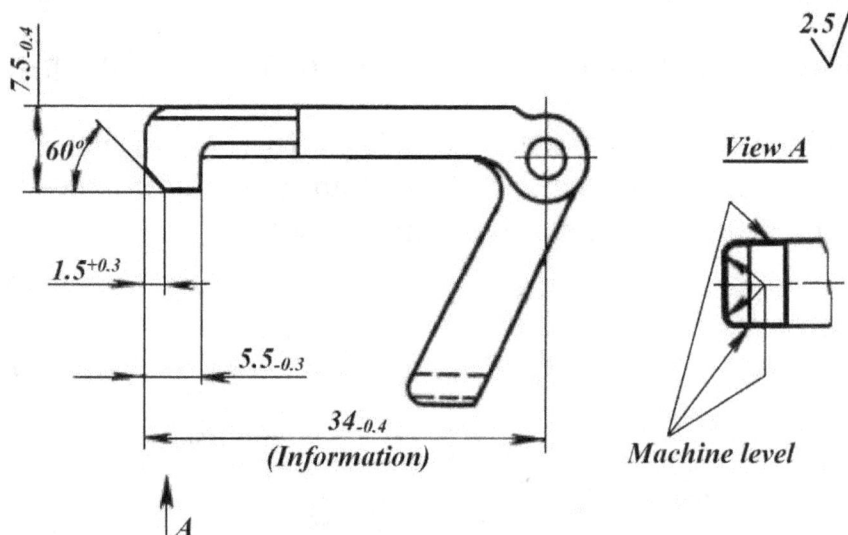

**Fig. 64.** Machining of the pawl on the tooth of the latch hook for machine gun RPKS74N1with night sight, after re-surfacing

## 13.12. Through cracks or fracture buttstock

See sec. 8.11 and 5.12.

86

# 14. REPAIR OF BIPOD FOR MACHINE GUN
## (Fig. 20)

## 14.1. Bending of the feet on the legs 1of the bipod

See the General Guidelines, ch. 3.

## 14.2. Tight rotation of the bipod base 6 on the barrel

See the General Guidelines, ch. 3.

## 14.3. Break in the legs 1of the bipod

See the General Guidelines, ch. 3.

## 14.4. Bending of the legs 1 of the bipod

Straighten legs of the bipod. Dents on legs resulting from the changes without disfiguring their appearance are allowed.

## 14.5. Legs 1 of the bipod are not retained in the stowed position

Latch *2* for the bipod legs should securely hold the legs in the folded (stowed) position and with shaking gun should not become unfastened.

If there is a bend in the middle of the legs latch, straighten latch. When bending the folded end of the latch, straighten it on a mandrel with a diameter of 24 mm.

If a break occurs or it is not possible to straighten the latch, to replace it as specified in sec. 5.16.4 and 5.16.5.

# 15. REPAIR OF MAGAZINE

## 15.1. Magazine floor plate 6 is not retained on the magazine housing 1

See the General Guidelines, ch. 3.

## 15.2. Magazine is difficult to fill with cartridges

See the General Guidelines, ch. 3.

## 15.3. Cartridges are not retained in the magazine

See the General Guidelines, ch. 3.

### 15.4. Magazine is not held in the receiver by the magazine catch

See the General Guidelines, ch. 3 and sec. 8.17.

### 15.5. Cartridges fail to feed from the magazine into the chamber of the barrel

Cause of the problem and how to resolve them, see sec. 8.18.

## 16. REPAIR BAYONET-KNIFE
(Fig. 65)

### 16.1. Bayonet is not retained on the weapon

Without pressing the bayonet latch button *17* and without the sheath *12* on the knife, the knife must be connected to the weapon by hand pressure and be securely held on by the latch.

Being able to remove the bayonet without pressing the latch is not allowed; movement of the bayonet on the bayonet lug is allowed.

When there is deterioration of or break in the latch spring *1*, replace the bad spring.

After replacing the spring, stake the latch button *17* on the threaded end at two points.

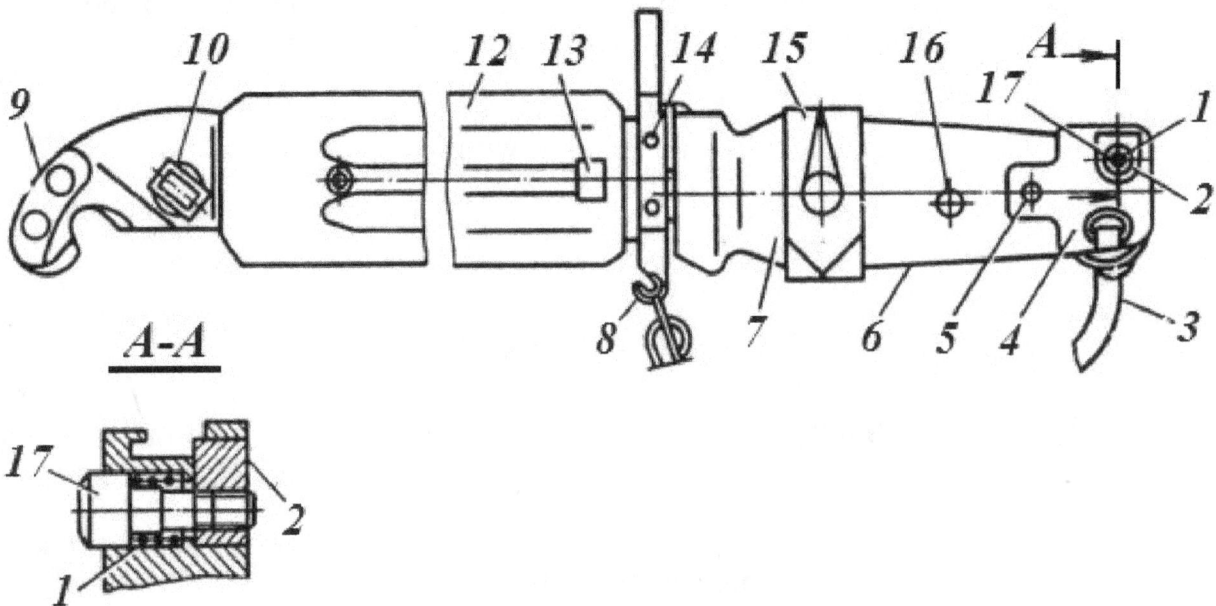

**Fig. 65.** Bayonet 6H4 for assault rifles:

*1* - latch spring 1-7; *2* - latch base 1-6; *3* – wrist strap assembly Sb 1-3; *4* - pommel 1-12; *5* - pommel screw 1-5; *6* - handle of a knife-bayonet 1-11; *7* knife-bayonet Sb 1; *8* – hilt (cross guard) 1-2; *9* – wire cutter anvil 2-11; *10* – wire cutter pivot 2-2; *12* - scabbard assembly Sb 2, *13* – retainer spring 2-8; *14* hilt (cross guard) pin 1-3, *15* – hanger assembly Sb 2-3; *16* – handle pin 1-9; *17* - latch button 1-8

## 16.2. Assembled bayonet is not held in scabbard

Bayonet shall be removable from the scabbard *12* with a visible effort.

If the bayonet falls out of the scabbard, straighten or replace the retainer spring *13*.

## 16.3. Movement of the hilt (cross guard) on the blade of the bayonet

If the hilt (cross guard) *8* moves on the blade, replace the hilt (cross guard) pins *14*.

## 16.4. Movement of the handle on the blade bayonet or handle broken or split

If there is movement of the handle *6* on the bayonet blade, re-glue it as specified in sec. 5.15. If the handle *6* is broken or split, replace it as described in sec. 5.15.

## 16.5. Movement of the wire cutter anvil on the scabbard

If the wire cutter anvil 9 moves on the scabbard, tighten the rivets.

## 16.3. Bend or break in the tip of the blade

If there is a bend or break in the tip of the blade, sharpen it as per Fig. 66.

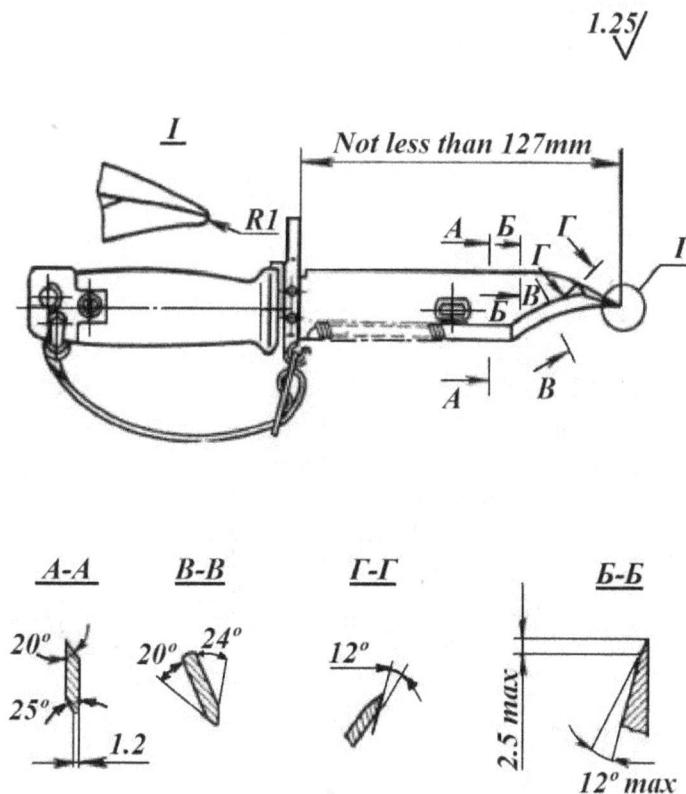

**Fig. 66.** Sharpening the bayonet blade

## 16.7. Chipping and dulling of the blade

Nicks with depth up to 1 mm are allowed.

If there are unacceptable nicks in and (or) dulling of the cutting edges of the blade, sharpen the edge on an abrasive wheel as per Fig. 66.

## 16.8. Worn or broken wrist strap or hanger

Put together a wrist strap assembly as per Fig. 145 or (and) a hanger assembly as per Fig. 147 and install.

# 17. REPAIR OF ACCESSORIES AND TOOLS

## 17.1. Bent cleaning rod

See the General Guidelines, ch. 3.

## 17.2. Fracture of the cleaning rod or damage to the threads of the cleaning rod

See the General Guidelines, ch. 3.

Re cut threads as per Fig. 67. Shortening of the cleaning rod is allowed, for assault AK74 and AKS74 as far as to 368 mm, for machine guns - as far as to 540 mm, for assault rifle AKS74U - as far as to 175 mm.

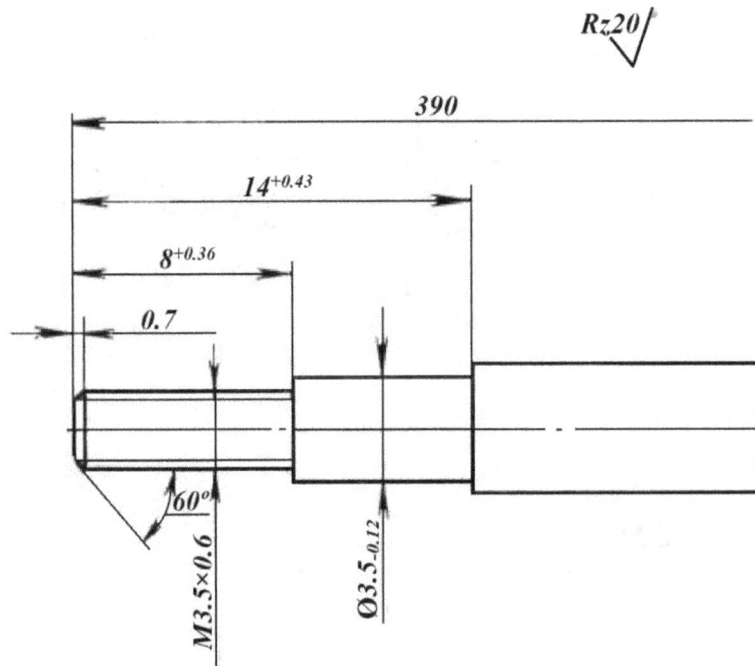

**Fig. 67.** Reworking threaded end of the cleaning rod

### 17.3. Loss of oil from the oil bottle

See the General Guidelines, ch. 3.

If a plastic oiler is punctured, replace the bottle.

### 17.4. Bent punch, screwdriver/front sight elevation tool

See the General Guidelines, ch. 3.

## 18. INSPECTION AND TESTING OF REFURBISHED PRODUCTS

18.1. Each weapon that goes through the medium level weapon and parts repair and restoration process at the army and the front organization levels, is subject to the following inspections and tests:

visual inspection as specified in sec. 4.2;

maintenance checks as specified in sec. 4.3;

verification of battle readiness, as specified in the instruction manual of the weapon;

test fire the weapon to check the interaction of parts and mechanisms in two stages, fire a 10 shot burst followed by 2-3 single shots, during which malfunctions are not acceptable.

18.2. For weapons equipped with night sights, this is done after checking the battle readiness of the sighting device, as specified in the instruction manual of the device.

18.3. After maintenance is carried out:

verify by troubleshooting that the problem(s) with which the weapon was received have been fixed by the repair;

check the technical condition of the weapon to the extent specified in the guide for operating the weapon;

check interaction of parts and mechanisms of the weapon using 10 training rounds (loaded in a magazine); by operating the bolt carrier, empty the magazine, malfunctions are not allowed;

check the weapon for battle readiness after performing any troubleshooting specified in sec. 6.1-6.7, 6.12, 7.1-7.3, 7.5, 7.7, 7.9 and 8.6 for the AKS74U;

test fire the weapon to check the interaction of parts and mechanisms after performing any troubleshooting specified in sec. 9.2, 9.5 and 9.6; Tests are carried in two stages, fire a 10 shots burst followed by 2-3 single shots, during which malfunctions are not acceptable.

18.4. After carrying out technical service № 2 all weapons undergo maintenance checks as specified in Section. 4.3, and 2% of the products, or at least two units per working day (shift), are subject to the control testing for shooting accuracy and precision for battle (battle readiness verification), as indicated in the guide for use of the weapon, and checking on the interaction of in two stages of a 10 shot burst, followed by 2-3 single shots, during which malfunctions are not acceptable.

# A SUMMARY STATEMENT OF APPLICABILITY OF GENERAL AND SPECIAL TOOLS USED FOR MEDIUM LEVEL REPAIR OF WEAPONS

| Name and designation | Purpose and brief description | Location | Note |
|---|---|---|---|
| **1. STANDARD TOOLS** | | | |
| Scales common spring, 0-6 kg | To test the trigger pull with the hammer cocked | From the repair depot stock | |
| Ruler 300 GOST 427-75 | l=300 mm | Same | |
| Ruler verification 200 GOST 8026-75 | l=200 mm | » | |
| Micrometer 0-25 GOST 6507-78 | | » | |
| Square UP-2-160 GOST 3749-66 | | » | |
| Caliper ShTs-11-250-0,05 GOST 166-80 | | » | |
| Probe 2 Cl. № 2 GOST 882-75 | | » | |
| Probe 2 Cl. № 3 GOST 882-75 | | » | |
| Clamp sliding GOST 22401-83 6910-0067 | 1.8-8 mm | » | |
| Chisel metalworking 2810-0187 GOST 7211-72 | 16×60°, l=160 mm | » | |
| **Wrenches for round dies** | | | |
| Clamp 6910-0152 GOST 22395-77 | Ø 20 mm | From the repair depot stock | |
| Clamp 6910-0161GOST 22395-77 | Ø 25 mm | Same | |
| Clamp 6910-0162 GOST 22395-77 | Ø 30 mm | » | |
| Staking tool 8343-0036 GOST 7213-72 | 3 mm | » | |
| Number stamps 7858-0072 GOST 25726-83 | 3 mm | » | |
| Lateral arms 7814-0132 GOST 22308-77 | l=125 mm | » | |

| Name and designation | Purpose and brief description | Location | Note |
|---|---|---|---|
| Drilling machine electric manual IE 1033 | 36 V, 200 Hz, with drilling capability up to a diameter of 14 mm | From the repair depot stock | |
| **Taps, machine, hand** | | | |
| Tap 2621-2401 GOST 3266-81 | M3×0,5 | Same | |
| Tap 2621-2425 GOST 3266-81 | M4×0,7 | » | |
| Tap 2621-2457 GOST 3266-81 | M5×0,8 | » | |
| Tap 2621-2481 GOST 3266-81 | M6×1,0 | » | |
| **Bench hammers** | | | |
| Hammer 7850-0102 GOST 2310-77 | 0.4 kg | » | |
| Hammer Steel 10 GOST 1050-74 E | 0.4 kg | » | |
| Needle file set GOST 1513-77 E | complete | » | |
| **Files** | | | |
| Files 2820-0023 GOST 1465-80 | № 3 - 250 mm | » | |
| Files 2820-0060 GOST 1465-80 | № 5 - 128 mm | » | |
| Files 2821-0115 GOST 1465-80 | № 4 - 200 mm | » | |
| Files 2822-0022 GOST 1465-80 | № 2 - 250 mm | » | |
| **Screwdriver mechanic and assembly** | | | |
| Screwdriver 7810-0394 GOST 17199-71 | 1X6,5 | » | |

*Appendix 1 (continued)*

| Name and designation | Purpose and brief description | Location | Note |
|---|---|---|---|
| **Round dies for metric thread** | | | |
| Die 2650-1485 GOST 9740-71 | M3×0,5 | From the repair depot stock | |
| | | Same | |
| Die 2650-1521 GOST 9740-71 | M4×0,7 | » | |
| Die 2650-1551 GOST 9740-71 | M5×0,8 | » | |
| Die 2650-1581 GOST 9740-71 | M6×1,0 | » | |
| Combination pliers 7814-0091 GOST 5547-75 | l = 160 mm | » | |
| Jig saw frame GOST 17270-71 6920-0021 E | For blade lengths 250 and 300 mm | » | |
| Rasp half round, notching № 1 3806-0062 GOST 6876-79 | l = 250 mm | » | |
| Hand vise 7802-0033 GOST 7226-72 E | Width of the jaws 45 mm | » | |
| Triangular scraper with handle | | | |
| Scriber 7840-0021 GOST 24473-80 E | for marking | | |

## 2. SPECIAL TOOLS AND ACCESSORIES

| Name and designation | Purpose and brief description | Location | Note |
|---|---|---|---|
| 2 1. Temporary magazine axis pin | For fitting magazine to magazine catch | Manufactured by the repair depot per Fig. 68 | |
| 2.2. Punches | For disassembly | Same, per Fig. 69 | |
| 2.3. Cotton swab | For the lubrication of the bore | From complete spare parts kit (SPTA) | |
| 2.4. Gauge, firing pin protrusion (1.4; 1.52 mm) 6И17.К-1 | See column 1 | From complete set of special tools | |

*Appendix 1 (continued)*

| Name and designation | Purpose and brief description | Location | Note |
|---|---|---|---|
| 2.5. Gauge, no-go, muzzle erosion (5.5 mm) 6И17.К-2 | See column 1 | From the complete set of special tools | |
| 2.6. Gauge, headspace (pass/go) (31.7 mm) 6И17.К-3 | Same | Same | |
| 2.7. Gauge, headspace (no-go) (31.85 mm) 6И17.К-4 | » | » | |
| 2.8. Gauge, headspace (rejection/field) (32 mm) 6И17.К-5 | » | » | |
| 2.9. Gauge, extractor go/no-go (1.65; 2 mm) 6И17К-7 | » | » | |
| 2.10. Gauge, muzzle brake alignment 6И17.К-8 | » | » | Fig. 70 (for reference) |
| 2.11. Gauge, flash hider alignment 6И17 К-9 | » | » | Fig. 71 (for reference) |
| 2.12. Gauge, ring for checking bolt to barrel chamber gap | » | Manufactured by the repair depot per Fig. 72 | |
| 2.13. Mandrel for repairing the muzzle brake and flash hider | » | From the complete set of special tools | Fig. 73 (for reference) |
| 2.14. Mandrel for repairing receiver cover | » | Manufactured by the repair depot per Fig. 74 | |
| 2.15. Mandrel for repairing the gas tube | » | Same, per Fig. 75 | |
| 2.16. Mandrel for repairing the back end of the gas tube | » | Same, per Fig. 76 | |
| 2.17. Mandrel for removing unwanted movement of the gas tube latch repairing | » | Same, per Fig. 77 | |

| Name and designation | Purpose and brief description | Location | Note |
|---|---|---|---|
| 2.18. Screwdriver/front sight wrench | For adjusting the front sight elevation | From complete spare parts kit (SPTA) | |
| 2.19. Cleaning kit case with lid | To aid in cleaning the barrel | Same | |
| 2.20. Tool for performing windage adjustments of front sight 6И17.Sb 1 | See column 1 | From the complete set of special tools | |
| 2.21. Device for resizing muzzle brake and flash hider 6И17.Sb 2 | Same | Same | Fig. 78—85 (for reference) |
| 2.22. Cleaning jag | | From complete spare parts kit (SPTA) | |
| 2.23. Rod for checking bolt alignment | See column 1 | Manufactured by the repair depot per Fig. 86 | |
| 2.24. Device for attaching to the muzzle to check bolt alignment | Same | Same, per Fig. 87 | |
| 2.25. Training cartridges (5.45-мм) | To check the mechanical operation | From the repair depot stock | |
| 2.26. Gauge for checking the auto-sear engagement with the bolt carrier | Same | Same, per Fig. 88 | |
| 2.27. Cleaning rod for RPK74 | To aid in cleaning the barrel | From complete spare parts kit (SPTA) | |
| 2.28. Tool for setting the front latch spring for the metal buttstock | See column 1 | Manufactured by the repair depot per Fig. 158 | |

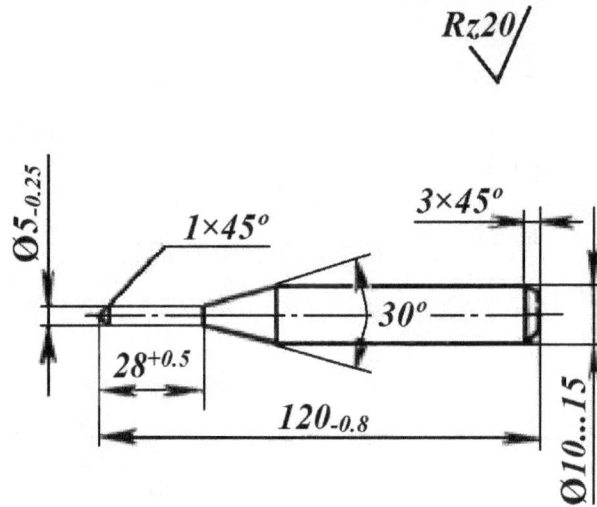

$Rz20$

**Fig. 68.** Temporary magazine catch pin

Material: steel 50, tempered to HRCs 38,5- 45,5. Phosphated

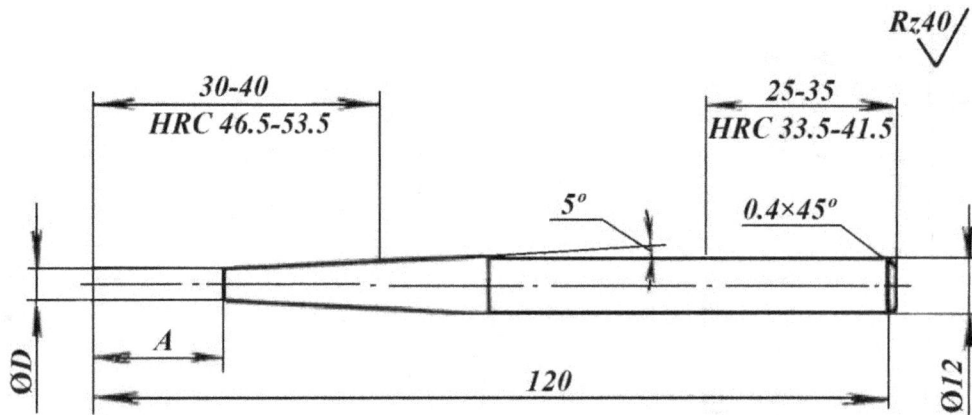

$Rz40$

| $D$, mm | $1.4_{-0.2}$ | $2.3_{-0.2}$ | $3.3_{-0.2}$ | $4.3_{-0.3}$ | $6_{-0.3}$ | $8_{-0.4}$ |
|---------|--------------|--------------|--------------|--------------|------------|------------|
| $A$, mm | 15 | 15 | 30 | 30 | 40 | 50 |

**Fig. 69.** Punches

Material: steel U8A, tempered. Phosphated

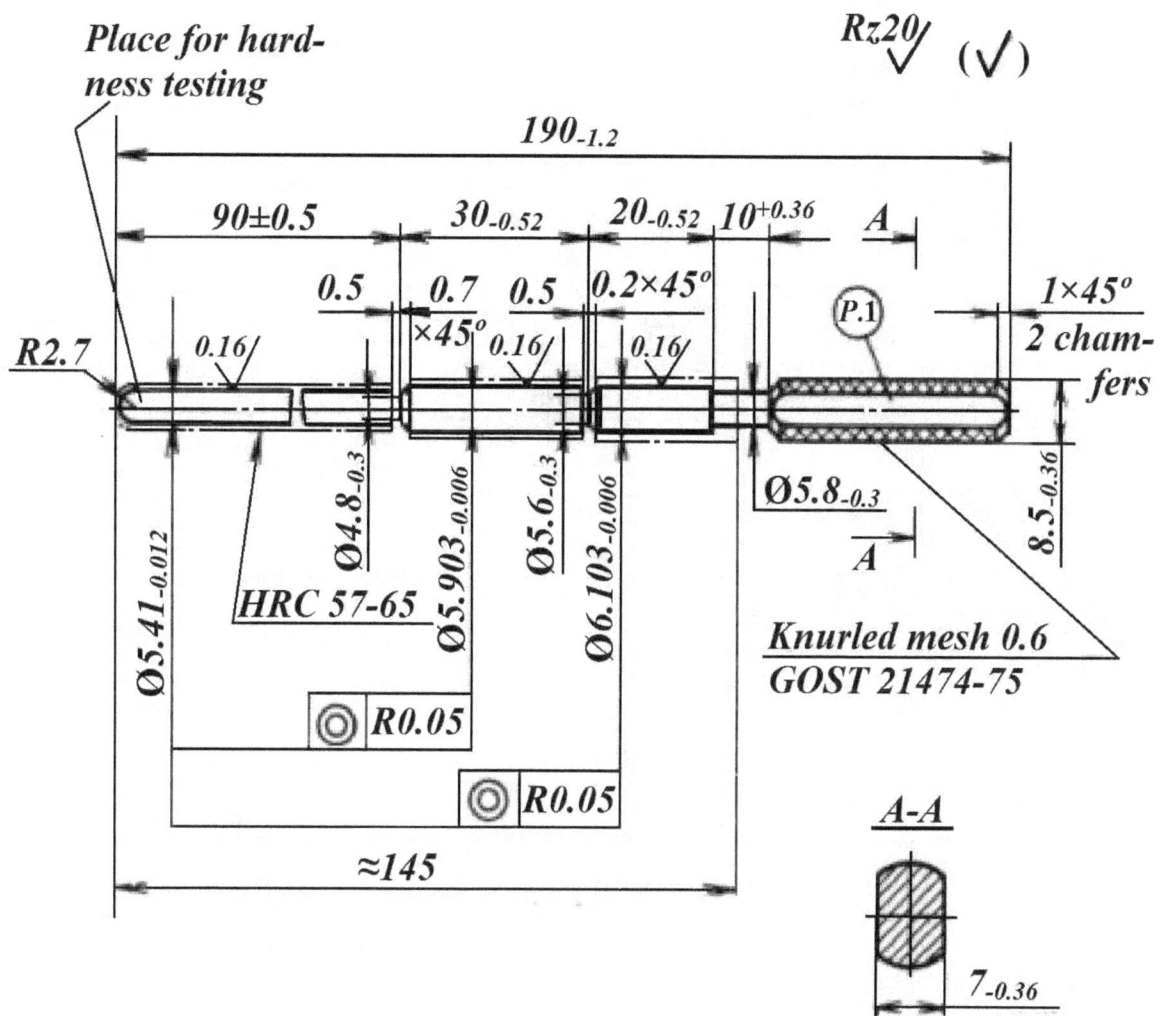

Place for hardness testing

Rz20/ (√)

190$_{-1.2}$

90±0.5   30$_{-0.52}$   20$_{-0.52}$   10$^{+0.36}$   A

0.5   0.7   0.5   0.2×45°   1×45°
     ×45°                    2 chamfers

R2.7   0.16/   0.16/   0.16/   (P.1)

Ø5.41$_{-0.012}$   Ø4.8$_{-0.3}$   Ø5.903$_{-0.006}$   Ø5.6$_{-0.3}$   Ø6.103$_{-0.006}$   Ø5.8$_{-0.3}$   8.5$_{-0.36}$

HRC 57-65

A   A

⊚ R0.05

⊚ R0.05

Knurled mesh 0.6
GOST 21474-75

≈145

A-A

7$_{-0.36}$

mm

| Nominal Size and marking | Manufactured size | Wear inspected to |
|---|---|---|
| 6.6 | 6.603$_{-0.006}$ | -- |
| 6.3ПР | 6.303$_{-0.006}$ | -- |
| 5.4 | 5.41$_{-0.012}$ | 5.392 |

**Fig. 70.** Gauge to check the alignment of the muzzle brake 6И17. К-8

Marked as 6И17 К-8 6.3ПР
Material: steel 9HS GOST 5950-73

99

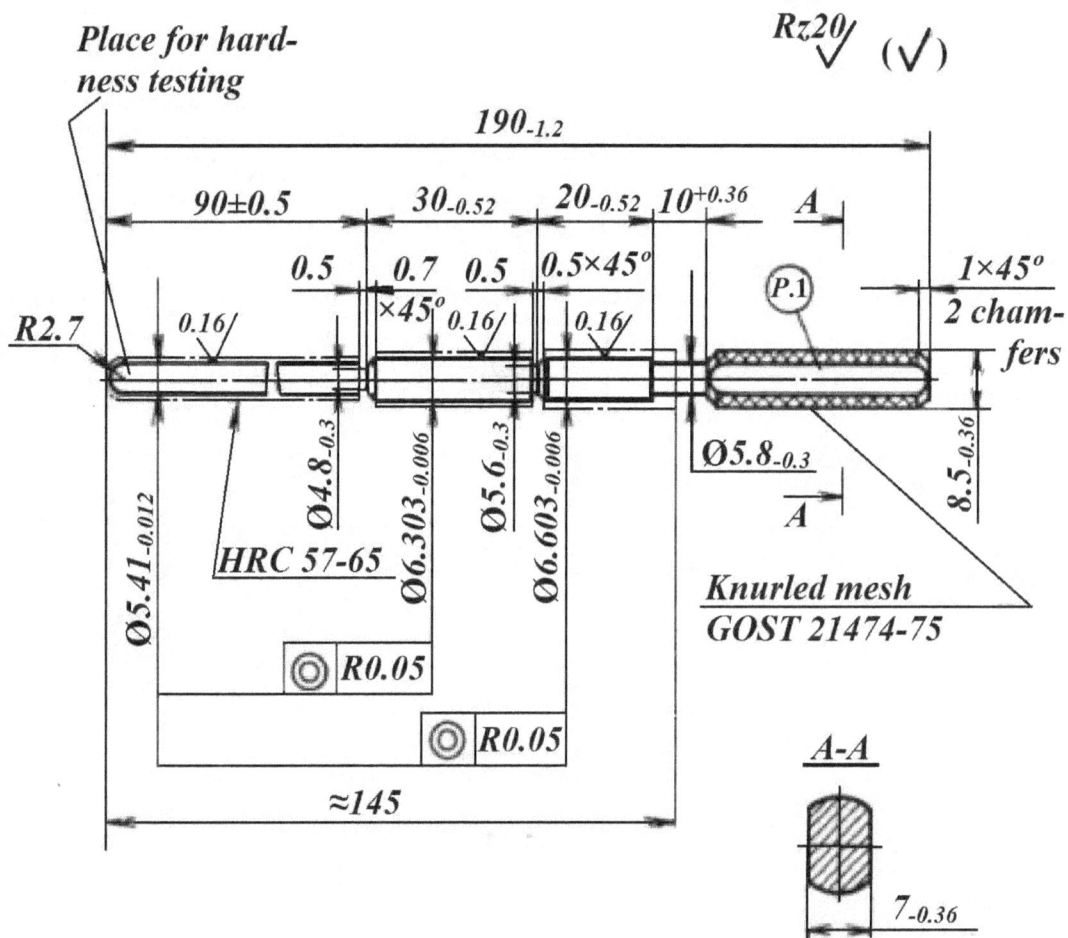

Place for hardness testing

$Rz20$ / ( √ )

$190_{-1.2}$

$90\pm0.5$  $30_{-0.52}$  $20_{-0.52}$  $10^{+0.36}$  $A$

$0.5$  $0.7$  $0.5$  $0.5\times45°$  $1\times45°$
$\times45°$  $0.16$ /  $0.16$ /  2 chamfers

$R2.7$  $0.16$ /

$P.1$

$\varnothing5.41_{-0.012}$

$HRC\ 57\text{-}65$

$\varnothing4.8_{-0.3}$  $\varnothing6.303_{-0.006}$  $\varnothing5.6_{-0.3}$  $\varnothing6.603_{-0.006}$

$\varnothing5.8_{-0.3}$

$8.5_{-0.36}$

$A$

◎ $R0.05$

◎ $R0.05$

Knurled mesh
GOST 21474-75

$\approx145$

A-A

$7_{-0.36}$

**mm**

| Nominal Size and marking | Manufactured size | Wear inspected to |
|---|---|---|
| 6.1 | $6.103_{-0.006}$ | -- |
| 5.9ПР | $5.903_{-0.006}$ | -- |
| 5.4 | $5.41_{-0.012}$ | 5.392 |

**Fig. 71.** Gauge to check the alignment of the muzzle brake 6И17. К-9

Marked as 6И17 К-9 5.9ПР
Material: steel 9HS GOST 5950-73

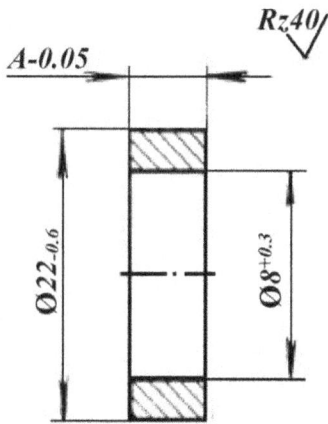

**Fig. 72** Ring 2 and Ring 2.5
Etch on perimeter of ring 2 or ring 2,5
$A = 2$ and $A = 2.5$ mm

Material: steel HRC 40, tempered to 35.5-38.5, phosphated

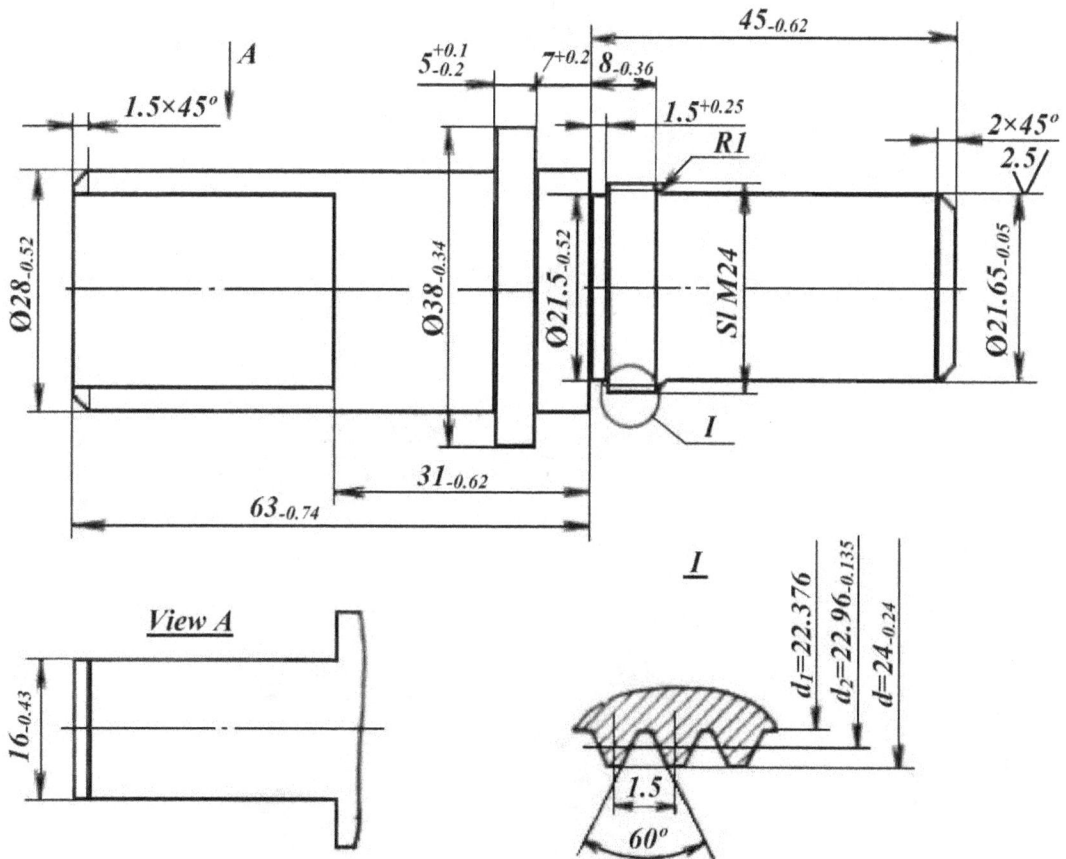

View A

**Fig. 73.** Mandrel for fixing the muzzle brake and the flash hider
Material: steel 50, tempered to HRC 38.5-45.5. Phosphated

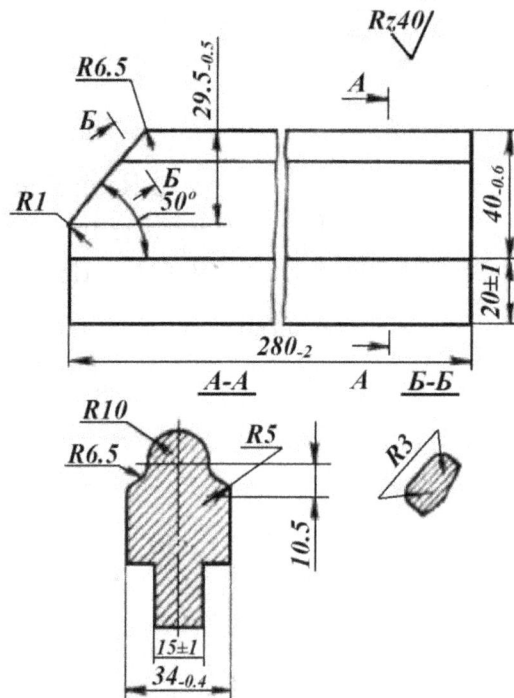

**Fig. 74.** Mandrel for receiver cover

Material: steel 50, tempered to HRCs 33.5-38.5. Phosphated

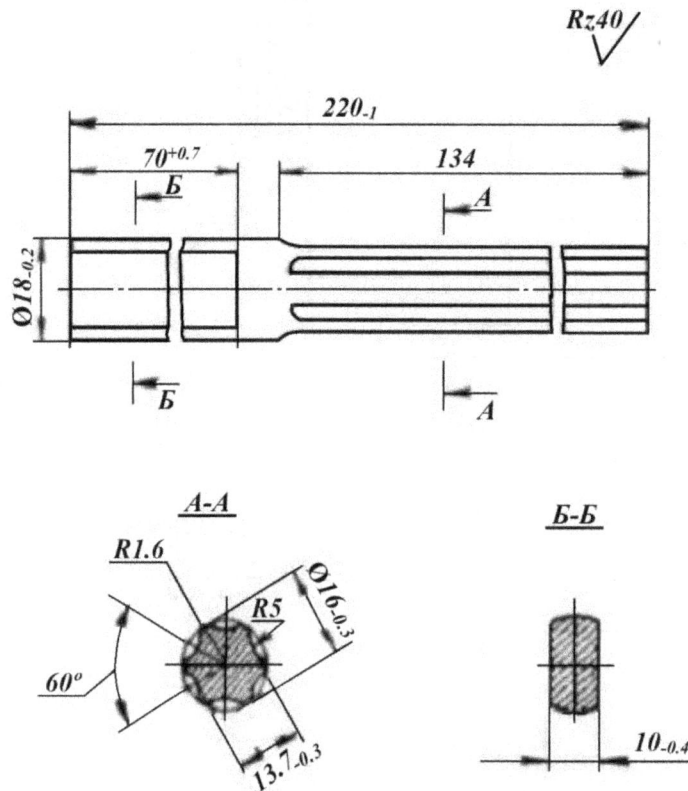

**Fig. 75.** Tool for gas tube

Material: steel 50, tempered to HRCs 45.5-53.5. Phosphated

102

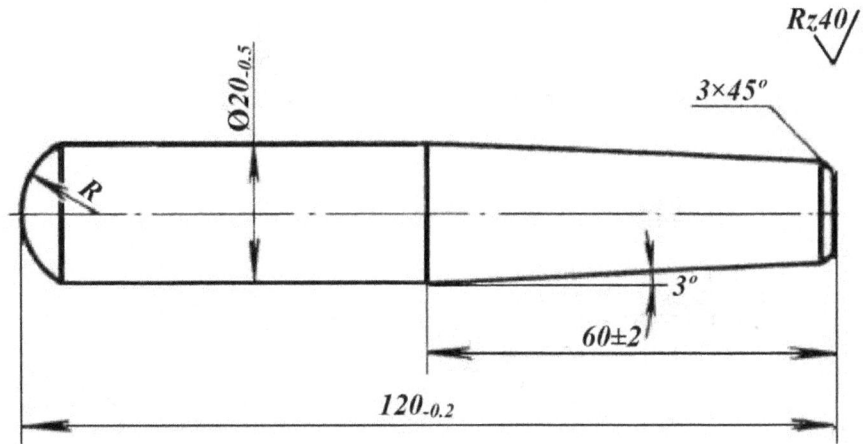

**Fig. 76.** Mandrel for the rear end of the gas tube

Material: steel 45; tempered to HRC 45.5-53.5. Phosphated

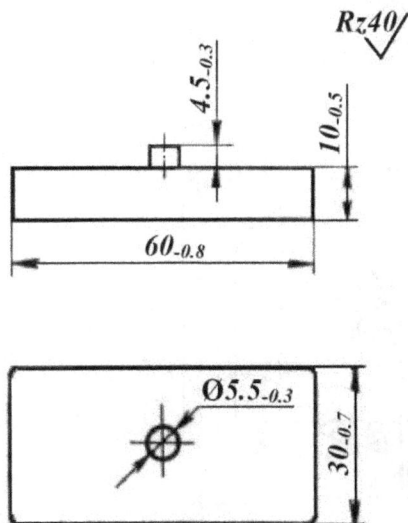

**Fig. 77.** Mandrel to help remove movement of the gas tube latch

Material: steel 45, tempered to HRC 45.5-5.5. Phosphated

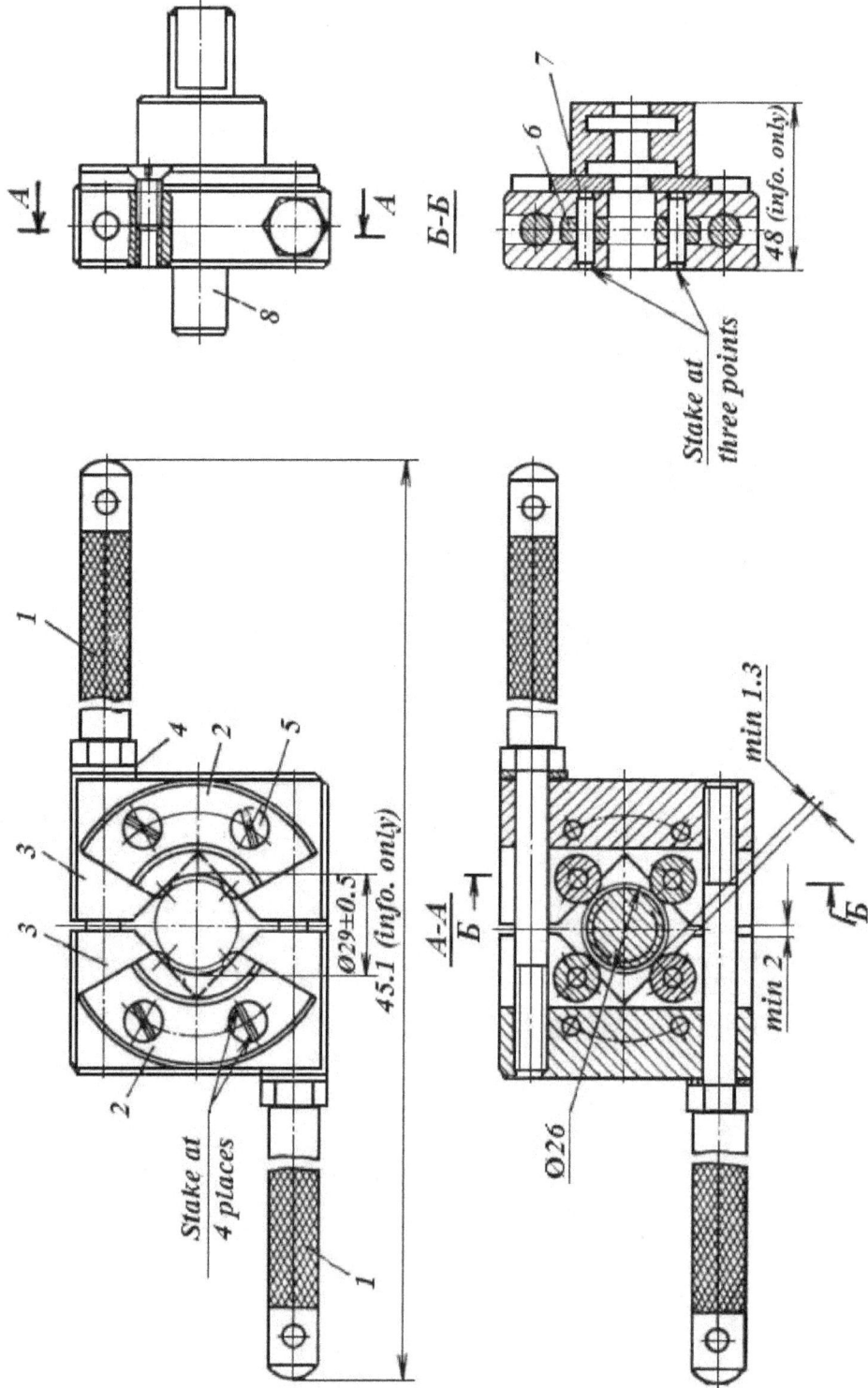

**Fig. 78.** Device 6И17.Sb 2 crimping roller for muzzle brakes and flash hiders for assault rifles

*1* - torque bar (Fig. 82); *2* - arc (Fig. 81); *3*- body (Fig. 79); *4* - washer (Fig. 85); *5* - screw (Fig. 83); *6* - roller (Fig. 80); *7* - axis pin (Fig. 84); *8*- mandrel (Fig. 73)

Б-Б

48 (info. only)

Stake at three points

Stake at 4 places

∅29±0.5

45.1 (info. only)

A-A
Б

∅26

min 1.3

min 2

104

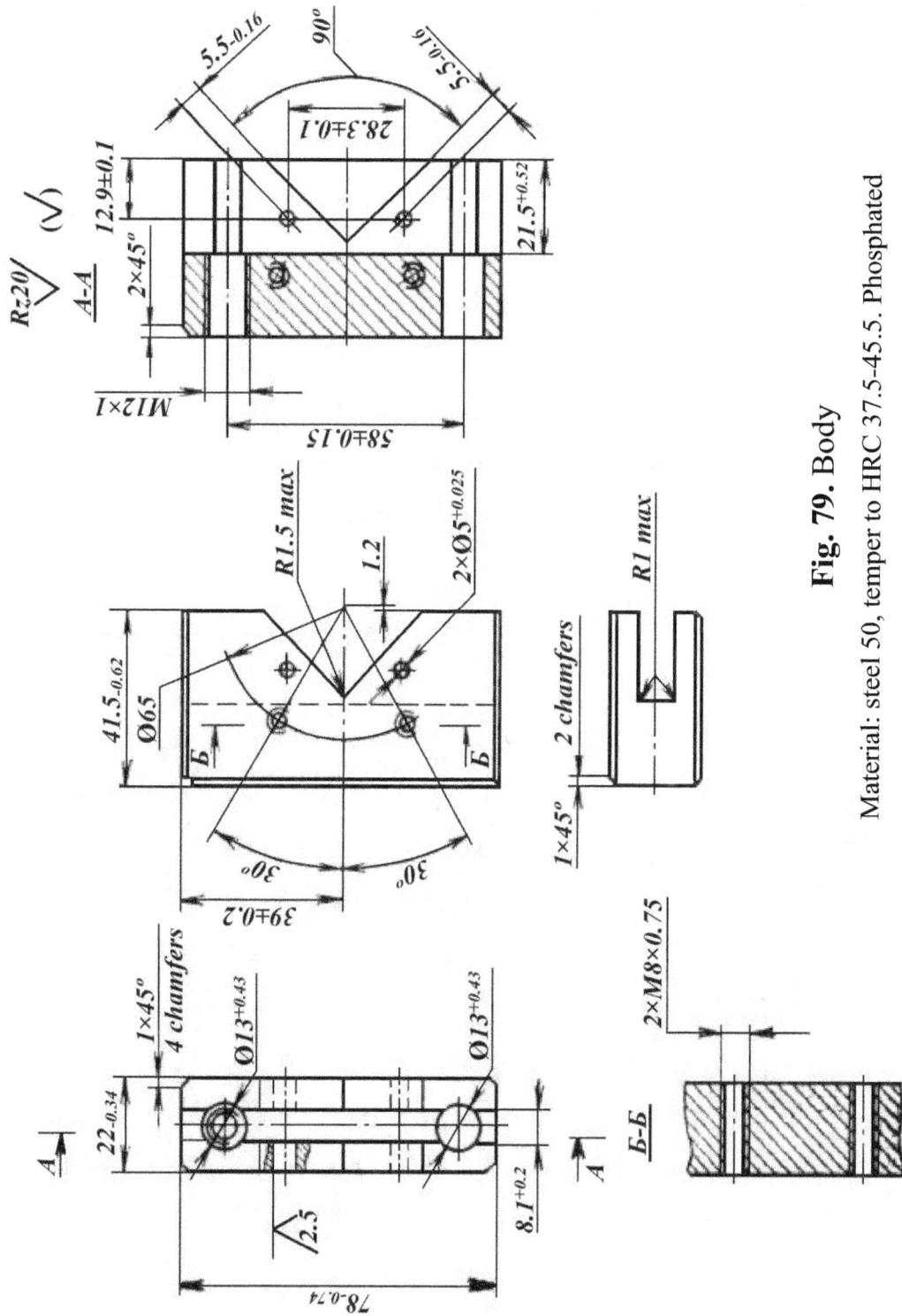

**Fig. 79.** Body

Material: steel 50, temper to HRC 37.5-45.5. Phosphated

105

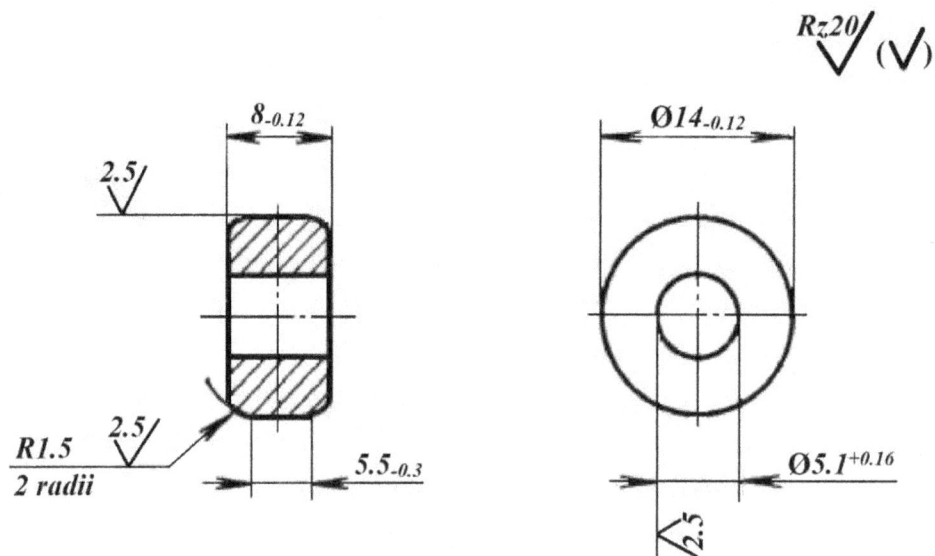

**Fig. 80.** Roller

Material: steel U8A, temper to HRC 55-60. Phosphated

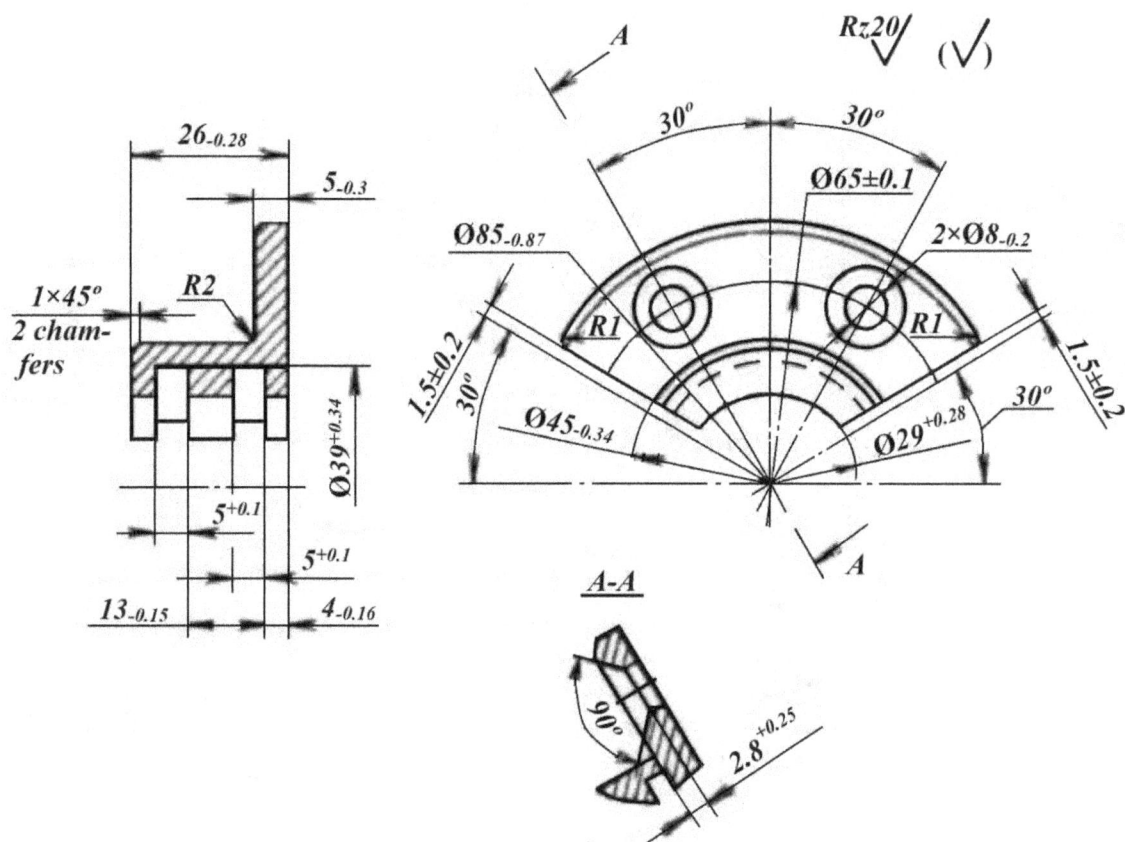

**Fig. 81.** Arc

Material: steel HRC 50, tempered to 38.5-43.5. Phosphated

106

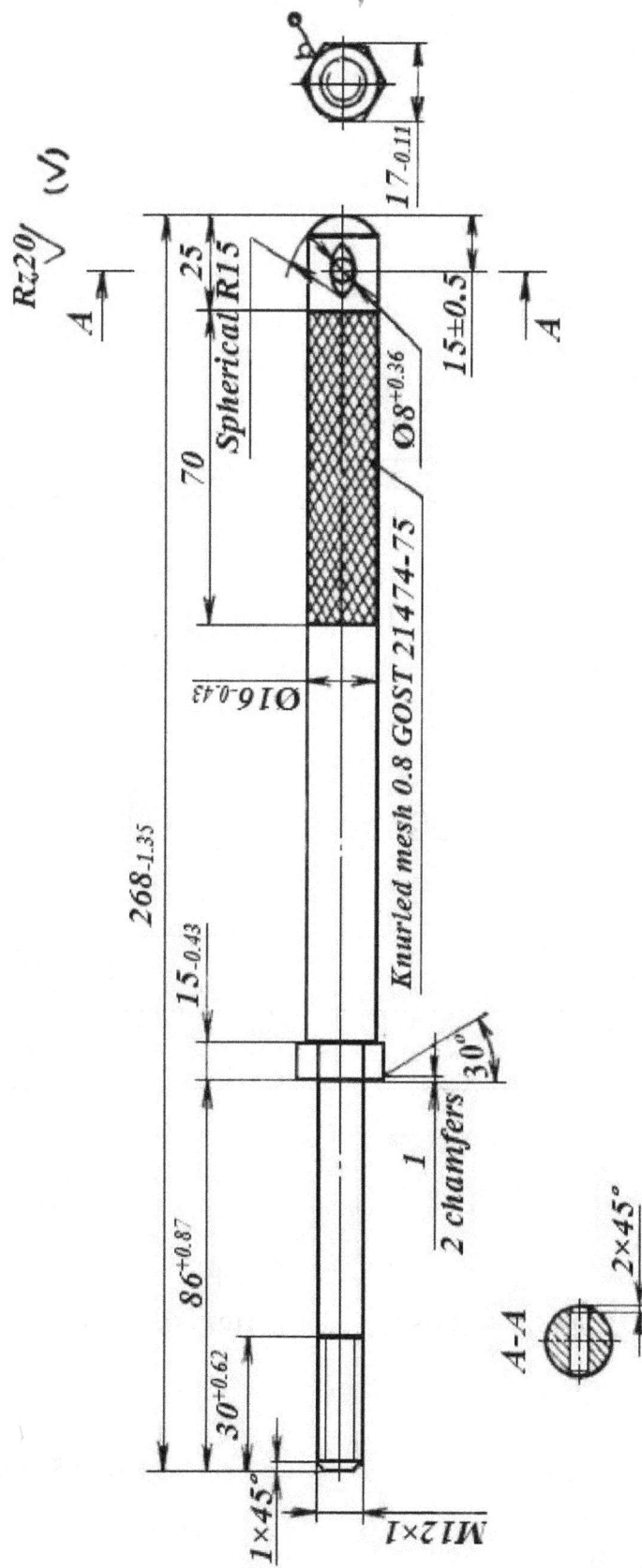

**Fig. 82.** Torque Bar

Material: steel 35, tempered to HRC 34-41.5. Phosphated

107

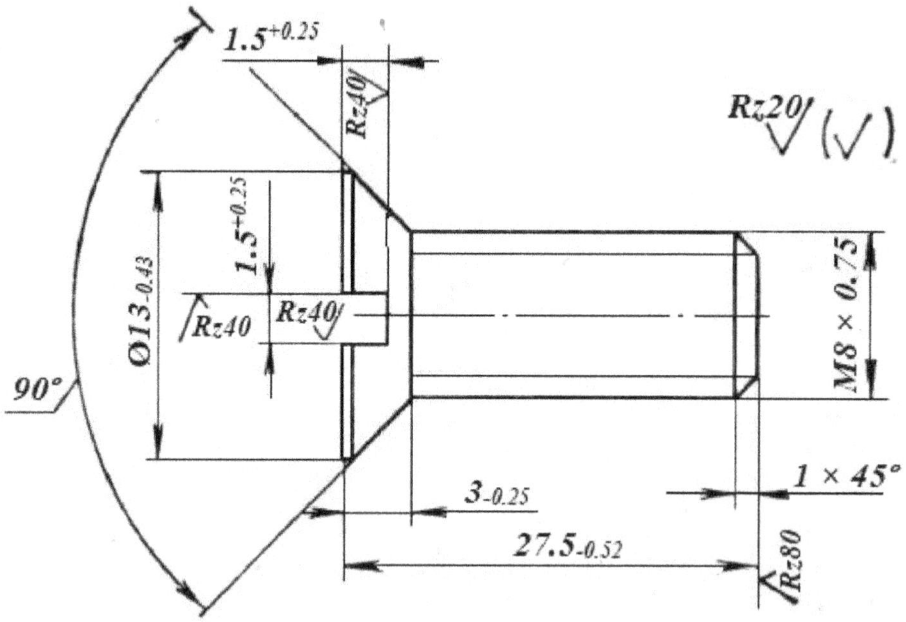

**Fig. 83.** Screw

Material: steel 35, tempered to 34-41.5 HRC. Phosphated

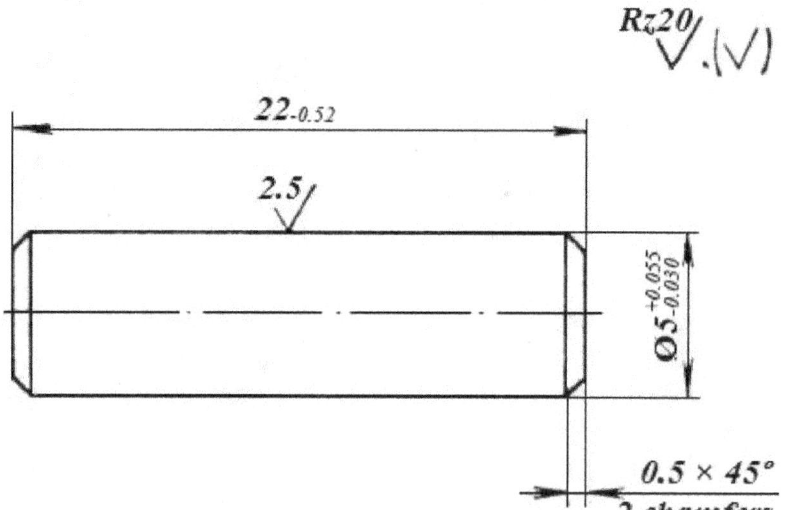

**Fig. 84.** Axis pin

Material: steel U8A, temper to HRC 56-61. Phosphated

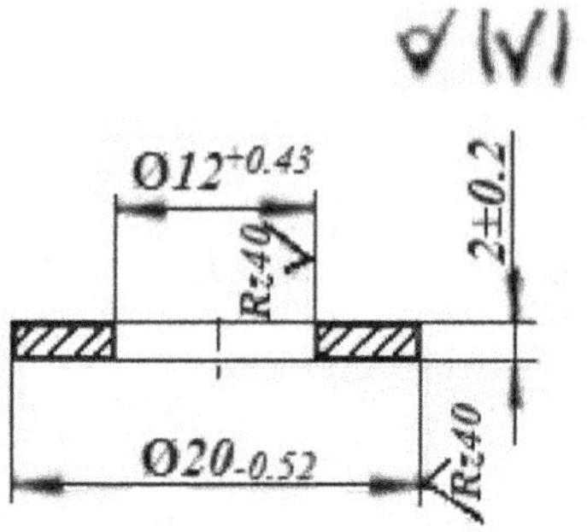

**Fig. 85**. Washer

Material: steel 40. Phosphated

108

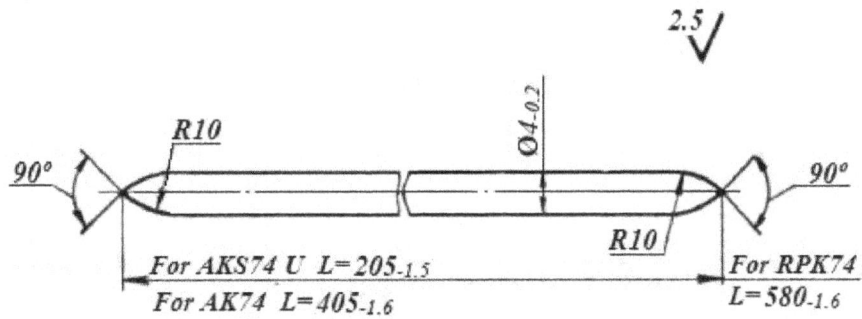

**Fig. 86.** rod to check bolt alignment

Material: steel HRC 50, tempered to 49.5-54.5. Phosphated

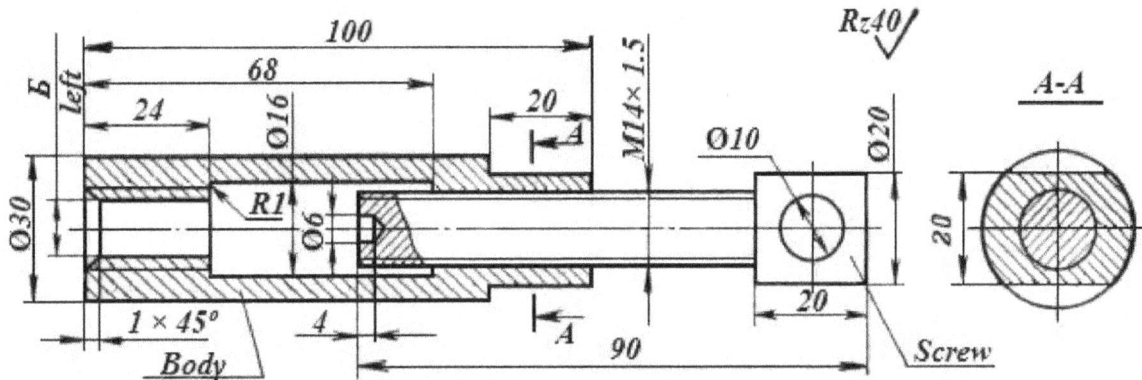

**Fig. 87.** Deveice for attaching to the mussle to check the bolt alignment

Material: Steel 50. tempered to HRC 33 5-38 5 phosphated
Size Б: 6P18 for -M14 × 1, for 6P20 - M24 × 1.5

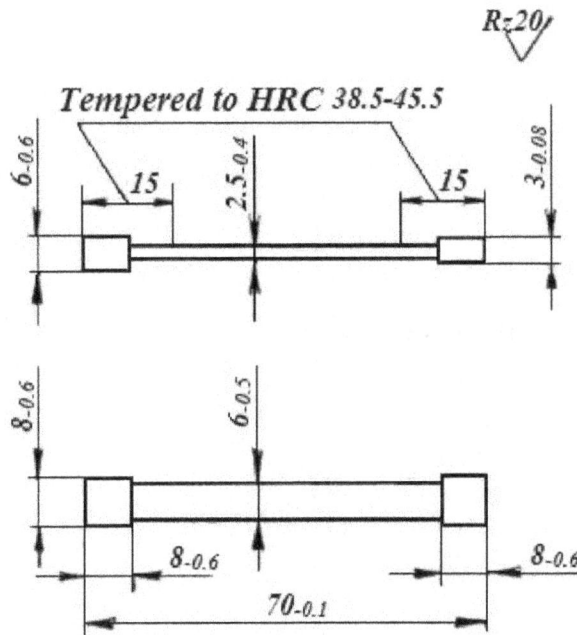

**Fig. 88.** Gauge for checking auto-sear engagement

Material: steel 50. Phosphated

109

# NUMERICAL DESIGNATION AND FIGURES FOR ASSEMBLIES AND PARTS OF 5.45 MM KALASHNIKOV ASSAULT RIFLES AND LIGHT MACHINE GUNS, MANUFACTURED W/O TECHNICAL FLOW CHARTS

| Designation | Name | Figure Number |
|---|---|---|
| **From 5.45mm Kalashnikov assault rifle AK74 (6P20)** | | |
| 0-10 | Disconnector spring | 89 |
| 0-12 | Auto-sear spring | 90 |
| 0-13 | Magazine catch axis pin | 91 |
| 0-16 | Grip nut | 92 |
| 0-17 | Bolt bounce retarder latch axis pin | 93 |
| 0-19 | Grip screw | 94 |
| 0-23 | Sight leaf spring | 95 |
| 0-25 | Firing mechanism axis pin | 96 |
| 0-27 | Trigger axis pin bushing | 97 |
| 1-28 | Lower handguard retainer latch | 98 |
| 1-31 | Front sight base | 99 |
| 1-32 | Front sight post | 100 |
| 1-33 | Muzzle device retainer pin retaining pin | 101 |
| 1-37 | Lower handguard retainer | 102 |
| 1-38 | Muzzle device retainer pin spring | 89 |
| 1-41 | Upper handguard spring | 104 |
| 1-45 | Gas tube tensioning spring | 105 |
| 1-52 | Barrel pin | 106 |
| 2-4 | Elevation slide latch spring | 89 |
| 3-3 | Gas piston pin | 103 |
| 3-9 | Firing pin retaining pin | 107 |
| 3-10 | Extractor axis pin | 108 |
| 4-4 | Recoil spring retainer for loop type recoil spring guide rod | 109 |
| 4-5 | Recoil spring guide loop type front rod | 110 |
| 5-5 | Cleaning kit case spring | 111 |
| 5-10 | Cleaning kit trapdoor spring | 112 |
| 5-11 | Cleaning kit trapdoor axis pin | 113 |
| **From 5.45mm Kalashnikov assault rifle AKS74 (6P21)** | | |
| 0-36 | Rear stock latch spring | 89 |
| 0-37 | Rear stock latch retainer pin | 114 |
| 0-39 | Front stock latch spring | 115 |
| 0-40 | Front stock latch axis pin | 116 |
| 0-41 | Folding stock axis pin | 117 |
| 0-42 | Front stock latch hook | 118 |
| Sb 5-1 | Sling swivel assembly | 119 |
| 5-6 | Sling swivel hinge | 120 |
| 5-7 | Sling loop | 121 |
| 5-13 | Sling swivel assembly washer | 122 |

| Designation | Name | Figure Number |
|---|---|---|
| | **From 5.45mm Kalashnikov assault rifle AKS74 (6P21)** | |
| 0-21 | Receiver cover axis pin | 123 |
| 1-17 | Front sight post | 124 |
| 1-31 | Front sight base | 99 |
| 1-35 | Flash hider retainer pin retaining pin | 103 |
| 1-36 | Gas tube retainer plunger pin | 125 |
| 1-37 | Flash hider retainer pin | 126 |
| 1-38 | Flash hider retainer pin spring | 127 |
| 1-41 | Upper handguard spring | 128 |
| 1-22 | Gas tube retainer spring | 89 |
| 7-32 | Rear sight leaf axis pin | 129 |
| 7-33 | Rear sight leaf spring | 130 |
| | **From 5.45mm Kalashnikov light machine gun RPK74 (6P18)** | |
| 1-28 | Lower handguard retainer latch | 131 |
| 1-37 | Muzzle deveice retainer pin | 132 |
| 1-38 | Muzzle deveice retainer pin spring | 89 |
| 2-6 | Rear sight windage adjustment lock knob | 133 |
| 2-7 | Rear sight windage adjustment screw | 134 |
| 2-8 | Rear sight windage adjustment tension spring | 89 |
| 2-9 | Rear sight windage adjustment nut | 135 |
| 2-10 | Rear sight windage adjustment nut pin | 113 |
| 4-4 | Recoil spring retainer for straight rod type recoil spring guide rod | 136 |
| 9-7 | Bipod legs latch | 137 |
| 9-8 | Bipod legs latch axis pin | 113 |
| 9-10 | Bipod axis pin | 138 |
| 9-11 | Bipod spring | 89 |
| | **From 5.45mm Kalashnikov light machine gun RPKS74 (6P19)** | |
| Sb 1-10 | Sling swivel assembly | 130 |
| 0-26 | Latch hook axis pin | 140 |
| 0-27 | Latch hook spring | 141 |
| 1-52 | Stock latch | 142 |
| 1-53 | Stock latch spring | 89 |
| 1-54 | Stock latch axis pin | 143 |
| 1-55 | Stock axis pin | 113 |
| 1-56 | Sling loop | 121 |
| 1-57 | Sling swivel hinge | 144 |
| | **From Bayonet 6H4** | |
| Sb 1-3 | Wrist strap assembly | 145 |
| Sb 2-2 | Keeper strap assembly | 146 |
| Sb 2-2 | Hanger assembly | 147 |

| Designation | Name | Figure Number |
|---|---|---|
| 1-3 | Hilt (cross guard) pin | 103 |
| 1-7 | Latch spring | 89 |
| 1-9 | Handle pin | 148 |
| 1-14 | Wrist strap | 149 |
| 1-18 | Wrist strap buckle | 150 |
| 2-7 | Hanger assembly belt loop strap | 151 |
| 2-14 | Hanger assembly keeper strap stud button | 152 |
| 2-15 | Hanger assembly washer | 153 |
| 2-16 | Hanger assembly keeper strap | 154 |
| 2-19 | Hanger assembly metal suspension strap | 155 |
| 2-20 | Hanger assembly D-ring | 156 |
|  | Hanger assembly rivet | 153 |

## From accessories (6Yu20)

| Item 5 | Punch | 157 |
|---|---|---|

**Fig. 89.** Helical Springs

Material: wire GOST 9389-75 I. Winding right. Annealed at 240-260 ° C

$R_z40/(\sqrt{})$

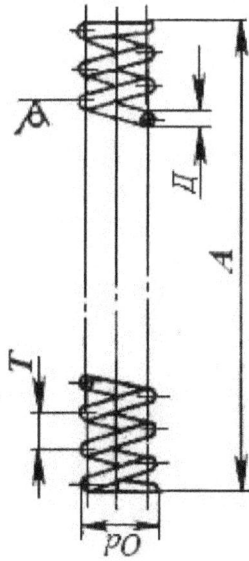

| Part № | Name | A. Length mm | Step T. mm | Wire diameter Д. mm | The outer diameter of the spring OD mm | Number of active coils | Total number of coils | Expanded length of the spring. mm |
|---|---|---|---|---|---|---|---|---|
| 6P18.1-38 | Spring, flash hider retainer RPK | $16^{+0.5}_{-1.5}$ | 1.55 | 0.5 | $3.5_{-0.2}$ | 10 | 12±0.5 | 113 |
| 6P18.2-8 | Spring, windage adjustment tension | 11.5±2 | 2.12 | 0.56 | $7.4_{-0.3}$ | 5 | 7±0.5 | 180 |
| 6P18.9-11 | Spring, bipod | $67^{+2}_{-1}$ | 3.7 | 1.5 | $10_{-0.35}$ | 16.5 | 18.5±0.5 | 510 |
| 6P19.1-53 | Spring, stock latch RPKS74 | 19.5±2 | 2.4 | 0.9 | $5.8_{-0.3}$ | 7.5 | 9.5±0.5 | 150 |
| 6P20.0-10 | Spring, disconnector | $20^{+1}_{-1.5}$ | 1.43 | 0.6 | $3.6_{-0.2}$ | 13 | 15±0.5 | 133 |
| 6P20.1-38 | Spring, muzzle device retainer, AK74 | $12^{+0.5}_{-1.5}$ | 1.5 | 0.5 | $3.6_{-0.2}$ | 5.5 | 7.5±0.5 | 76 |
| 6P20.2-4 | Spring, elevation slide latch | $10^{+1.5}_{-1.0}$ | 2.1 | 0.56 | $4.8_{-0.2}$ | 4 | 6±0.5 | 85 |
| 6P21.0-36 | Spring, rear stock latch, AKS74 | 66±3 | 6.4 | 1.2 | $13_{-0.5}$ | 10 | 12±1 | 500 |
| 6P26.1-22 | Spring, gas tube retainer AKS74U | 29 | 2.2 | 1.1 | $6.8_{-0.2}$ | 12 | 12±0.5 | 210 |
| 6H4.1-7 | Spring, bayonet latch | 16±1 | 3.75 | 1 | $9_{-0.2}$ | 4 | 6±0.3 | 151 |

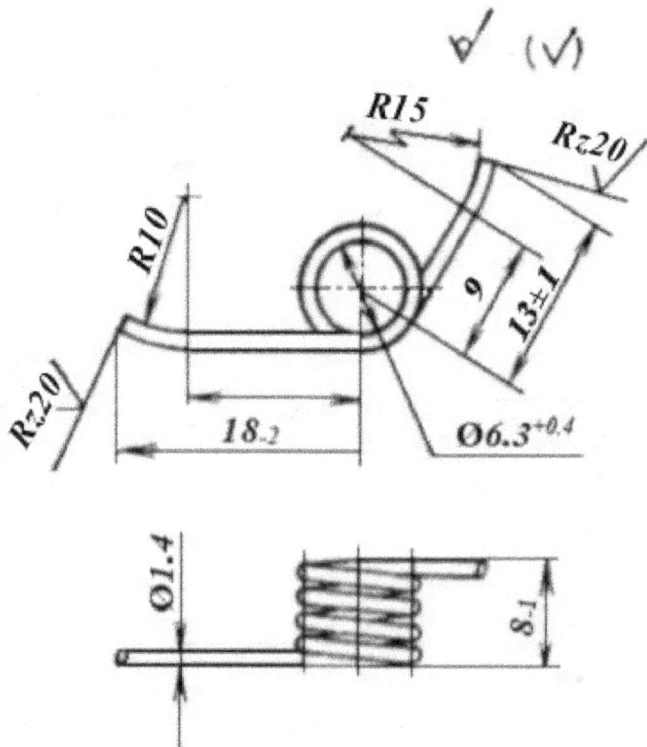

**Fig. 90.** Magazine catch spring
6P20.0 12

Material: wire I-1,4 GOST 9389-75. Annealed
at 240- 260 ° C
Winding left. Number of turns, 4. Expanded
length 135 mm

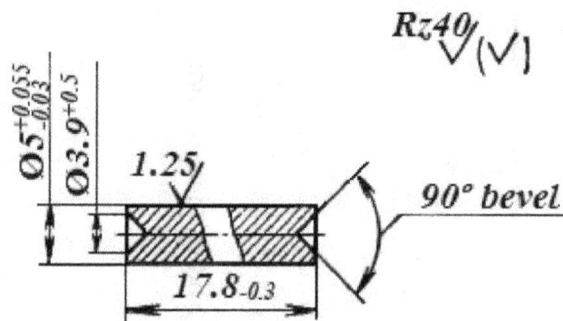

**Fig. 91.** Magazine catch axis pin 6P20.0-13

Material: steel 50. Tempered to HRC 38.6-45.5. Phosphated

114

RZ40/ (∨)

10-0.36

⌀22-0.52

12-0.24

8.5-0.36

View Б

1.75 min on
both sides

Rz80

3-0.25

15-0.43

10-0.43

A

20°

20°

A-A
M6

1

60°

Б

Rz80

A

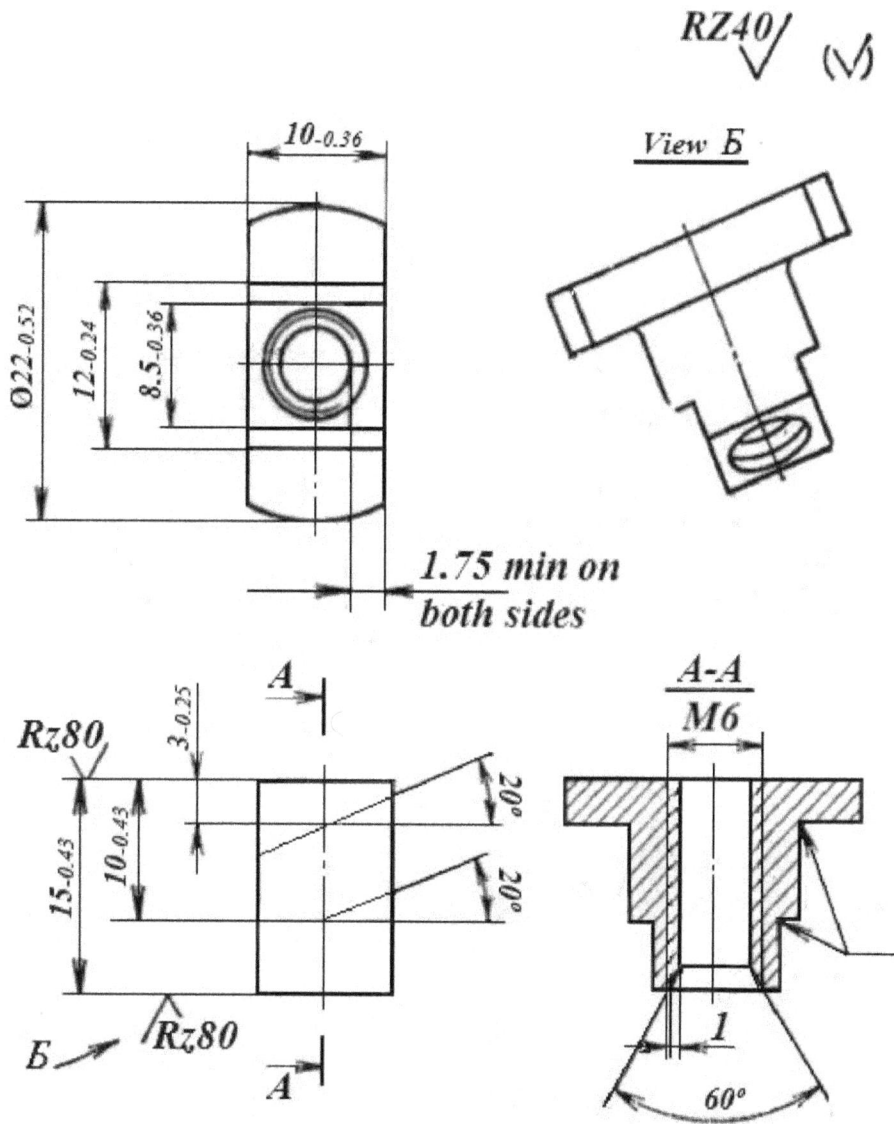

**Fig. 92.** Grip nut 6P20.0-16

Material: steel 45. Tempered to HRC 38.5-45.5. Phosphated and lacquered

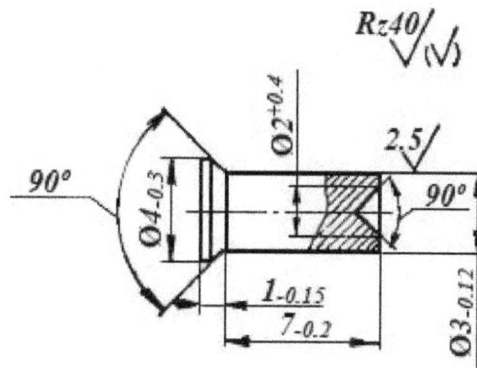

Rz40/ (∨)

90°

⌀4-0.3

⌀2+0.4

2.5/

90°

1-0.15

7-0.2

⌀3-0.12

**Fig. 93.** Axis 6P20.0-17

Material: steel ZOHRA. Tempered to HV 412-540. Phosphated

115

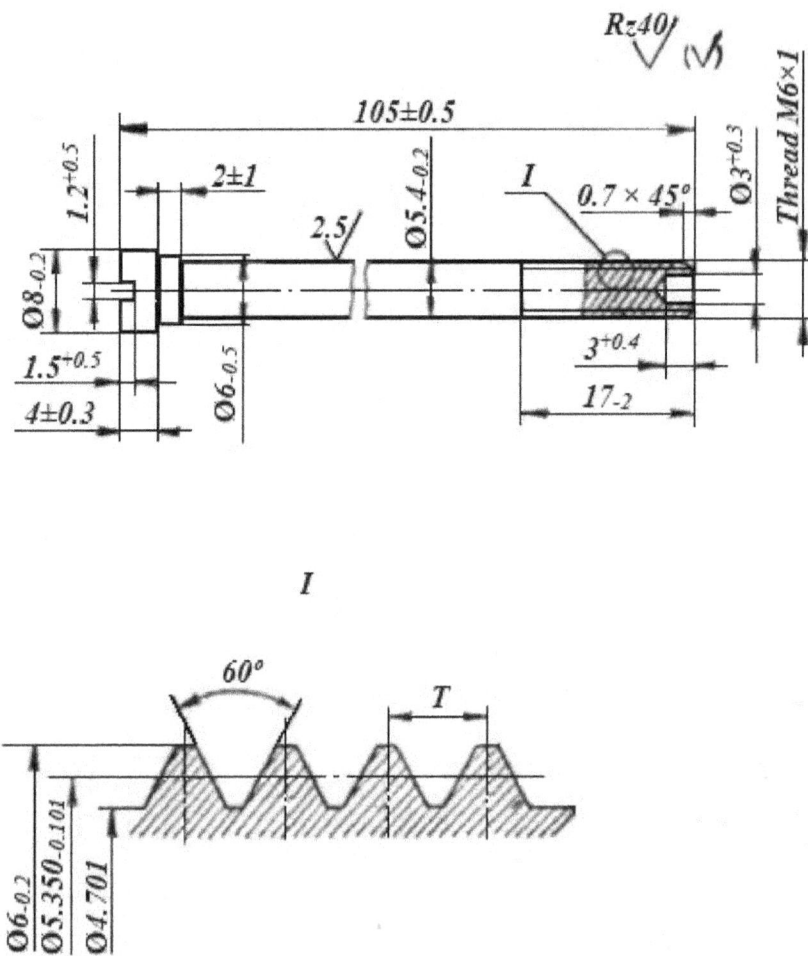

**Fig. 94.** Grip screw 6P20.0-19

Material: steel 50. Phosphated and lacquered

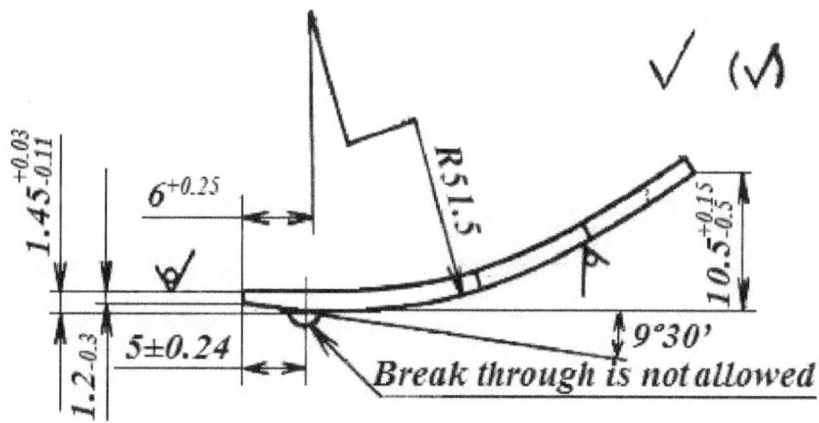

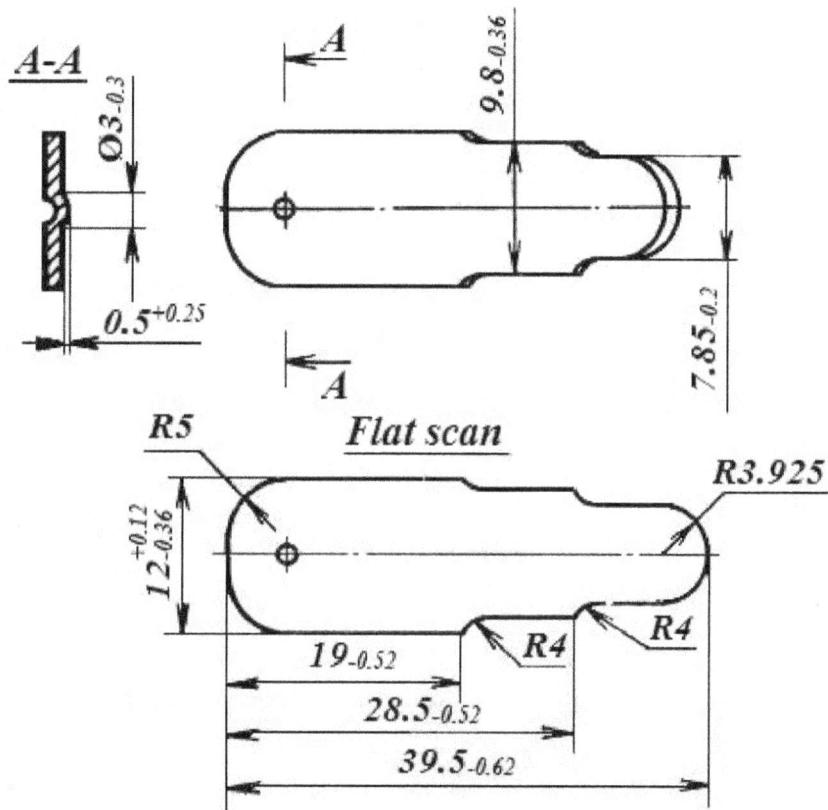

**Fig. 95.** Sight leaf spring 6P20.0-23

Material: steel U8A. Tempered to HRC 47.5-53. Phosphated and lacquered

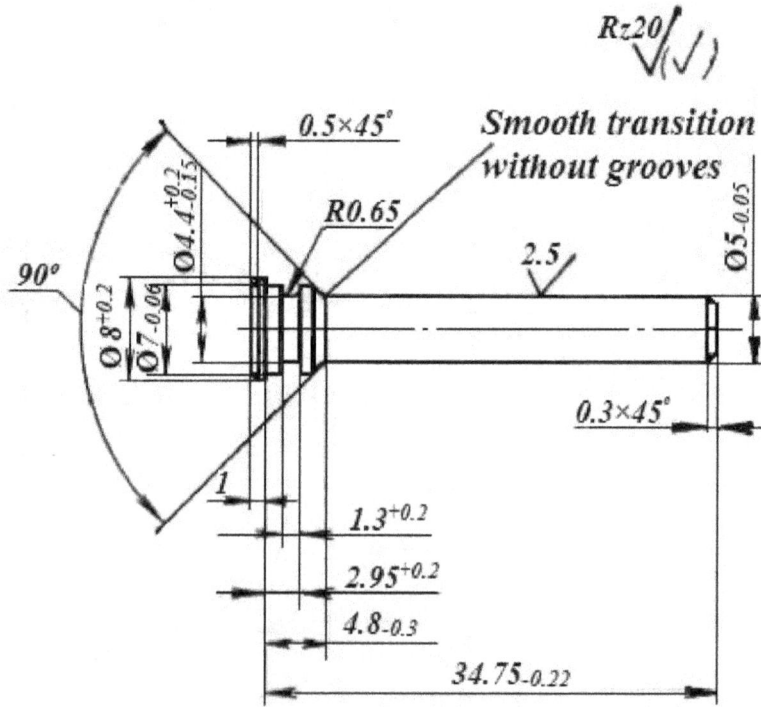

**Fig. 96.** Firing mechanism axis pin 6P20.0-25

Material: steel 50. Tempered to HRC 41.5-47.5. Phosphated

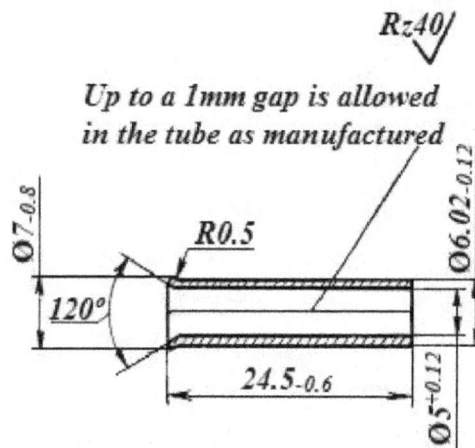

**Fig. 97.** Trigger axis pin bushing 6P20.0-27

Material: steel 50. Tempered to HV 341- 391. Phosphated

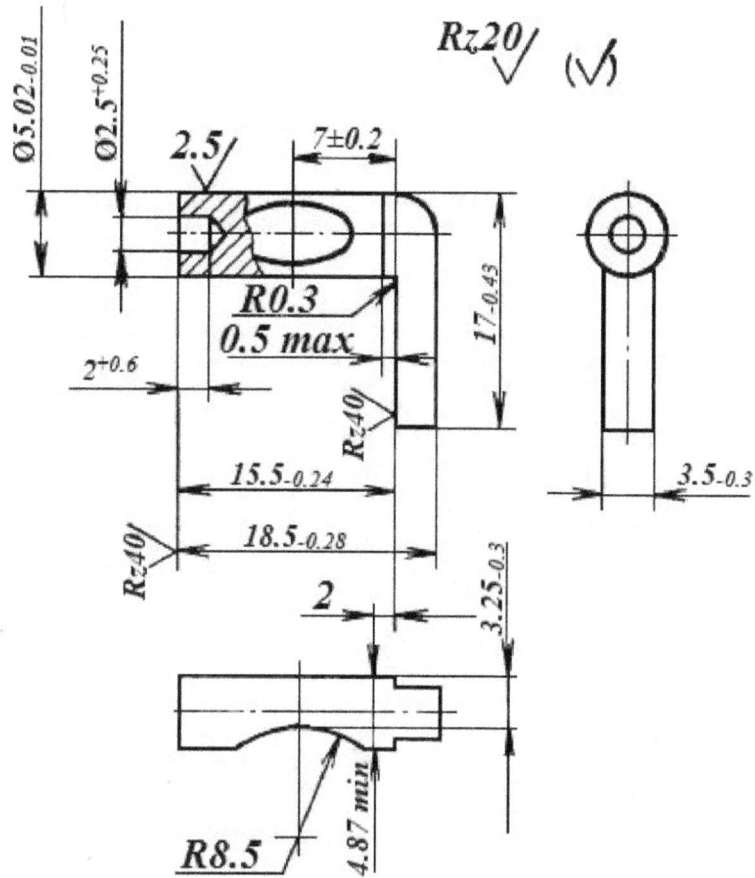

**Fig. 98.** Lower handguard retainer latch 6P20.1-28

Material: steel 40. Tempered to HRC 34-38.5. Phosphated

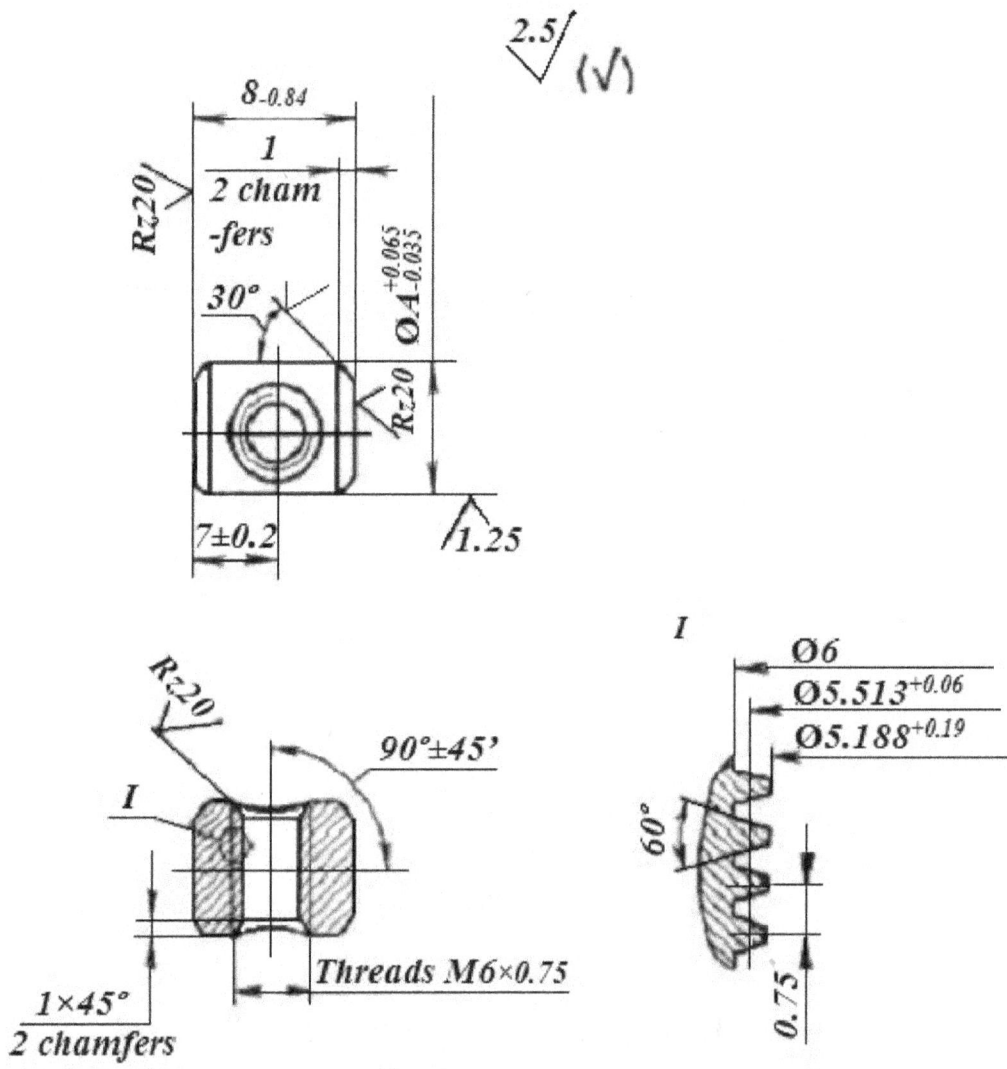

| Diameter | Group | |
|---|---|---|
| | 1 | 2 |
| A, mm | 10.05 | 10.065 |

| Part № | Dimension B, mm |
|---|---|
| 6P20.1-31 | 14 |
| 6P26.1-31 | 18 |

**Fig. 99.** Front sight base 6P20.1-31 and the front sight base AKSU 6P26.1-31

Material: steel 50. Tempered to HRC 43.5-49.5. Oxidized

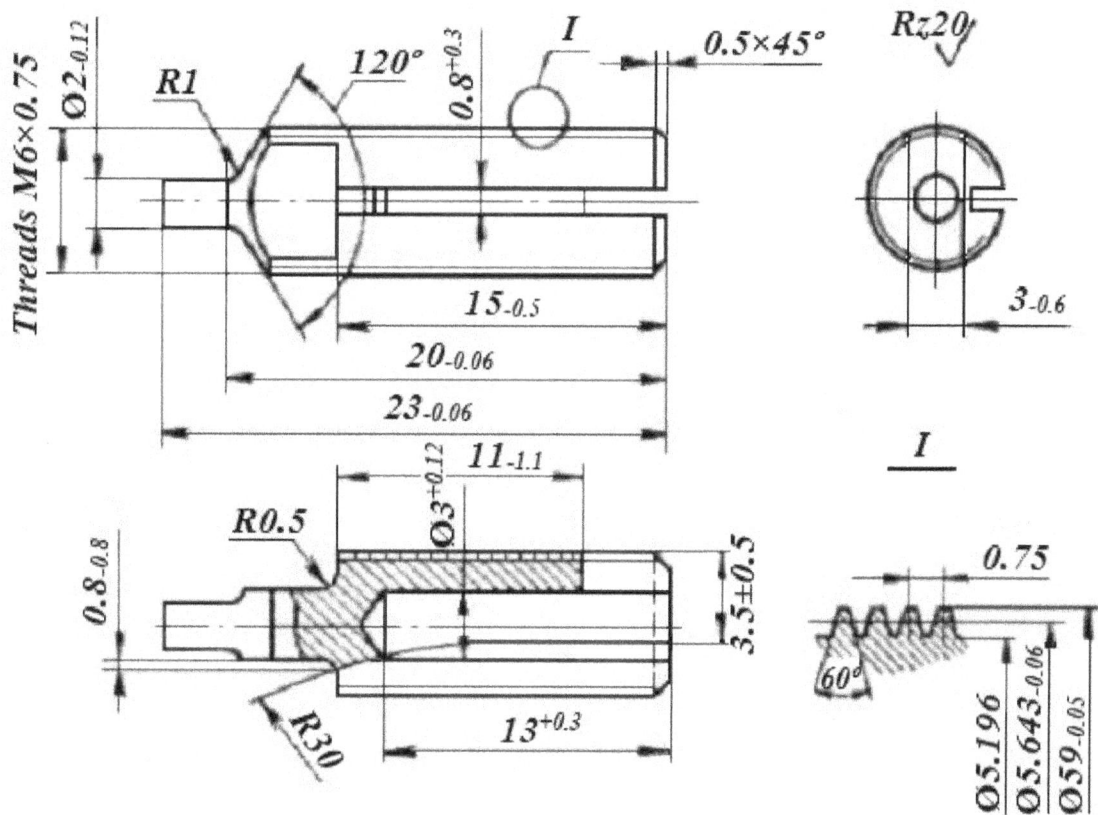

**Fig. 100.** Front sight post 6P20.1-32

Material: steel ZOHRA. Tempered to HRC 41.5-49.5. Phosphated

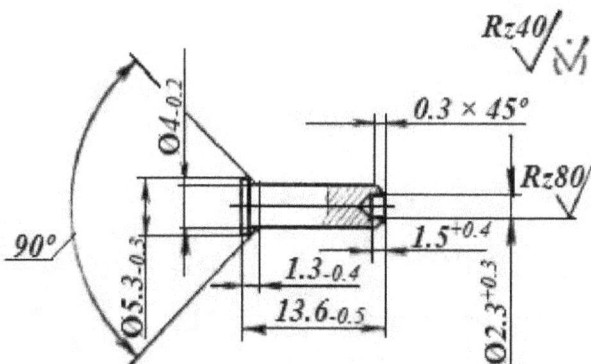

**Fig. 101.** Retaining pin for muzzle brake retainer 6P20.1-33

Material: steel 35. Phosphated and lacquered

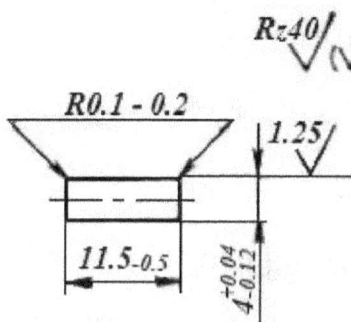

**Fig. 102.** Muzzle brake retainer pin 6P20.1-37

Material: steel 50. Tempered to HRC 38.5-45. Phosphated

121

$Rz80/$
$(\sqrt{})$

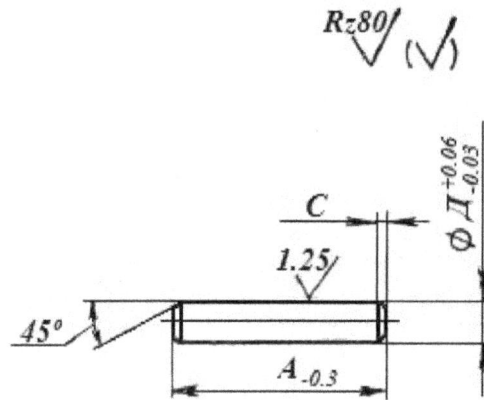

| Part № | Name | Dimension, мм | | | Термообработка |
|---|---|---|---|---|---|
| | | Д | A | C | |
| 6H4.1-3 | Hilt (crossgaurd) pin | 3,5 | 16.5 | 0.3 | HRC 32 -38.5 |
| 6P20.3-3 | Gas piston pin | 3 | 19 | 0.5 | |
| 6P26.1-35 | Retaining pins AKSU | 2.47; 2.5; 2.53 | 8.2 | 0.3 | HRC 43.5 – 49.5 |

**Fig. 103.** Pins

Material: steel 50. Phosphated

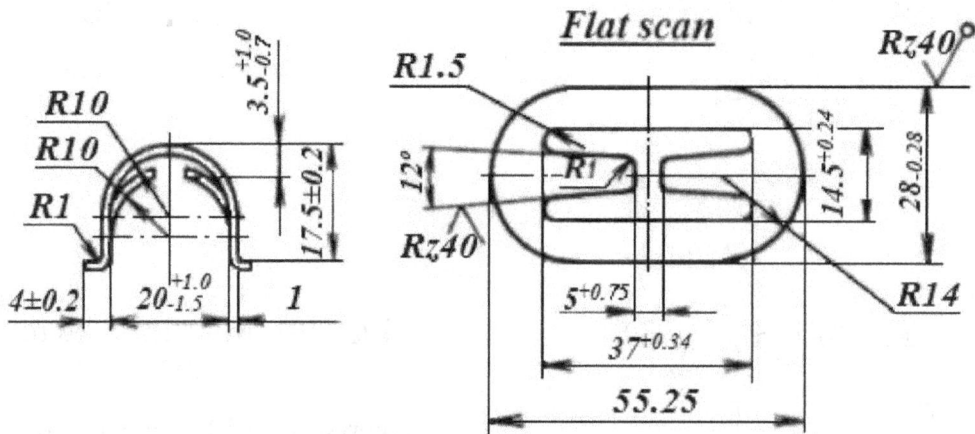

**Fig. 104.** Upper handguard retainer spring 6P20.1-41

Material: steel tape 50. Tempered to HRC 43.5-49.5. Phosphated and lacquered

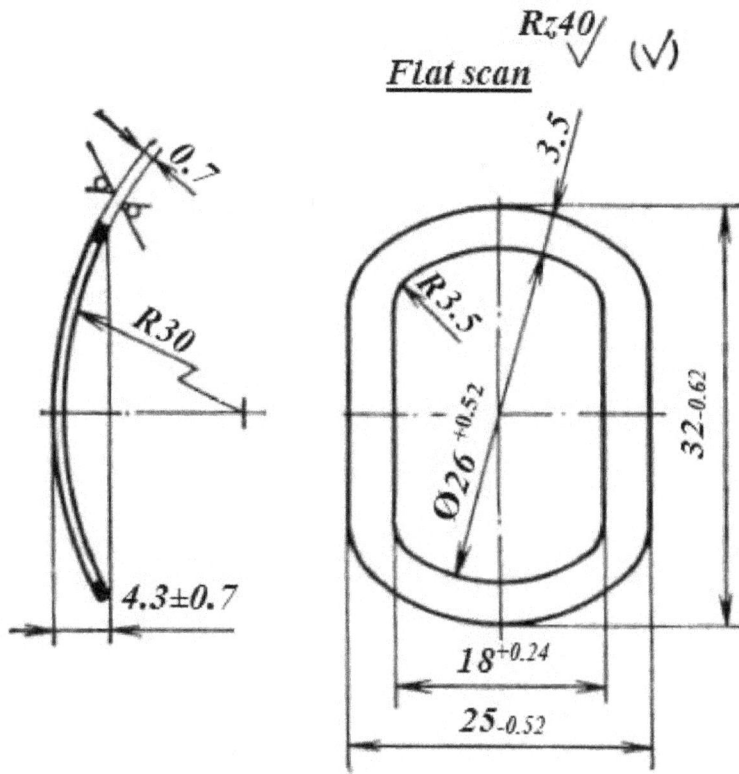

**Fig. 105.** Gas tube tensioning spring 6P20.1-45

Material: ribbon 50HFA-S-0.7 GOST 2283-79. Tempered to HRC 73.5-76. Phosphated and lacquered

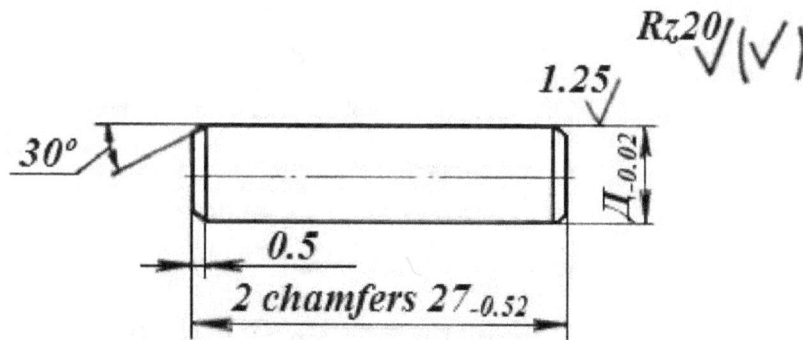

| Diameter | Group | | |
|---|---|---|---|
| | 1 | 2 | 3 |
| Д, мм | 7,065 | 7,095 | 7,565 |

**Fig. 106.** Barrel pin 6P20.1-52

Material: steel 50. Tempered to HRC 40.5-48. Phosphated

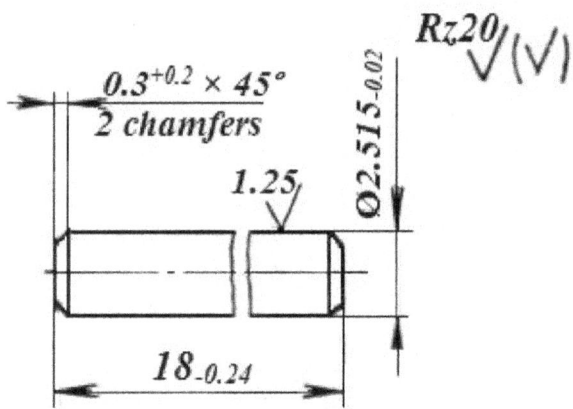

**Fig. 107.** Firing pin retaining pin 6P20.3-9

Material: steel 50. Tempered to HPCC 38.5-45.5.
Phosphated

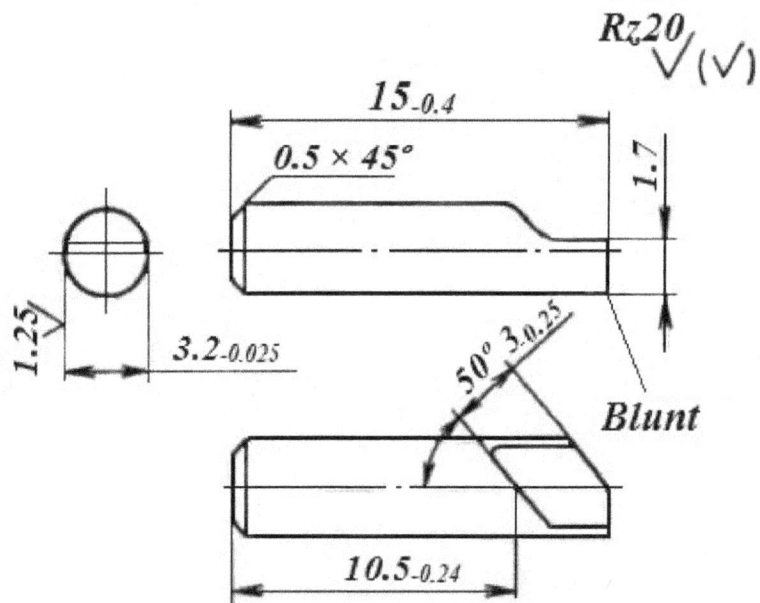

**Fig. 108.** Extractor axis pin 6P20.3-10

Material: steel 50. Tempered to HRC 38,5-45,5. Phosphated

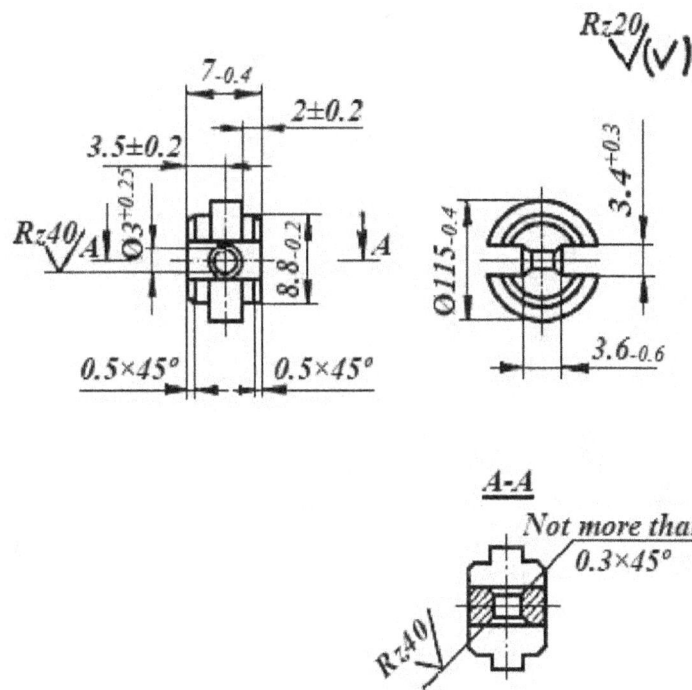

**Fig. 109.** Recoil spring retainer cap 6P20.4-4

Material: steel 50 Tempered to HRA 68-73. Phosphated and lacquered

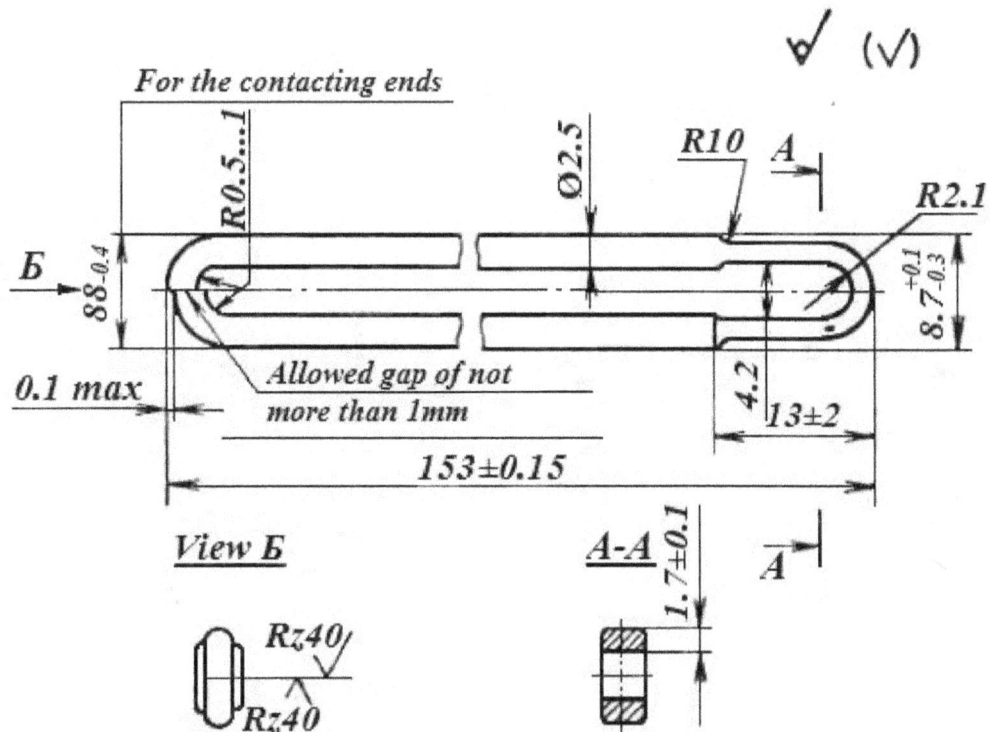

**Fig. 110.** Recoil spring forward guide rod 6P20.4-5

Material: wire GOST 17305-71 50 2.5. Tempered to HRC 38,5-45.5. Phosphated and lacquered

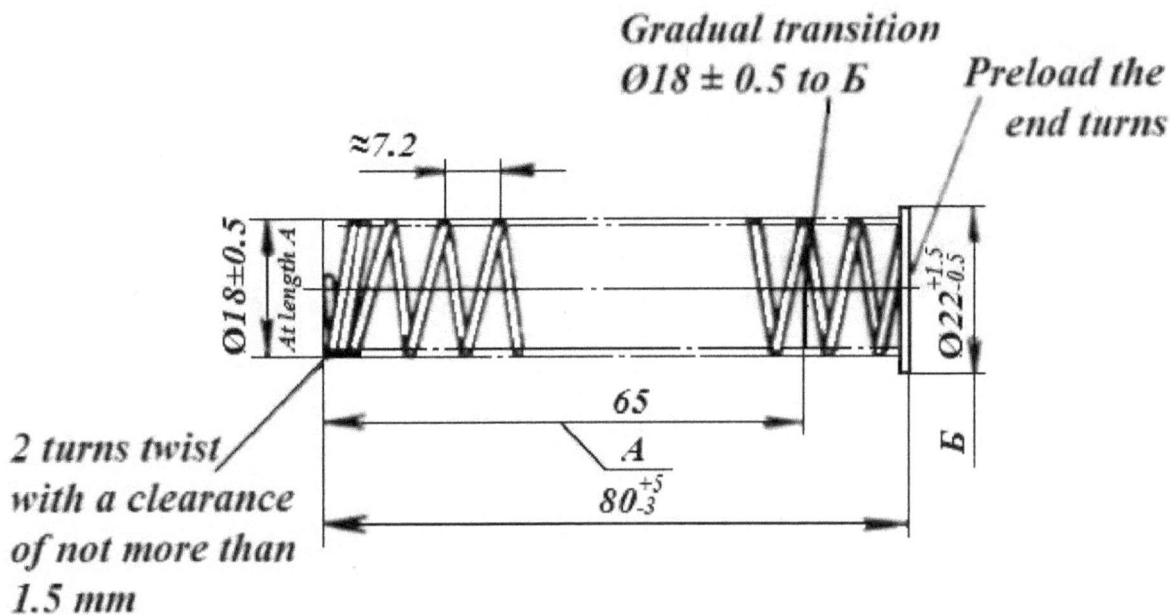

**Fig. 111.** Cleaning kit case retainer spring 6P20.5-5

Material: wire GOST 9389-75 1-1. Annealed at 240-260 ° C. Winding left. Number of coils 13 ± 1. Expanded length of 766 mm

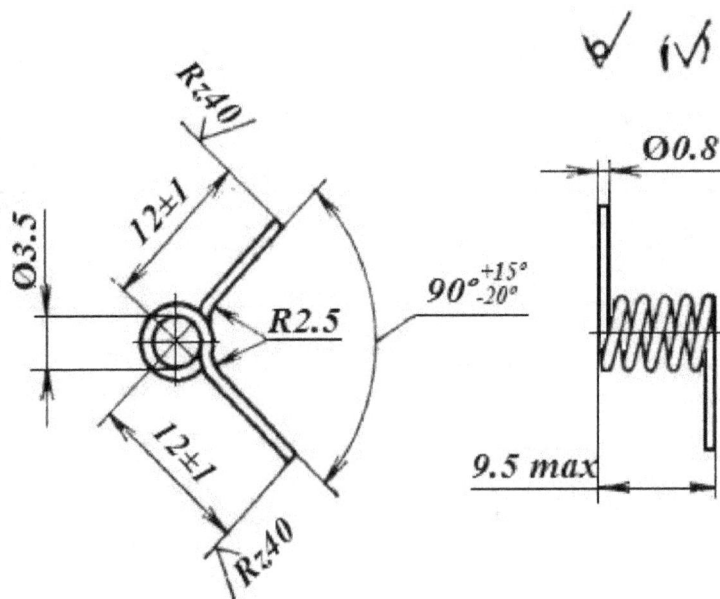

**Fig. 112.** Spring cover 6P20.5-10

Material: wire 1-0,8 GOST 9389-75. Annealed at 240-260 ° C. Winding left. Number of coils 9. Expanded length 140 mm

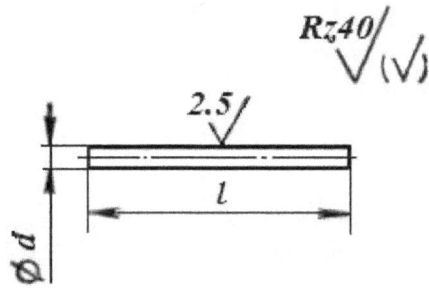

| Part № | Name | Dimension, мм | | Annealing |
|---|---|---|---|---|
| | | $d$ | $l$ | |
| 6P19.1-55 | Folding stock axis pin RPKS74 | $d*_{-0.05}$ | $29_{-0,6}$ | Tempered to HRC 39 - 45.5 |
| 6P18.2-10 | Windage nut pin RPK74 | $1.5_{-0.12}$ | | Hv 300-390 |
| 6P18.9-8 | Bipod latch axis pin RPK74 | $2.5_{-0.05}$ | | |
| 6P20.5-11 | Trapdoor axis pin | $2.5_{-0.12}$ | | |

d * - diameter of axis pin actual size of the hole.

**Fig. 113.** Axis pins and pins

Material: steel 50. Phosphated

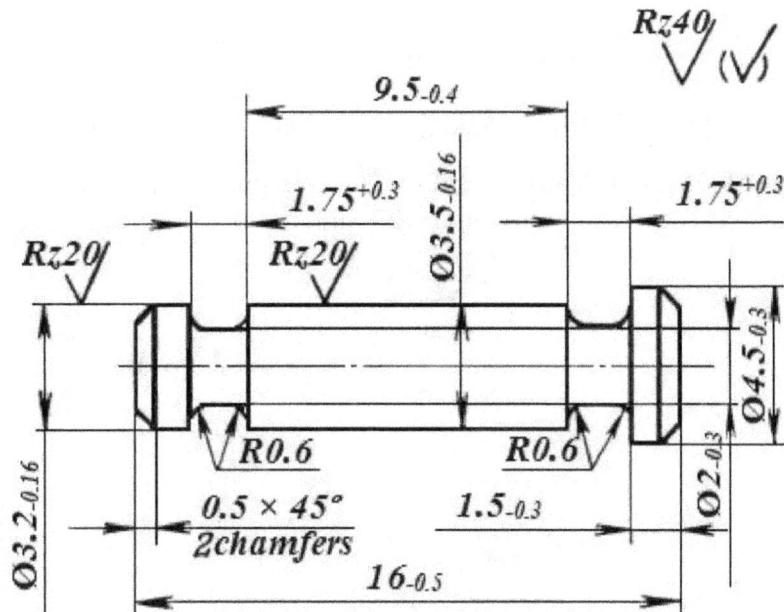

**Fig. 114.** Folding stock rear latch retainer pin 6P21.0-37

Material: Steel 50. Tempered to HRC 38.5-45.5. Phosphated

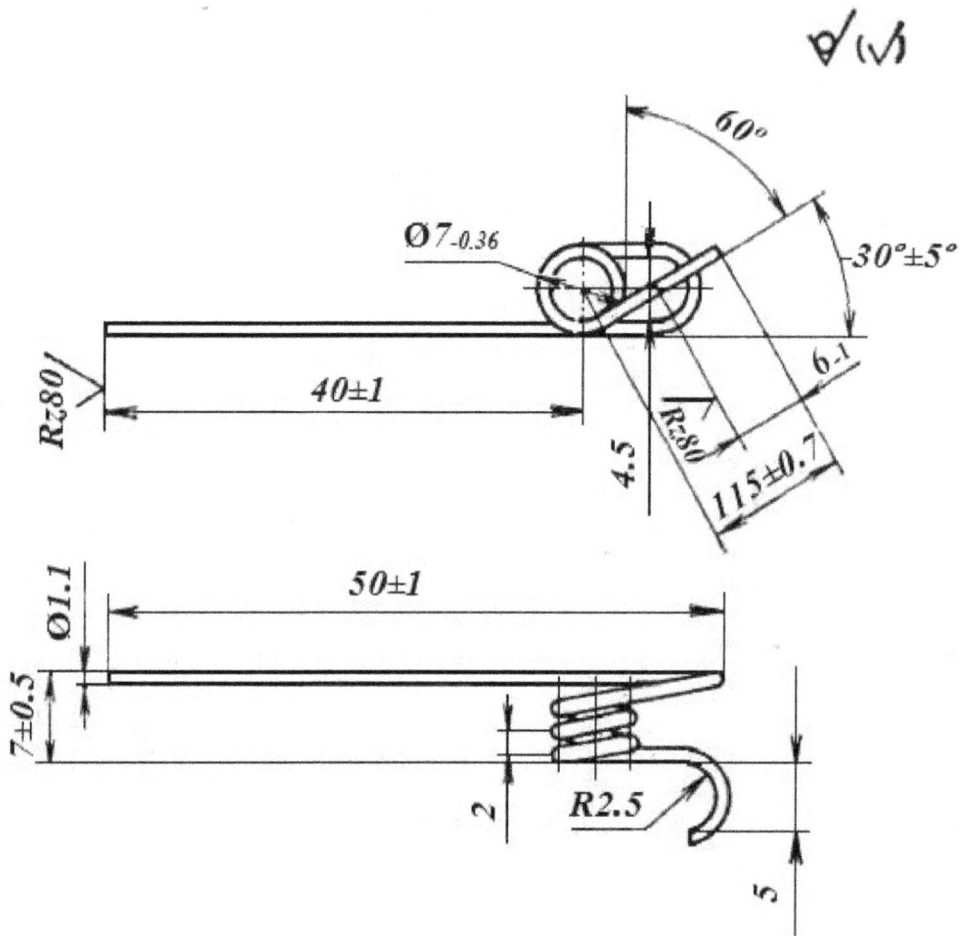

**Fig. 115.** Folding stock front latch spring 6P21.0-39

Material: wire GOST 9389-75 1-1.1. Vacation 240-260ºC. Wrapped right. Number of coils 3. Expanded length 127 mm

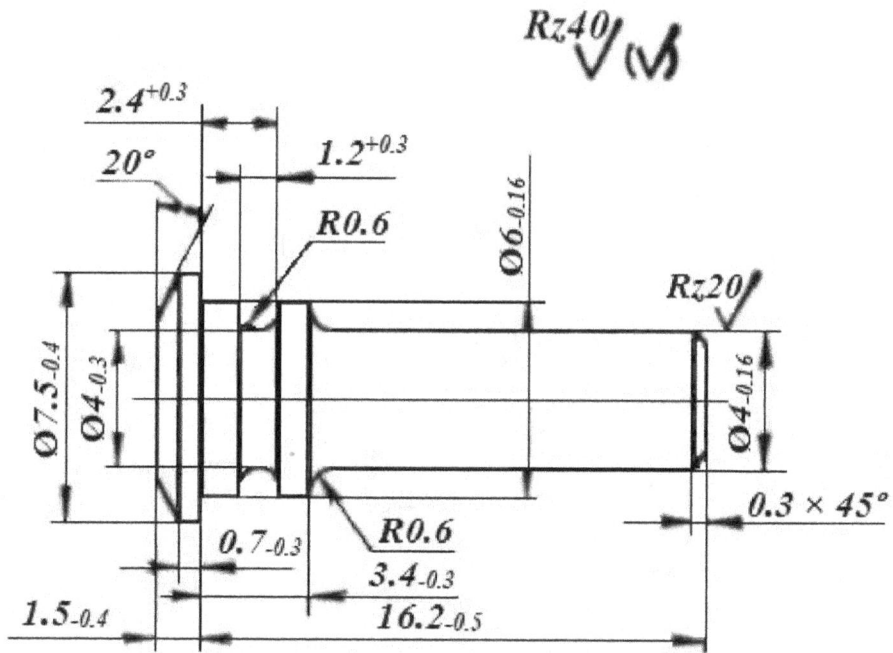

**Fig. 116.** Folding stock front latch axis pin 6P21.0-40

Material: steel 50. Tempered to HRC 38,5-45,5. Phosphated

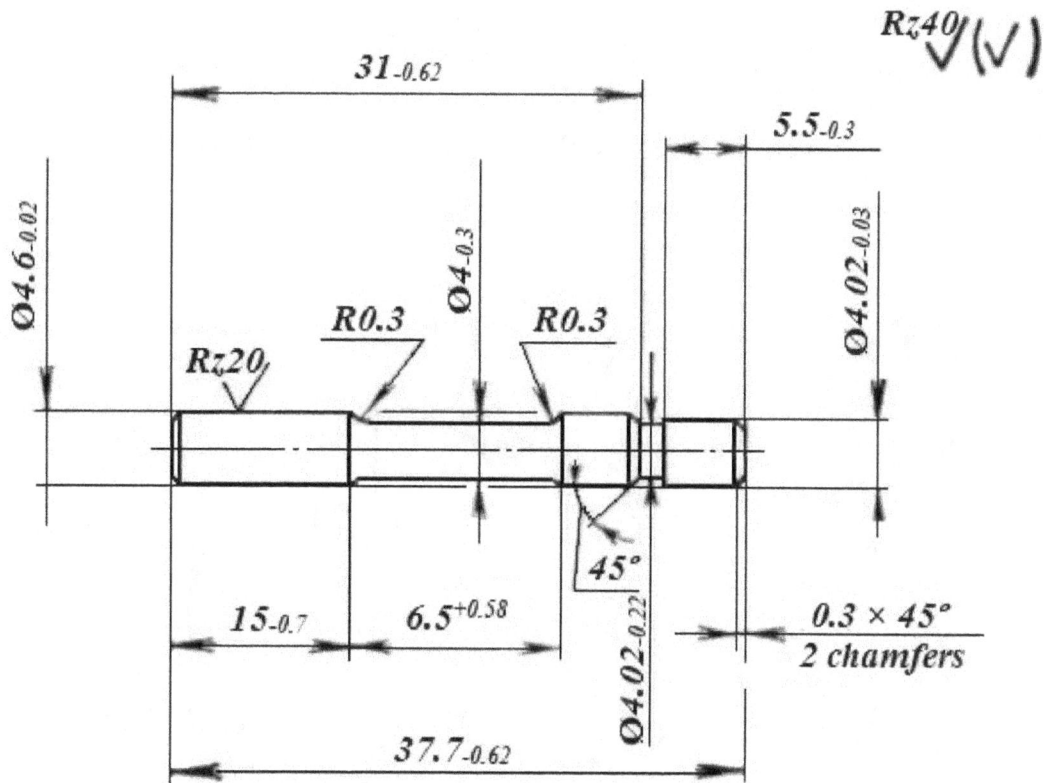

**Fig. 117.** Folding stock axis pin 6P21.0-41

Material: steel 50. Tempered to HRC 38.5-45.5. Phosphated

A-A

15°

4.7-0.16

R9

R0.5

Rz20

1-0.4

2-0.4

Rz20

R0.3

51°

4-0.16

Rz40 (√)

5.5-0.48

0.75

4-0.3

2.5±0.1

19-0.52

A

R4

13.8±0.1

60°

R4

Ø4+0.16

25°

R4.5

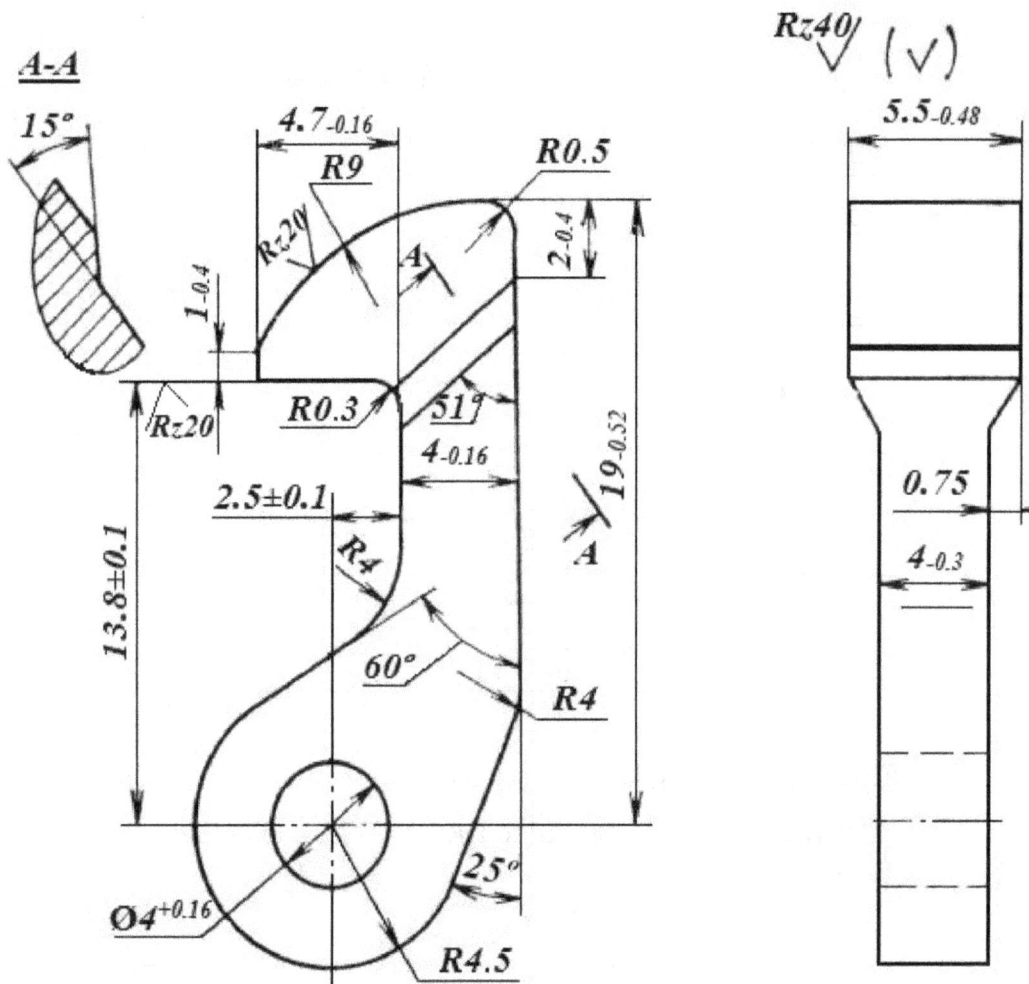

**Fig. 118.** Folding stock front latch hook 6P21.0-42

Material: Steel 60. Tempered to HRC 28-40. Phosphated and lacquered

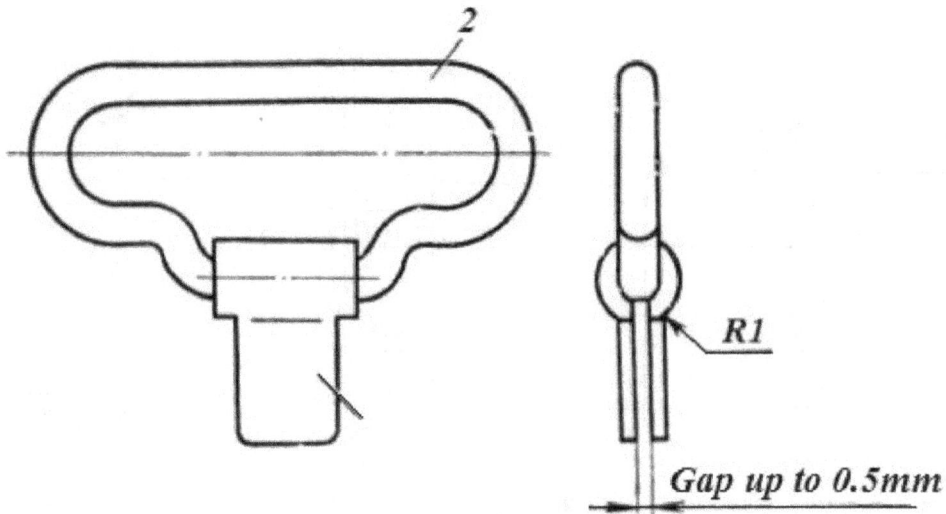

2

R1

Gap up to 0.5mm

**Fig. 119.** Sling swivel assembly for folding stock 6P21.Sb 5-1

*1* – sling loop 6P21.5-6, *2* – sling swivel hinge 6P21 5-7

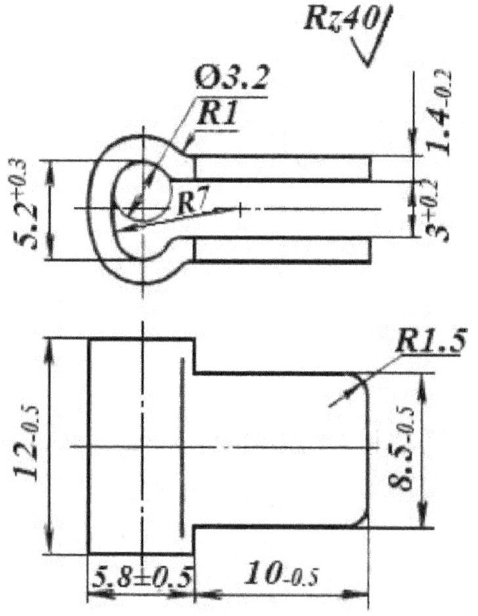

**Fig. 120.** Sling swivel hinge for folding stock 6P21.5-6

Material: steel 40. Phosphated

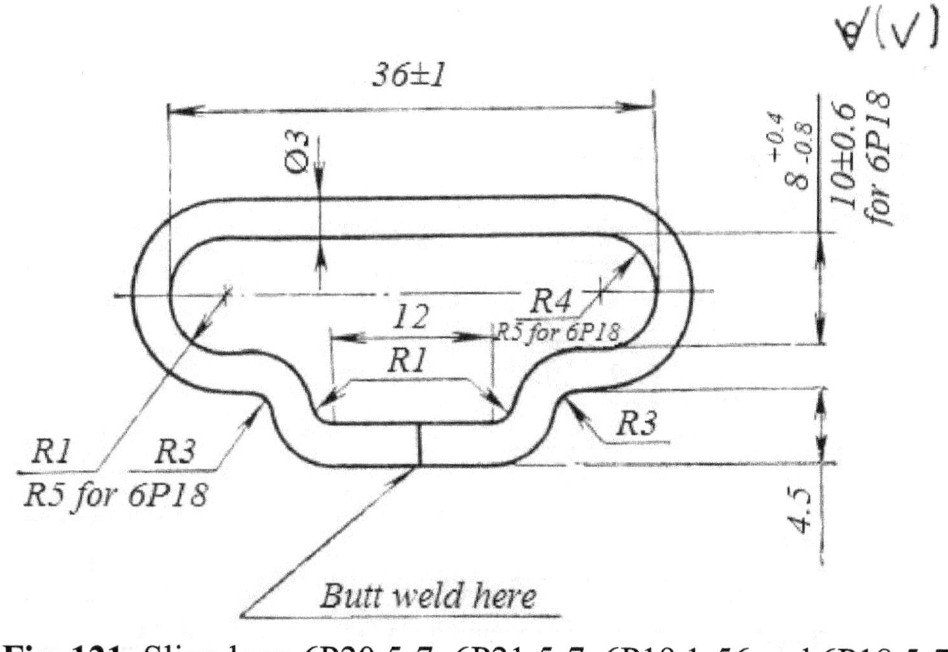

**Fig. 121.** Sling loop 6P20.5-7, 6P21.5-7, 6P19.1-56 and 6P18.5-7

Material: wire GOST 17305-71 3-40. Tempered to HRC 38.5-45.5. Phosphated

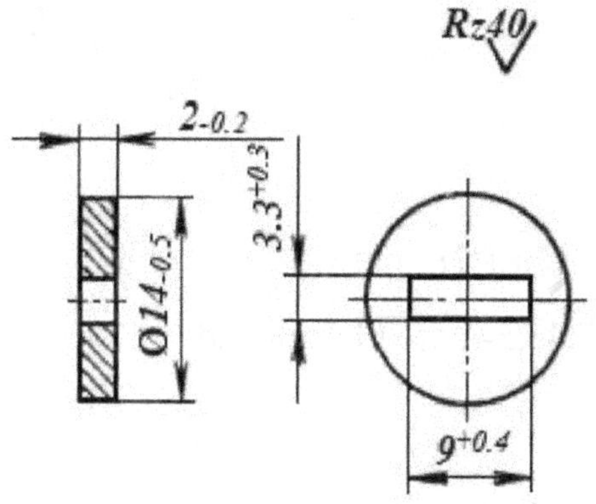

**Fig. 122.** Washer 6P21.5-13

Material: steel 40. Phosphated

131

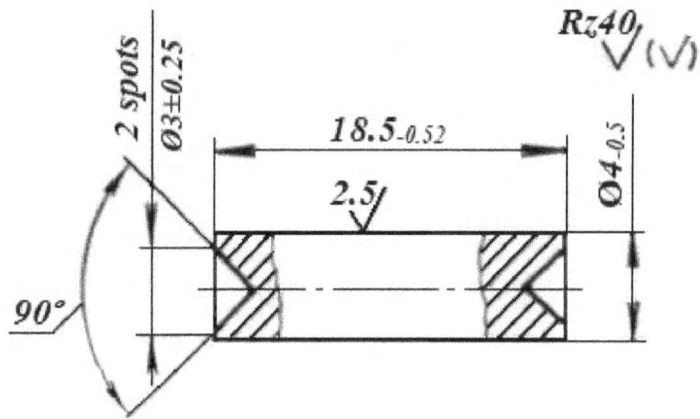

**Fig. 123.** Receiver cover axis pin AKSU 6P26.0-21

Material: Steel 50. Tempered to HRC 38,5-45,5. Phosphated

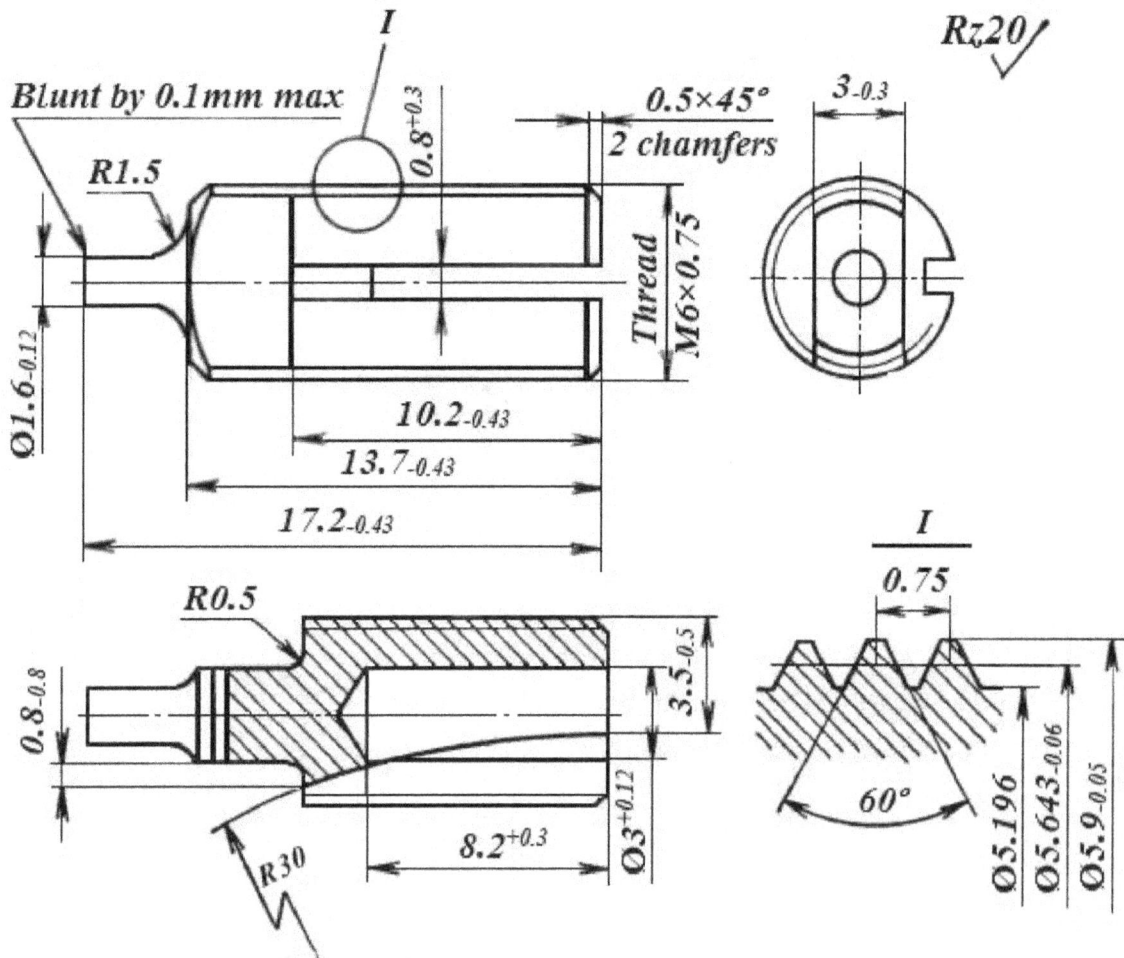

**Fig. 124.** Front sight post AKSU 6P26.1-17

Material: steel ZOHRA. Tempered to HRC 41,5-49,5. Phosphated

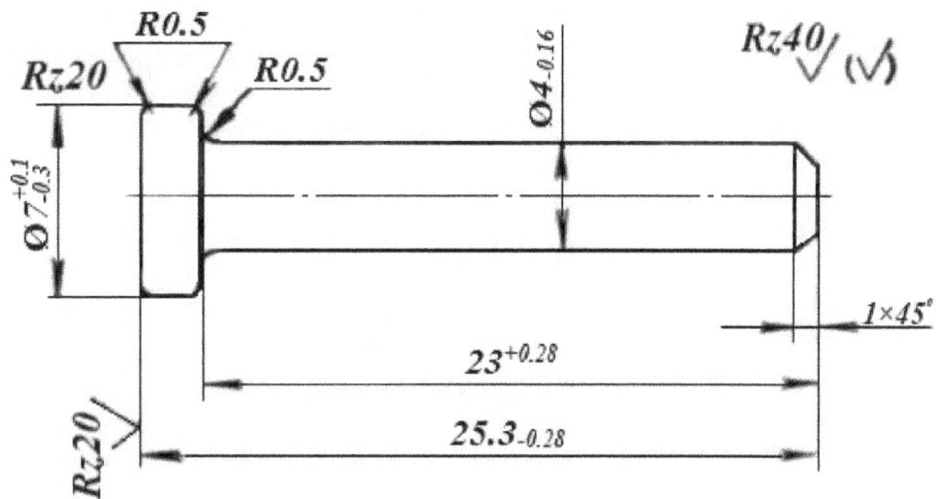

**Fig. 125.** Gas tube retainer plunger pin AKSU 6P26.1-36
Material: steel 50. Tempered to HRC 38.5-45.5. Phosphated

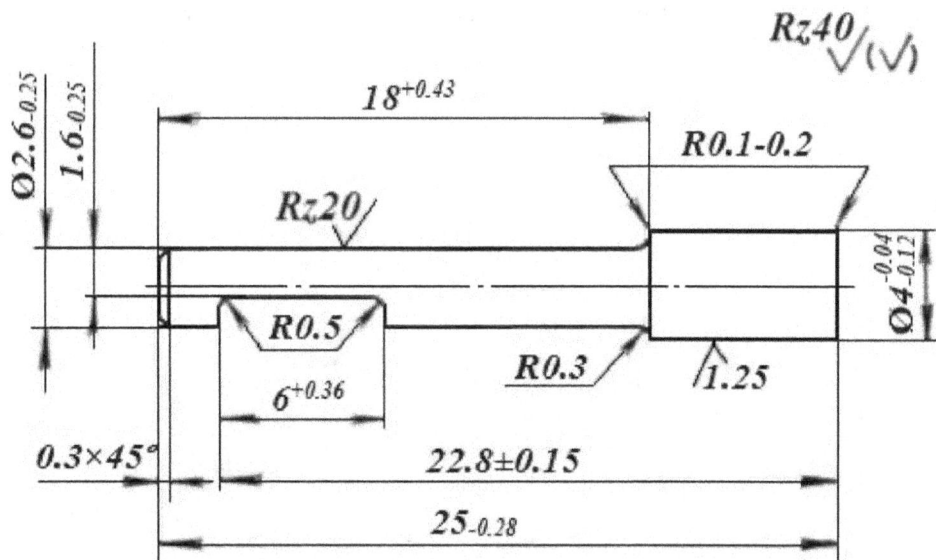

**Fig. 126.** Flash hider retainer pin AKSU 6P26.1-37
Material: steel 50. Tempered to HRC 38.5-45.5. Phosphated

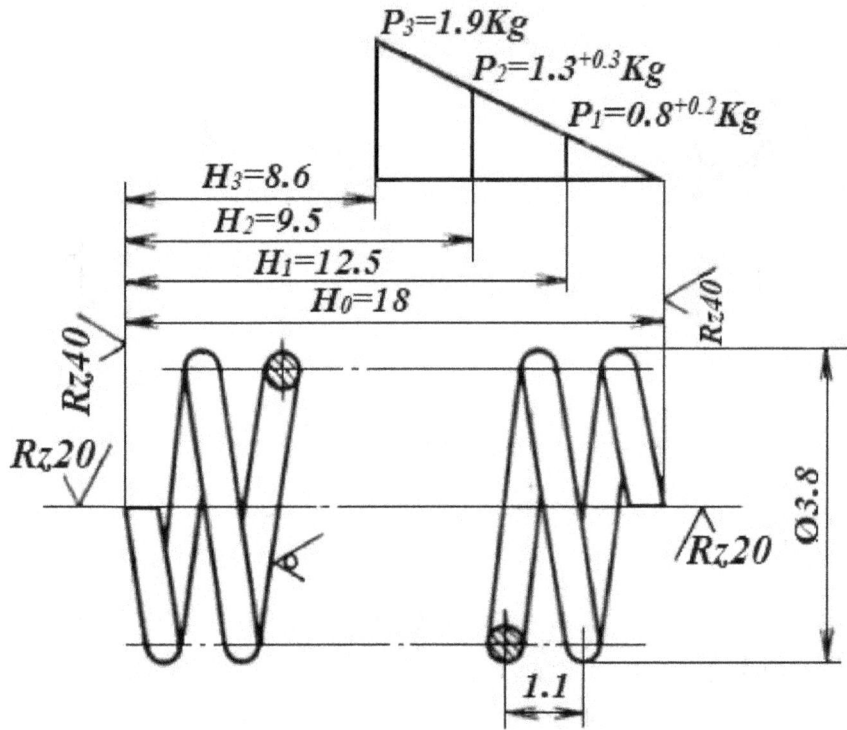

**Fig. 127.** Flash hider retainer spring AKSU 6P26.1-38

Material: wire V-0.51 TU3-1002-77. Number of coils 14-15. Tempered at a temperature $(460 \pm 10)$ ° C for 10 min. Compress COLD to deform to the point of contact of the coils for 24 hours. The diameter of the control sleeve during compression is 3.9 mm

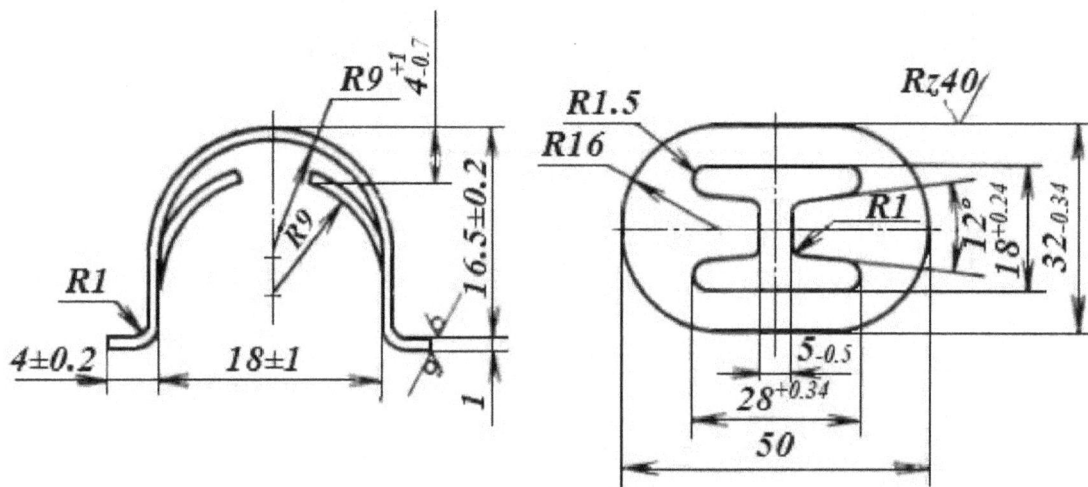

**Fig. 128.** Upper handguard retainer spring for AKSU 6P26.1-41

Material: steel Tempered to 50 HRC 43.5-49.5. Phosphated and lacquered

134

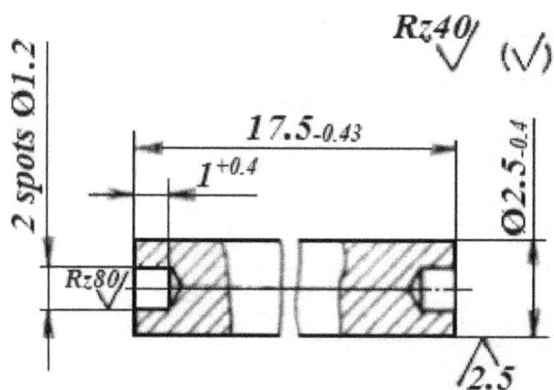

**Fig. 129.** Rear sight leaf axis pin AKSU 6P26.7-32

Material: steel 50. Tempered to HRC 36.5-42.5. Phosphated

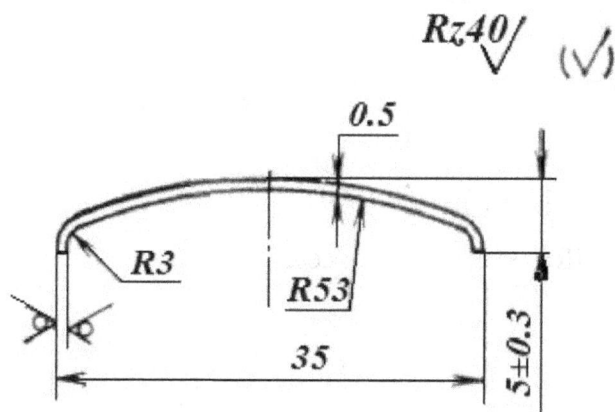

**Fig. 130.** Rear sight leaf spring AKSU 6P26.7-33

Material: steel 50HFA-S-0.5×12 GOST 2283-79. Tempered to HRC 73.5-76. Oxidized

**Flat scan**

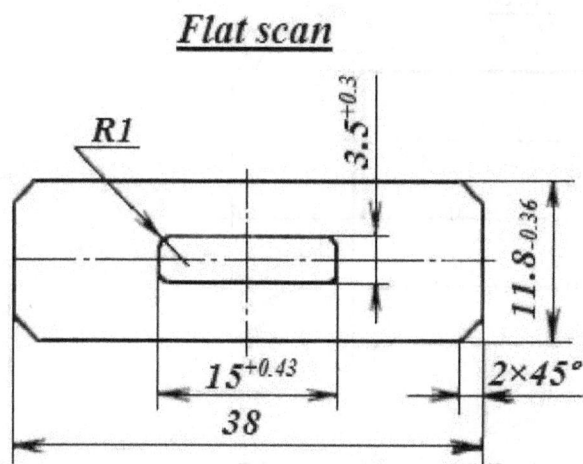

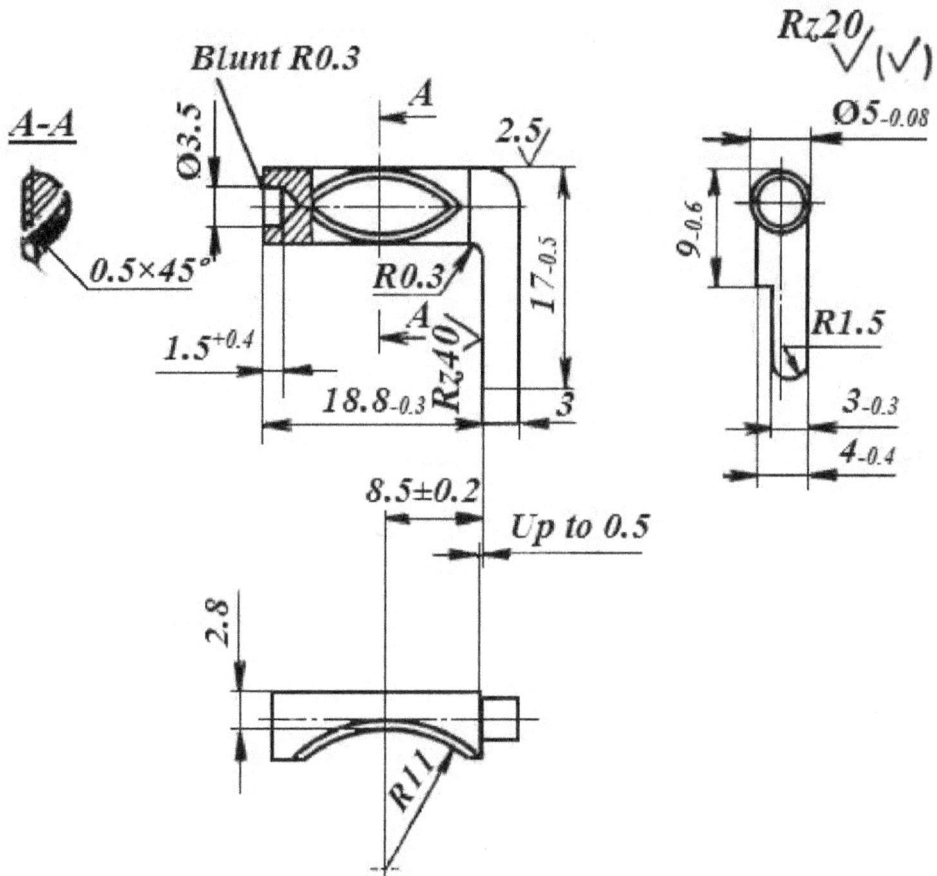

**Fig. 131.** Lower handguard retainer latch RPK74 6P18.1-28

Material: steel 50, Tempered to HRC 34-39. Phosphated

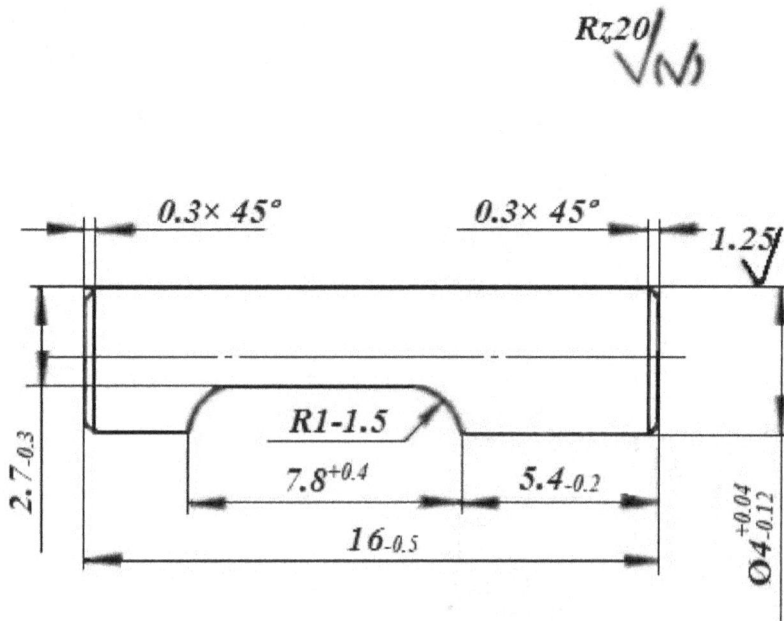

**Fig. 132.** Flash hider retainer pin RPK74 6P18.1-37

Material: steel 50. Tempered to HRC 39-45,5. Phosphated

136

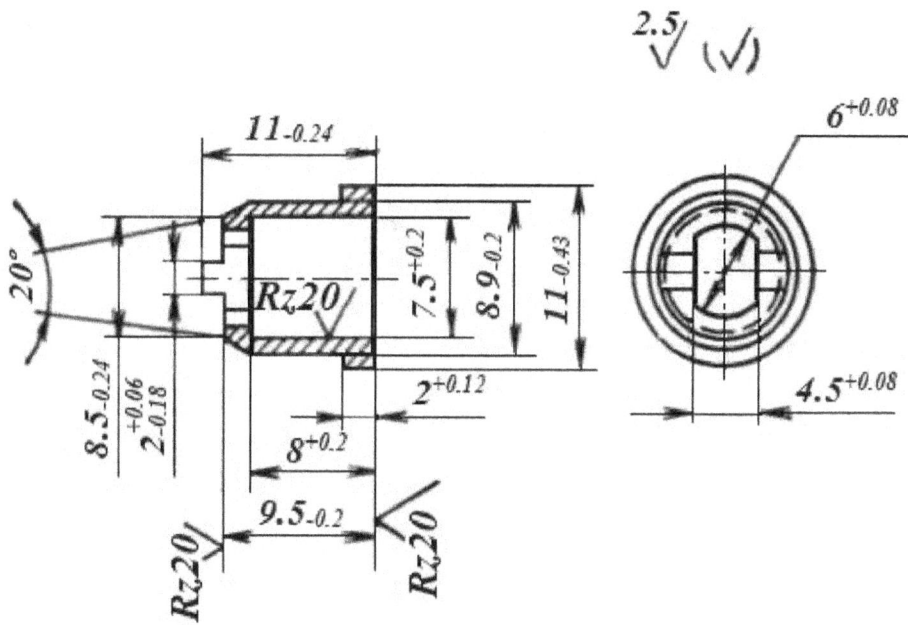

**Fig. 133.** Windage adjustment lock knob RPK74 6P18.2-6

Material: steel 50. Tempered to HRA 69-72.5. Phosphated

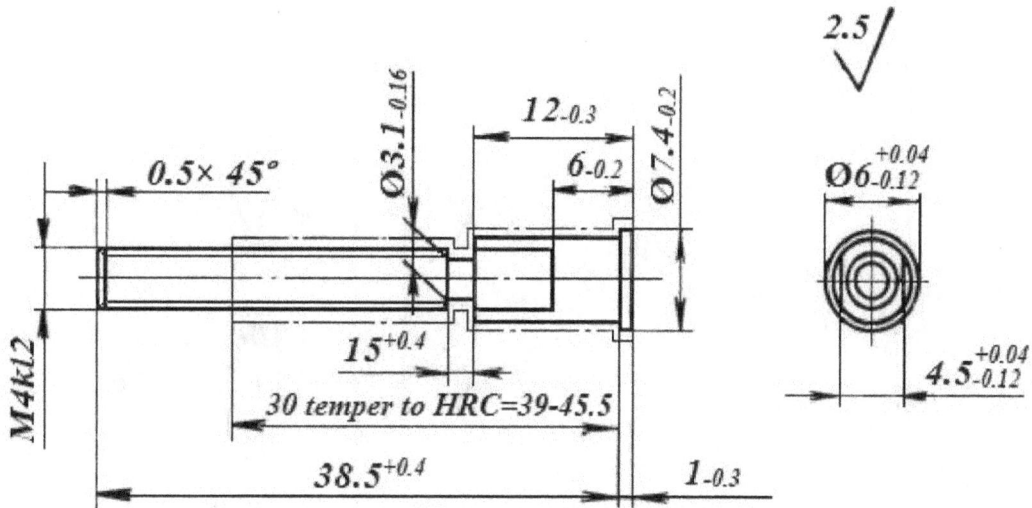

**Fig. 134.** Windage adjustment screw RPK74 6P18.2-7

Material: steel 50. Phosphated

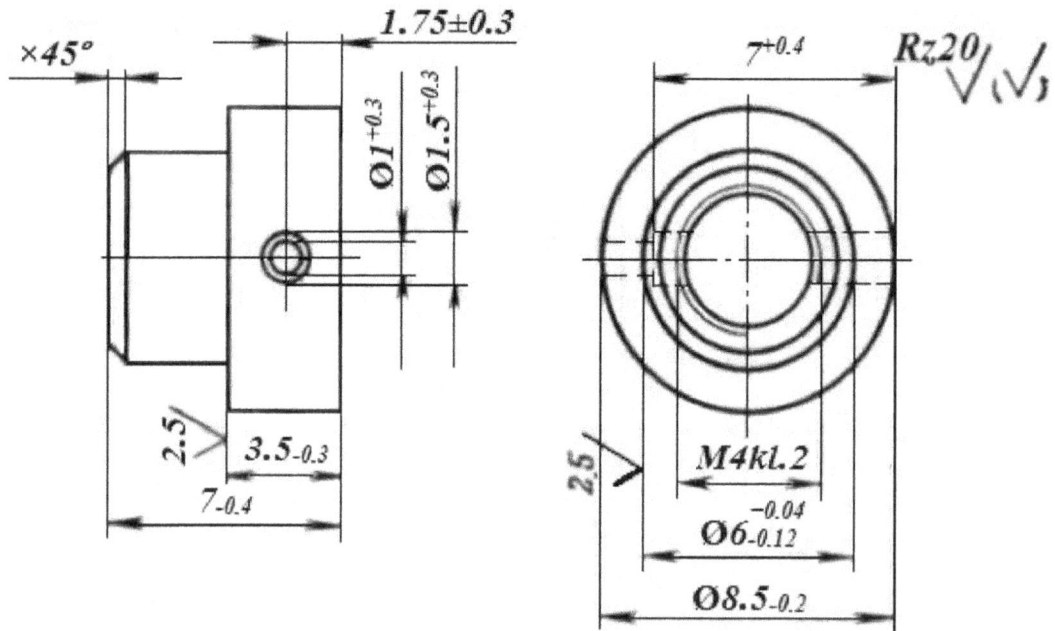

**Fig. 135.** Windage adjustment nut RPK74 6P18.2-9

Material: steel 50. Tempered to HRA 69-72.5. Phosphated and coated with varnish on the outer surface

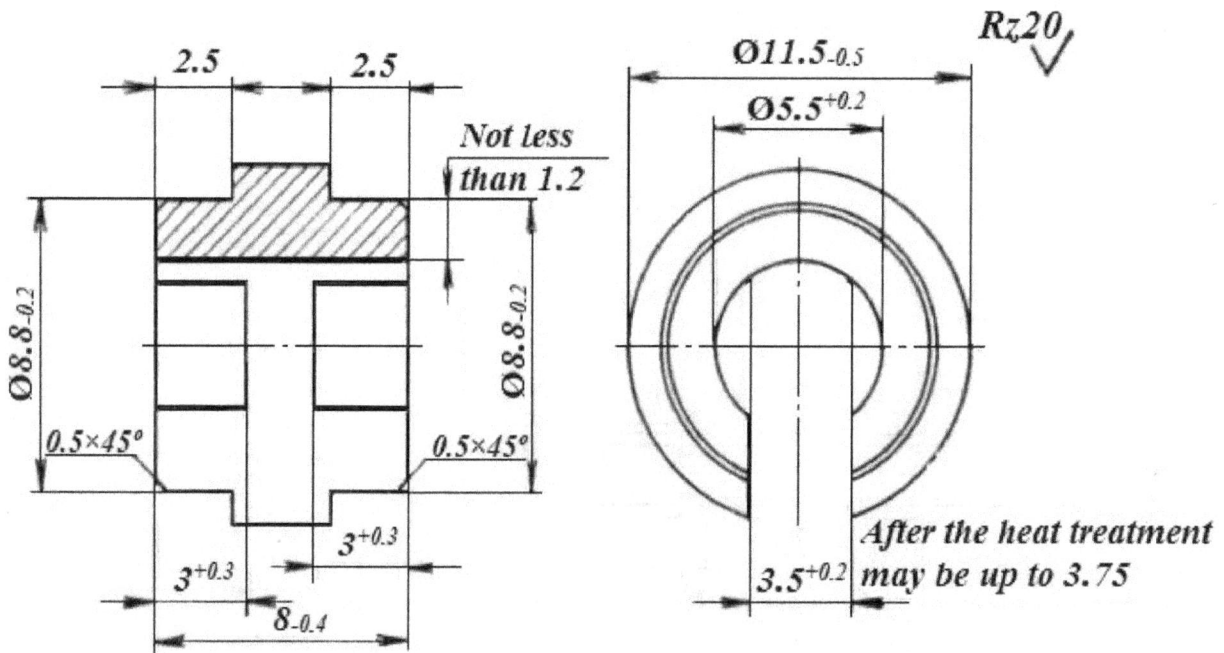

**Fig. 136.** Recoil spring retainer cap for RPK74 6P18.4-4

Material: steel 50. Tempered to HRA 69-73. Phosphated

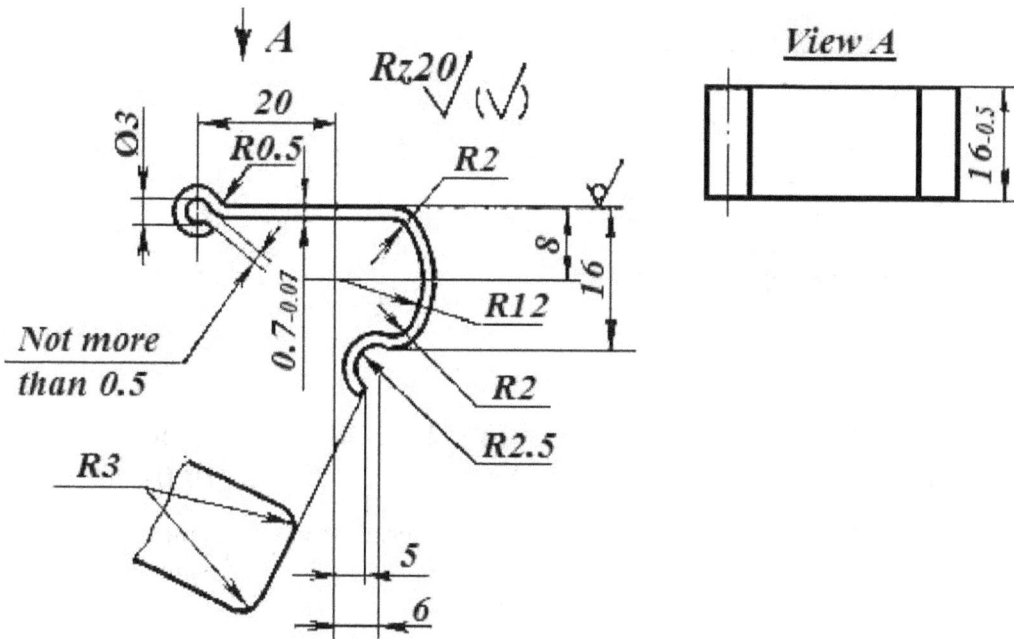

**Fig. 137.** Bipod latch RPK74 6P18.9-7

Material: steel 50. Tempered to HRA 71.5-74.5. Phosphated and lacquered

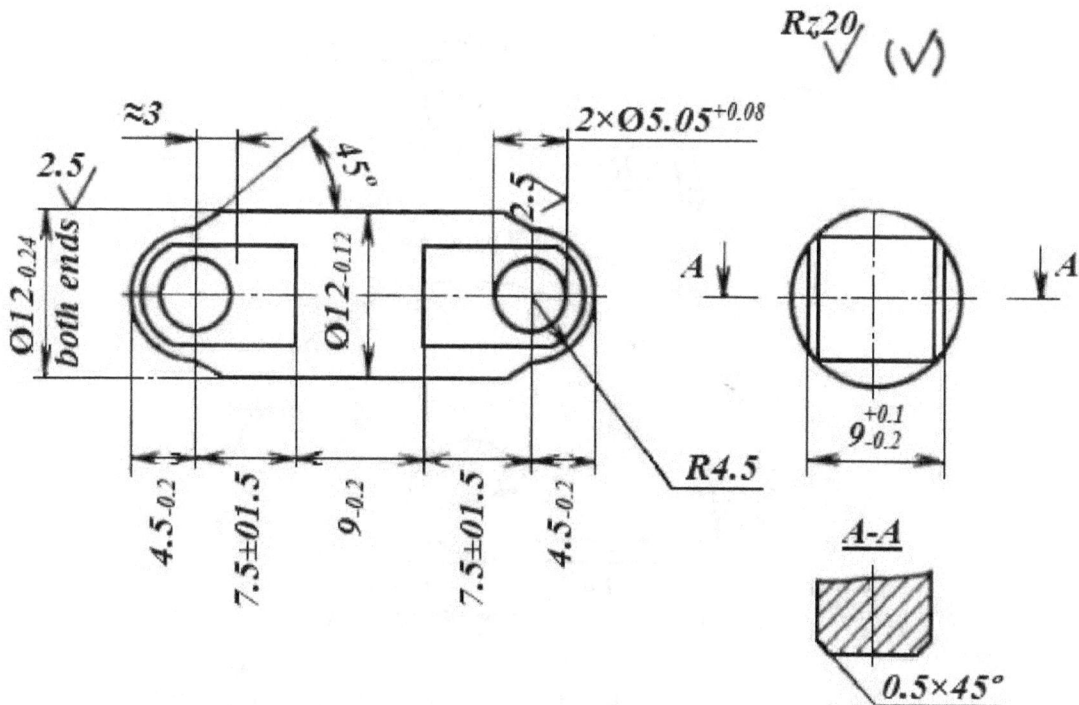

**Fig. 138.** Bipod axis pin RPK74 6P18.9-10

Material: steel 50. Tempered to HRCa 39-45.5. Phosphated

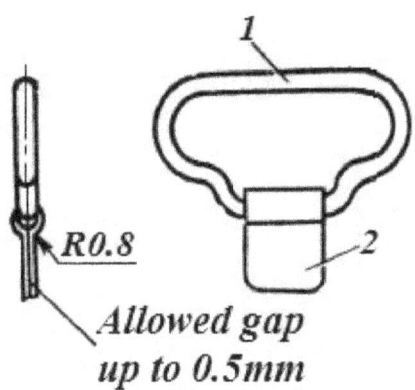

**Fig. 139.** Sling swivel assembly RPKS74
6P19.S6 1-10:

*1* – sling loop 6P19.1-56; *2* – sling swivel hinge
6P19.1-57

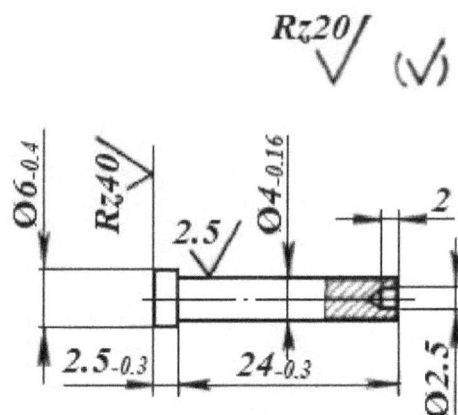

**Fig. 140**. Stock latch hook axis pin RPK74S
6P19.0-26

Material: steel 50. Tempered to HRC 30-34.
Phosphated

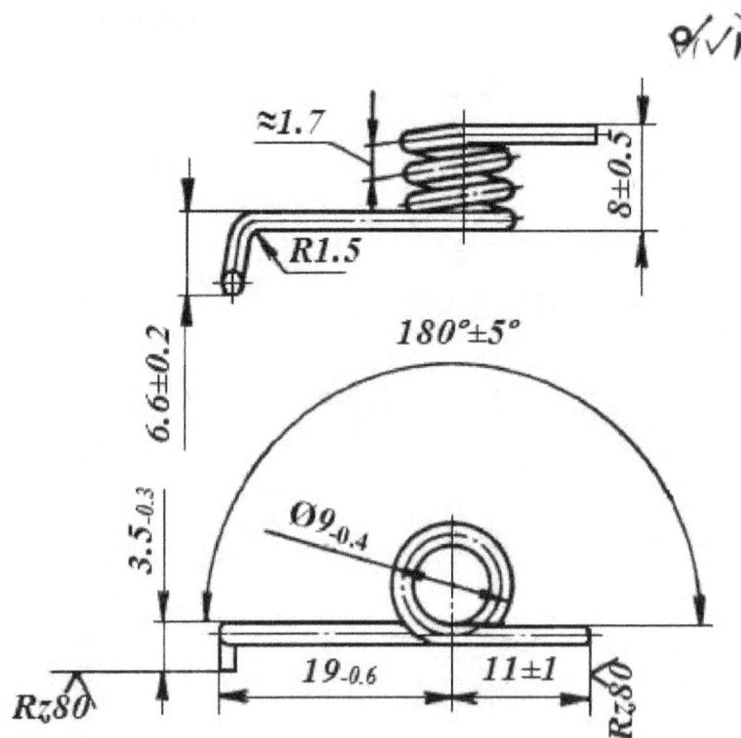

Fig. 141. Stock latch hook spring RPK74S 6P19.0-27

Material: wire 1-1.6. Annealed at 240-250 ° C. Wrapped right. Nuber of coils 4. Expanded length 131 mm

$Rz20$ $\sqrt{(\sqrt{})}$

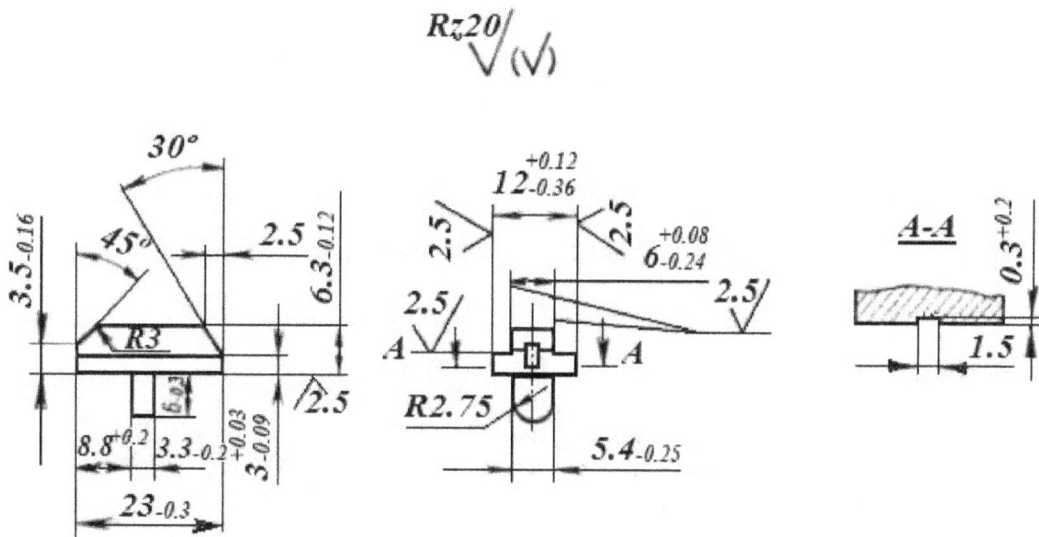

**Fig. 142.** Stock latch RPKS74 6P19.1-52

Material: sgal 50. Tempered to HRCa 39-45,5. Phosphated

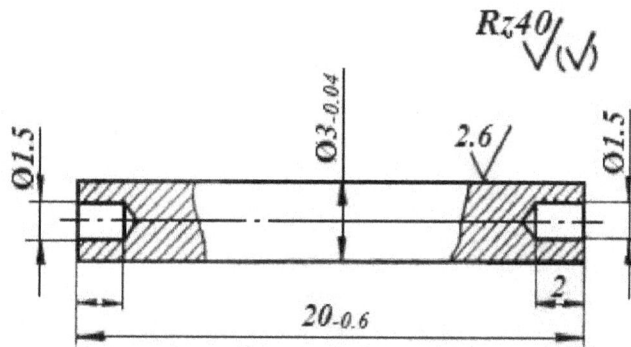

$Rz40$ $\sqrt{(\sqrt{})}$

**Fig. 143.** Stock latch pin RPKS74 6P19.1-54

Material: steel 50. Tempered to HRCs 34-39. Phosphated

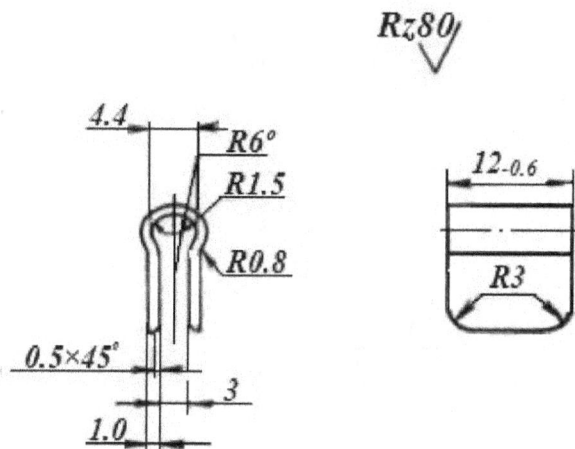

$Rz80$ $\sqrt{}$

Fig. 144. Sling swivel hinge RPKS74 6P19.1-57

Material: steel 50. Length 25 mm unfolded

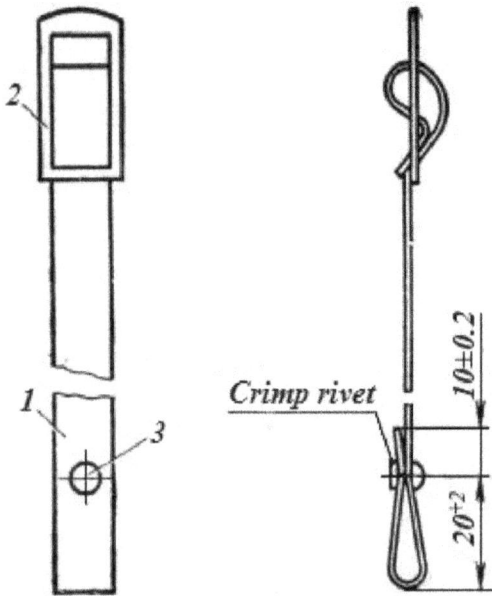

**Fig. 145.** Wrist strap assembly 6H4.Sb 1-3:

*1*- strap 6H4.1-14; *2* - buckle 6H4.1-18; *3* - rivet

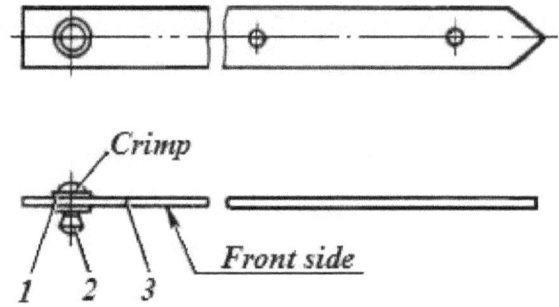

**Fig. 146.** Retainer strap assembly
6H4.Sb 2-2:

*1* - washer 6H4.2-15; *2* - button stud 6H4.2-14; *3* - strap 6H4.2-16

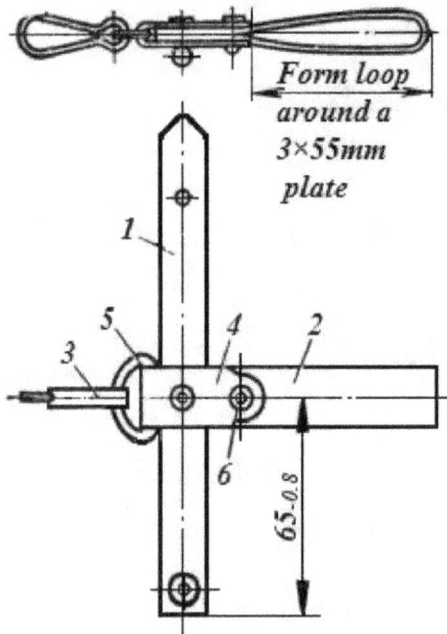

**Fig. 147.** Hanger assembly 6H4.Sb 2-3:

*1* – retainer strap assembly 6H4.Sb 2-2; *2* - strap 6H4.2-7; *3* – snap hook 6H4.2-10; *4* - suspension plate 6H4.2-19; *5* – D-ring 6H4.2-20; *6* - rivet

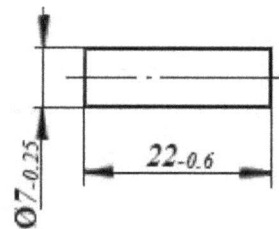

**Fig. 148.** Handle pin 6H4.1-9

Press material AG-4-V
GOST 20437-76

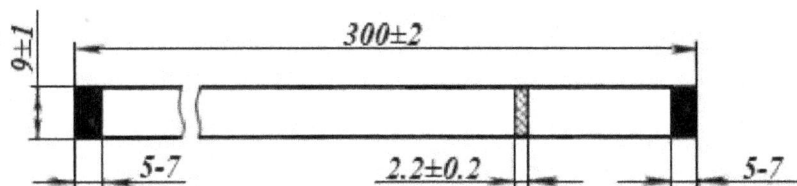

**Fig. 149.** Wrist strap 6H4.1-14

Material: heavy strap webbing LRT bilayer with filling, width 9 mm
GOST 16996-71
Sew the ends of the belt sheathing, then soak with glue number 88-N

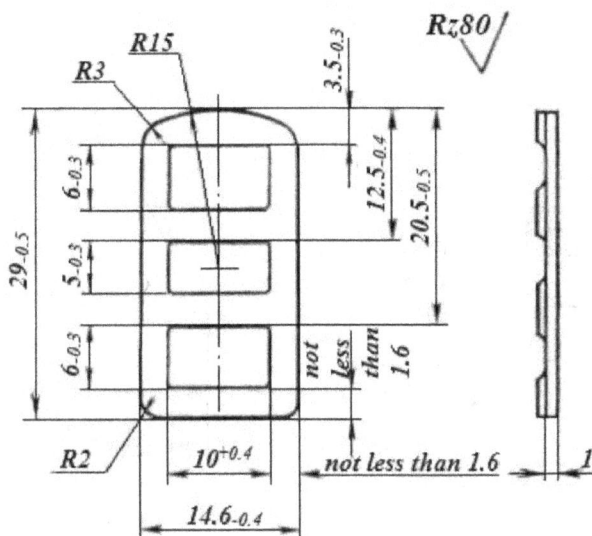

**Fig. 150.** Wrist strap buckle 6H4.1-18

Material: steel 40. Tempered to HRA 67-71. Phosphated and lacquered

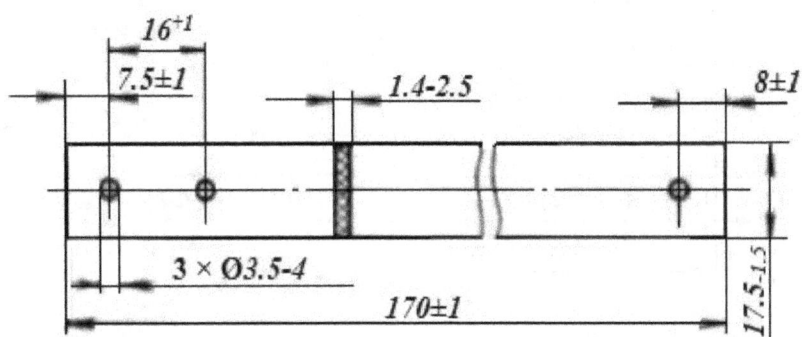

**Fig. 151.** Hanger belt loop strap 6H4.2-7

Material: Harness and saddle leather smooth or pebbled, brown GOST 1904-81

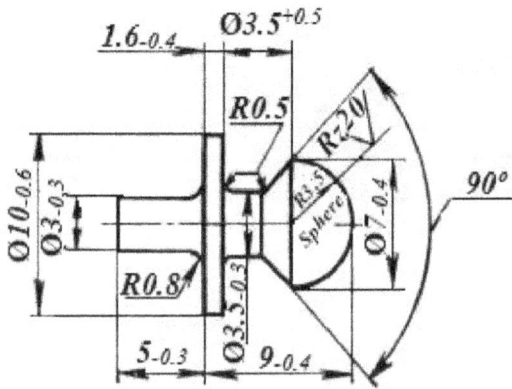

**Fig. 152.** Button stud 6H4.2-14

Material: steel 15. Phosphated and lacquered

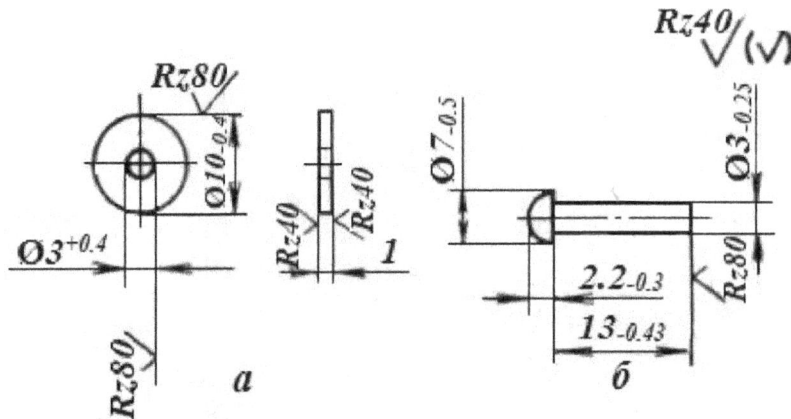

**Fig. 153.** Washers 6H4.2-15 (a), and   rivet 6H4 6Sh46.1-17 (b)

Material washer: steel 40. Phosphated and lacquered
Material rivet: Steel 15. Phosphated

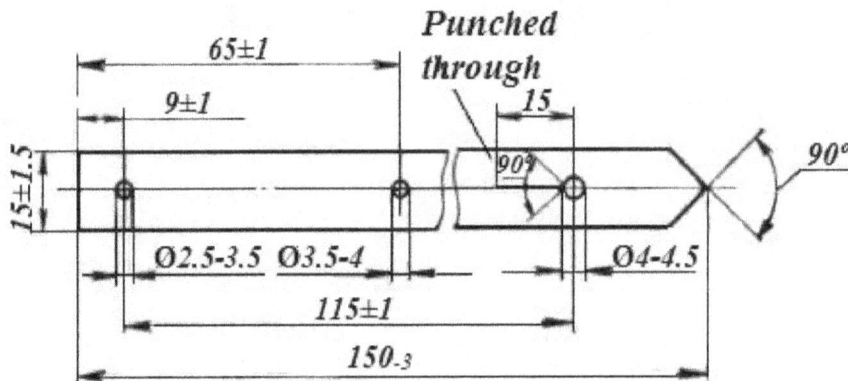

**Fig. 154.** Strap 6H4.2-16

Material: Harness and saddle leather smooth or pebbled, brown GOST 1904-81.
Thickness of 1.4-2.5 mm

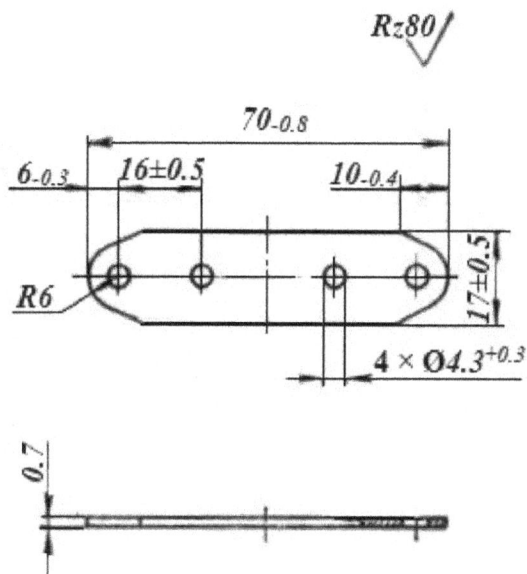

**Fig. 155.** Suspension plate 6H4.2-19

Material: steel 20. Phosphated and lacquered

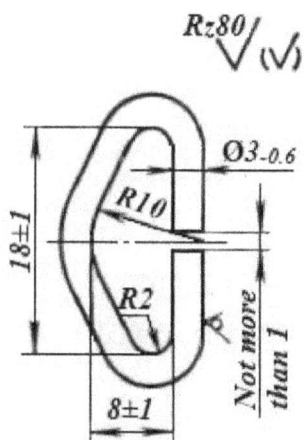

**Fig, 156.** D-ring 6H4.2-20

Material: wire 3-4V GOST 5663-79. Phosphated and lacquered

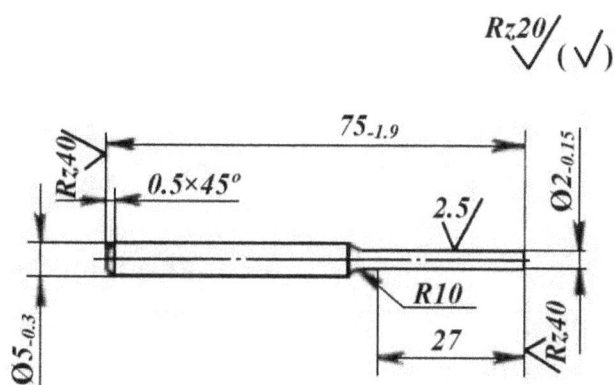

**Fig. 157.** Punch, cleaning kit

Material: steel 55. Tempered to HRCj 48,5-53,5. Phosphated in lacquered

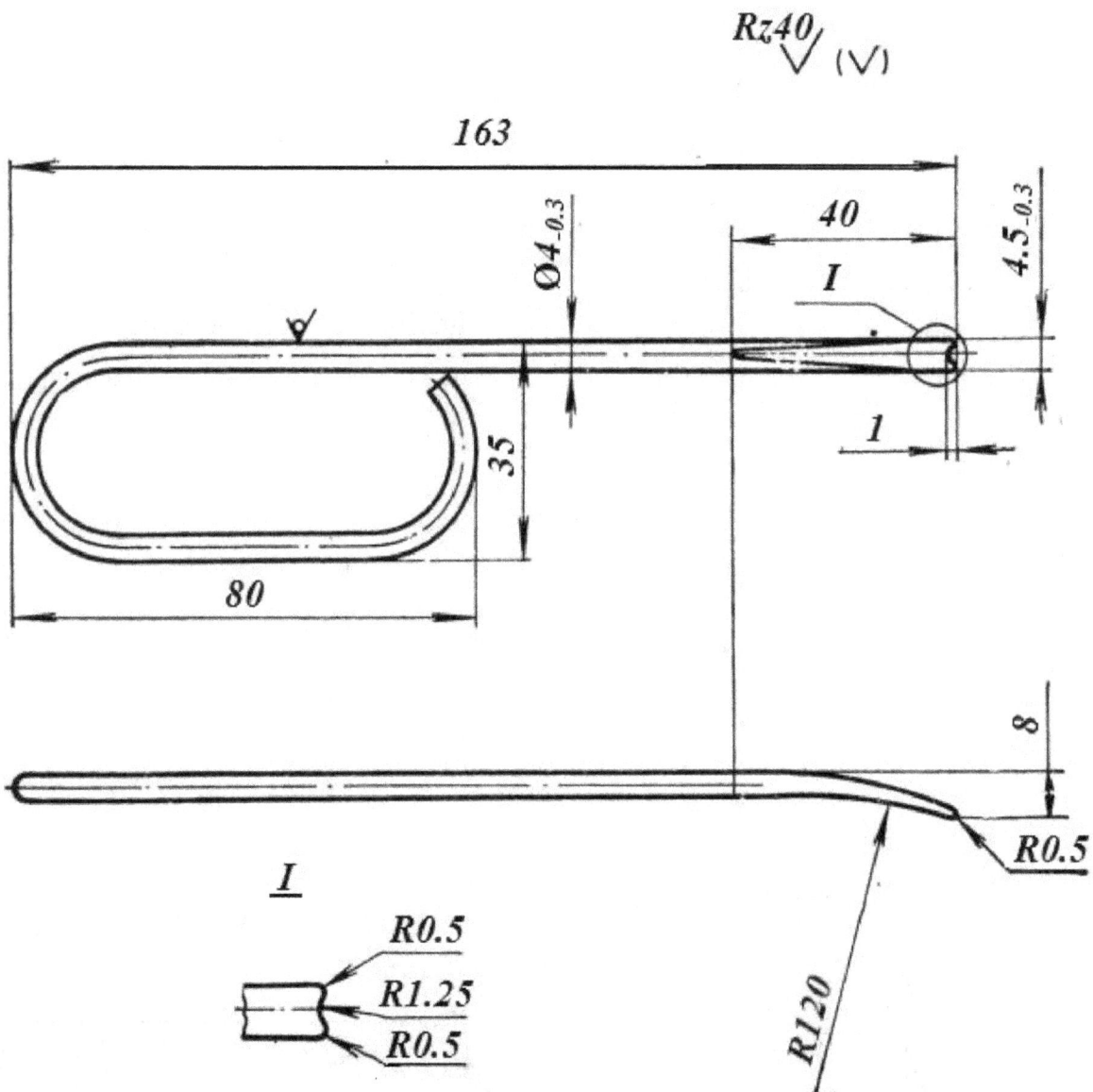

**Fig. 158**. Fork setting metal folding stock latch spring

Material: steel 35-50. Tempered to HRC 39.5-43.5. Phosphated

## MANUFACTURE OF POUCHES AND CASES

1. Pouches and cases for weapons and accessories are manufactured from the drawings in this appendix:

pouch for magazines for assault rifle AK74 (6Sh46), Fig. 159;

pouch for magazines for light machine gun RPK74 (6Sh51), Fig. 185:

case for shortened assault rifle AKS74 (6Sh21), Fig. 207;

case for shortened assault rifle AKS74U (6Sh64), Fig. 214;

case for Kalashnikov light machine gun with folding stock RPKS74 (6Sh22), Fig. 223.

2. Materials.

Linen canvas tarpaulin, technical grade for severe use, combined with an impregnation of № 1, art. 11102 GOST 15530-76

Substitute. Synthetic linen canvas for severe use, combined with an impregnation of № 1 and 2, art. 11204 GOST 15530-76.

Fabric, rain repellent, pressure coated, impregnated with VO art. 3104 GOST 7297-75.

Felt, coarse GOST 6418-81.

Leather, harness GOST 1904-81.

Ribbon, synthetic linen, binding, khaki color, 15mm OST 17-148-72.

Ribbon, belting, heavy, LRT, bilayer with filling, protective khaki color GOST 16996-71.

Cotton thread, khaki color № 0 GOST 6309-80.

Webbing. TPT, protective khaki color, 2nd grade, art. 63-T MRTU 17-386-67.

3. Parts of the canvas, fabric and ribbon lines are sewn with thread using stitch lngth of 2-3 mm.

The joints must be no gaps with the same interference both lines; the ends of the sutures to fix the back line.

Dotted lines in the figures show the positions of the joints; dimensions up to dotted lines are for hem seams.

4. Individual pouches and cases should be produced from a single piece of cloth taking into account the cutting of their component parts.

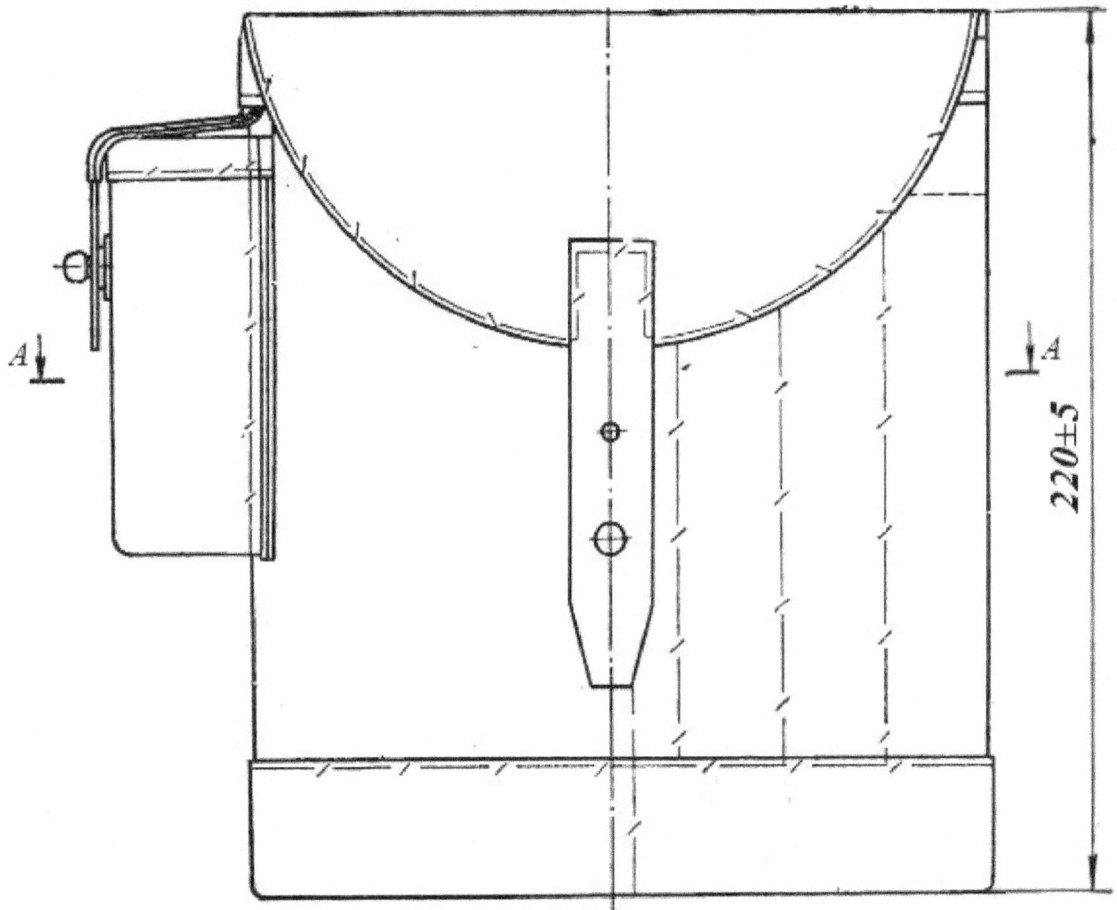

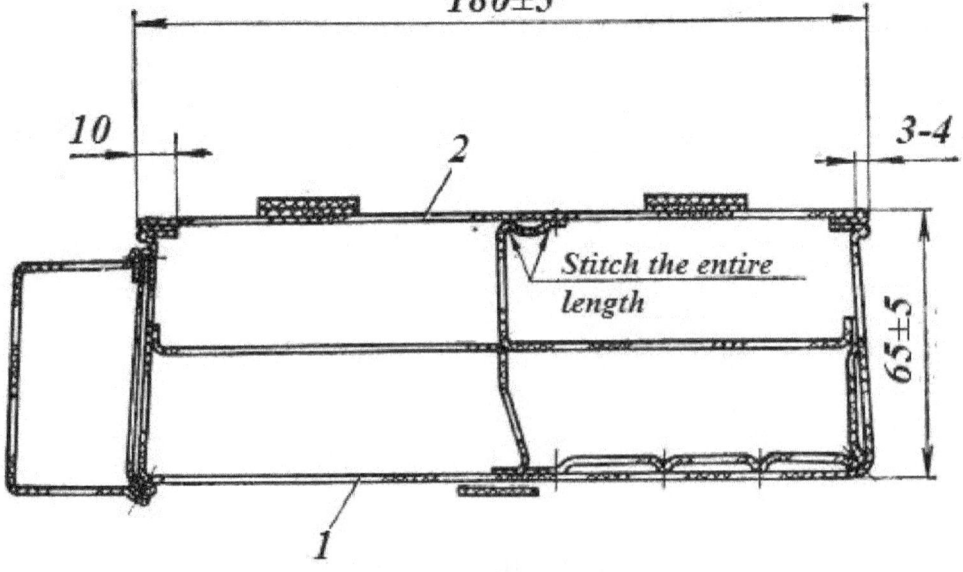

**Fig. 159** Magazine pouch 5.45mm Kalashnikov assault rifles AK74 (6SH46):

*1* - front panel assembly Sb 1 (Fig. 160); *2* rear panel assembly Sb 2; (Fig. 177)

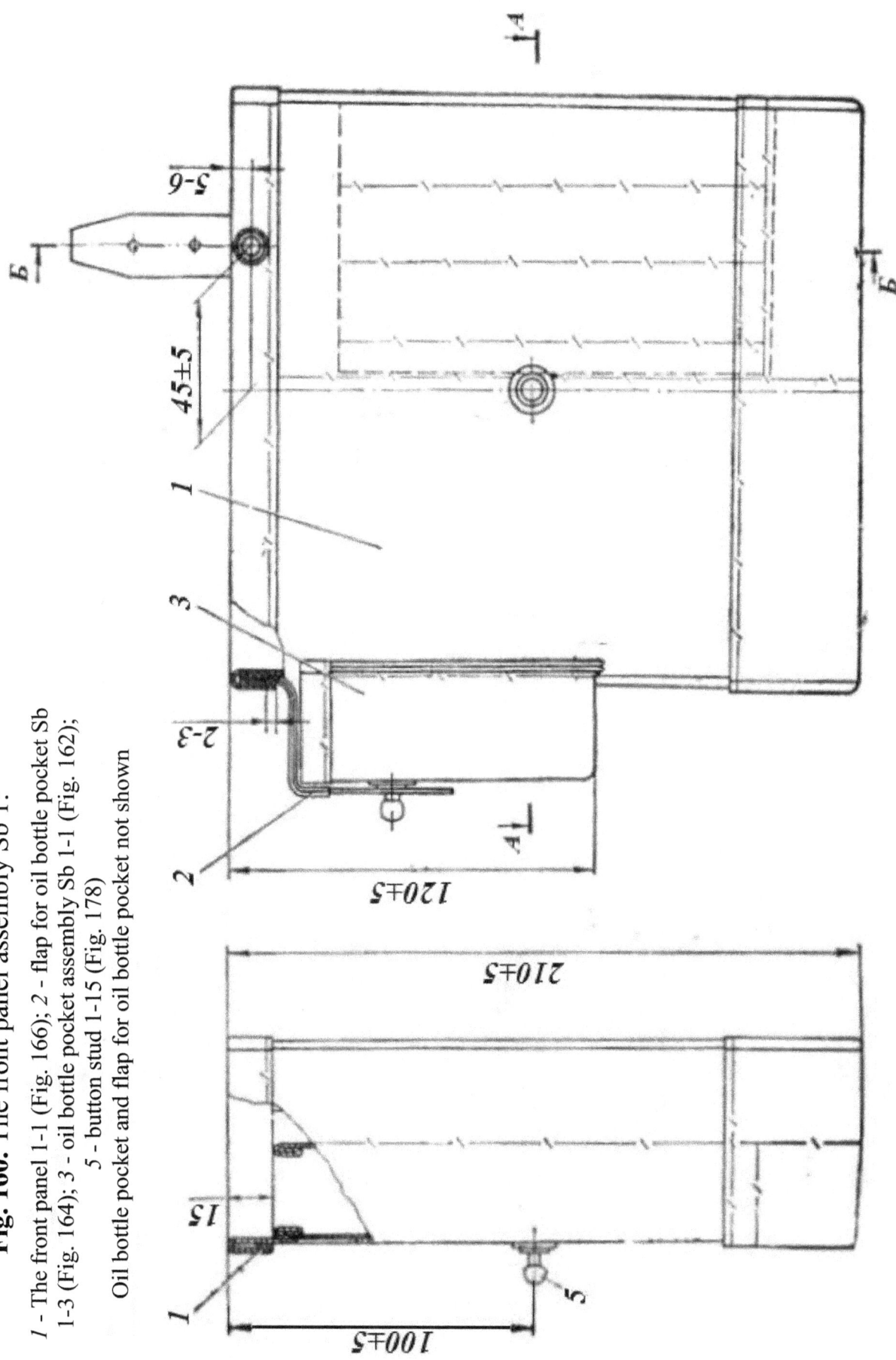

**Fig. 160.** The front panel assembly Sb 1:

*1* - The front panel 1-1 (Fig. 166); *2* - flap for oil bottle pocket Sb 1-3 (Fig. 164); *3* - oil bottle pocket assembly Sb 1-1 (Fig. 162); *5* - button stud 1-15 (Fig. 178)

Oil bottle pocket and flap for oil bottle pocket not shown

149

A-A (see Fig. 160)

Stitch the entire length

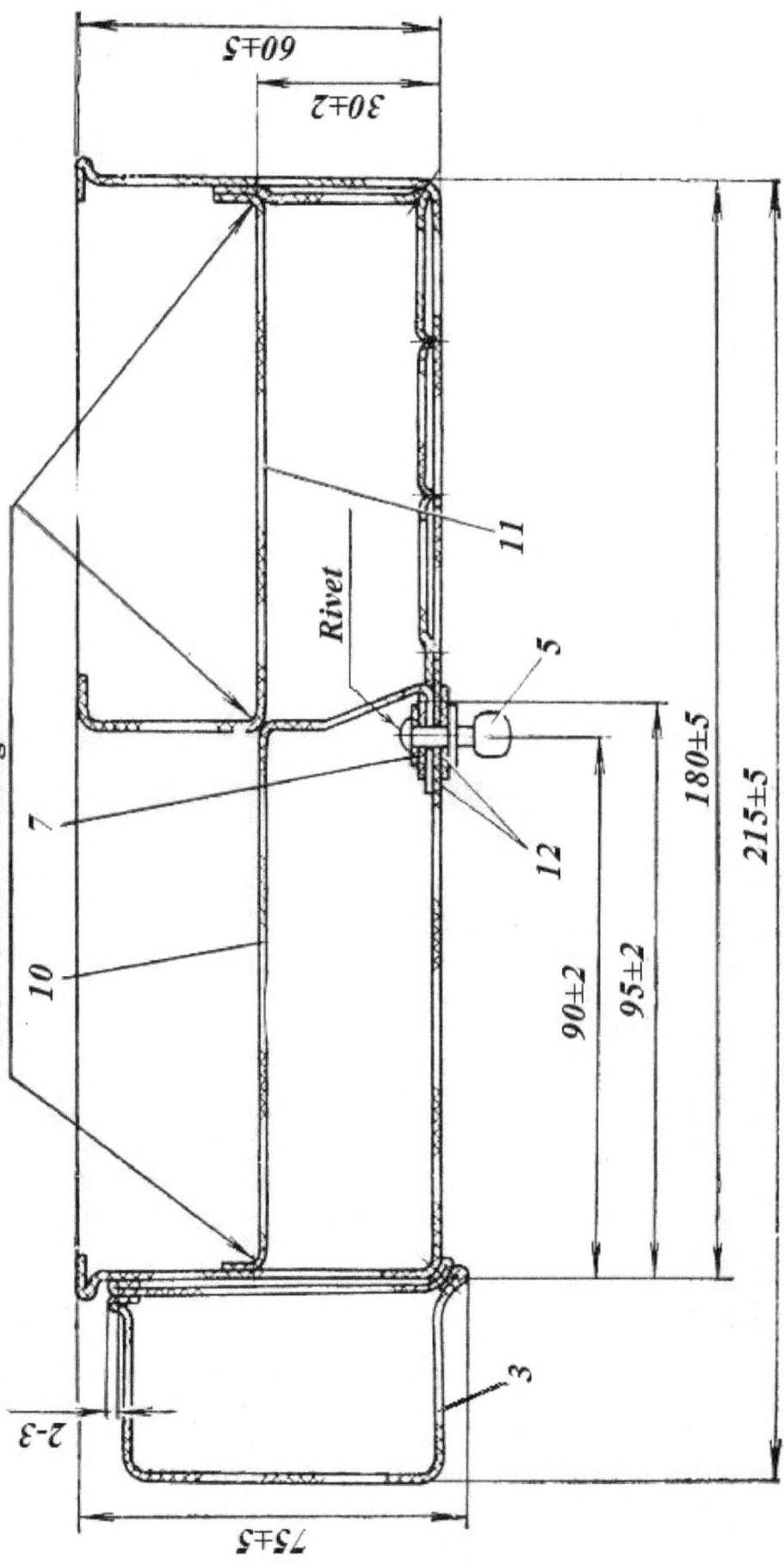

Rivet

11

5

7

12

10

3

60∓5

30∓2

215±5

180±5

95±2

90±2

75∓5

2-3

150

**Б-Б** *(see Fig. 160)*

*175±3*

*2-3*

*2-3*

*Rivet*

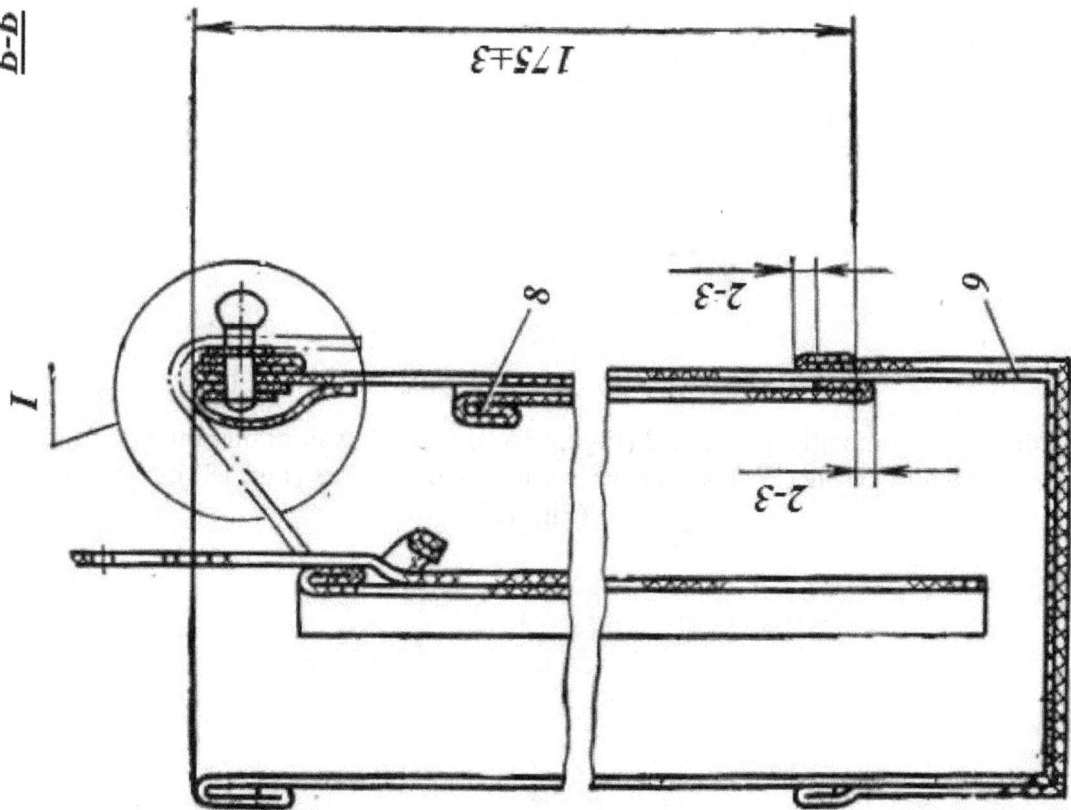

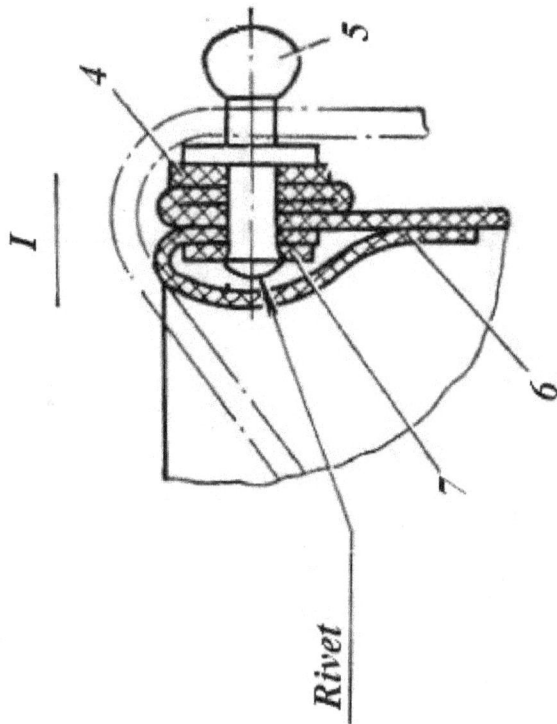

**Fig. 161.** Front panel assembly Sb 1 :

*3* – oil bottle pocket assembly Sb 1-1 (Fig. 162); *4* - leather washer 1-14 (Fig. 175); *5* – button stud 1-15 (Fig. 176); *6* - pad under the washer 1-19 (Fig. 182); *7*- washer 6Sh46.1-17 (Fig. 153); *8* – stripper clip pocket 1-5 (Fig. 169); *9* – front wall reinforcement pocket 1-2 (Fig. 166); *10* - partition (Fig.173 1-10); *11* - right partition assembly Sb 1-2 (Fig. 163); *12* - leather washer 1-20 (Fig. 183)

Button stud 5 and washers 7 and 12 are set after sewing on reinforcement pocket 9 and partition 10

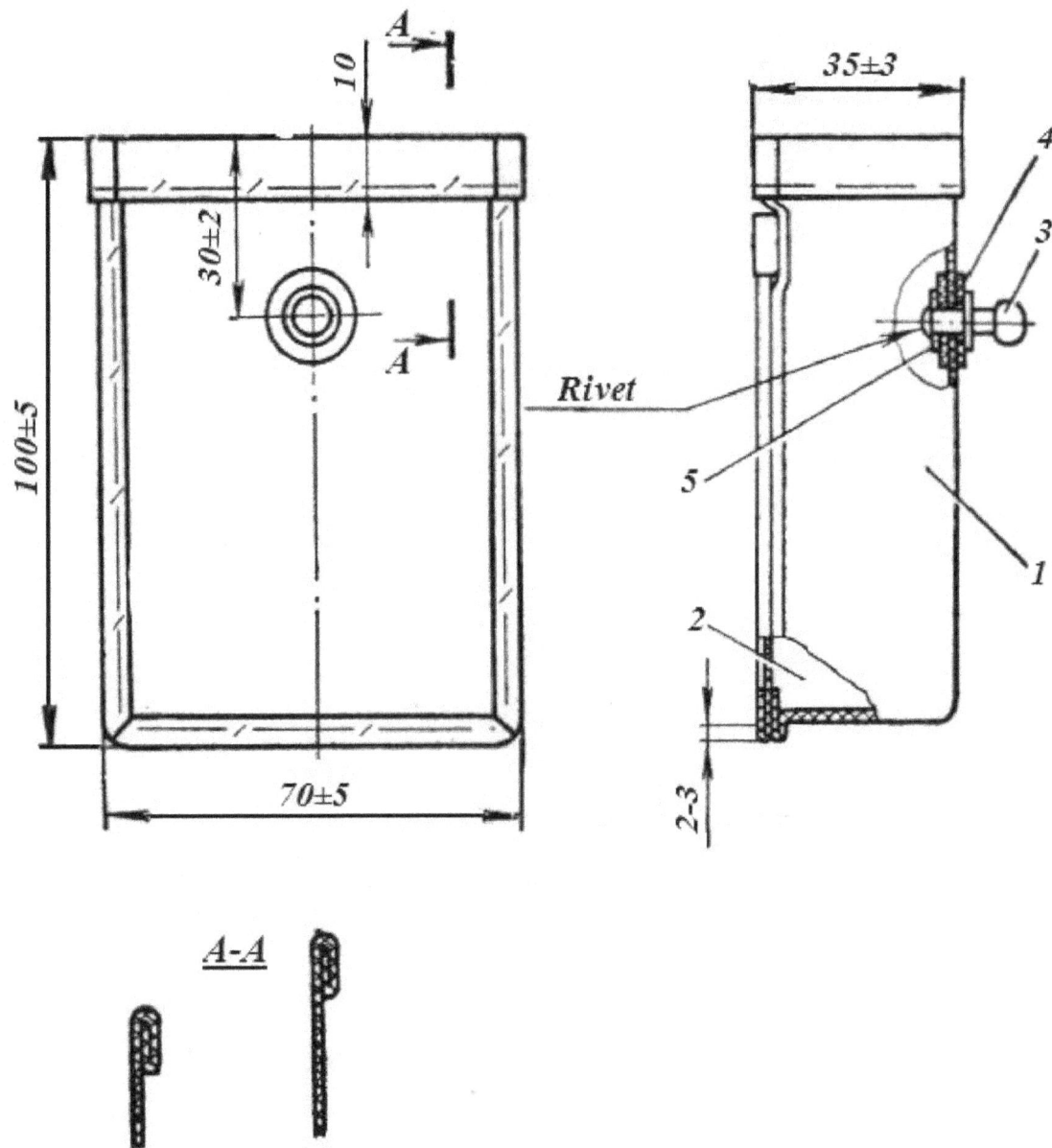

**Fig. 162.** Oil bottle pocket assembly Sb 1-1:

*1* - front wall of oil bottle pocket 1-3 (Figure 167); *2* - back wall of oil bottle pocket 1-4 (Figure 168); *3* – button stud 1-5 (Fig. 176); *4* - leather washer 1-20, 2 pieces (Fig. 183); *5* - washer 6Sh46.1-17 (Fig. 153)

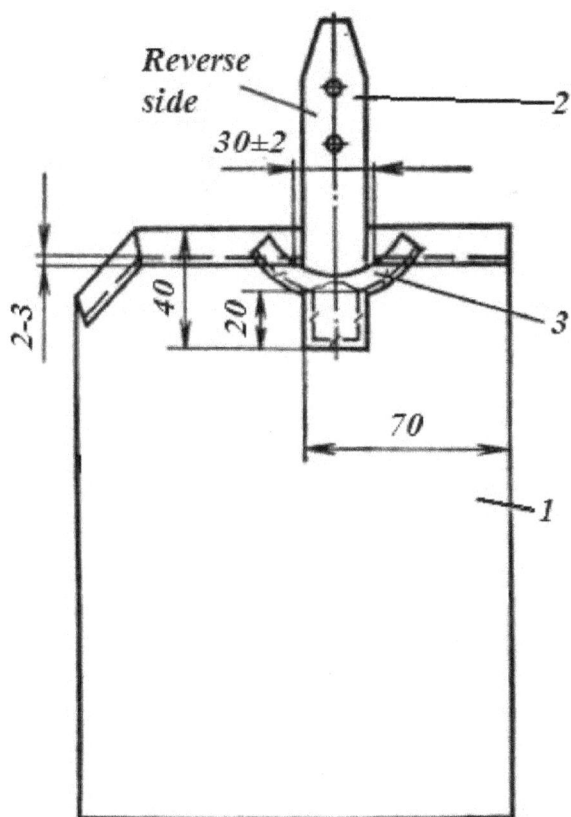

**Fig. 163.** Right partition assembly Sb 1-2:

*1* - partition 1-11 (Fig. 173); *2* – cell security strap 1-13 (Fig. 174); *3* – loop, tape binding, impregnated, khaki 15 × 80 mm
Prior to sewing on loop 3 fold the width of the tape double and stitch

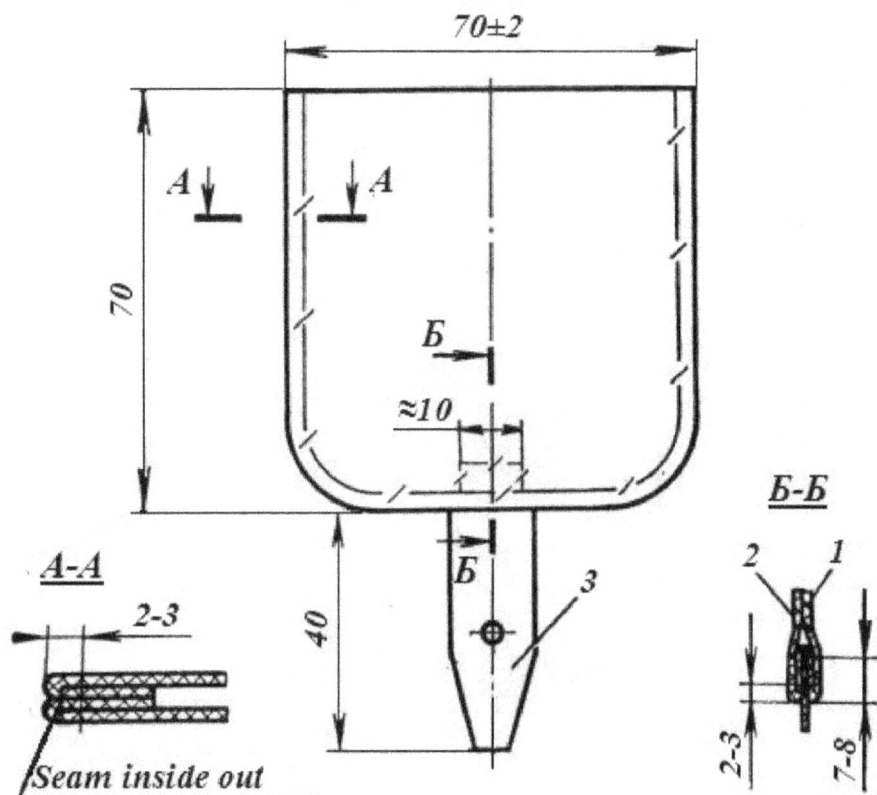

**Fig. 164.** Flap assembly for oil bottle pocket Sb 1-3:
1 – flap for oil bottle pocket 1-7 (Fig. 170); 2 - lining for flap for oil bottle pocket 1-8 (Fig. 171); 3 - closure strap 1-9 (Fig. 172)

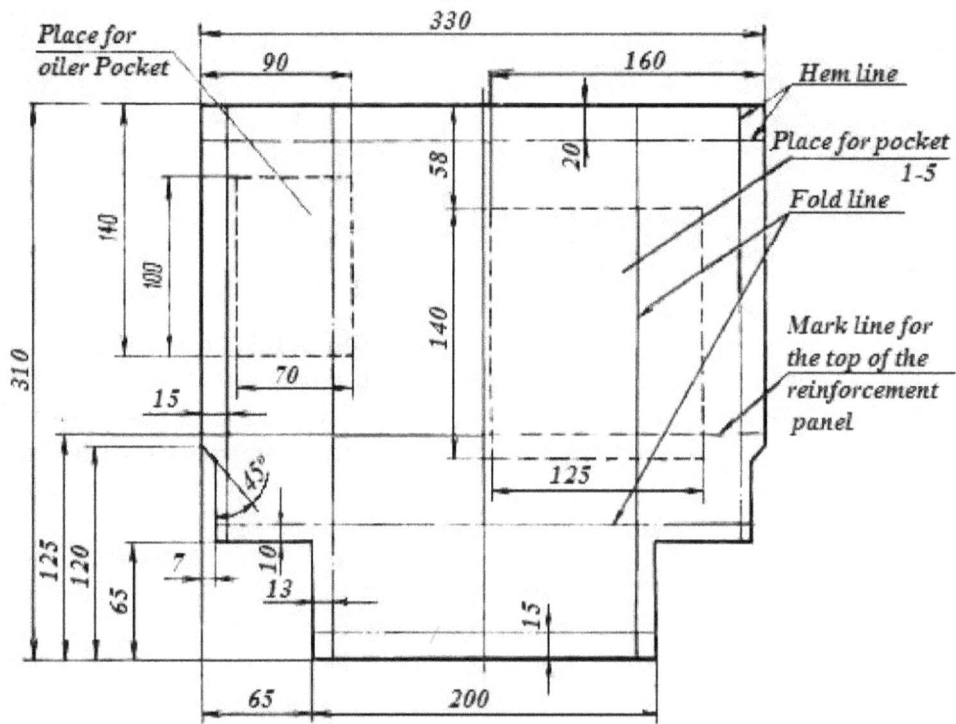

**Fig. 165.** Front panel 1-1

Material: canvas

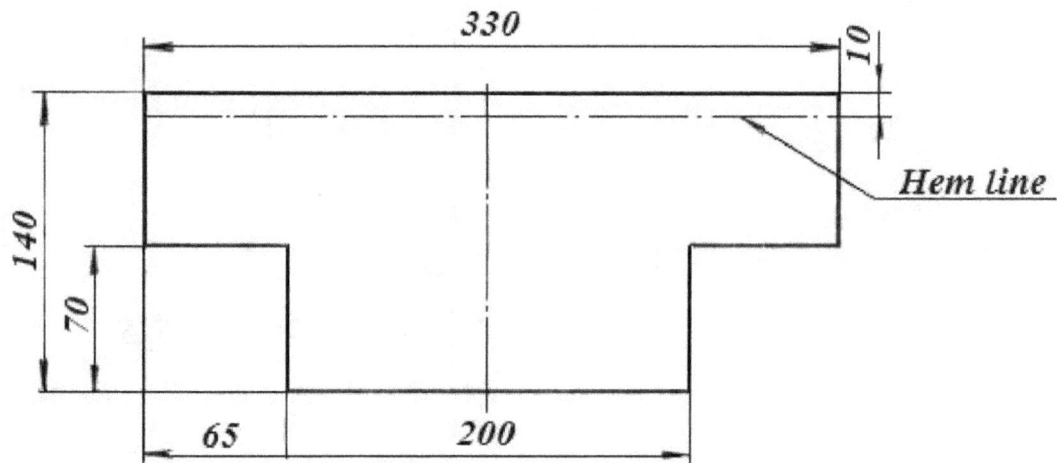

**Fig. 166.** Front panel reinforcement 1-2

Material: canvas

154

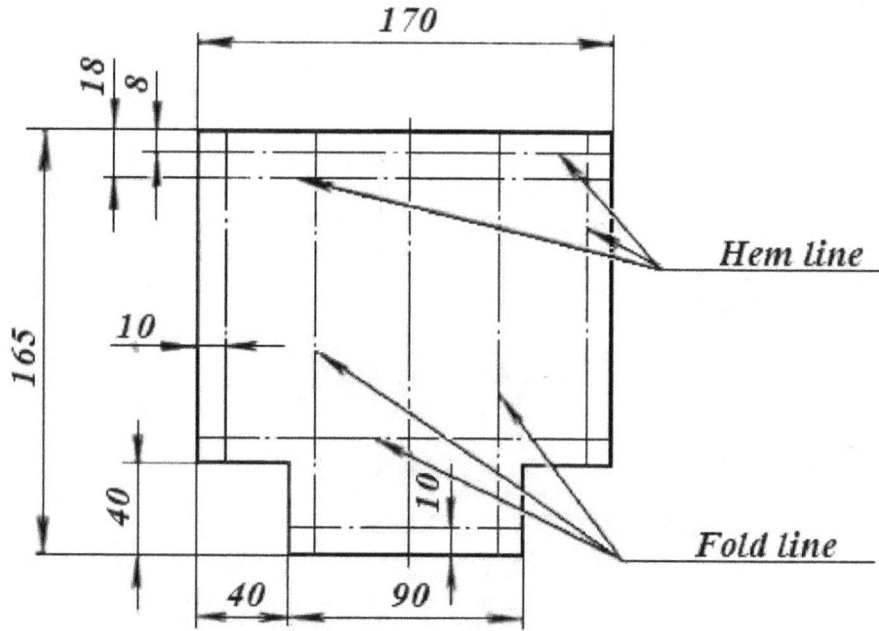

**Fig. 167.** Front wall of oil bottle pocket 1-3
Material: canvas

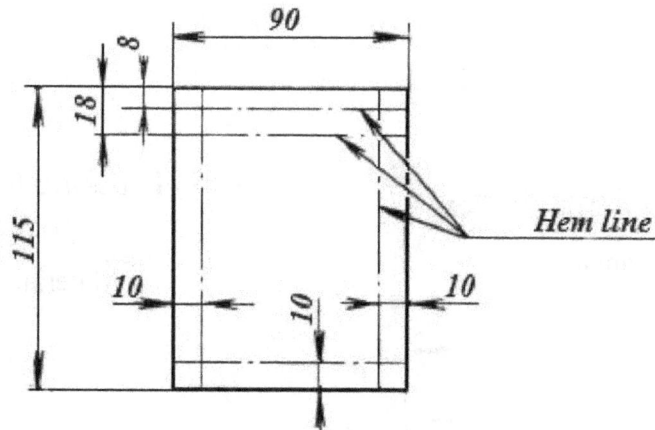

**Fig. 168.** Back wall of oil bottle pocket 1-4
Material: canvas

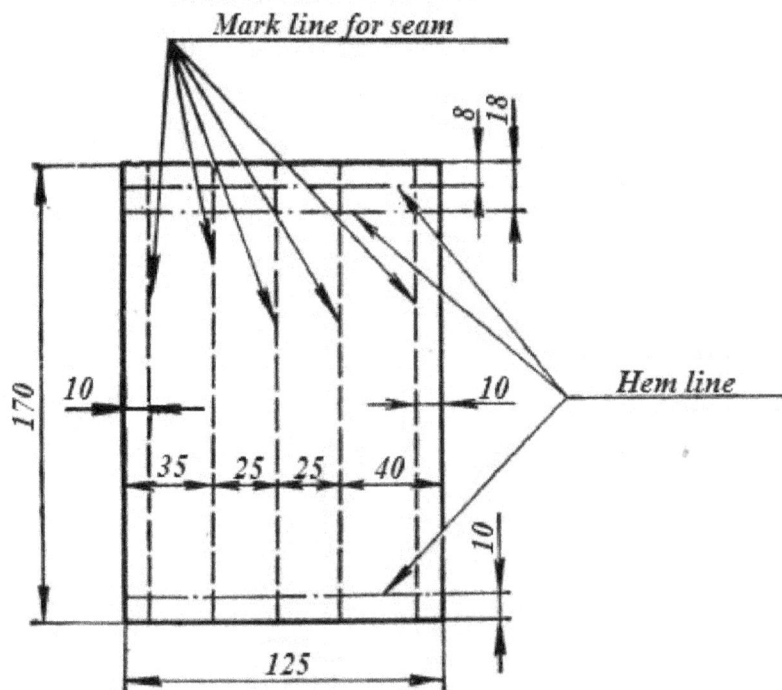

**Fig. 169.** Stripper clip pocket 1-5

Material: canvas

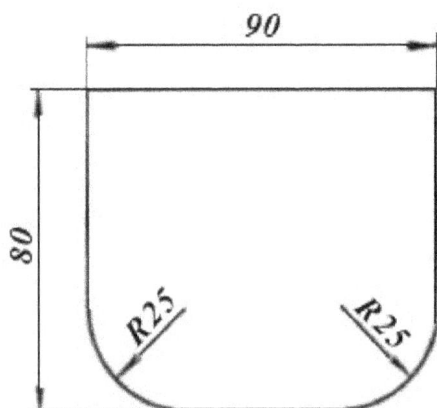

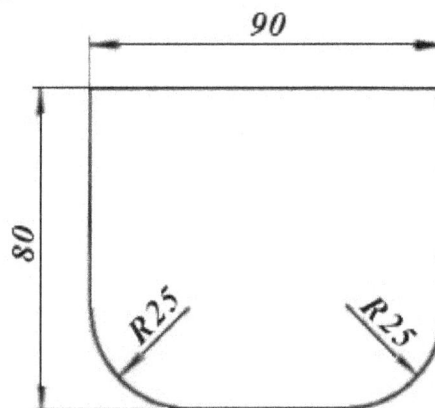

**Fig. 170.** Flap for oil bottle pocket 1-7

Material: canvas

**Fig. 171.** Lining for flap for oil bottle pocket 1-8

Material: tent linen

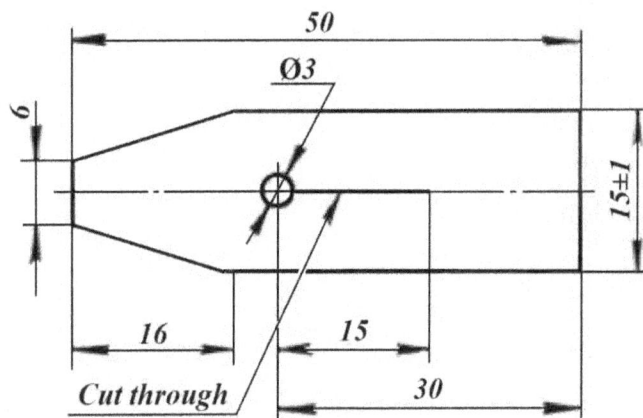

**Fig. 172.** Closure strap 1-9

Material: harness leather type L GOST 1904-81, thickness of $(1,8 \pm 0,2)$ mm

156

## Piece 1-11

200

18
8

Hem line

160

55

15 30

8

30

18

Fold line

Mark line for seam

10

## Piece 1-10

200

150

10

8

18

Hem line

45

15

Mark line for seam

Fold line

Mark line for seam

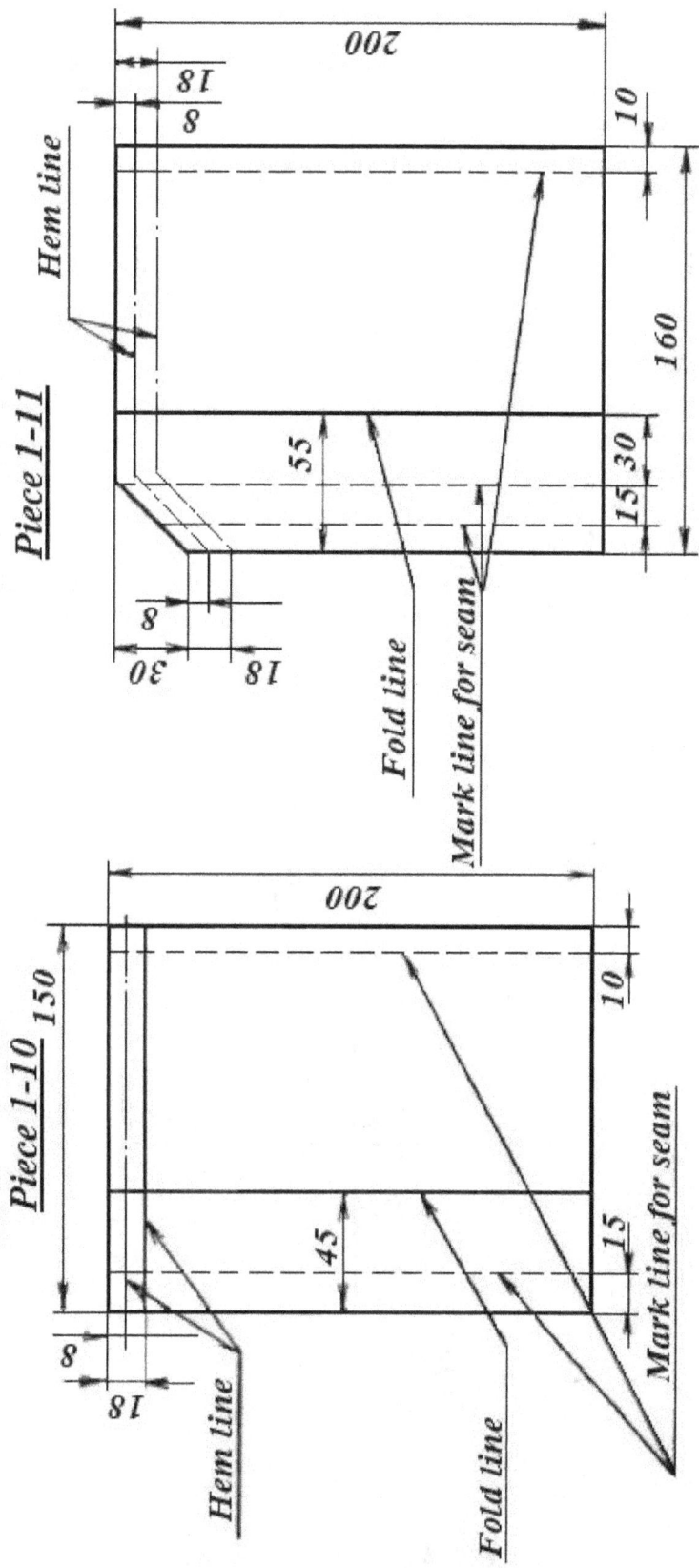

**Fig. 173.** Partitions 1-10, 1-11
Material: canvas

157

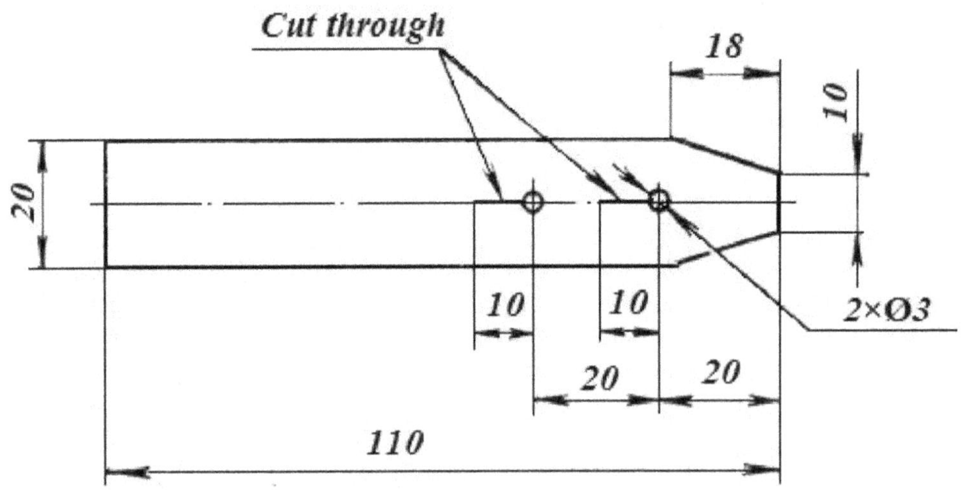

**Fig. 174.** Cell security strap 1-13

Material: harness leather type L GOST 1904-81, thickness of $(1{,}8 \pm 0{,}2)$ mm

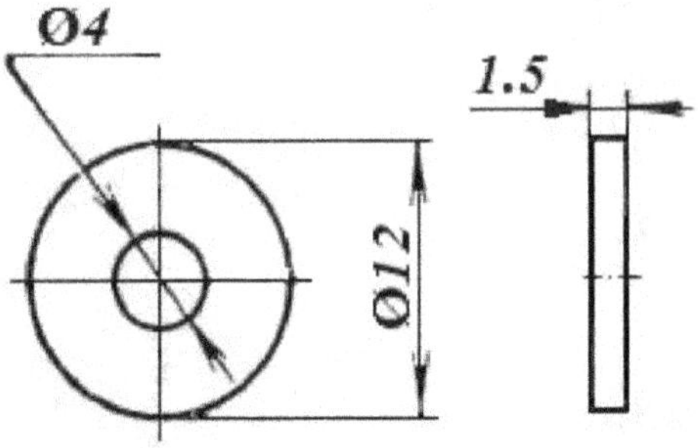

**Fig. 175.** Leather washer 1-14

Material: harness leather GOST 1904 Ya-1

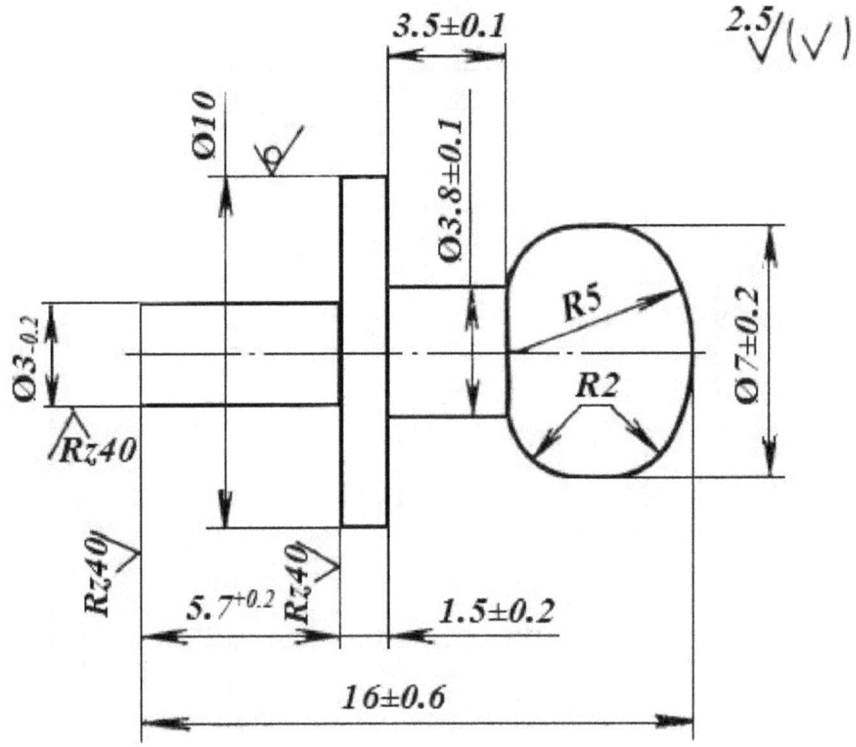

**Fig. 176.** Button stud 1-15

Material: steel 20. Phosphated and lacquered

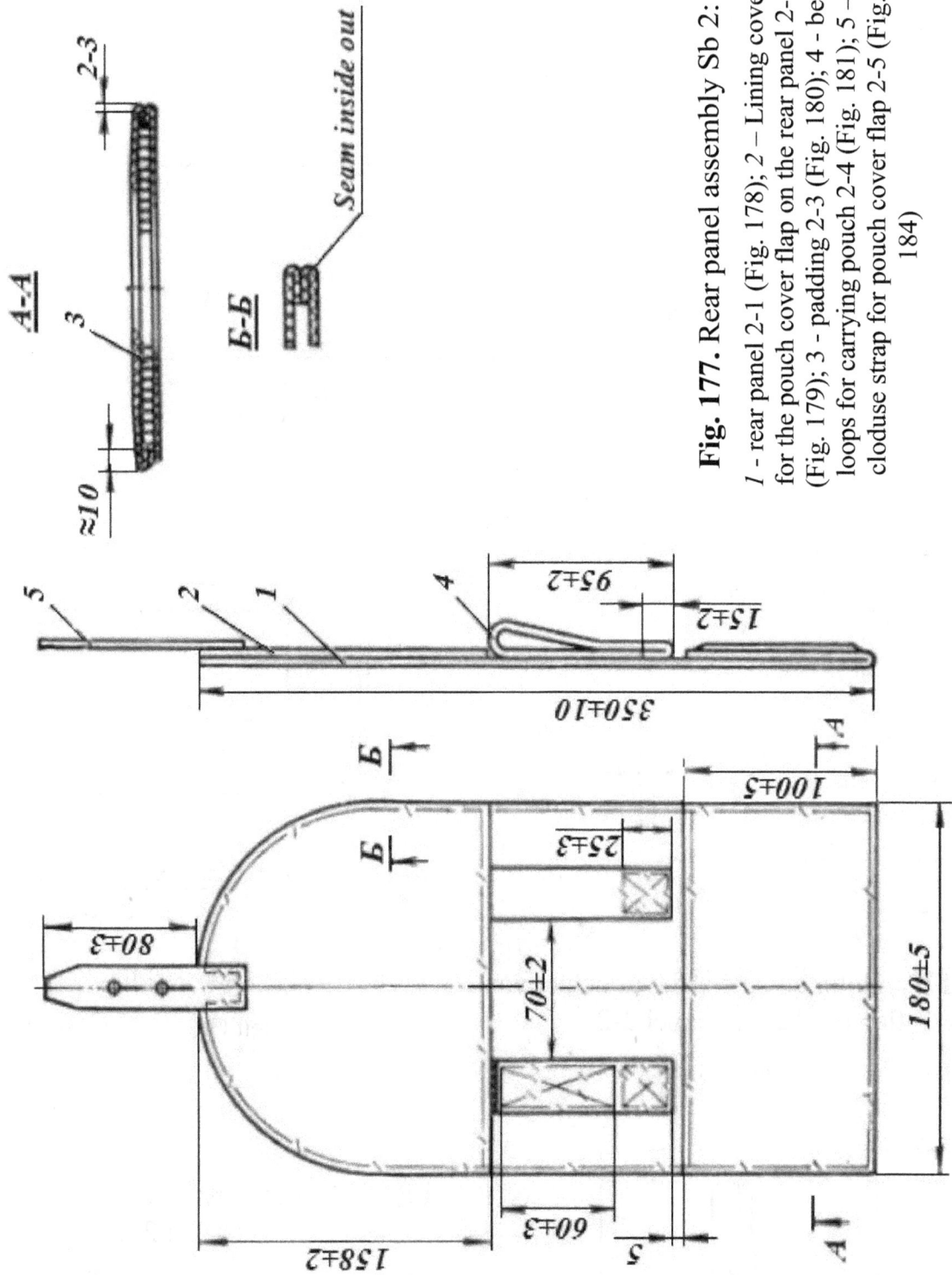

**Fig. 177.** Rear panel assembly Sb 2:

*1* - rear panel 2-1 (Fig. 178); *2* – Lining cover for the pouch cover flap on the rear panel 2-2 (Fig. 179); *3* - padding 2-3 (Fig. 180); *4* - belt loops for carrying pouch 2-4 (Fig. 181); *5* – cloduse strap for pouch cover flap 2-5 (Fig. 184)

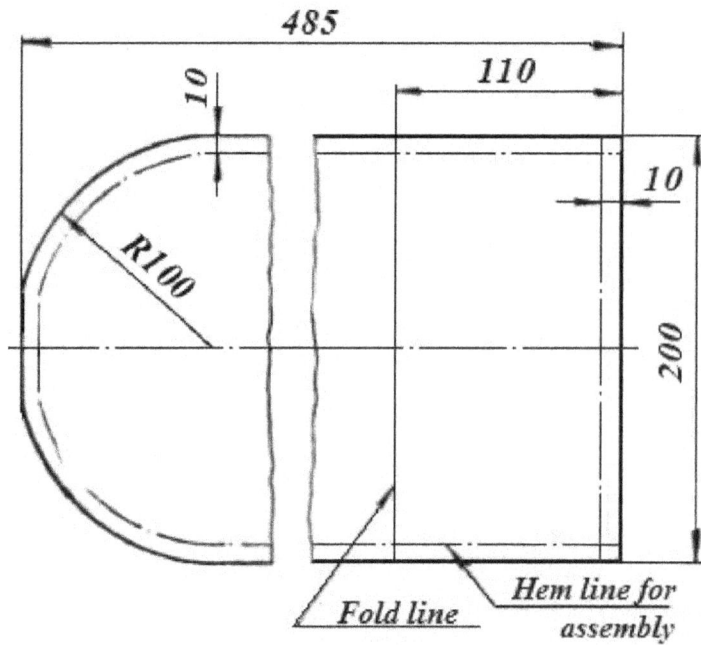

**Fig. 178.** Rear panel 2-1

Material: canvas

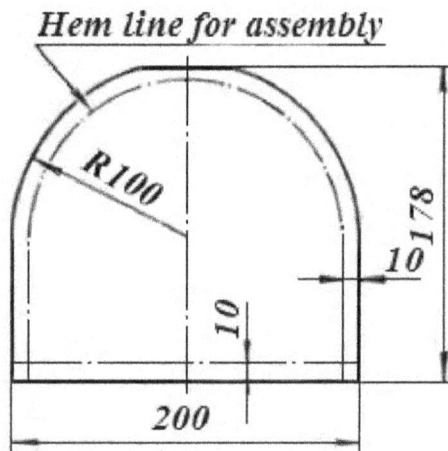

**Fig. 179.** Outer cover for the pouch cover flap on the rear panel 2-2

Material: canvas, tarpaulin

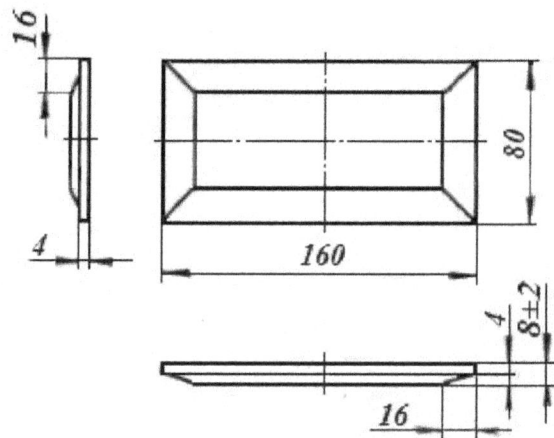

**Fig. 180.** Padding 2-3

Material: felt GPrB8 GOST 6418-81

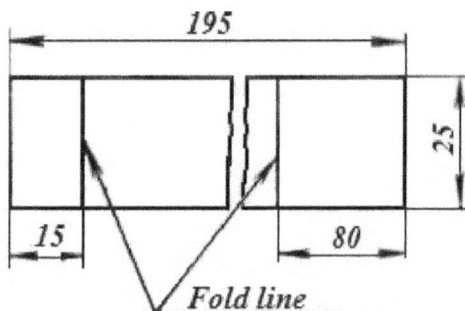

**Fig. 181.** Strap for belt loop for carrying pouch 2-4

Material: ribbon, belt, heavy LRT bilayer with filling, khaki GOST 16996-71

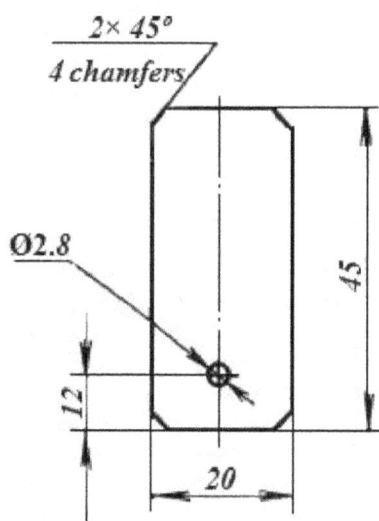

**Fig. 182.** Cover behind washer 1-19

Material: harness leather GOST 1904-81 thickness of 0.8-1.2 mm

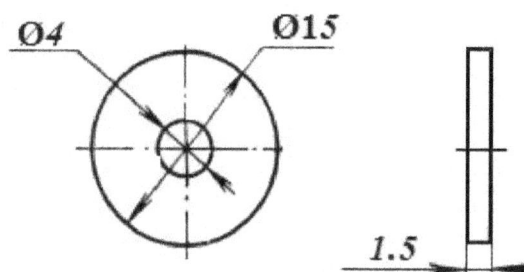

**Fig. 183.** Leather washer 1-20

Material: harness leather GOST 1904-81

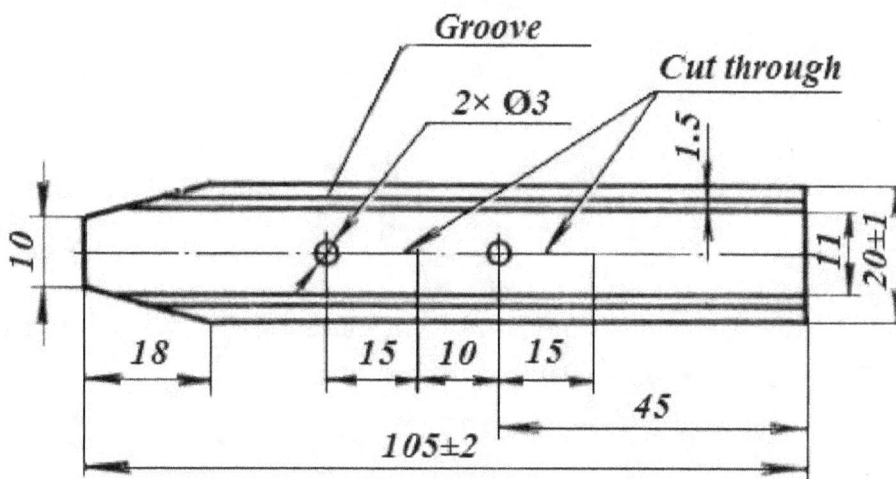

**Fig. 184.** Closure strap for the pouch cover 2-5

Material: harness leather type L GOST 1904-81, thickness of $(2 \pm 0.2)$ mm

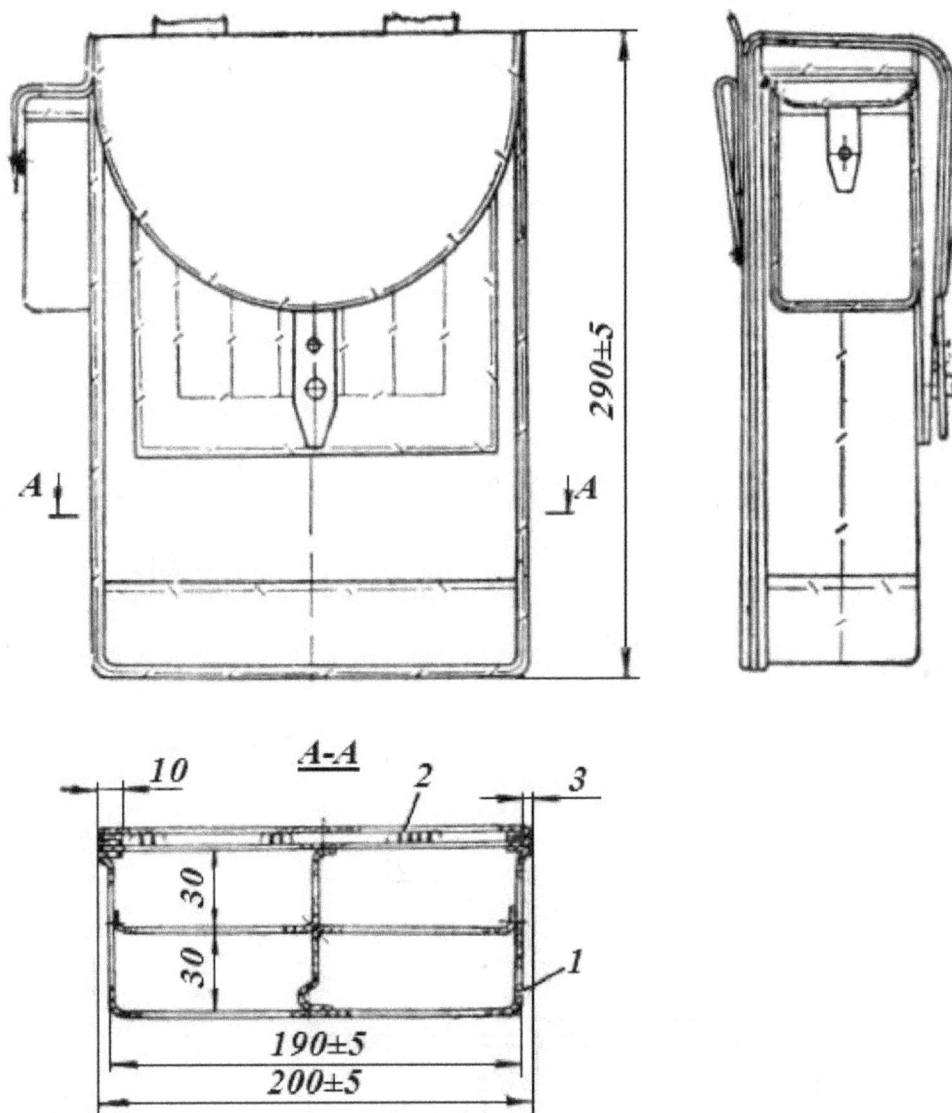

**Fig. 185.** Magazine pouch 5.45mm light machine gun Kalashnikov RPK74 (index item 6Sh51):

*1* - front panel assembly Sb 1 (Fig. 186); *2* - rear panel assembly Sb 2 (Fig. 195)

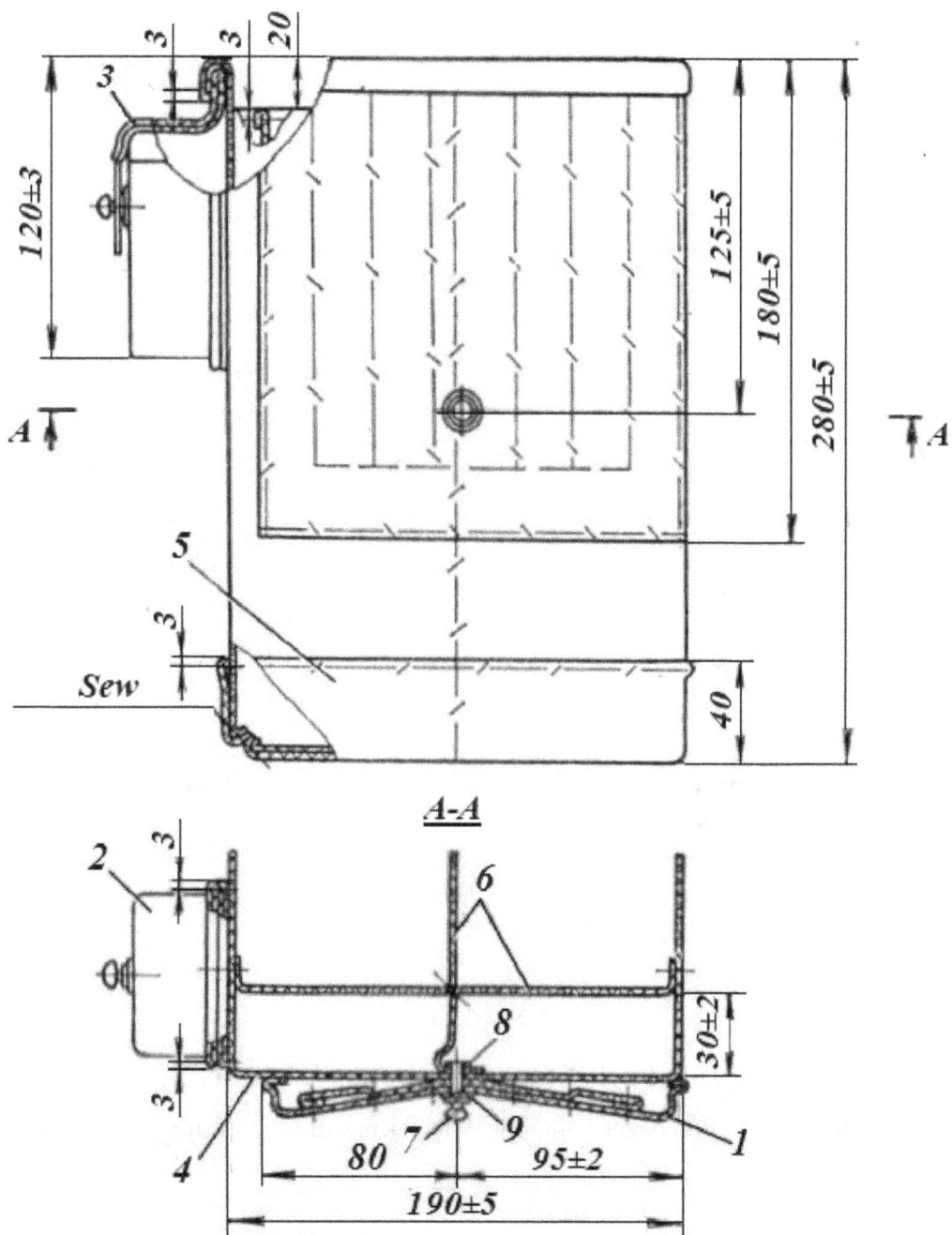

**Fig. 186.** The front wall assembly Sb 1:

*1* - pocket for stripper clips Sb 1-1 (Fig. 187); *2* – oil bottle pocket assembly Sb 1-2 (Fig. 188); *3* – oil bottle pocket cover flap assembly Sb 1-3 (Fig. 164); *4* - front panel 1-1 (Fig. 190); *5* – reinforcement for front panel 1-2 (Fig. 191); *6* - partition 1-3, 2 pcs. (Fig. 192); *7* – button stud 1-17 (Fig. 206); *8* – washer 6Sh46.1-17 (Fig 153); *9* - leather washer 1-20 (Fig. 183)

Assemblies *2* and *3* are to be sewn as per the mark up for the front panel *4*. For pocket *1* position the groove as per the mark up for the front panel. At 12 kg force, pulling out of the button stud *7* is not allowed

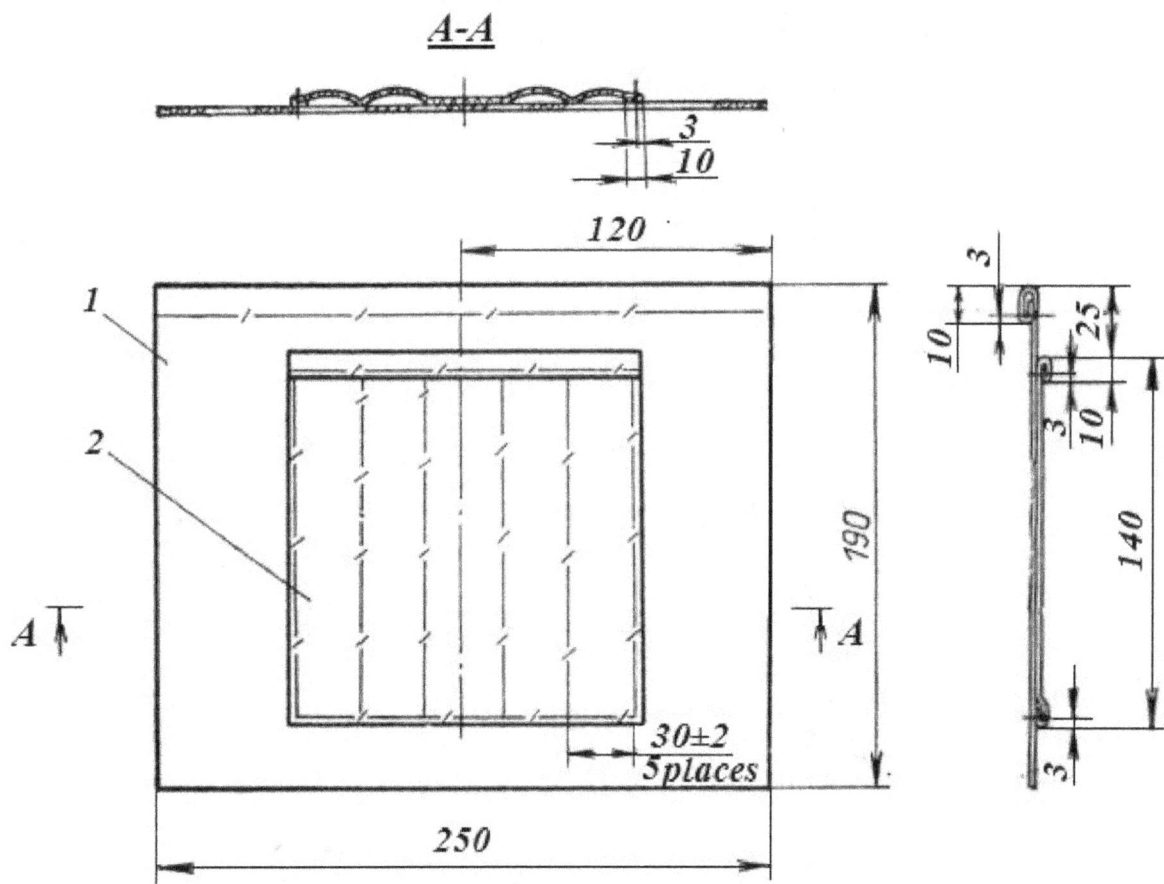

**Fig. 187.** Pocket for stripper clips assembly Sb 1-1:

*1* – panel for striper clip pocket 1-4 (Fig. 193); *2* - partition for stripper clips 1-6 (Fig. 194)

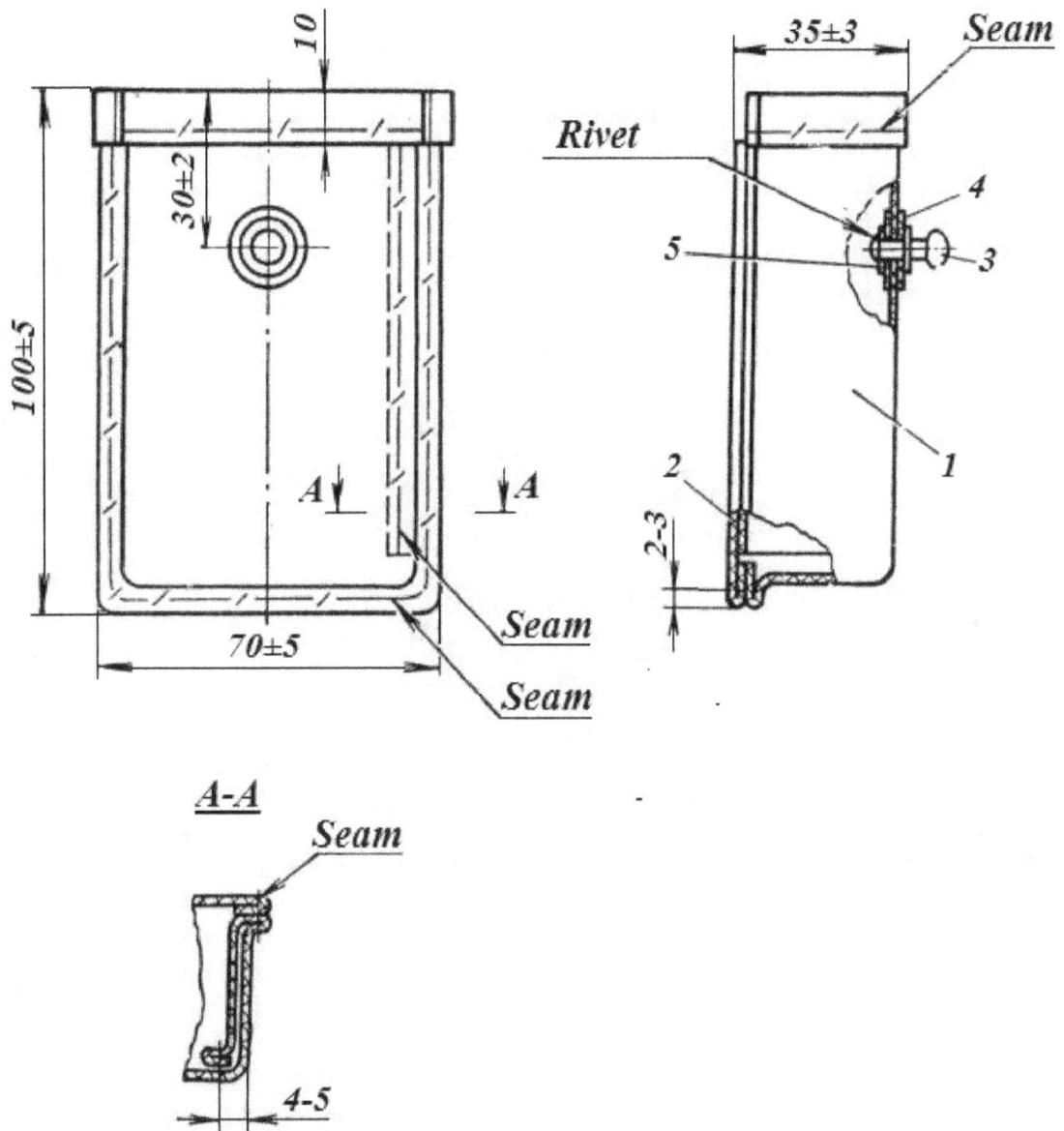

**Fig. 188.** Oil bottle pocket assembly Sb 1-2:

*1* - front panel for oil bottle pocket 1-6 (Fig. 189); *2* - rear panel for oil bottle pocket 1-4 (Fig. 168); *3* – button stud 1-17 (Fig. 206); *4* - leather washer 1-20, 2 pcs. (Fig. 183); *5* - washer 6Sh46 1-17 (Fig. 153)

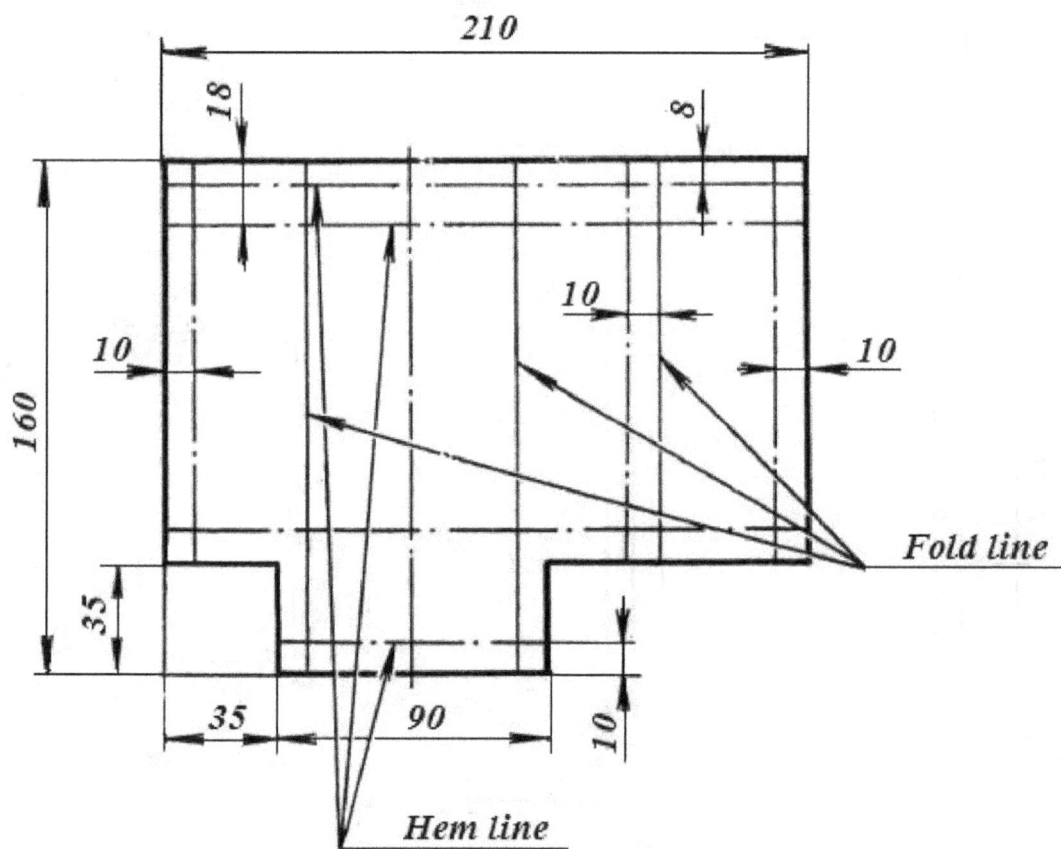

**Fig. 189.** Front panel for oil bottle pocket 1-6

Material: canvas

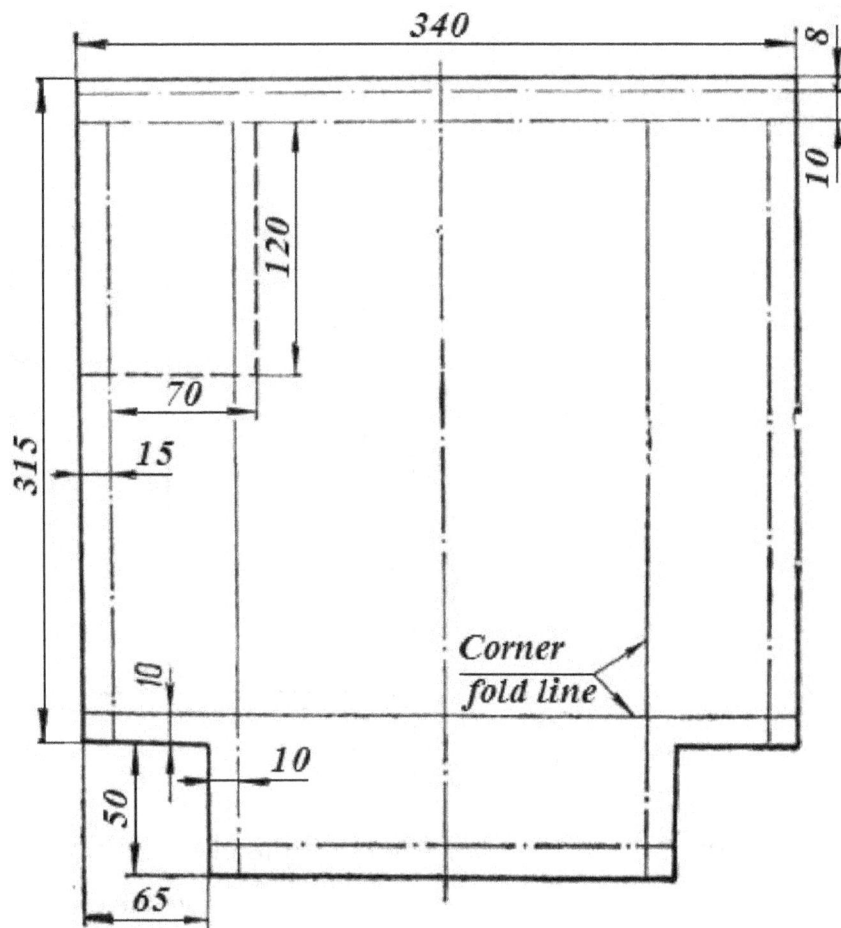

**Fig. 190.** Front panel 1-1

Material: canvas. Dimensions 70 and 120 indicate stitch lines for pocket Sb 1-2

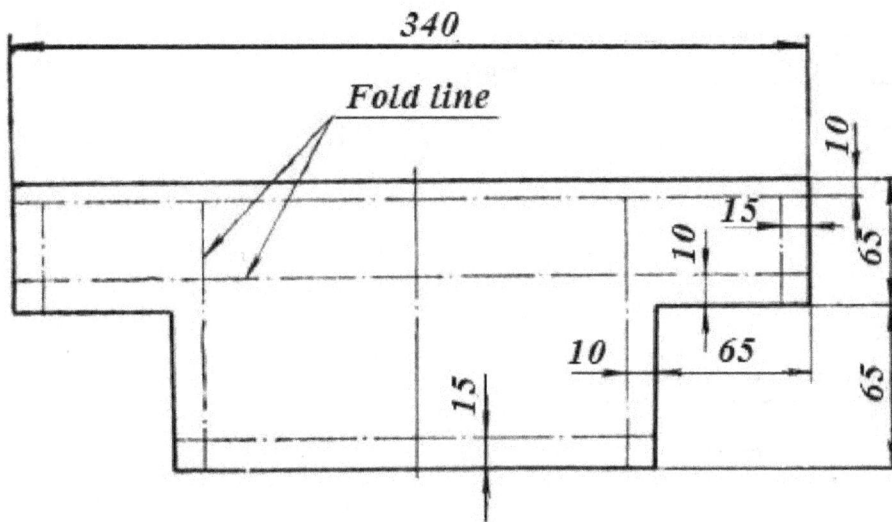

**Fig. 191.** Reinforcement panel for front panel 1-2

Material: canvas

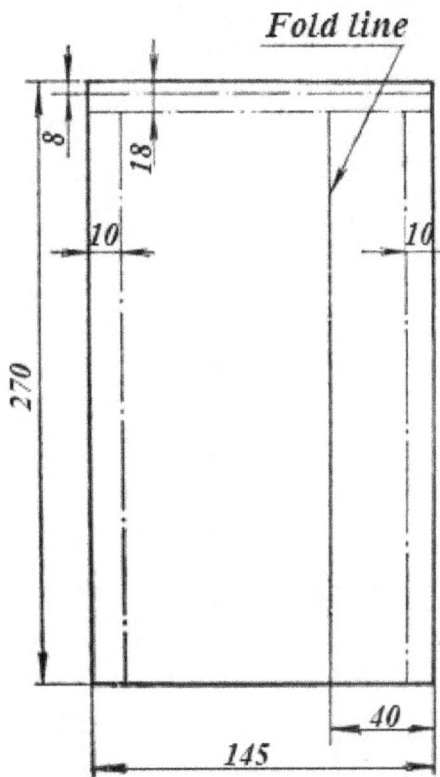

**Fig.192.** Partition 1-3

Material: canvas

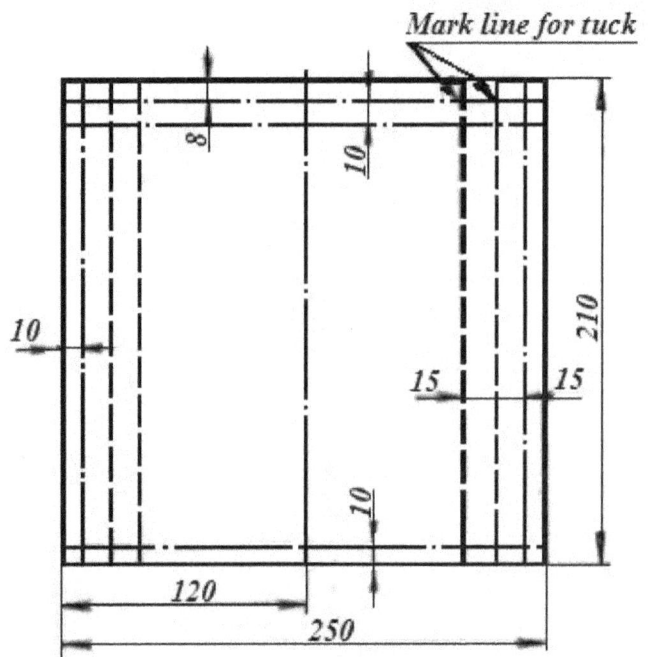

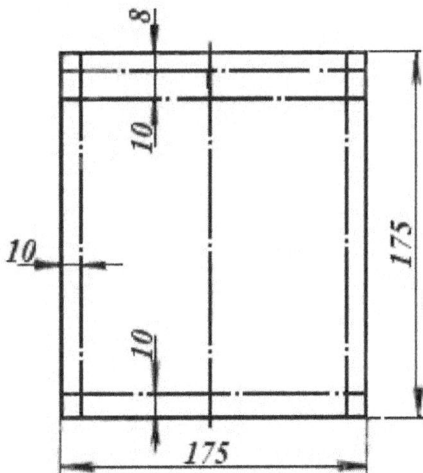

**Fig. 193.** Panel for stripper clip pocket 1-4

Material: canvas

**Fig. 194.** Partition for stripper clips 1-5

Material: canvas

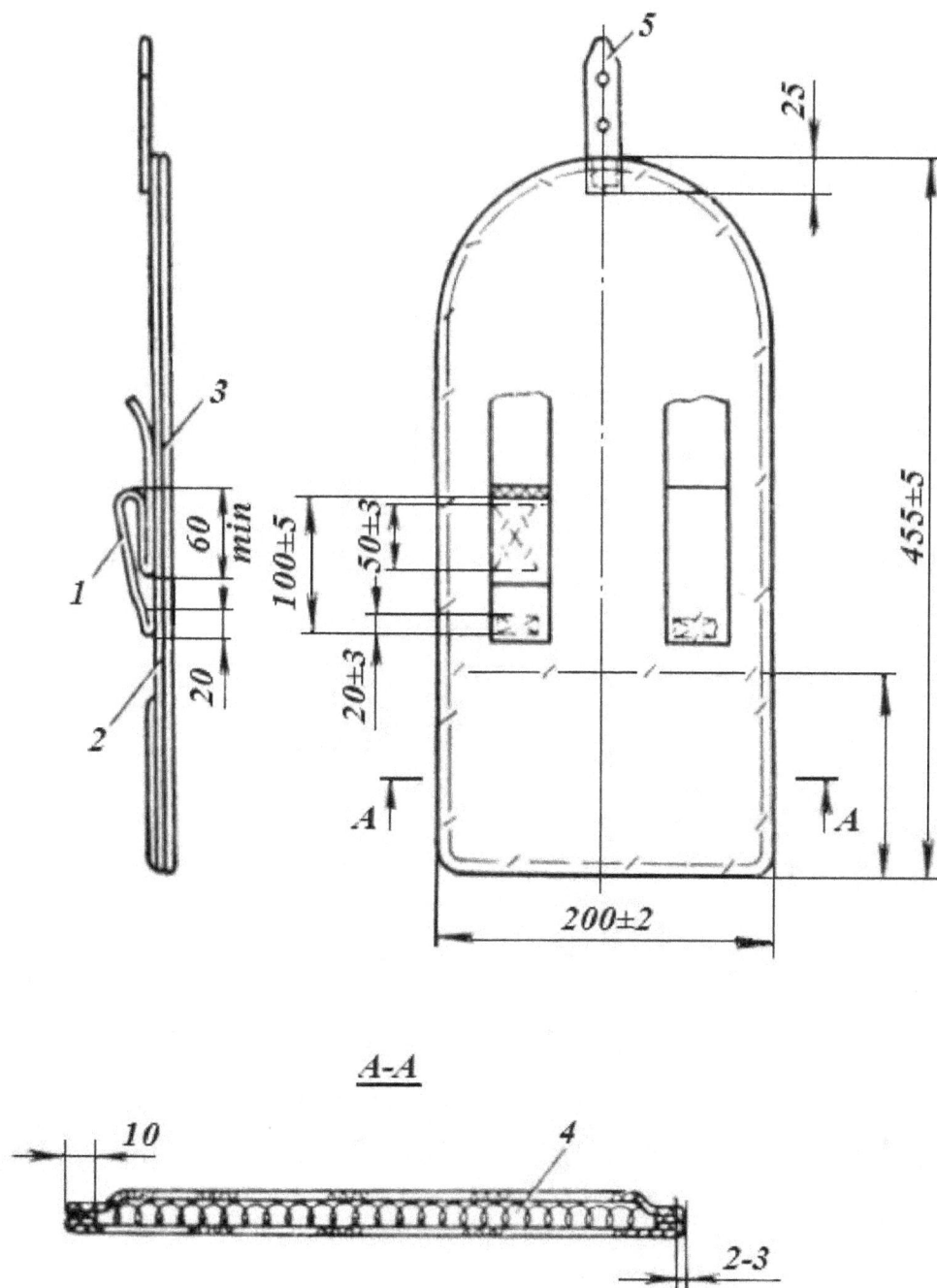

**Fig. 195.** Rear panel assembly Sb 2:

*1* – belt loop and shoulder strap assembly 6Sh51.Sb 1-3 (Fig. 199); *2* - rear panel 2-1 (Fig. 196); *3* - lining cover for the rear panel 2-2 (Fig. 197); *4* - padding 2-3 (Fig. 198); *5* – closure strap for pouch cover 2-5 (Fig. 184)

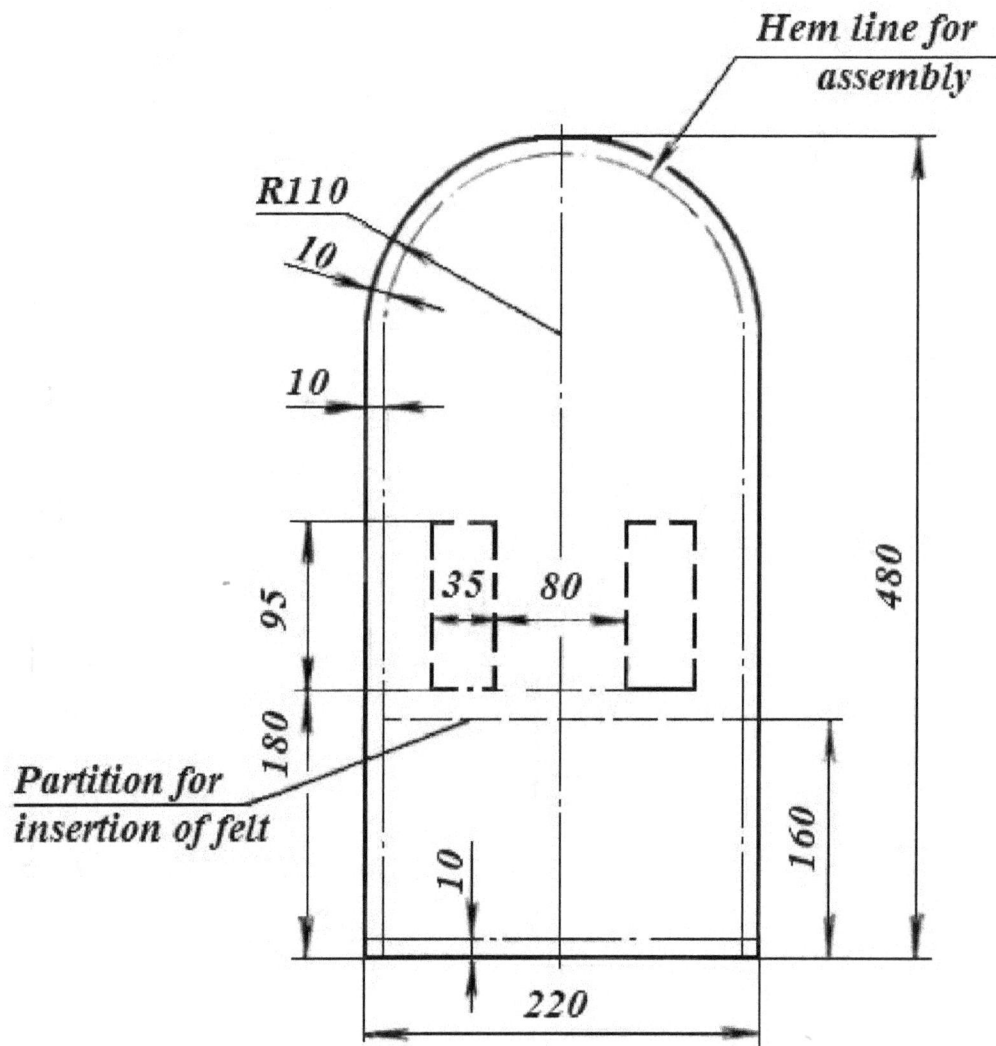

**Fig. 196.** Rear panel 2-1

Material: canvas. Sizes 35, 80 and 95 for stitch lines for belt loops and shoulder strap.

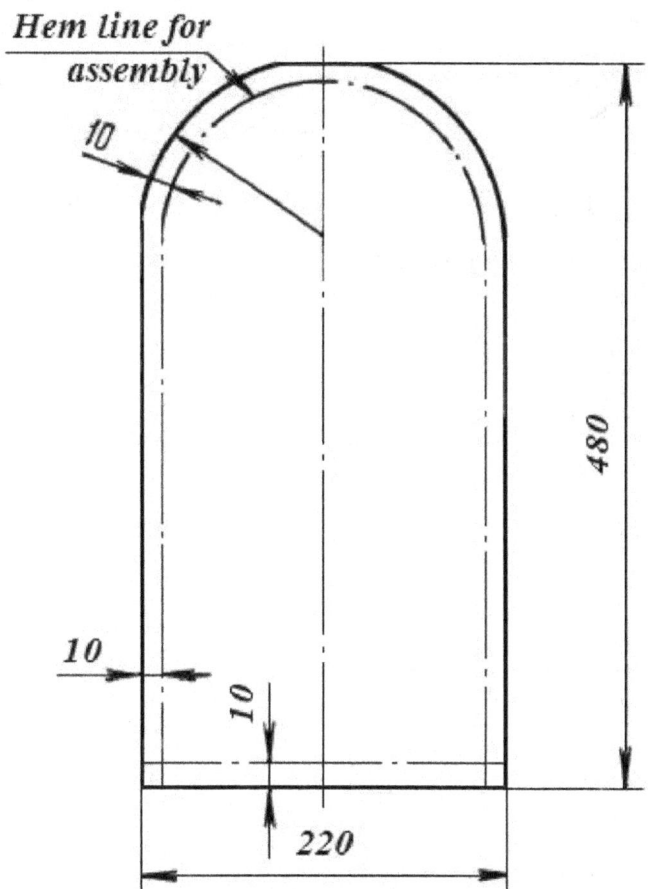

**Fig. 197.** Lining cover for the rear panel 2-2

Material: canvas. Tuck to lay to the left

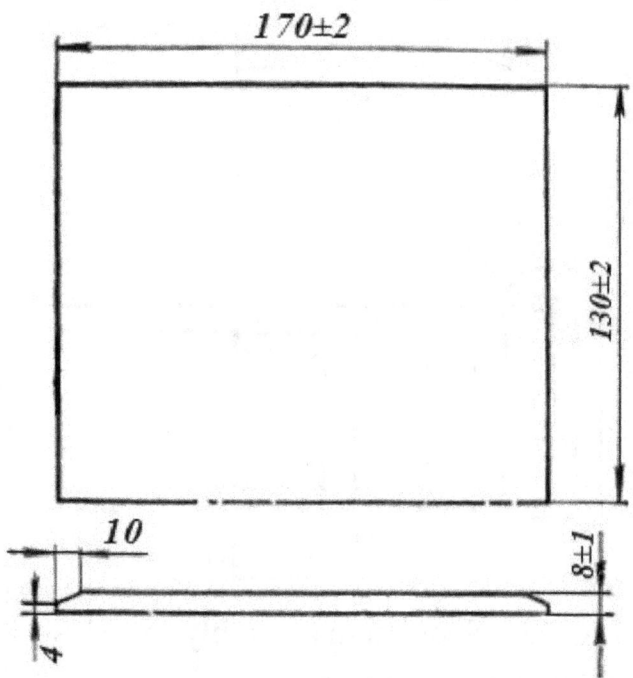

**Fig. 198.** Padding 2-3

Material: felt, coarse GOST 6418-81

171

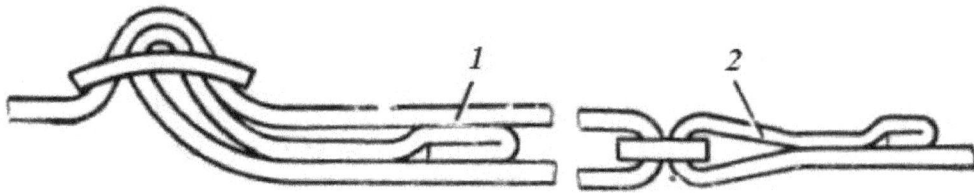

**Fig. 199.** The belt assembly 6Sh51.Sb 1-3:

*1* - shoulder strap assembly 6Sh51.Sb 1-4 (Fig. 200); *2* - short strap assembly
6Sh51.Sb 1-5 (Fig. 201)

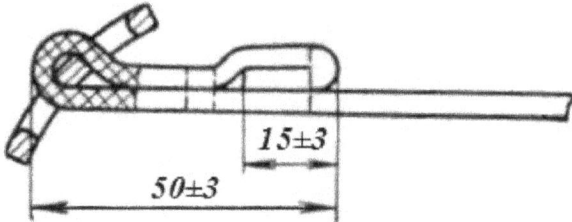

**Fig. 200.** Shoulder strap assembly
6SH51 Sb 1-4:

*1* - shoulder strap 6Sh51.Sb 1- 4 (Fig. 202);
*2* – double slot buckle 6SH51.2-7 (Fig.
204);
100 mm lines of 22-24 stitches. Sewing
should be tight and without distortions

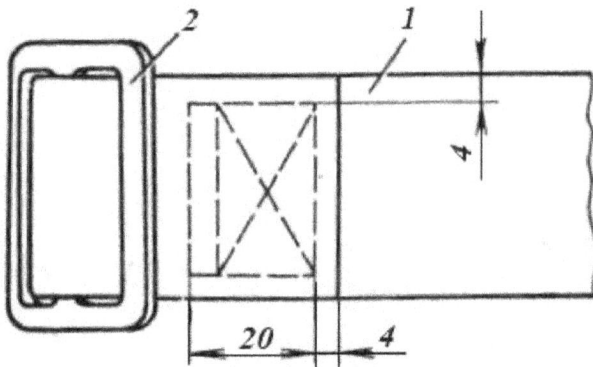

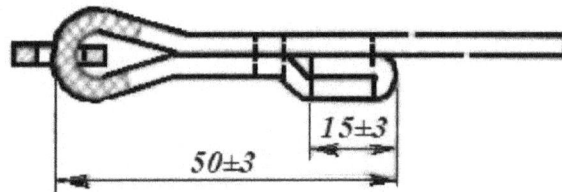

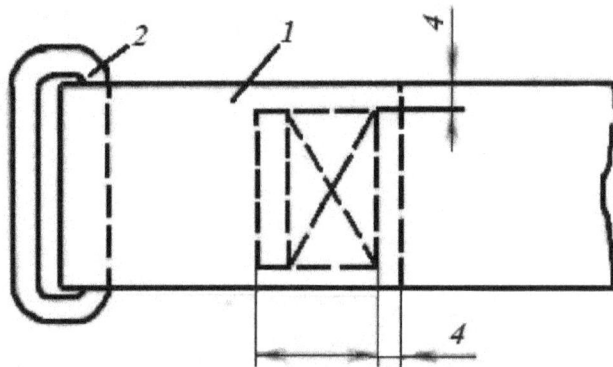

**Fig. 201.** Short strap assembly 6Sh51.Sb 1-5:

*1* - short strap 6SH51.2-6 (Fig. 203); *2* – single slot buckle 6SH51.2-8 (Fig. 205)
100 mm lines of 22-24 stitches. Sewing should be tight and without distortions

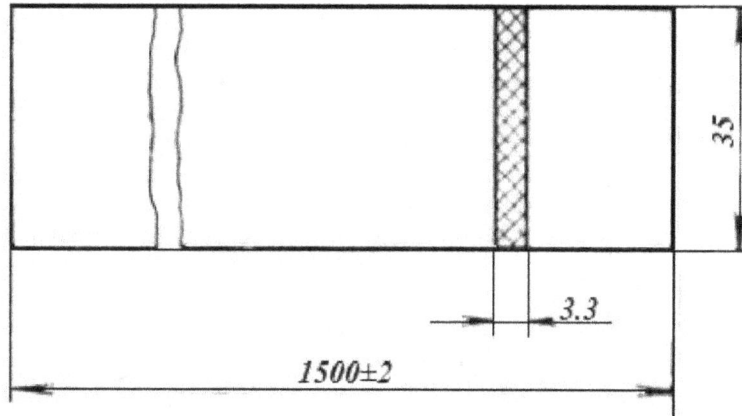

**Fig. 202.** Shoulder Strap 6SH51.2-4

Material: webbing TPT

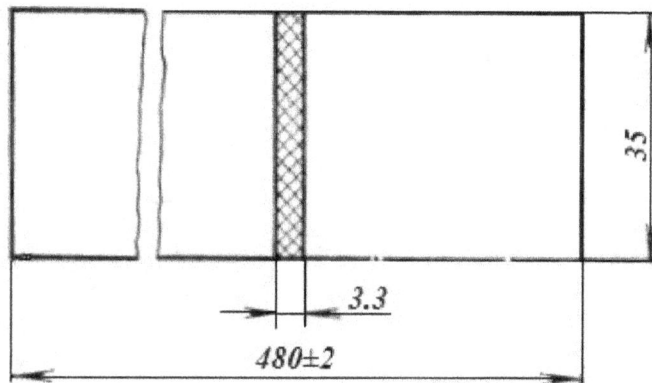

**Fig. 203.** Short Strap 6SH51.2-6

Material: webbing TPT

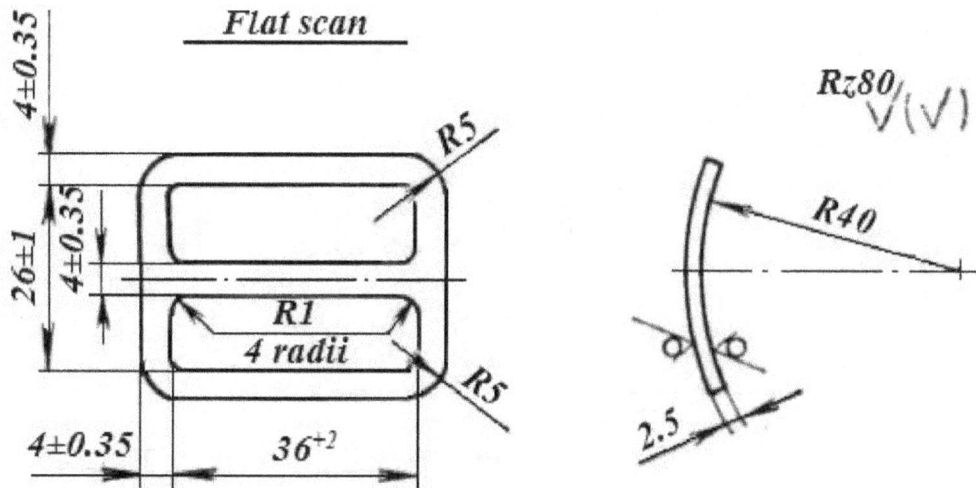

**Fig. 204.** Double slot buckle 6SH51.2-7

Material: steel 20. Phosphated and lacquered

173

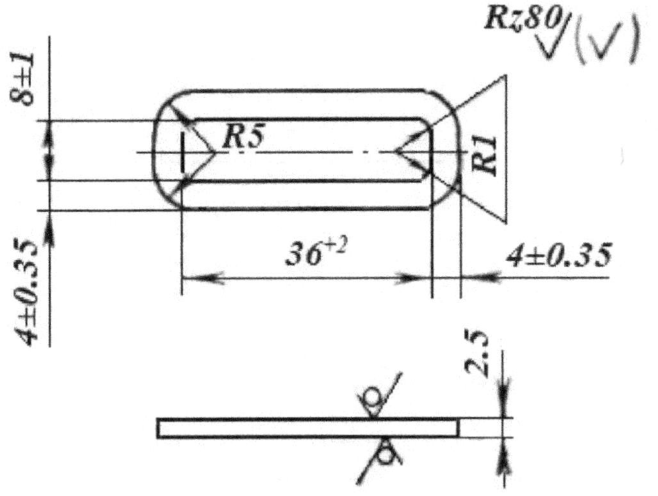

**Fig. 205.** Single slot buckle 6SH51.2-8

Material: steel 20. Phosphated and lacquered

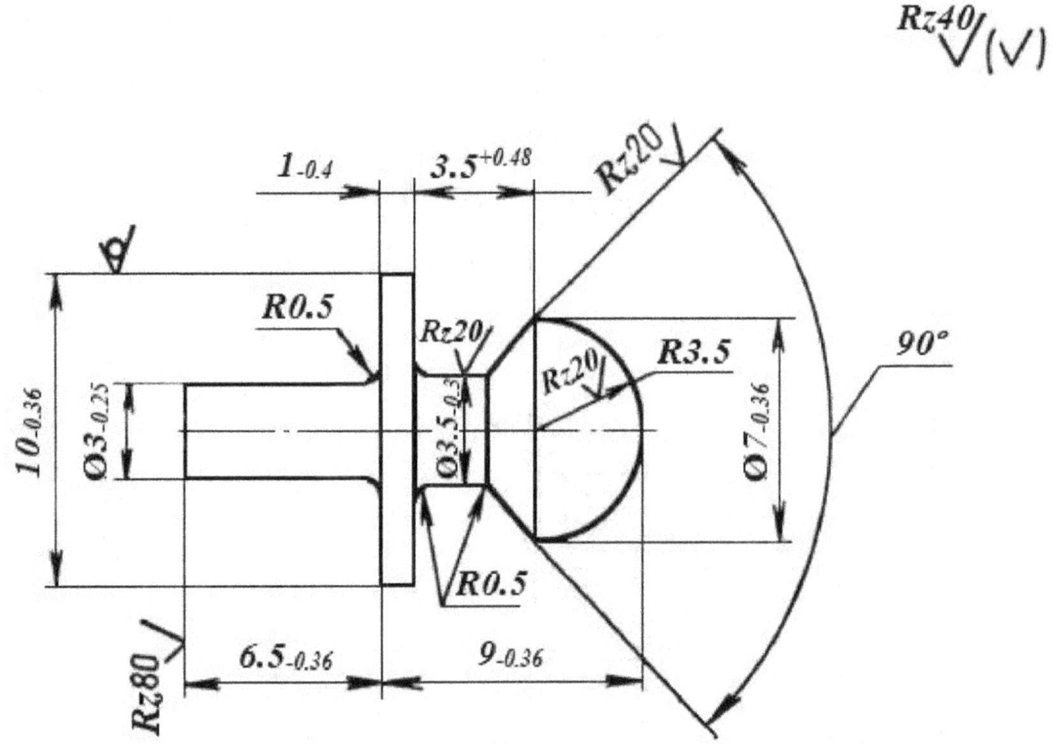

**Fig. 206.** Button stud 1-17

Material: steel 20. Phosphated and lacquered

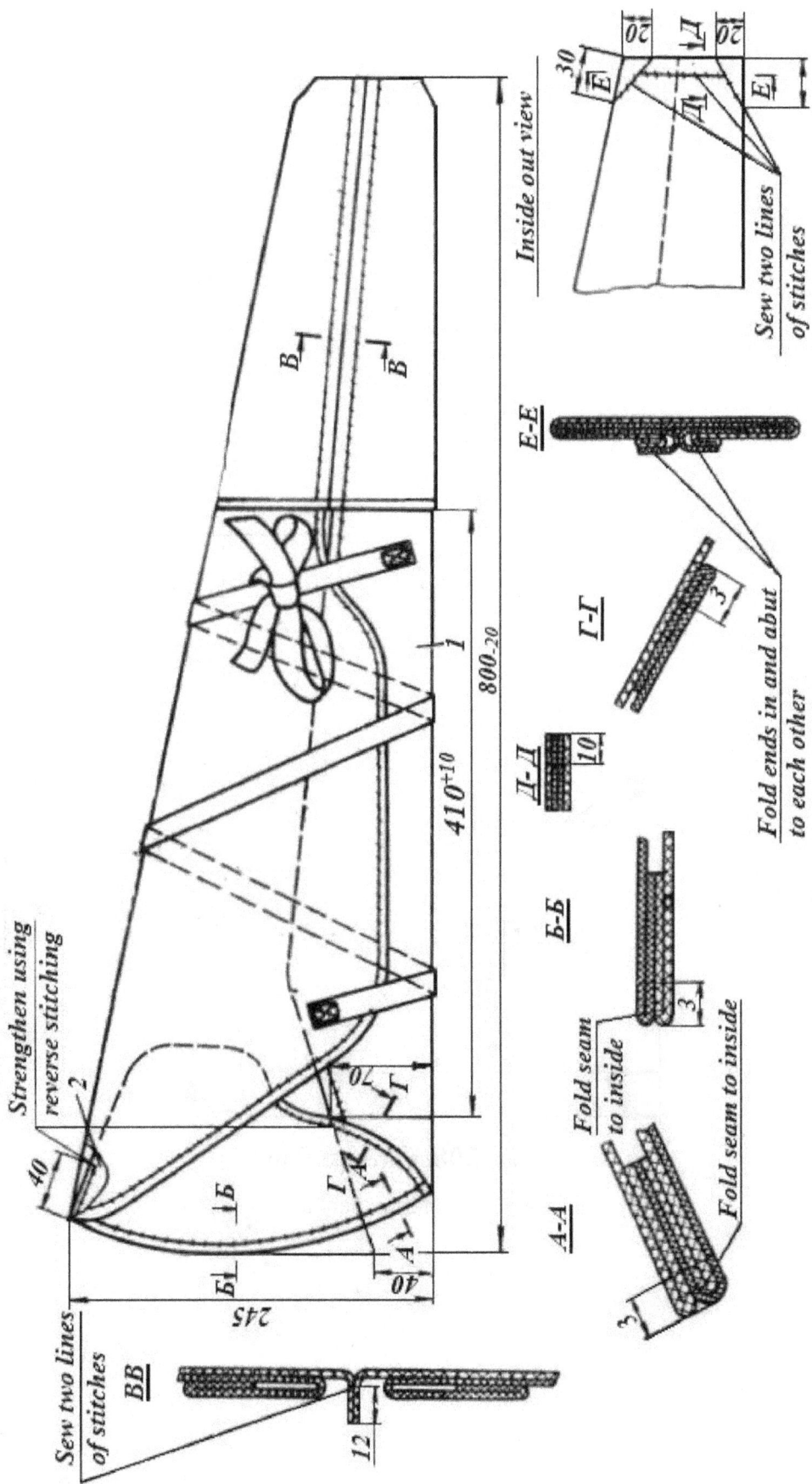

**Fig, 207.** Case for assault rifle AKS74 (Index item 6Sh21):

*1* – body of case Sb 1 (Fig. 209); *2* – closure flap 0-1 (Fig. 208)

*Inside out view*

*Sew two lines of stitches*

*Fold ends in and abut to each other*

*Strengthen using reverse stitching*

*Sew two lines of stitches*

*Fold seam to inside*

*Fold seam to inside*

*Е-Е*

*Г-Г*

*Д-Д*

*Б-Б*

*А-А*

*ВВ*

$800_{-20}$

$410^{+10}$

245

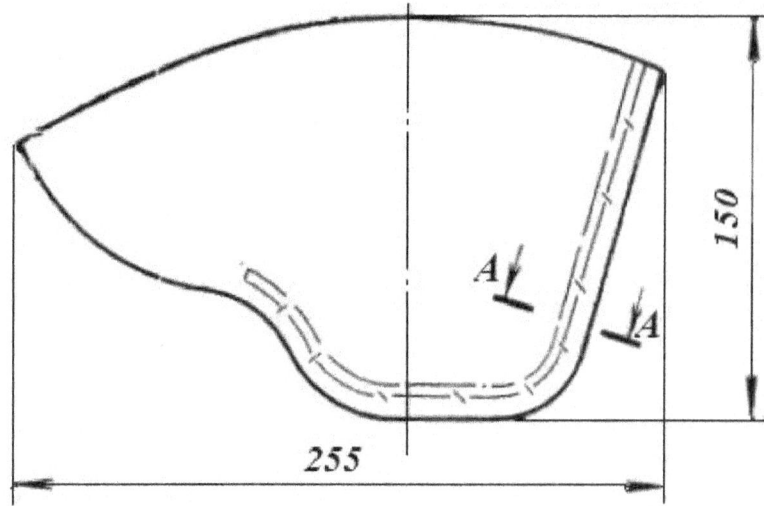

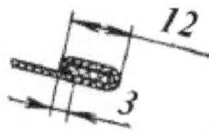

A-A

Flat scan

Dimensions for the hem seam

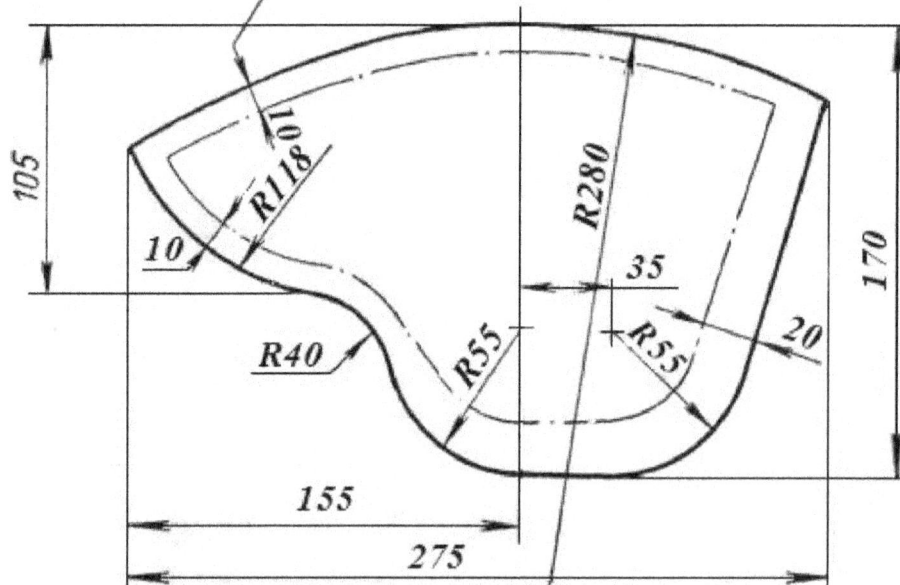

**Fig. 208.** Closure flap 0-1

Material: canvas

**Fig. 209.** Case basic assembly Sb 1:

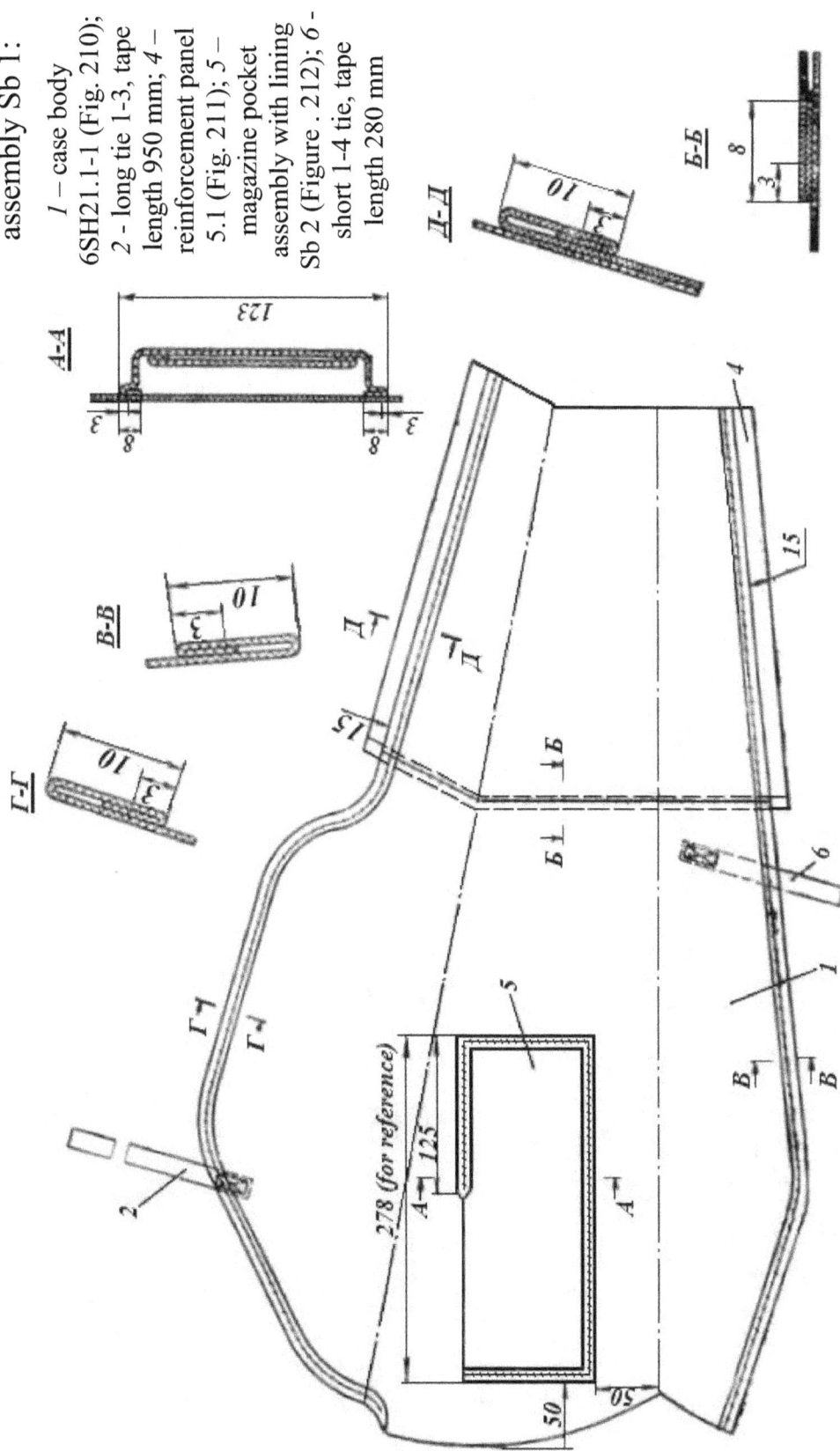

*1 – case body 6SH21.1-1 (Fig. 210); 2 - long tie 1-3, tape length 950 mm; 4 – reinforcement panel 5.1 (Fig. 211); 5 – magazine pocket assembly with lining Sb 2 (Figure . 212); 6 - short 1-4 tie, tape length 280 mm*

177

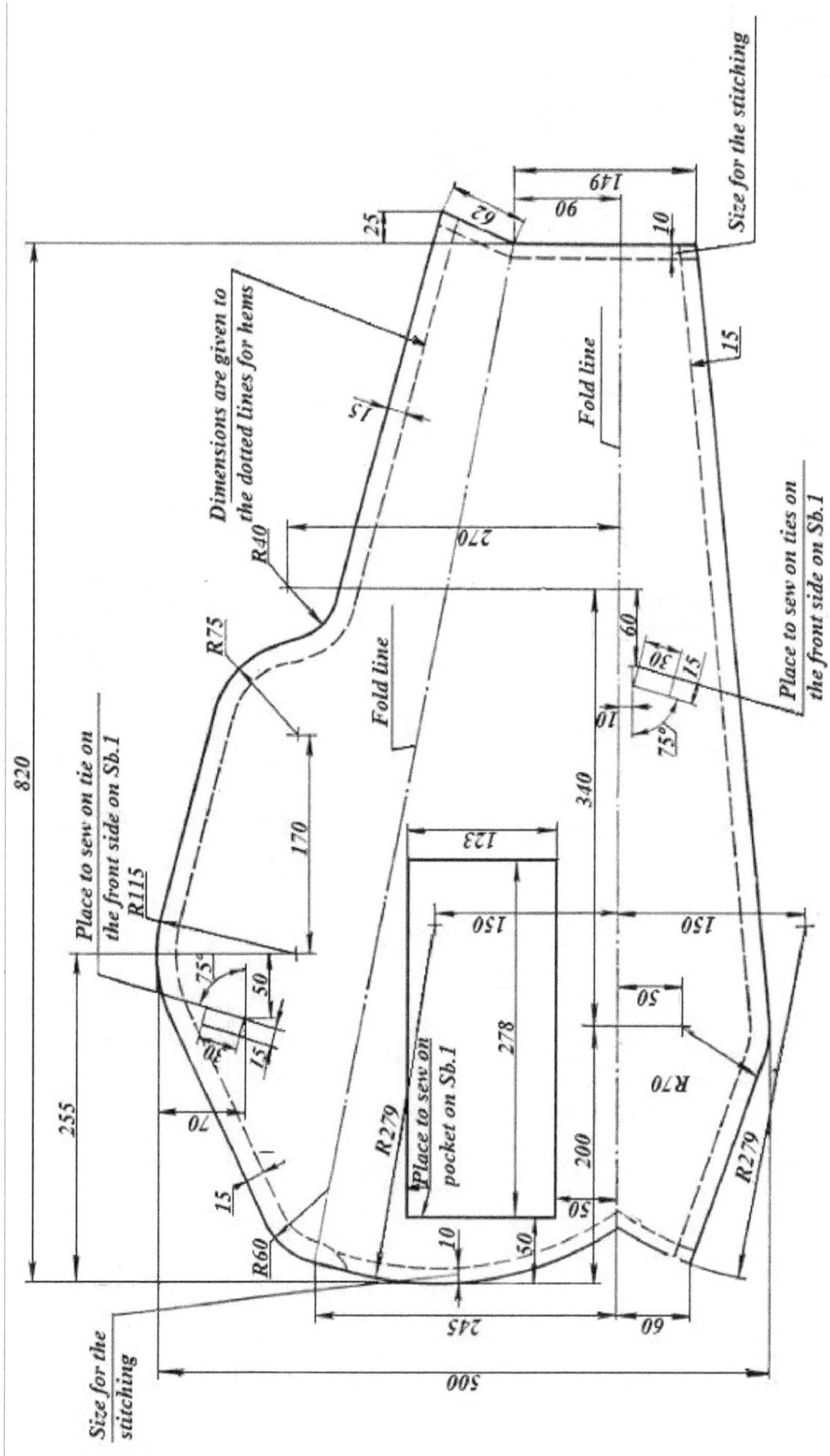

**Fig. 210.** Case opened out 6Sh21.1-1:
Material: canvas

Dimensions are given to the dotted lines for hems

Place to sew on tie on the front side on Sb.1

Place to sew on pocket on Sb.1

Place to sew on ties on the front side on Sb.1

Size for the stitching

Size for the stitching

Fold line

Fold line

820

500

255

170

270

340

200

278

150

150

149

90

62

50

60

60

50

50

50

70

70

245

123

15

15

15

15

15

25

10

10

10

10

30

30

75°

75°

R40

R75

R115

R60

R70

R279

R279

R279

178

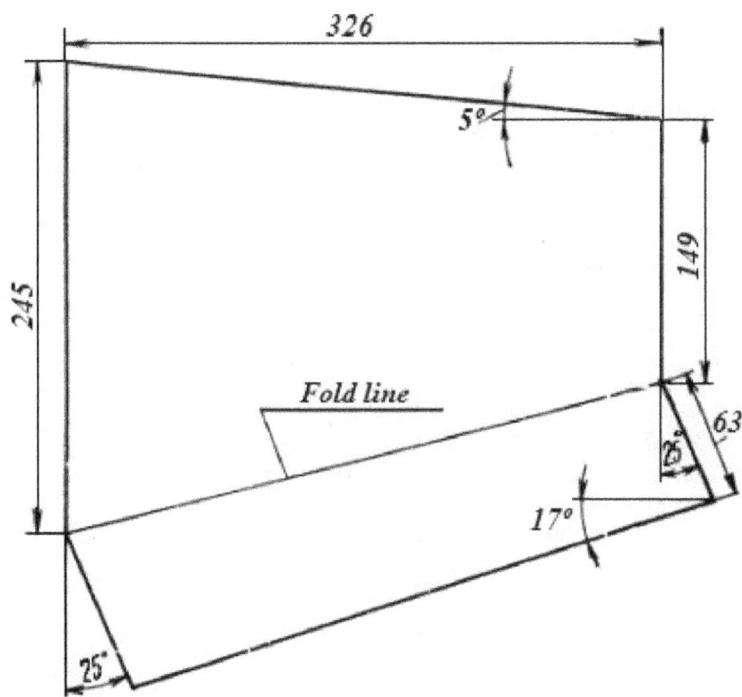

**Fig. 211.** Reinforcement panel 1-5 for case for assault rifle AKS74

Material: canvas

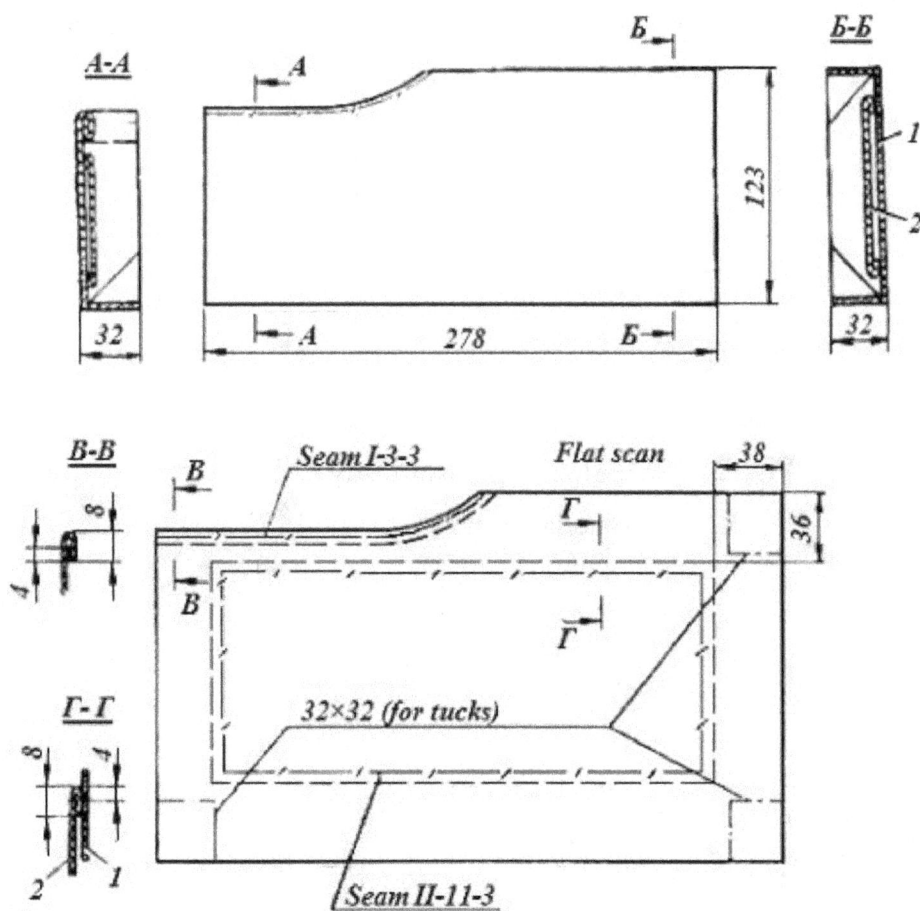

**Fig. 212.** Magazine pocket body with lining Sb 2:

1 – Magazine pocket 2-1 (Fig. 213); 2 – pocket lining 2-2, canvas 130 X 290 mi (135 × 282 mm)

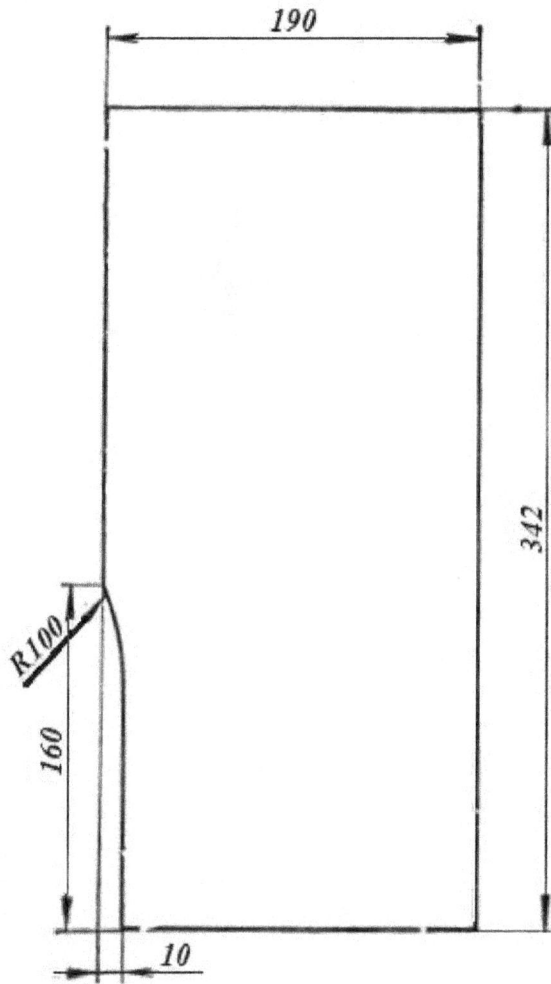

**Fig. 213.** Magazine pocket body 2-1

Material: canvas

**Fig, 214.** Case for assault rifle AKS74U (Index item 6Sh66):

*1 – body of case Sb 1 (Fig. 215); 2 – case bottom assembly Sb 3 (Fig. 218); 3 – closure flap 0-1 (Fig. 208)*

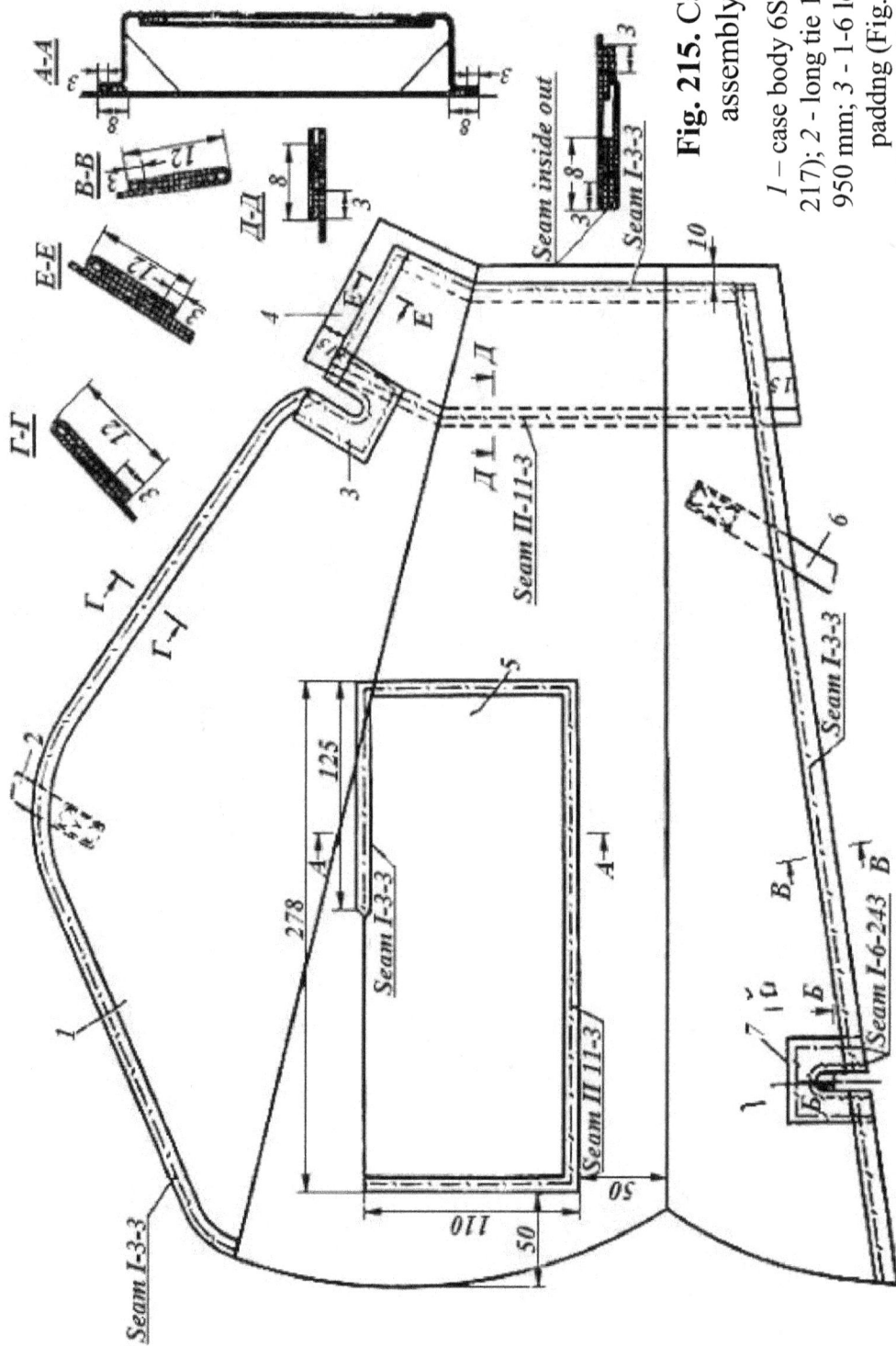

**Fig. 215.** Case basic assembly Sb 1;

*1* – case body 6SH64.1-1 (Fig. 217); *2* - long tie 1-3, tape length 950 mm; *3* - 1-6 lower sling slot paddng (Fig. 218); *4* - reinforcement 1-5 (Fig. 219); *5* - magazine pocket with lining Sb 2 (Fig. 212); *6* - short 1-4 tie, tape length 280 mm; *7* - upper sling slot padding 1-2 (Fig. 220)

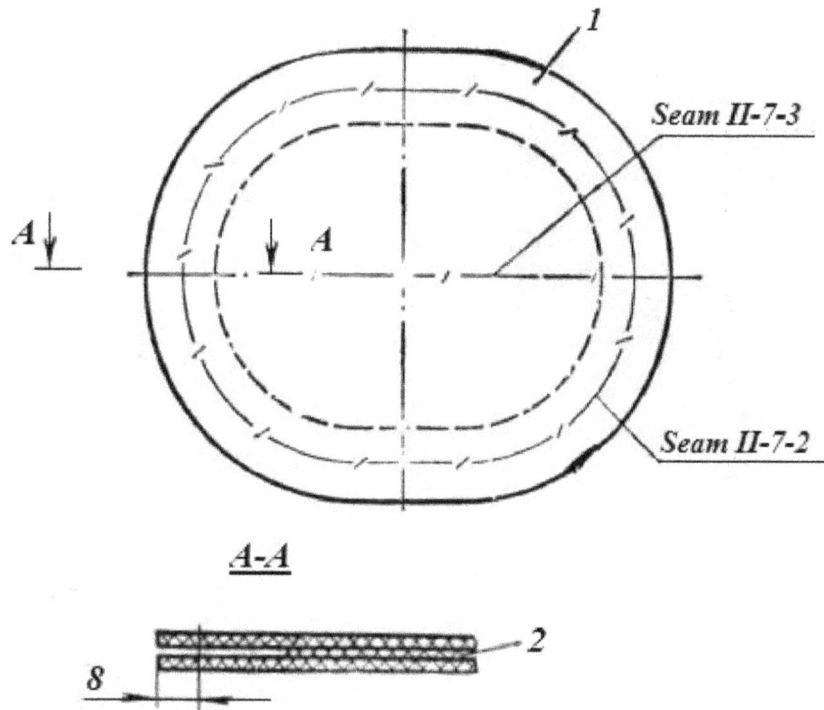

**Fig. 216.** Bottom assembly for the case Sb 3:

*1* - bottom of the case 3-1, 2 pcs. (Fig. 221); *2* – padding for the bottom of the case 3-2 (Fig. 222)

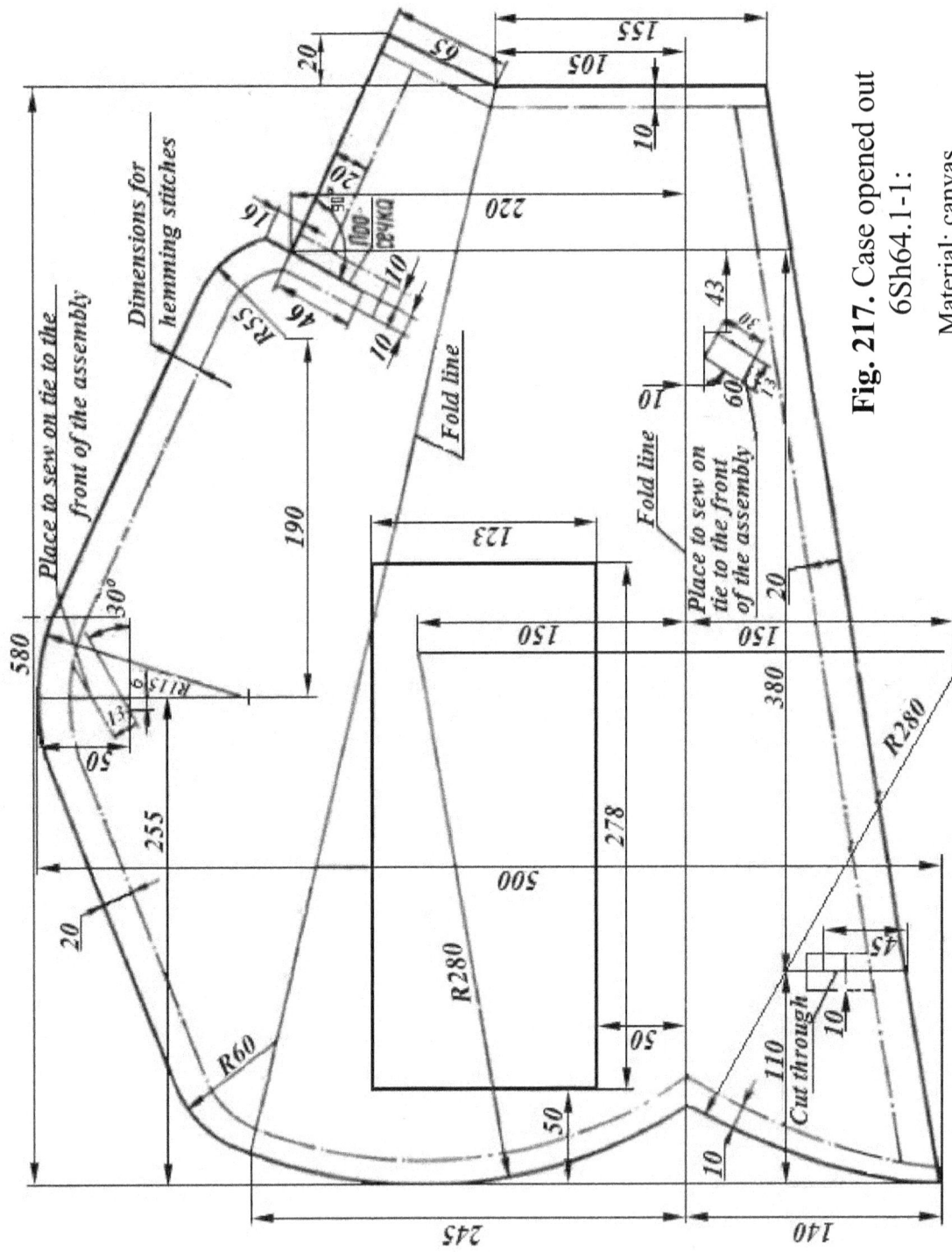

**Fig. 217.** Case opened out
6Sh64.1-1:

Material: canvas

Dimensions for hemming stitches

Place to sew on tie to the front of the assembly

Place to sew on tie to the front of the assembly

Fold line

Fold line

Cut through

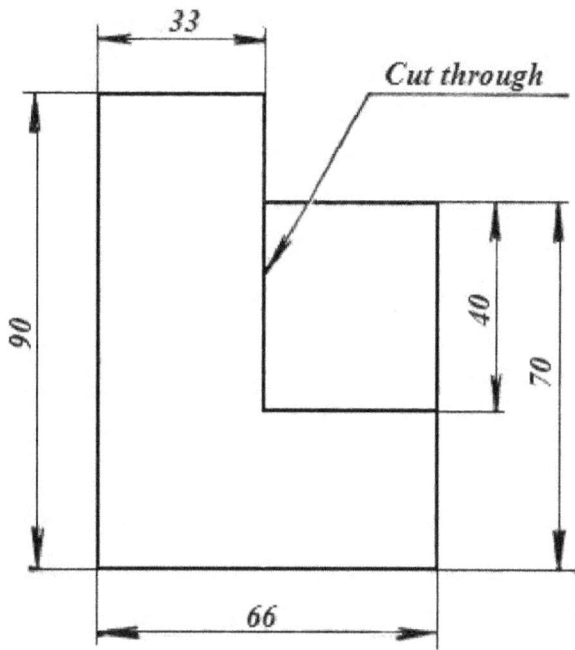

**Fig. 218.** Lower sling slot padding 1-6 for case for assault rifle AKS74U

Material: linen

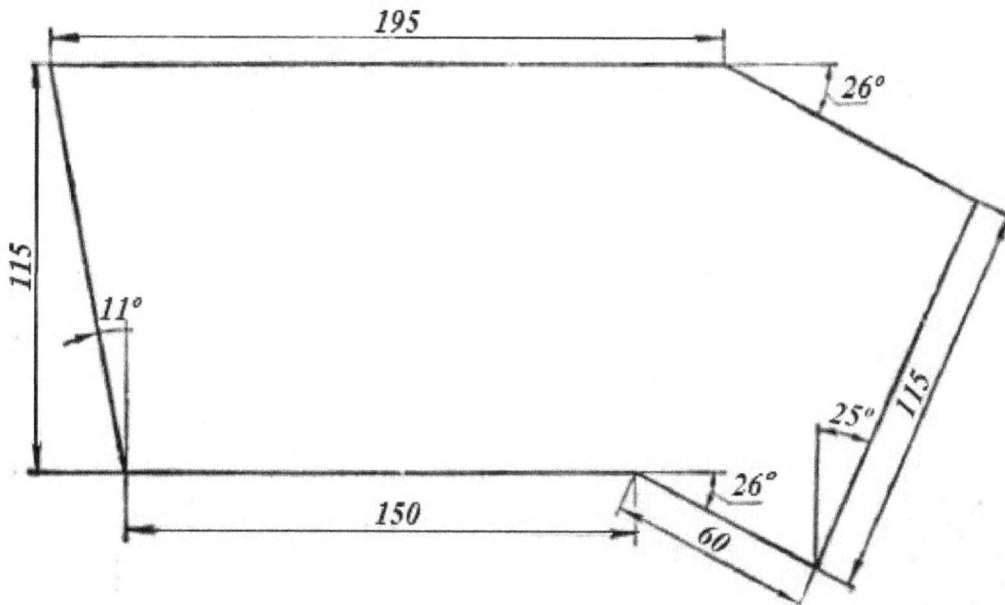

**Fig. 219.** Reinforcement 1-5 for case for assault rifle AKS74U

Material: canvas

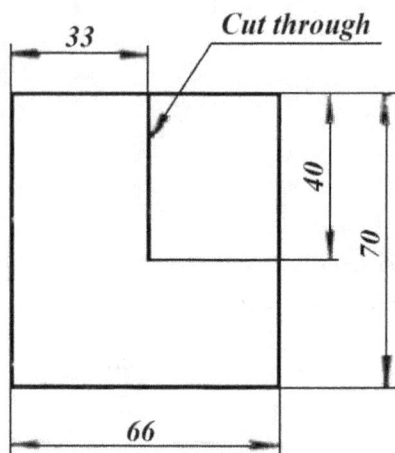

**Fig. 220.** Upper sling slot padding 1-2

Material: linen

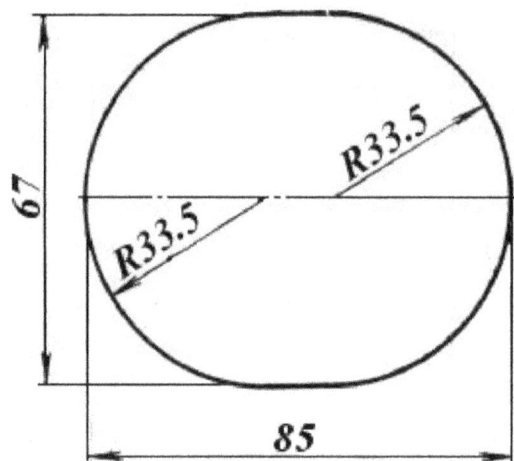

**Fig. 221.** Bottom of the case

Material: canvas

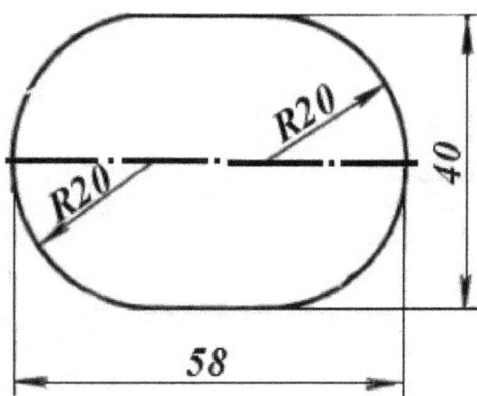

**Fig. 222.** Padding for bottom of the case

Material: canvas

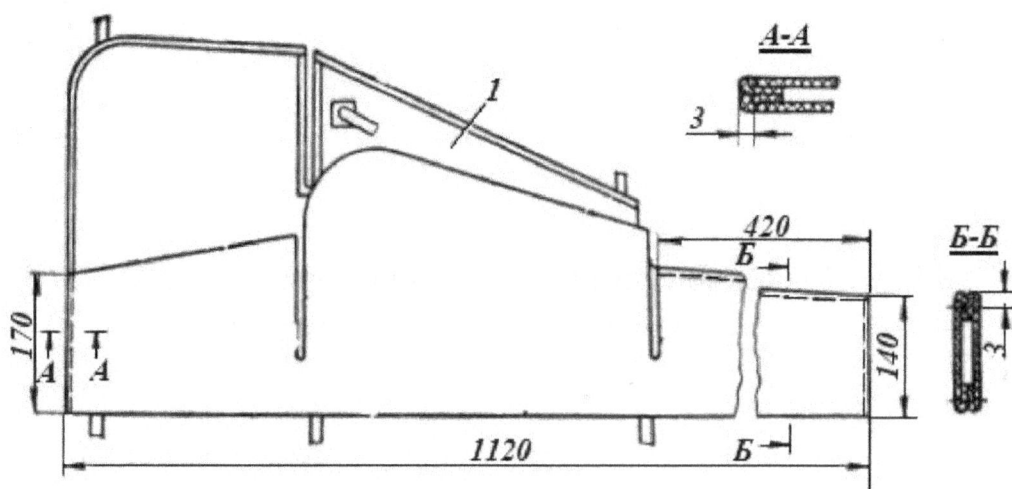

**Fig. 223.** Case for Kalashnikov light machine gun with folding buttstock (6Sh22):

*1* - case assembly Sb 1-1 (Fig. 224)

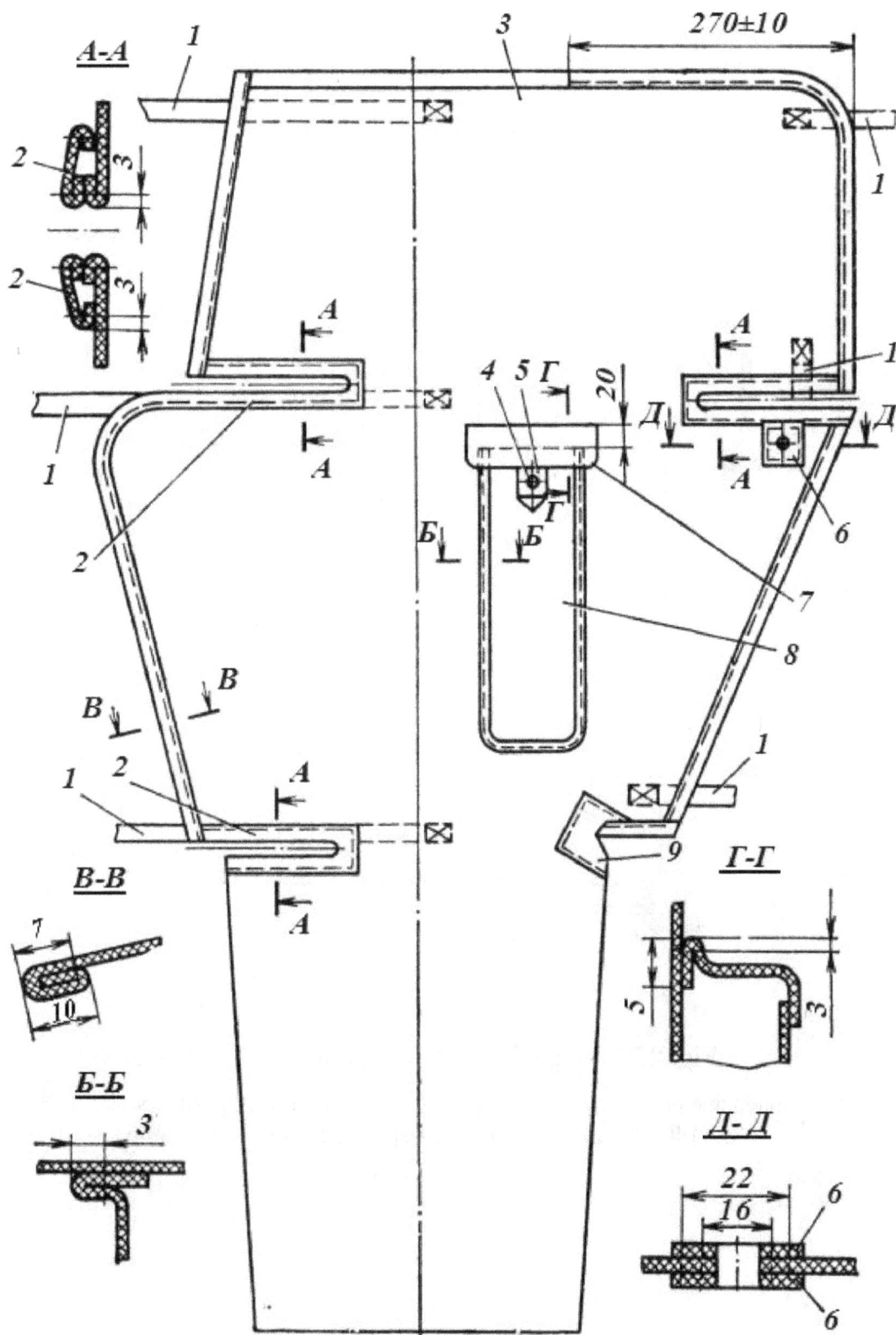

**Fig. 224.** Case assembly Sb 1-1:

*1* – tie 1-3, tape 400 mm, 6 pcs .; *2* – sling slot reinforcement 1-5, 3 pcs. (Fig. 229); *3* – case body 1-1 (Fig. 226); *4* – button, aluminum; *5* - hinge for magazine pocket flap 1-9 (Fig. 230); *6* – washer 1-4, 2 pcs. (Fig. 228); *7* – magazine pocket flap assembly Sb 1-2 (Fig. 225); *8* – magazine pocket 1-2 (Fig. 227); *9* – sling slot reinforcement, small 1-10 (Fig. 231)

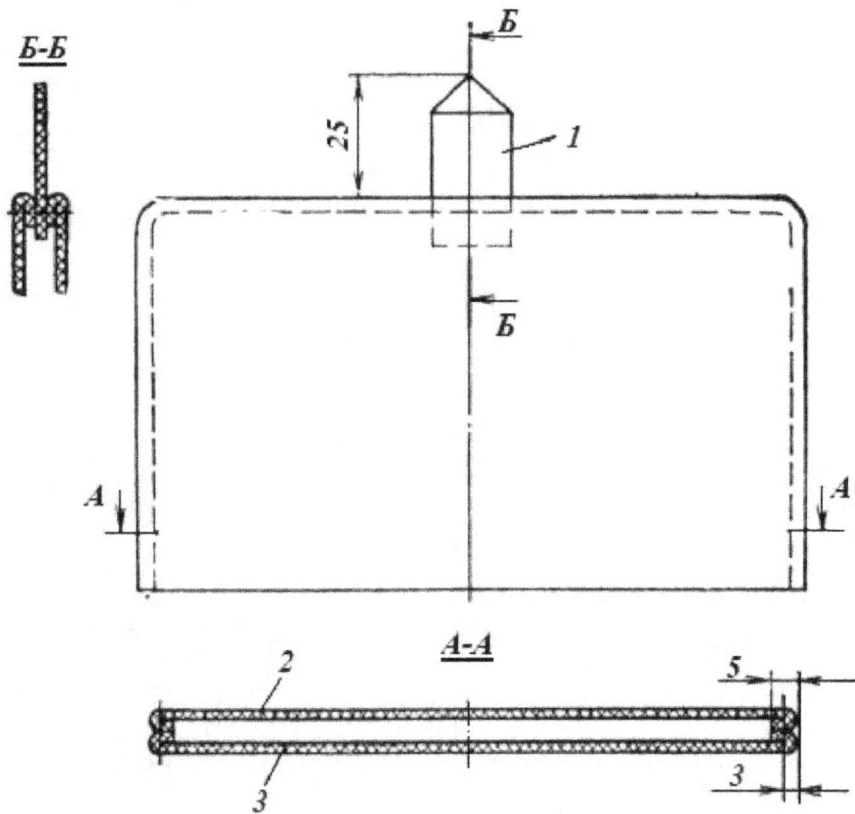

**Fig. 225.** Magazine pocket flap assembly Sb 1-2:

*1*- loop for magazine pocket flap 1-9 (Fig. 230); *2* - lining for magazine pocket flap 1-8, linen 80X140; *3* – magazine pocket flap 1-7, canvas 80 × 40 mm

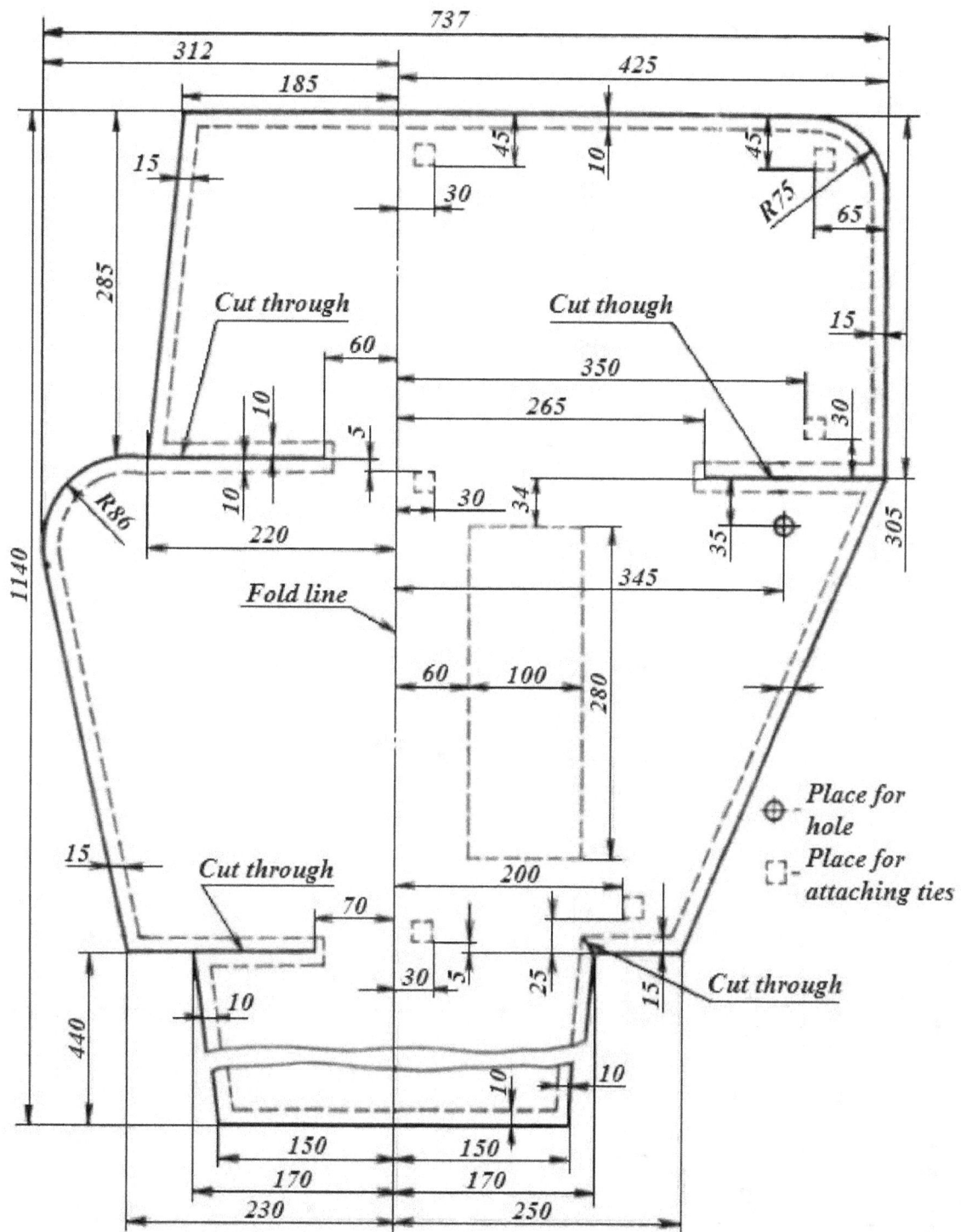

**Fig. 226.** Case opened out:

Material: canvas

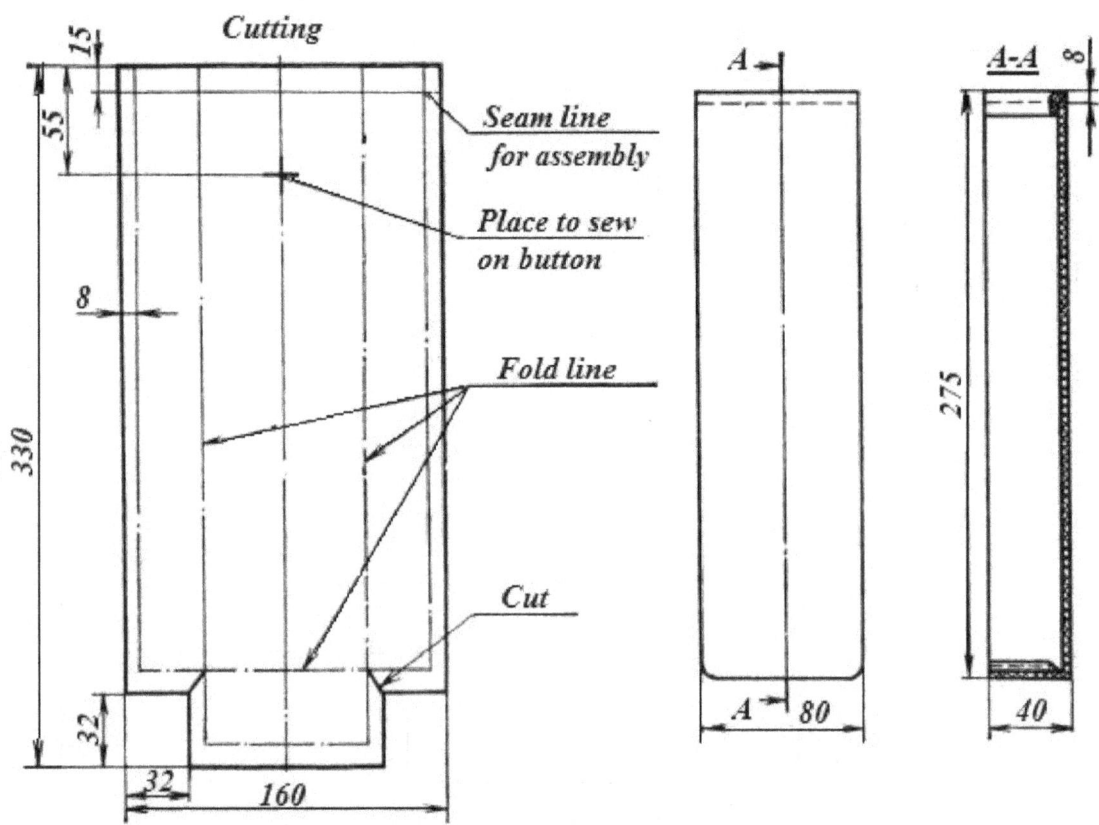

**Fig. 227.** Magazine pocket body 2-1

Material: canvas

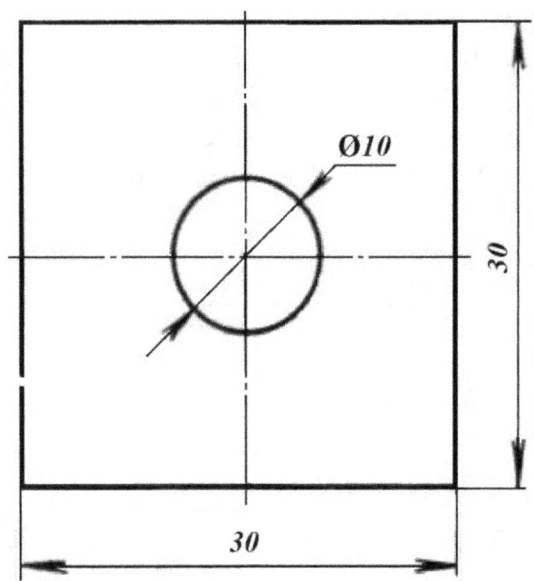

**Fig. 228.** Washer 1-4

Material: harness leather type L, 1st grade
GOST 1904-81

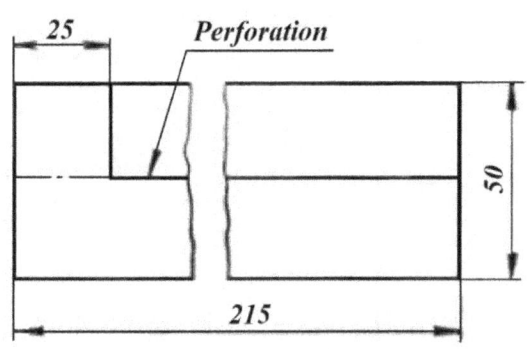

**Fig. 229.** Sling slot reinforcement 1-5

Material: linen

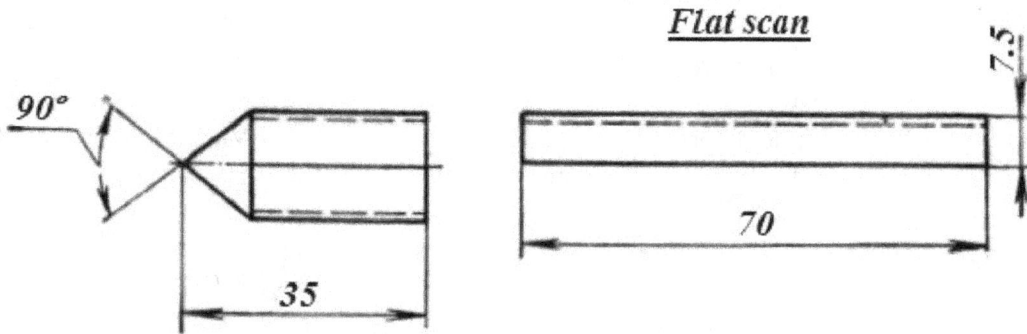

**Fig. 230.** Loop for magazine pocket flap 1-9

Material: webbing

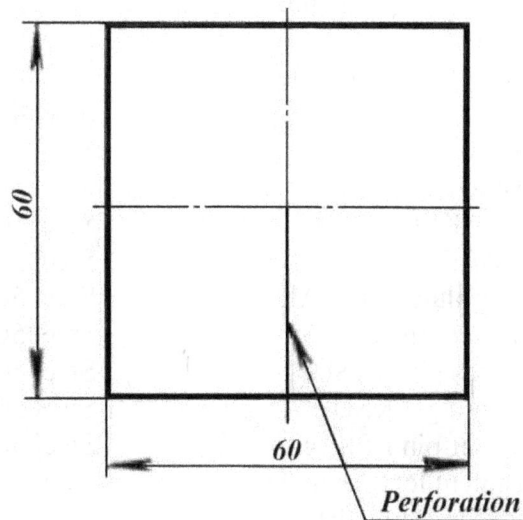

**Fig. 231.** Sling slot reinforcement, small 1-10

Material: linen

*APPENDIX 4*

191

# STATEMENT OF ALLOWED SUBSTITUTES FOR MATERIALS USED FOR WEAPON PARTS FOR REPAIR PER FIGURES IN THIS TEXT OF THIS MANUAL

| Designation | Name | Material grade | |
|---|---|---|---|
| | | per drawing | allowed |
| 6P20.0-13 | Axis pin for magazine catch | Steel 50 | Steel 45 |
| 6P20.0-16 | Grip nut | Steel 45 | Steel 40 |
| 6P20.0-17 | Axis pin for retarder catch | Steel 3OXPA | Steel 50 |
| 6P20.0-19 | Grip screw | Steel 50 | Steel 45 |
| 6P20.0-23 | Rear sight leaf spring | Steel У8A | Steel 55 |
| 6P20.0-25 | Axis pin for firing mechanism | Steel 50 | Steel 45 |
| 6P20.0-27 | Trigger axis pin bushing | Steel 50 | Steel 40 |
| 6P20.1-31 | Front sight base | Steel 50 | Steel 45 |
| 6P20.1-32 | Front sight post | Steel 3OXPA | Steel 50 |
| 6P20.1-33 | Retaining pin for muzzle device Muzzle | Steel 35 | Steel 30 |
| 6P20.1-37 | brake retainer pin | Steel 50 | Steel 3OXPA |
| 6P20.1-41 | Upper handguard retainer spring | Steel 50 | Steel У8A |
| 6P20.1-45 | Gas tube tensioning spring | Steel 50XФA | Steel У8A |
| 6P20.1-52 | Barrel pin | Steel 50 | Steel 45 |
| 6P20.3-3 | Gas piston pin | Steel 50 | Steel 45 |
| 6P20.4-4 | Recoil spring retainer cap | Steel 50 | Steel 45 |
| 6P20.5-7 | Sling loop | Steel 40 | Steel 35 |
| 6P20.5-11 | Trapdoor axis pin | Steel 50 | Steel 40 |
| 6P21.0-37 | Folding stock rear latch retainer pin | Steel 50 | Steel 45 |
| 6P21.0-40 | Folding stock front latch axis pin | Steel 50 | Steel 45 |
| 6P21.0-41 | Folding stock axis pin | Steel 50 | Steel 45 |
| 6P21.5-6 | Sling swivel hinge for folding stock | Steel 40 | Steel 35 |
| 6P21.5-7 | Sling loop | Steel 40 | Steel 35 |
| 6P26.0-21 | Receiver cover axis pin AKSU | Steel 50 | Steel 45 |
| 6P26.1-17 | Front sight post AKSU | Steel 3OXPA | Steel 50 |
| 6P26.1-31 | Front sight base AKSU | Steel 50 | Steel 45 |
| 6P26.1-35 | Retaining pins AKSU | Steel 50 | Steel 45 |
| 6P26.1-36 | Gas tube retainer plunger pin AKSU | Steel 50 | Steel 45 |
| 6P26.1-37 | Flash hider retainer pin AKSU | Steel 50 | Steel 45 |
| 6P26.7-32 | Rear sight leaf axis pin AKSU | Steel 50 | Steel 45 |
| 6P26.7-33 | Rear sight leaf spring AKSU | Steel 50XФA | Steel У8A |
| 6P18.1-37 | Flash hider retainer pin RPK74 | Steel 50 | Steel 45 |
| 6P18.2-6 | Windage adjustment lock knob RPK74 | Steel 50 | Steel 45 |
| 6P18.2-7 | Windage adjustment screw RPK74 | Steel 50 | Steel 45 |
| 6P18.2-9 | Windage adjustment nut RPK74 | Steel 50 | Steel 45 |
| 6P18.2-10 | Windage adjustment nut pin RPK74 | Steel 50 | Steel 45 |
| 6P18.4-4 | Recoil spring retainer cap for RPK74 | Steel 50 | Steel 45 |
| 6P18.9-7 | Bipod latch RPK74 | Steel 50 | Steel 45 |
| 6P18.9-10 | Bipod axis pin RPK74 | Steel 50 | Steel 45 |

*Appendix 4 (continued*

| Designation | Name | Material grade | |
|---|---|---|---|
| | | per drawing | allowed |
| 6P19.0-26 | Stock latch hook axis pin RPK74S | Steel 50 | Steel 45 |
| 6P19.1-52 | Stock latch RPKS74 | Steel 50 | Steel 3OXPA |
| 6P19.1-54 | Stock latch pin RPKS74 | Steel 50 | Steel 45 |
| 6P19.1-55 | Folding stock axis pin RPKS74 | Steel 50 | Steel 3OXPA |
| 6P19.1-56 | Sling loop RPKS74 | Steel 40 | Steel 35 |
| 6P19.1-57 | Sling swivel hinge RPKS74 | Steel 50 | Steel 45 |
| 6H4.1-3 | Hilt (cross guard) pin for bayonet | Steel 50 | Steel 45 |
| 6H4.1-18 | Wrist strap buckle for bayonet wrist strap | Steel 40 | Steel 35 |
| 6H4.2-15 | Washer for bayonet hanger assembly | Steel 40 | Steel 35 |
| 6H4.2-20 | D-ring for bayonet hanger assembly | Steel 45 | Steel 35 |

# STATEMENT OF APPLICABILITY AND INTERCHANGEABILITY OF PARTS BY WEAPON

| Designation | Old designation | Name | AK74 | AKS74 | AKS74U | RPK74 | RPKS74 | Level of interchangeability |
|---|---|---|---|---|---|---|---|---|
| 6P20.Sb 0-1 | | Firing mechanism | + | + | – | + | + | |
| 6P26.Sb 0-1 | | Same | – | – | + | – | – | |
| 6P20.Sb 0-2 | | Retarder assembly | + | + | – | + | + | I |
| 6P20.Sb 0-6 | | Muzzle brake | + | + | – | – | – | PI |
| 6P18.0-1 | 6P2.0-1V | Receiver cover RPK74 | – | – | – | + | + | |
| 6P20.0-1 | 6P1.0-1 | Same AK74 | + | + | – | – | – | |
| 6P20.0-2 | 6P1.0-1V | » | + | + | – | – | – | |
| 6P20.0-3 | | Hammer | + | + | + | + | + | I |
| 6P20.0-4 6P20.0-32 | 6P1.0-3 | Mainspring | + | + | + | + | + | I |
| 6P20.0-5 6P20.0-15 | | Retarder base | + | + | – | + | + | PI |
| 6P20.0-6 | | Auto-sear | + | + | + | + | + | I |
| 6P20.0-8 6P20.0-29 | 6P1.0-6 | Auto-sear spring | + | + | + | + | + | I |
| 6P20.0-7 | | Trigger | + | + | + | + | + | I |
| 6P20.0-9 | 6P1.0-7 | Retarder latch | + | + | – | + | + | I |
| | | Disconnector | + | + | + | + | + | |

| Designation | Old designation | Name | Applies to | | | | | Level of interchangeability |
|---|---|---|---|---|---|---|---|---|
| | | | assault rifles | | | machine guns | | |
| | | | AK74 | AKS74 | AKS74U | RPK74 | RPKS74 | |
| 6P20.0-10 | 56-A-212.0-10 | Disconnector spring | + | + | + | + | + | I |
| 6P20.0-11 | 6P1.0-11 | Magazine catch | + | + | + | + | + | I |
| 6P20.0-12 | 56-A-212.0-12 | Magazine catch spring | + | + | + | + | + | I |
| 6P20.0-13 | 56-A-212.0-13 | Magazine catch axis pin | + | + | + | + | + | I |
| 6P20.0-15 / 6P20.0-5 | | Auto-sear | + | + | + | + | + | I |
| 6P20.0-16 | | Grip nut | + | + | + | + | + | I |
| 6P20.0-17 | 6P1.0-17 | Retarder catch axis pin | + | + | + | + | + | I |
| 6P20.0-19 | 56-A-212.0-19 | Grip screw | + | + | + | + | + | I |
| 6P20.0-20 | | Muzzle Brake | + | + | - | - | - | PI |
| 6P26.0-20 | | Flash hider AKSU | - | - | + | - | - | PI |
| 6P26.0-21 | | Receiver cover axis pin AKSU | - | - | + | - | - | I |
| 6P20.0-23 | 56-A-212.0-23 | Rear sight leaf spring | + | + | - | + | + | I |
| 6P19.0-25 | 6P8.0-25 | Stock latch hook RPKS74 | - | - | - | - | + | I |
| 6P20.0-25 | 56-A-212.0-25 | Firing mechanism axis pin | + | + | + | + | + | I |
| 6P19.0-26 | 6P8.0-26 | Stock latch hook axis pin RPKS74 | - | - | - | - | + | I |
| 6P19.0-27 | | Stock latch hook spring RPKS74 | - | - | - | - | + | I |
| 6P20.0-27 | | Trigger axis pin bushing | + | + | + | + | + | I |
| 6P20.0-28 | | Retarder spring | + | + | + | + | + | I |
| 6P20.0-29 / 6P20.0-8 | | Trigger | + | + | + | + | + | I |

| Designation | Old designation | Name | AK74 | AKS74 | AKS74U | RPK74 | RPKS74 | Level of interchangeability |
|---|---|---|:--:|:--:|:--:|:--:|:--:|:--:|
| 6P20.0-32 } 6P20.0-4 | | Retarder base | + | + | - | + | + | PI |
| 6P21.0-35 | | Folding stock rear stock latch AKS74 | - | + | + | - | - | I |
| 6P21.0-36 | | Folding stock rear latch spring AKS74 | - | + | + | - | - | I |
| 6P21.0-37 | | Folding stock rear latch retainer pin AKS74 | - | + | + | - | - | I |
| 6P26.0-39 | | Trigger limiter/spacer AKSU | - | - | + | - | - | I |
| 6P21.0-39 | | Folding stock front latch spring AKS74 | - | + | + | - | - | I |
| 6P21.0-40 | | Folding stock front latch axis pin AKS74 | - | + | + | - | - | I |
| 6P21.0-41 | | Folding stock axis pin AKS74 | - | + | + | - | - | I |
| 6P21.0-42 } | | Folding stock front latch hook AKS74 | - | + | + | - | - | I |
| 6P21.0-44 } | | Same | - | + | - | - | - | I |
| 6P18.Sb 1-2 | 6P2.Sb 1-2 | Upper handguard/gas tube assembly RPK74 | - | - | - | + | + | |
| 6P20.Sb 1-2 | | Same AK74 | + | + | - | + | + | |
| 6P26.Sb 1-2 | | Upper handguard/gas tube assembly AKSU | - | - | + | - | - | |
| 6P20.Sb 1-3 | | Selector lever assembly | + | + | + | + | + | PI |
| 6P18.Sb 1-6 | | Gas tube latch assembly RPK74 | - | - | - | + | + | |
| 6P20.Sb 1-6 | 56- A-212.Sb 1-6 | Same | + | + | - | - | - | |
| 6P19.Sb 1-10 | | Sling swivel assembly RPKS74 | - | - | + | - | + | |
| 6P18.Sb 1-12 | 6P1.Sb 1-6 | Gas tube assembly RPK74 | - | + | - | + | + | |
| 6P20.Sb 1-12 | 6P8.Sb 1-10 | Same AK74 | + | + | - | - | - | |
| 6P26.Sb 1-13 | | Gas tube assembly AKSU | - | - | + | - | - | |

| Designation | Old designation | Name | Applies to — assault rifles | | | Applies to — machine guns | | Level of interchangeability |
|---|---|---|---|---|---|---|---|---|
| | | | AK74 | AKS74 | AKS74U | RPK74 | RPKS74 | |
| 6P18.Sb 1-13 | | Bipod assembly RPK74 | – | – | – | + | + | PI |
| 6P18.Sb 1-14 | | Same | – | – | – | + | + | I |
| 6P18.1-15 | 6P2.1-15 | Barrel pin RPK74 | – | – | – | + | + | |
| 6P26.1-17 | | Front sight post AKSU | + | – | + | – | – | |
| 6P20.1-22 | 56-A-212.1-22 | Gas tube lock arm | – | + | – | + | + | I |
| 6P26.1-22 | | Gas tube retainer spring AKSU | – | – | + | – | – | |
| 6P18.1-28 | 6P2.1-28 | Lower handguard retainer latch RPK74 | + | – | – | + | + | |
| 6P20.1-28 | 6P1.1-28 | Same AK74 | + | + | + | – | – | |
| 6P20.1-31 | 56-A-212.1-31 | Front sight base | – | + | – | + | + | |
| 6P26.1-31 | | Same AKSU | + | – | + | – | – | |
| 6P20.1-32 | 56-A-212.1-32 | Front sight post AKSU | + | + | – | + | + | PI |
| 6P20.1-33 | | Retaining pin for muzzle brake retainer | + | + | – | – | – | PI |
| 6P18.1-34 | 56-A-212.1-34 | Rear sight block pin RPK74 | – | – | – | + | + | I |
| 6P20.1-34 | 6P1.1-34 | Same AK74 | + | + | + | – | – | PI |
| 6P26.1-35 | | Retaining pin AKSU | – | – | + | – | – | PI |
| 6P20.1-35 | 6P1.1-35 | Washer | + | + | – | + | + | I |
| 6P18.1-36 | 56-A-242.1-36 | Gas tube lock shaft RPK74 | – | – | – | + | + | |
| 6P20.1-36 | 6P1.1-36 | Same AK74 | + | + | – | – | – | |
| 6P26.1-36 | | Gas tube retainer plunger pin AKSU | – | – | + | – | – | |
| 6P20.1-37 | | Muzzle brake retainer pin | + | + | – | – | – | I |

| Designation | Old designation | Name | AK74 | AKS74 | AKS74U | RPK74 | RPKS74 | Level of interchangeability |
|---|---|---|:--:|:--:|:--:|:--:|:--:|:--:|
| | | | assault rifles | | | machine guns | | |
| 6P18.1-37 | 56-A-212 1-37 | Flash hider retainer pin RPK74 | - | - | - | + | + | I |
| 6P26.1-37 | | Flash hider retainer pin AKSU | - | - | + | - | - | I |
| 6P18.1-38 | 56-A-212.1-38 | Muzzle deveice retainer spring RPK74 | - | - | - | + | - | I |
| 6P20.1-38 | 6P1.1-38 | Same AK74 | + | + | - | - | + | I |
| 6P26.1-38 | | Flash hider retainer spring AKSU | - | - | + | - | - | I |
| 6P18.1-40 | 56-A-212.1-40B | Upper handguard RPK74 | - | - | - | + | + | PI |
| 6P20.1-40 | | Same AK74 | + | + | - | - | - | PI |
| 6P26.1 40 | | » AKSU | - | - | + | - | - | |
| 6P20.1-41 | 56-A-212.1-41 | Upper handguard retainer spring | + | + | - | - | + | PI |
| 6P26.1-41 | | Same AKSU | - | - | + | - | - | |
| 6P18.1-44 | 6P2.1-44 | Cleaning rod guide ring RPK74 | - | - | - | + | + | I |
| 6P20.1-45 | | Gas tube tensioning spring latch | + | + | - | - | - | I |
| 6P19.1-52 | 6P8.1-52 | Stock latch RPKS74 | - | - | - | - | + | I |
| 6P20.1-52 | | Barrel pin | + | + | + | - | - | I |
| 6P19.1-53 | 6P8.1-53 | Spring, stock latch RPKS74 | - | - | - | - | + | PI |
| 6P19.1-54 | 6P8.1-54 | Stock latch pin RPKS74 | - | - | - | - | + | PI |
| 6P19.1-55 | 6P8.1-55 | Folding stock axis pin RPKS74 | - | - | - | - | + | I |
| 6P19.1-56 | 6P8.1-56 | Sling loop RPKS74 | - | - | - | - | + | |
| 6P19.1-57 | 6P8.1-57 | Sling swivel hinge RPKS74 | - | - | - | - | + | |
| 6P18.1-61 } 6P18.1-70 | | Flash hider RPK74 | - | - | - | + | + | I |

| Designation | Old designation | Name | AK74 | AKS74 | AKS74U | RPK74 | RPKS74 | Level of interchangeability |
|---|---|---|---|---|---|---|---|---|
| 6P18.Sb 2 | 6P2.Sb 2 | Rear sight leaf assembly RPK74 | – | – | – | + | + | PI |
| 6P20.Sb 2 | 6P1.Sb 2 | Same AK74 | + | + | – | – | – | PI |
| 6P18.2-1 | 6P2.2-1 | Rear sight leaf RPK74 | – | – | – | + | + | PI |
| 6P20.2-1 | 6P1.2-1 | Same AK74 | + | + | – | – | – | PI |
| 6P20.2-2 | 56-A-212.2-1 | Rear sight elevation slide | + | + | – | + | + | PI |
| 6P20.2-3 | 56-A-212.2-3 | Rear sight elevation slide latch | + | + | – | + | + | PI |
| 6P20.2-4 | 56-A-212.2-4 | Rear sight elevation slide latch spring | + | + | – | + | + | I |
| 6P18.2-5 | 6P2.2-5 | Rear sight blade RPK74 | – | – | – | + | + | I |
| 6P18.2-6 | 6P2.2-6 | Windage adjustment lock knob RPK74 | – | – | – | + | + | I |
| 6P18.2-7 | 6P2.2-7 | Windage adjustment screw RPK74 | – | – | – | + | + | I |
| 6P18.2-8 | 6P2.2-8 | Spring, windage adjustment tension | – | – | – | + | + | I |
| 6P18.2-9 | 6P2.2-9 | Windage adjustment nut RPK74 | – | – | – | + | + |  |
| 6P18.2-10 | 6P2.2-10 | Windage adjustment nut pin RPK74 | + | + | – | + | + | I |
| 6P20.Sb 3 |  | Bolt carrier with bolt assembly | + | + | – | + | + |  |
| 6P26.Sb 3 |  | Same AKSU | – | – | + | – | – |  |
| 6P20.Sb 3-1 |  | Bolt carrier assembly | + | + | – | + | + | PI |
| 6P26.Sb 3-1 |  | Same AKSU | – | – | + | – | – | PI |
| 6P20.Sb 3-2 |  | Bolt assembly | + | + | + | + | + | PI |
| 6P20.3-1 |  | Bolt carrier | + | + | – | + | + | PI |
| 6P26.3-1 |  | Same AKSU | – | – | + | – | – | PI |

| Designation | Old designation | Name | AK74 | AKS74 | AKS74U | RPK74 | RPKS74 | Level of interchangeability |
|---|---|---|---|---|---|---|---|---|
| | | | assault rifles | | | machine guns | | |
| 6P20.3-2 | | Gas piston | + | + | – | + | + | PI |
| 6P26.3-2 | | Same AKSU | – | – | + | – | – | PI |
| 6P20.3-3 | 56-A-212.3-3 | Gs piston pin | + | + | + | + | + | I |
| 6P20.3-4 | | Same | + | + | – | + | + | I |
| 6P20.3-5 | | Bolt | + | + | + | + | + | PI |
| 6P20.3-7 | | Firing pin | + | + | + | + | + | PI |
| 6P20.3-9 | | Extractor spring | + | + | + | + | + | I |
| 6P20.3-10 | | Firing pin retaining pin | + | + | + | + | + | I |
| 6P20.3-11 | | Extractor axis pin | + | + | + | + | + | I |
| | | Extractor | + | + | + | + | + | PI |
| 6P18.Sb 4 | | Recoil mechanism assembly RPK74 | – | – | – | + | + | |
| 6P20.Sb 4 | | Same AK74 | + | + | – | – | – | PI |
| 6P26.Sb 4 | | » AKSU | – | – | + | – | – | |
| 6P18.Sb 4-1 | | Recoil spring guide RPK74 | – | – | – | + | + | PI |
| 6P20.Sb 4-1 | | Same AK74 | + | + | – | – | – | PI |
| 6P26.Sb 4-1 | | » AKSU | – | – | + | – | – | I |
| 6P18.4-3 | | Recoil spring RPK74 | – | – | – | + | + | I |
| 6P20.4-3 | 6P1.4-3 | Same AK74 | + | + | – | – | – | I |
| 6P18.4-4 | | Recoil spring retainer cap RPK74 | – | – | – | + | + | I |
| 6P20.4-4 | 6P1.4-4 | Same AK74 | + | + | + | – | – | I |

| Designation | Old designation | Name | AK74 | AKS74 | AKS74U | RPK74 | RPKS74 | Level of interchangeability |
|---|---|---|:---:|:---:|:---:|:---:|:---:|:---:|
| 6P18.4-5 | | Forward guide rod for recoil spring RPK74 | - | - | - | + | + | I |
| 6P20.4-5 | 6P 1.4-5 | Forward guide rod for recoil spring AK74 | + | + | + | - | - | I |
| 6P18.Sb 5 | 6P2 Sb 5 | Buttstock assembly RPKS74 | - | - | - | + | - | |
| 6P19.Sb 5 | 6P8.Sb 5 | Same RPKS74 | - | - | - | - | + | |
| 6P20.Sb 5 | | » AK74 | + | - | - | - | - | |
| 6P21.Sb 5 | | » AKS74 | - | + | - | - | - | |
| 6P26.Sb 5 | | » AKS74U | - | - | + | - | - | |
| 6P20.Sb 5-1 | 6P1.Sb 5-1 | Sling swivel assembly | + | - | - | - | - | I |
| 6P21.Sb 5-1 | | Same AKS74 | - | + | + | - | - | I |
| 6P18.Sb 5-2 | 6P2.Sb 5-2 | Cleaning kit trap door assembly RPK74 | - | - | - | + | + | |
| 6P20.Sb 5-2 | | Cleaning kit trap door assembly AK74 | + | - | - | - | - | |
| 6P21.Sb 5-2 | | Metal folding buttstock AK74 | - | + | - | - | - | |
| 6P18.Sb 5-3 | 6P2.Sb 5-3 | Sling swivel assembly RPK74 | - | - | - | + | - | I |
| 6P18.5-1 | 6P2.5-1 | Buttstock RPK74 | - | - | - | + | - | |
| 6P19.5-1 | 6P8.5-1 | Same RPKS74 | - | - | - | - | + | |
| 6P20.5-1 | | » AK74 | + | - | - | - | - | |
| 6P20.5-3 | 56-A-212.5-3 | Buttstock / butt plate screw | + | - | - | + | + | I |
| 6P20.5-4 | 6P1.5-4 | Sling swivel screw | + | - | - | + | - | I |

*Appendix 5 (continued)*

| Designation | Old designation | Name | AK74 | AKS74 | AKS74U | RPK74 | RPKS74 | Level of interchangeability |
|---|---|---|:--:|:--:|:--:|:--:|:--:|:--:|
| | | | **assault rifles** | | | **machine guns** | | |
| 6P20.5-5 | 56-A 212 5 5 | Cleaning kit case retainer spring | + | - | - | + | + | I |
| 6P20.5-6 | 6P1.5-6 | Sling swivel base upper plate | + | - | - | - | - | |
| 6P21.5-6 | | Sling swivel hinge AKS74 | - | + | + | - | - | |
| 6P20.5-7 | 6P1.5-7 | Sling loop AK74 | + | - | - | - | - | |
| 6P21.5-7 | | Sling loop AKS74 | - | + | + | - | - | |
| 6P18.5-7 | 6P2.5-7 | Same RPK74 | - | - | - | + | + | I |
| 6P20.5-8 | 56-A-212.5-8A | Trapdoor | + | - | - | + | + | I |
| 6P18.5-9 | 6P2.5-9 | Trapdoor hinger RPK74 | - | - | - | + | + | |
| 6P20.5 9 | | Same AK74 | + | - | - | - | - | |
| 6P20.5-10 | 56-A-212.5-10 | Trapdoor spring | + | - | - | + | + | PI |
| 6P18.5-10 | 6P2. 5-10 | Sling swivel base RPK74 | - | - | - | + | + | |
| 6P20.5-11 | | Trapdoor axis pin | + | - | - | + | + | |
| 6P20.5-12 | 6P1. 5-12 | Sling swivel base lower plate | + | + | + | - | - | |
| 6P21.5-13 | | Washer for metal stock sling swivel AKS74 | - | + | + | - | - | |
| 6P20.5-16 | | Butt plate | + | - | - | - | - | I |
| 6P18.Sb 6 | 6P2.Sb 6 | Lower handguard assembly RPK74 | - | - | - | + | + | |
| 6P20.Sb 6 | | Same AK74 | + | + | - | - | - | I |
| 6P26.Sb 6 | | » AKSU | - | - | + | - | - | PI |

| Designation | Old designation | Name | AK74 | AKS74 | AKS74U | RPK74 | RPKS74 | Level of interchangeability |
|---|---|---|---|---|---|---|---|---|
| 6P20.6-4 | | Lower handguard spring | + | + | + | – | – | I |
| 6P20.Sb 14 | | Butt stock (plastic) assembly | + | – | – | – | – | |
| 6P20.Sb 7-1 | | Sling swivel assembly | + | – | – | – | – | |
| 6P26.Sb 7 | | Receiver cover assembly AKSU | – | – | + | – | – | |
| 6P26.7-31 | | | – | – | + | – | – | |
| 6P26.7-34 | | Rear sight leaf AKSU | – | – | + | – | – | |
| 6P26.7-32 | | Rear sight leaf axis pin AKSU | – | – | + | – | – | |
| 6P26.7-33 | | Rear sight leaf spring AKSU | – | – | + | – | – | |
| 6P18.Sb 8 | 6P1.Sb 8 | Pistol grip | + | – | – | + | + | PI |
| 6P20.Sb 8 | 6P1.Sb 8B | Same | – | – | – | – | – | PI |
| 6P21.Sb 8 | 6P4.Sb 9 | » | – | + | + | – | – | PI |
| 6P18.Sb 9-3 | 6P2.Sb 9-3 | Bipod latch assembly | – | – | – | + | + | I |
| 6P18.9-7 | 6P2.9-7 | Bipod latch | – | – | – | + | + | I |
| 6P18.9 8 | 6P2.9-8 | Bipod latch axis pin | – | – | – | + | + | I |
| 6P18.9 10 | 6P2.9-10 | Bipopd axis pin | – | – | – | + | + | I |
| 6P18.9 11 | 6P2.9-11 | Bipod spring | – | – | – | + | + | I |

Appendix 5 (continued)

| Designation | Name | Applicability | | | Interchangeability |
|---|---|---|---|---|---|
| | | 6L18 | 6L20 | 6L23 | |
| 6L18.Sb 0-1 | Magazine body 45 rd Bakelite | + | - | - | I |
| 6L23.Sb 1 | Same 30rd injection molded | - | - | + | I |
| 6L20.Sb 0-2 | Magazine follower assembly | + | + | + | I |
| 6L20.Sb 0-3 | Magazine lock plate assembly | + | + | + | I |
| 6L18.Sb 0-4 | Magazine lock plate spring 45 rd magazine | + | - | - | I |
| 6L20.Sb 0-4 | Same 30 rd magazine | - | + | + | I |
| 6L20.Sb 0-5 | Magazine body 30rd Bakelite | - | + | - | I |
| 6L18.0-1 | Magazine follower 45rd magazine | + | - | - | I |
| 6L23.0-1 | Same 30rd injection molded | - | + | + | I |
| 6L18.0-2 | Magaazine lock plate 45rd magazine | + | - | - | I |
| 6L23.0-2 | Same 30rd injection molded | - | + | + | I |
| 6L18.0-9 | Magazine spring 45rd magazine | + | - | - | I |
| 6L20.0-9 | Same 30rd magazine | - | + | + | I |
| 6L20.0-11 | Magazine floor plate | + | + | + | I |
| 6L18.Sb | Magazine for 5.45 mm light machine gun Kalashnikov | | | | I |
| 6L20.Sb | Magaxine for 5.45 mm assault rifle Kalashnikov | | | | I |
| 6L23.Sb | Magazine injection molded for 5.45m assault rifle Kalashnikov [this is the polymer magazine] | | | | I |

Notes: 1. Legend: I - interchangeable, PI - practically interchangeable. 2. Instructions on replacing components products are given in Sec. 5.

## SOME DIFFERENCES IN NAMES FOR PARTS USED IN THIS TRANSLATION AND THE LITERAL TRANSLATION FROM THE RUSSIAN WORDING USED IN THE ORIGINAL MANUAL

| Name used in translation | Name used in original manual |
|---|---|
| auto-sear | auto timer |
| bipod legs | struts for bipod |
| disconector | sear |
| extractor | ejector |
| ejector | deflector |
| firing mechanism | trigger mechanism |
| firing pin | striker |
| gas piston | stem |
| gas tube | base of the handguard |
| gas tube lock | check handguard |
| grip screw | screw connection |
| lower handguard | forearm |
| lower handguard retainer | check ring forearm |
| pistol grip or grip | handle |
| rear sight leaf | sighting plank |
| recoil mechanism assembly | return mechanism |
| recoil spring | return spring |

*[Note: in the original manual this appendix listed names used in the operation manual for parts vs. names used in the drawings and texts of the original Russian version of this manual. The author believed it made more sense to present some of the differeneces between this translation and a more literal translation in this section.]*

# TECHNICAL MAINTENANCE FOR
# ASSAULT RIFLES AND LIGHT MACHINE GUNS

## 1. General information

1.1. Assault rifles and machine guns are maintained in order to keep them in combat readiness, warning of issues and early detection and elimination of detected faults are exposed during technical maintenance

1.2. Technical maintenance for assault rifles and machine guns includes:
visual inspection;
routine maintenance;
maintenance level №1;
maintenance level № 2;
seasonal maintenance.

1.3. Maintenance of optical and night sights, fixed (installed on the assault rifles and light machine guns) to the weapon is conducted per the timing and level specified in the documentation for these sights.

## 2. Testing assault rifles and light machine guns

2.1. Testing of assault rifles and light machine guns is carried out by officials in the terms established by the Internal Service VS USSR, as well as before shooting, and issuing in order to carry out combat missions.

2.2. Soldiers and sergeants make sure that the assault rifles and light machine guns, are inspected every day and, in addition, before going for use on guard duty; before going for use in a class; during cleaning; and, in a combat situation - periodically during the day and before use on a combat mission.

2.3 Procedure and scope of the inspection of weapons are set out in the Operation Manual for 5.45mm Kalashnikov Assault Rifles (AK74, AKS74, AK74N, AKS74N) and 5.45-mm Kalashnikov light machine guns (RPK74, RPKS74, RPK74N, RPKS74N) and in the Operation Manual for 5 45-mm Kalashnikov Shortened Assault Rifle AKS74U (AKS74UN2); in the future they will be referred to the Manuals.

2.4. Defetcts identified during the inspection must be repaired immediately in the division. Ifthe weapon cannot be repaired in the division, send the weapon to the repair depot.

### 3. Routine maintenance assault rifles and light machine guns

3.1. Routine maintenance is carried out on the weapon:

after exercises in the field without firing;

after guard duty;

in preparation for firing;

after firing live and (or) blanks in combat situations and (or) during prolonged exercises during a lull in battle and during breaks in the exercises;

if the weapon has not been used but has been stored in a pyramid stack - at least once every 7 days, and in hot and dry climate - every 2-4 days.

3.2. Routine maintenance of weapons performed by unit personnel it in designated areas.

3.3. During the routine maintenance, the weapon is inspected, cleaned and lubricated with partial disassembly of weapon, as described in the manual for the weapon.

3.4. Monitoring of the routine maintenance is cttied out by officers of the unit.

### 4. Maintenance level №1 for assault rifles and light machine guns

4.1. Maintenance level №1 for the weapon is performed at least once a year, as well as:

after prolonged exercises and live firing;

after a long exposue to rain, water or snow;

after servere contamination;

when prepating the weapon for short-term storage.

4.2. Maintenance level №1 for the weapon is performed by unit personnel in designated areas with the assistance of experts, if necessary, from the repair depot.

4.3. When maintenance level №1 is performed, inspection and service are done concurrently; it is necessary that this is done by an individual versed in the full disassembly of the weapon and its parts.

During the maintanance the repair service technician inspects and verifies the weapon using military gauges, as well as eliminates any identified faults that do not require weapons be sent to the repair depot.

When necessary, combat readiness checks are done.

4.4. Maintenance organization, management and control for the maintenance level №1 are provided by the company commander (battery), who also holds a weapons control inspection after maintenance.

## 5. Maintenance level №2 for assault rifles and light machine guns

5.1. Maintenance level №2 is performed depending on the intensity and conditions of use of weapons at least once in 4 years.

Maintenance level №2 is recommended to be combined with the next scheduled maintenance level №1.

5.2. Maintenance level №2 for weapons carried out by experts from the repair depot under supervision of the unit leadership in designated areas. When this is done complete disassembly of a sample of the weapons is performed.

5.3. When maintenance level №2 is performed, perform the work for maintenance level №1, and check of the weapons by a specialist from the repair depot is done at the level specified in the check list for technical condition of the weapon (Sect. 4.3 of this Manual).

5.4. Maintenance level №2 for weapons is performed by the plan of the military unit (PAB service). The company commander (battery) organizes the maintenance level №2 and directs it, and inspects sample weapons after maintenance as specified in this manual.

If the maintenance level №2 is performed for a light machine gun, the company commander (battery) notes it on the form.

## 6. Seasonal maintenance for assault rifles and light machine guns

6.1. Seasonal mainteanance for weapons is performed in the areas of deployment of the unit, and provides lubricant for the transition from summer to winter and from winter to summer.

6.2. Seasonal maintenance should be combined with the next Maintenance №1 or №2.

6.3. When seasonal maintenance is performed, perform all the work for maintenance №1, and in addition:
the weapon is completely disassembled according to the manual;
after complete disassembly of the weapon the metal parts are washed in liquid rifle solvent and wiped dry with a cloth;
lubricated with lubricant for the weapons provided for the upcoming season of operation;
for weapons with night sights, batteries are cleaned, filled with electrolyte and made fresh via a controled discharge-charge cycle;

6.4. Seasonal maintenance of weapons is performed by the owners in the subdivision in the designated areas.

Service of the batteries performed in the repair depot of the unit.

6.5. Seasonal maintenance of weapons units is performed under the plan of the military unit.

The company commander (battery) organizes the seasonal maintenance and directs it, and inspects sample weapons after maintenance as specified in this manual.

# RATE OF APPLICATION FOR MATERIALS AND SPARE PARTS FOR MEDIUM LEVEL REPAIRS

## 5.45mm KALASHNIKOV ASSAULT RIFLES (6P20, 6P21, 6P26, 6P20N1, 6P21N1, 6P26N2) AND 5.45-mm KALASHNIKOV LIGHT MACHINE GUNS (6P18, 6P19, 6P18N1, 6P19N1)

## RATE OF APPLICATION OF SPARE PARTS FOR MEDIUM LEVEL REPAIRS 5.45MM KALASHNIKOV ASSAULT RIFLES (6P20, 6P21, 6P26, 6P20N1, 6P21N1, 6P26N2)

| Line № | Designation or standard № | OKP code | Suf. | Name | Number used in the weapon, pcs. | Rate of application of spare parts for repair of 100 weapons | | |
|---|---|---|---|---|---|---|---|---|
| | | | | | | 6P20 | 6P21 | 6P26 |
| 1 | 6P20.0-5 or | 7114130154 | 01 | Auto-sear | 1 | 1 | 1 | 1 |
| | 6P20.0-15 | 7114130167 | 07 | Ssame | 1 | 1 | 1 | 1 |
| 2 | 6P20.Sb 5-1 | 7114130326 | 10 | Sling swivel assembly | 1 | 5 | — | — |
| 3 | 6P21.Sb 5-1 | 7114130732 | 00 | Same AKS74 | 1 | — | 5 | 5 |
| 4 | 6P20.0-19 | 7114130175 | 07 | Grip screw | 1 | 3 | 3 | 3 |
| 5 | 6P20.0-27 | 7114130181 | 09 | Trigger axis pin bushing | 1 | 4 | 4 | 4 |
| 6 | 6P20.3-11 | 7114130295 | 00 | Extractor | 1 | 10 | 10 | 10 |
| 7 | 6P20.0-16 | 7114130168 | 06 | Grip nut | 1 | 2 | 2 | 2 |
| 8 | 6P20.Sb 0-2 | 7114130133 | 06 | Retarder assembly | 1 | 1 | 1 | 1 |
| 9 | 6P20.3-4 | 7114130286 | 01 | Bolt body | 1 | 1 | 1 | 1 |
| 10 | 6P20.Sb 3-2 | 7114130272 | 07 | Bolt assembly | 1 | 1 | 1 | — |
| 11 | 6P20.5-16 | 7114130341 | 00 | Butt plate | 1 | 1 | — | — |
| 12 | 6P20.0-7 | 7114130156 | 10 | Retarder latch | 1 | 1 | 1 | 1 |
| 13 | 6P20.0-11 | 7114130161 | 02 | Magazine catch | 1 | 1 | 1 | 1 |
| 14 | 6P21.0-42 or | 7114130718 | 09 | Folding stock front latch hook  AKS74 | 1 | — | 3 | 3 |
| | 6P21.0-44 | 7114130719 | 08 | Same | 1 | — | 3 | 3 |
| 15 | 6P20.2-3 | 7114130503 | 00 | Rear sight elevation slide latch | 1 | 2 | 2 | 3 |
| 16 | 6H4.2-10 | 7114120989 | 04 | Snap hook for bayonet hanger | 1 | 10 | 10 | — |
| 17 | 6P20.Sb 5-2 | 7114130327 | 09 | Cleaning kit trapdoor assembly AK74 | 1 | 3 | — | — |

| Line № | Designation or standard № | OKP code | Suf. | Name | Number used in the weapon, pcs. | Rate of application of spare parts for repair of 100 weapons | | |
|---|---|---|---|---|---|---|---|---|
| | | | | | | 6P20 | 6P21 | 6P26 |
| 18 | 6L20.0-11 | 7114131531 | 03 | Magazine floor plate | 1 | 2 | 2 | 3 |
| 19 | 6P20.0-1 | 7114130149 | 09 | Receiver cover | 1 | 1 | 1 | — |
| 20 | 6P26.Sb 7 | 7114132395 | 00 | Receiver cover assembly AKSU | 1 | — | — | 1 |
| 21 | 6P20.0-8 | 7114130157 | 09 | Trigger | 1 | 1 | 1 | 1 |
| or | 6P20.0-29 | 7114130183 | 07 | » | 1 | 1 | 1 | 1 |
| 22 | 6P20.0-2 | 7114130151 | 04 | Hammer | 1 | 1 | 1 | 1 |
| 23 | 6L20.Sb | 7114130001 | 06 | Magazine | 1 | 5 | 5 | 5 |
| or | 6L23.Sb | 7114130002 | 05 | Magazine injection molded | 1 | 5 | 5 | 5 |
| 24 | 6P20.Sb 4 | 7114110311 | 05 | Recoil mechanism assembly AK74 | 1 | 2 | 2 | — |
| 25 | 6P26.Sb 4 | 7114132301 | 00 | » AKSU | 1 | — | — | 2 |
| 26 | 6P20.Sb 0-1 | 7114130132 | 07 | Firing mechanism AK74 | 1 | 1 | 1 | — |
| 27 | 6P26.Sb 0-1 | 7114132011 | 07 | » AKSU | 1 | — | — | 1 |
| 28 | 6P20.4-4 | 7114130321 | 04 | Recoil spring retainer cap | 1 | 1 | 1 | — |
| 29 | 6P20.1-32 | 7114130239 | 08 | Front sight post AK74 | 1 | 5 | 5 | — |
| 30 | 6P26.1-17 | 7114132171 | 03 | » AKSU | 1 | — | — | 5 |
| 31 | 6P20.1-40 | 7114130251 | 01 | Upper handguard AK74 | 1 | 5 | 5 | — |
| 32 | 6P26.1-40 | 7114132195 | 06 | » AKSU | 1 | — | — | 5 |
| 33 | 6P20.Sb 1-12 | 7114130212 | 08 | Upper handguard/gas tube assembly AK74 | 1 | 2 | 2 | — |
| 34 | 6P26.Sb 1-2 | 7114132131 | 00 | Upper handguard/gas tube assembly AKSU | 1 | — | — | 2 |
| 35 | 6P20.Sb 4-1 | 7114130312 | 05 | Recoil spring guide AK74 | 1 | 1 | 1 | — |
| 36 | 6P26.Sb 4-1 | 7114132302 | 10 | Same AKSU | 1 | — | — | 1 |

| Line № | Designation or standard № | OKP code | Suf. | Name | Number used in the weapon, pcs. | 6P20 | 6P21 | 6P26 |
|---|---|---|---|---|---|---|---|---|
| 37 | 6P20.0-4 | 7114130153 | 02 | Retarder base | 1 | 1 | 1 | — |
|  | or | | | | | | | |
| 38 | 6P20.0-32 | 7114130187 | 03 | Same | 1 | 1 | 1 | — |
| 39 | 6P20.1-31 | 7114130238 | 09 | Front sight base AK74 | 1 | 1 | 1 | — |
|  | 6P26.1-31 | 7114132185 | 08 | Same AKSU | 1 | — | — | 1 |
| 40 | 6P26.0-39 | 7114132081 | 04 | Trigger limiter/spacer AKSU | 1 | — | — | 3 |
| 41 | 6P20.0-17 | 7114130169 | 05 | Retarder catch axis pin | 1 | 2 | 2 | 6 |
| 42 | 6P20.3-10 | 7114130294 | 01 | Extractor axis pin | 1 | 6 | 6 | 3 |
| 43 | 6P21.0-40 | 7114130716 | 00 | Folding stock front latch axis pin AKS74 | 1 | — | 3 | 5 |
| 44 | 6P20 0-13 | 7114130163 | 00 | Magazine catch axis pin | 1 | 5 | 5 | 5 |
| 45 | 6P26.0-21 | 7114132061 | 08 | Receiver cover axis pin AKSU | 1 | — | — | 5 |
| 46 | 6P20.5-11 | 7114130339 | 05 | Trapdoor cover axis pin | 1 | 5 | — | 5 |
| 47 | 6P21.0-41 | 7114130717 | 10 | Folding stock axis pin AKS74/AKSU | 1 | — | 5 | 5 |
| 48 | 6P20.0-25 | 7114130178 | 04 | Firing mechanism axis pin | 3 | 5 | 5 | 5 |
| 49 | 6P26.7-32 | 7114132425 | 00 | Rear sight leaf axis pin AKSU | 1 | — | — | 1 |
| 50 | 6P20.Sb 1-3 | 7114130202 | 10 | Selector lever assembly | 1 | 1 | 1 | — |
| 51 | 6P26.0-20 | 7114132059 | 02 | Flash hider AKSU | 1 | — | — | 7 |
| 52 | 6P20.2-1 | 7114130501 | 02 | Rear sight leaf | 1 | 1 | 1 | — |
| 53 | 6P20.Sb 2 | 7114130268 | 03 | Rear sight leaf assembly | 1 | 1 | 1 | 1 |
| 54 | 6L20.Sb 0-2 | 7114131511 | 07 | Magazine follower assembly | 1 | 1 | 1 | 1 |
|  | or | | | | | | | |
| 55 | 6L23.0-1 | 7114131701 | 03 | Magazine follower injection molded | 1 | 1 | 1 | 1 |
| 56 | 6H4.Sb 2-3 | 7114120984 | 09 | Hanger assembly for bayonet | 1 | 5 | 5 | — |
|  | 6P20.Sb 5 | 7114130325 | 00 | Buttstock assembly AK74 | 1 | 3 | — | — |
| 57 | 6P21.Sb 5 | 7114130731 | 01 | Same AKS74 | 1 | — | 3 | — |
| 58 | 6P26.Sb 5 | 7114132341 | 03 | » AKSU | 1 | — | — | 3 |

| Line № | Designation or standard № | OKP code | Suf. | Name | Number used in the weapon, pcs. | Rate of application of spare parts for repair of 100 weapons | | |
|---|---|---|---|---|---|---|---|---|
| | | | | | | 6P20 | 6P21 | 6P26 |
| 59 | 6P20.0-6 | 7114130155 | 00 | Auto-sear spring | 1 | 2 | 2 | 2 |
| 60 | 6P20.0-3 | 7114130152 | 03 | Mainspring | 1 | 1 | 1 | 1 |
| 61 | 6P20.4-3 | 7114130319 | 09 | Recoil spring | 1 | 5 | 5 | 5 |
| 62 | 6P20.3-7 | 7114130289 | 09 | Extractore spring | 1 | 5 | 5 | 5— |
| 63 | 6P20.0-28 | 7114130182 | 08 | Retarder spring | 1 | 5 | 5 | 5 |
| 64 | 6P21.0-39 | 7114130715 | 01 | Folding stock front latch spring AKS74 | 1 | — | 5 | 2 |
| 65 | 6P20.0-12 | 7114130162 | 01 | Magazine catch spring | 1 | 2 | 2 | — |
| 66 | 6P20.2-4 | 7114130504 | 10 | Rear sight elevation slide latch spring | 1 | 3 | 3 | — |
| 67 | 6P20.5-10 | 7114130337 | 07 | Trapdoor cover spring | 1 | 2 | — | — |
| 68 | 6P20.1-45 | 7114130257 | 06 | Gas tube tensioning spring | 1 | 5 | 5 | — |
| 69 | 6P20.5-5 | 7114130335 | 09 | Cleaning kit case retainer spring | 1 | 1 | — | — |
| 70 | 6P20.0-23 | 7114130177 | 05 | Rear sight leaf spring | 1 | 1 | 1 | — |
| 71 | 6L23.0-2 together with 6L20.0-9 or | 7114131702 | 02 | Magazine lock plate injection molded | 1 | 2 | 2 | 2 |
| | 6L20.Sb 0-4 | 7114131528 | 09 | Magazine spring | 1 | 1 | 1 | 1 |
| 72 | 6P21.0-36 | 7114131513 | 05 | Magazine lock plate spring | 1 | 5 | 5 | 5 |
| 73 | 6P20.1-38 | 7114130712 | 04 | Folding stock rear latch spring AKS74 | 1 | — | 4 | 4 |
| 74 | 6P26.1-38 | 7114130248 | 07 | Muzzle deveice retainer spring | 1 | 3 | 3 | — |
| 75 | 6P26.1-22 | 7114132193 | 08 | Flash hider retainer spring AKSU | 1 | — | — | 10 |
| 76 | | 7114132176 | 09 | Gas tube retainer spring AKSU | 1 | — | — | 2 |
| 77 | 6P20.6-4 | 7114130347 | 05 | Lower handguard spring | 1 | 8 | 8 | 8 |
| 78 | 6P26.7-33 | 7114132426 | 10 | Rear sight leaf spring AKSU | 1 | — | — | 8 |
| | 6P20.0-10 | 7114130159 | 07 | Disconnector spring | 1 | 2 | 2 | 2 |

| Line № | Designation or standard № | OKP code | Suf. | Name | Number used in the weapon, pcs. | 6P20 | 6P21 | 6P26 |
|---|---|---|---|---|---|---|---|---|
| 79 | 6H4.Sb 1-3 | 7114120941 | 09 | Wrist strap assembly for bayonet | 1 | 4 | 4 | — |
| 80 | 6P20.Sb 8 | 7114130361 | 07 | Pistol grip AK74 | 1 | 1 | — | — |
| 81 | 6P21.Sb 8 | 7114130821 | 00 | Same AKS74 | 1 | — | 1 | — |
| 82 | 6P4.Sb 9 | 7114120681 | 10 | » | 1 | — | — | 3 |
| 33 | 6P20.4-5 | 7114130322 | 03 | Recoil spring forward guide rod | 1 | 1 | 1 | 1 |
| 84 | 6P20.0-20 | 7114130173 | 09 | Muzzle brake | 1 | 3 | 3 | — |
|  | or |  |  |  |  |  |  |  |
|  | 6P20.Sb 0-6 | 7114130137 | 02 | same | 1 | 3 | 3 | — |
| 85 | 6P20.3-5 | 7114130287 | 00 | Firing pim | 1 | 2 | 2 | 2 |
| 86 | 6H4.2-8 | 7114120987 | 04 | Bayonet retainer spring | 1 | 1 | 1 | — |
| 87 | 6P20.1-41 | 7114130252 | 00 | Upper handguard retainer spring AK74 | 1 | 12 | 12 | 12 |
| 88 | 6P26.1-41 | 7114132196 | 05 | Same AKSU | 1 | — | — | 4 |
| 89 | 6P26.1-36 | 7114132191 | IC | Gas tube retainer plunger pin AKSU | 1 | — | — | 7 |
| 90 | 6P26.1-37 | 7114132192 | 09 | Flash hider retainer pin AKSU | 1 | — | — | 3 |
| 91 | 6P21.0-35 | 7114130711 | 05 | Folding stock rear stock latch AKS74 | 1 | — | 3 | 3 |
| 92 | 6P20.1-37 | 7114130247 | 08 | Muzzle brake retainer pin | 1 | 3 | 3 | — |
| 93 | 6P20.2-2 | 7114130502 | 01 | Clamp straps pridelnyh | 1 | 2 | 2 | — |
| 94 | 6P20.Sb 6 | 7114130342 | 10 | Lower handguard assembly AK74 | 1 | 3 | 3 | — |
| 95 | 6P26.Sb 6 | 7114132375 | 04 | Same AKSU | 1 | — | — | 3 |
| 96 | 6P26.7-31 | 7114132424 | 01 | Rear sight leaf AKSU | 1 | — | — | 4 |
|  | or |  |  |  |  |  |  |  |
|  | 6P26.7-34 | 7114132427 | 09 | same | 1 | — | — | 4 |

216

| Line № | Designation or standard № | OKP code | Suf. | Name | Number used in the weapon, pcs. | Rate of application of spare parts for repair of 100 weapons | | |
|---|---|---|---|---|---|---|---|---|
| | | | | | | 6P20 | 6P21 | 6P26 |
| 97 | 6P20.1-28 | 7114130235 | 01 | Lower handguard retainer latch | 1 | 2 | 2 | 2 |
| 98 | 6P20.Sb 1-6 | 7114130205 | 07 | Gas tube latch assembly | 1 | 2 | 2 | — |
| 99 | 6P20.0-9 | 7114130158 | 08 | Disconnector | 1 | 1 | 1 | 1 |
| 100 | 6P20.3-9 | 7114130293 | 09 | Firing pin retaining pin | 1 | 5 | 5 | 5 |
| 101 | 6P21.0-37 | 7114130713 | 03 | Folding stock rear latch retainer pin AKS74 | 1 | — | 4 | 4 |
| 102 | 6P20.1-33 | 7114130242 | 02 | Muzzle brake retainer pin | 1 | 6 | 6 | — |
| 103 | 6P26.1-35 | 7114132189 | 04 | Retaining pin AKSU | 1 | — | — | 3 |
| 104 | 6P20.3-3 | 7114130284 | 03 | Gs piston pin | 1 | 2 | 2 | 2 |
| 105 | 6P20.3-2 | 7114130283 | 04 | Gas piston AK74 | 1 | 2 | 2 | — |
| 106 | 6P26.3-2 | 7114132276 | 06 | Same AKSU | 1 | — | — | 2 |
| 107 | 6P20.5-4 | 7114130333 | 00 | Sling swivel screw | 2 | 5 | — | — |
| 108 | 6P20.5-3 | 7114130329 | 07 | Buttstock / butt plate screw | 4 | 6 | — | — |

# RATE OF APPLICATION OF MATERIALS FOR MEDIUM LEVEL REPAIRS 5.45MM KALASHNIKOV ASSAULT RIFLES
## (6P20, 6P21, 6P26, 6P20N1, 6P21N1, 6P26N2)

| Material | OKP code | Material characteristics | | | Unit of measurement | Rate of application for repair of 100 weapons | | |
|---|---|---|---|---|---|---|---|---|
| | | type, grade | № of standard | variation (dimebsion, № of standard) | | 6P20 | 6P21 | 6P26 |
| **Rolled ferrous metal** | | | | | | | | |
| Steel hot-rolled structural carbon quality bars | 0950100000 | Steel 50 | GOST 1050-74 | Round Ø 50 mm GOST 2590-71 | kg | 0.104 | 0.173 | 0.162 |
| | | Steel 50 | GOST 1050-74 | Same, Ø 6.5 mm | kg | 0.194 | 0.194 | 0.194 |
| | | Steel 50 | GOST 1050-74 | Same, Ø 9.0 mm | kg | 0.271 | 0.301 | 0.339 |
| | | Steel 50 | GOST 1050-74 | Same, Ø 13.0 mm | kg | 0.029 | 0.029 | 0.029 |
| | | Steel 50 | GOST 1050-74 | Same, Ø 23.0 mm | kg | 0.110 | 0.110 | 0.110 |
| | | Steel 50 | GOST 1050-74 | Strip 14×25 mm GOST 103-76 | kg | — | 0.049 | 0.049 |
| Total... | | | | | kg | 0.708 | 0.856 | 0.883 |
| **Products further recast** | | | | | | | | |
| Steel billet carbon quality calibrated cold drawn | 1141000000 | Steel 50 | GOST 1051-73 | Round Ø 3.0 mm GOST 7417-75 | kg | 0.021 | 0.006 | 0.023 |
| | | Steel 15 | GOST 1051-73 | Same, Ø 10.5 mm | kg | 0.026 | 0.026 | — |
| Total... | | | | | kg | 0.047 | 0.032 | 0.023 |

| Material | OKP code | Material characteristics | | | Unit of measurement | Rate of application for repair of 100 weapons | | |
|---|---|---|---|---|---|---|---|---|
| | | type. grade | № of standard | variation (dimebsion, № of standard) | | 6P20 | 6P21 | 6P26 |
| **Hardware** | | | | | | | | |
| Carbon steel spring wire | 1221000000 | Grade 1 | GOST 9389-75 | Ø 0.5 mm GOST 9389-75 | кг | 0.001 | 0.001 | — |
| | | Grade 1 | GOST 9389-75 | Ø 0.56 mm GOST 9389-75 | кг | 0.001 | 0.001 | — |
| | | Grade 1 | GOST 9389-75 | Ø 0.6 mm GOST 9389-75 | кг | 0.002 | 0.002 | 0.002 |
| | | Grade 1 | GOST 9389-75 | Ø 0.8 mm GOST 9389-75 | кг | 0.003 | — | — |
| | | Grade 1 | GOST 9389-75 | Ø 1.0 mm GOST 9389-75 | кг | 0.028 | 0.005 | — |
| | | Grade 1 | GOST 9389-75 | Ø 1.1 mm GOST 9389-75 | кг | — | 0.007 | 0.014 |
| | | Grade 1 | GOST 9389-75 | Ø 1.2 mm GOST 9389-75 | кг | — | 0.021 | 0.021 |
| | | Grade 1 | GOST 9389-75 | Ø 1.4 mm GOST 9389-75 | кг | 0.008 | 0.008 | 0.008 |
| **Total...** | | | | | кг | 0.043 | 0.045 | 0.045 |
| Wire made of carbon structural steel | 1221000000 | Steel 50 | GOST 17305-71 | Ø 2.5 mm GOST 17305—71 | кг | 0.100 | 0.100 | 0.100 |
| | | Steel 40 | GOST 17305-71 | Ø 3.0 mm GOST 17305—71 | кг | 0.026 | 0.070 | 0.044 |
| **Total...** | | | | | кг | 0.126 | 0.170 | 0.144 |

| Material | OKP code | Material characteristics | | | Unit of measurement | Rate of application for repair of 100 weapons | | |
|---|---|---|---|---|---|---|---|---|
| | | type. grade | № of standard | variation (dimebsion. № of standard) | | 6P20 | 6P21 | 6P26 |
| Steel wire welding | 1211010000 | SV-08 | GOST 2246-70 | Ø 2 mm GOST 2246-70 | kg | 0.300 | 0.300 | 0.300 |
| Tape cold-rolled spring steel | 1231000000 | 50HFA | GOST 2283-79 | Tape 0.5×14 mm GOST 2283-79 | kg | — | — | 0.007 |
| | | 50HFA | GOST 2283-79 | Same, 0.7X28 mm | kg | 0.016 | 0.016 | — |
| | | U8A | GOST 2283-79 | Same, 1.45×14 mm | kg | 0.021 | 0.021 | — |
| Total... | | | | | kg | 0.037 | 0.037 | 0.007 |
| Tape cold-rolled carbon structural steel | 1231000000 | Srteel 50 | GOST 2284-79 | Tape 0.45×28 mm GOST 2284-79 | kg | 0.007 | 0.007 | 0.007 |
| | | Srteel 50 | GOST 2284-79 | Same, 0.7×20 mm | kg | 0.024 | 0.024 | — |
| | | Srteel 40 | GOST 2284-79 | Same, 1×16 mm | kg | 0.021 | 0.021 | — |
| | | Srteel 50 | GOST 2284-79 | Same, I X34 mm | kg | 0.043 | 0.043 | 0.041 |
| | | Srteel 40 | GOST 2284-79 | Same, 2×16 mm | kg | — | 0.012 | 0.012 |
| | | Srteel 40 | GOST 2284-79 | Same, 1.4×14 mm | kg | — | 0.018 | 0.018 |
| Total... | | | | | kg | 0.095 | 0.125 | 0.078 |
| Coated metal electrodes for manual metal arc welding and surfacing | 272000000 | | GOST 9467-75 | GOST 9466-75 | kg | 0.300 | 0.300 | 0.300 |
| **Chemical products** | | | | | | | | |
| Acetone technical grade | 2418110130 | 1st Grade | GOST 2768-84 | | kg | 0.050 | 0.050 | — |
| Ammonium carbonate pure | 2621160781 | Ch | GOST 3770-75 | | kg | 0.200 | 0.200 | 0.200 |

220

| Material | OKP code | Material characteristics | | | Unit of measurement | Rate of application for repair of 100 weapons | | |
|---|---|---|---|---|---|---|---|---|
| | | type, grade | № of standard | variation (dimebsion. № of standard) | | 6P20 | 6P21 | 6P26 |
| Calcium carbide | 2155310000 | A | GOST 1460-81 | | kg | 0.250 | 0.250 | 0.250 |
| Alcohol-soluble nigrosine | 2463229010 | | GOST 9307-78 E | | kg | 0.160 | 0.160 | 0.160 |
| Polyvinyl butyral | 2215120301 | PSh | GOST 9439-85 | | kg | 0.640 | 0.640 | 0.640 |
| Paste PHZ (such as GOI) medium | 2123241120 | № 3 | TU 6-18-178-80 | | kg | 0.010 | 0.010 | 0.010 |
| Polyethylenepolyamine technical grade | 2413450000 | A | TU 6-02-594-80 | | kg | 0.020 | 0.020 | 0.020 |
| Rectified ethyl alcohol technical grade | 9182100000 | | GOST 18300-72 | | kg | 0.015 | 0.015 | 0.015 |
| Phenol formaldehyde resin | 2225110302 | SOZh-309 (VIAM-B) | GOST 20907-75 | | kg | 0.200 | 0.200 | 0.200 |
| Two part epoxy, uncured | 2146140100 | ED-16 | GOST 10587-84 | | kg | 0.150 | 0.150 | 0.150 |
| Potassium dichromate technical grade | | | GOST 26528- E | | kg | 0.040 | 0.040 | 0.040 |
| **Paint and varnish products** | | | | | | | | |
| Primer phosphating | 2313630104 | VL-02 | GOST 12707-77 | | kg | 3.600 | 3.600 | 3.600 |
| Adhesive Phenol-polyvinyl-acetate | 2252110103 | BF-4 1st Grade | GOST 12172-74 | | kg | 0.100 | 0.100 | 0.100 |
| Lacquer black | 2311130600 | BT-577 | GOST 5631-79 | | kg | 0.050 | 0.050 | 0.050 |
| Varnish NTs-62 black | 2314110102 | | OST 6-10-391-74 | | kg | 0.050 | 0.050 | 0.050 |
| Varnish NTs-5119 | 2314113500 | | OST 6-10-392-76 | | kg | 1.000 | 0.500 | 0.500 |
| Polish ITs-5119 | 2314114100 | | OST 6-10-392-76 | | kg | 0.500 | 0.250 | 0.250 |
| Solvent | 2319130300 | 646 | GOST 18188-72 | | kg | 3.600 | 3.600 | 3.600 |

221

| Material | OKP code | Material characteristics | | | Unit of measurement | Rate of application for repair of 100 weapons | | |
| --- | --- | --- | --- | --- | --- | --- | --- | --- |
| | | type. grade | № of standard | variation (dimebsion. № of standard) | | 6P20 | 6P21 | 6P26 |
| Solvent carboniferous technical grade | 2415710130 | A | GOST 1928-79 | | kg | 4.800 | 4.800 | .800 |
| **Pulp and paper products** newsprint | 5431112200 | B | GOST 6445-74 E | | kg | 0.200 | 0.200 | 0.200 |
| **Products of the textile industry** Wiper rags assorted fine | 8181000000 | Art. 625 | TU 63 178-77-82 | | kg | 0.800 | 0.800 | 0.800 |
| Cotton wool, furniture | 8195331110 | Art. 11 | GOST 5679-74 | | kg | 0.100 | 0.100 | 0.100 |
| Webbing belt heavy two-layer with a filling | 8151410000 | LRT Art. 170 t-r | GOST 16996-71 | Width 9.0 mm | kg | 0.100 | 0.100 | — |
| Bleached household muslin | 8319600000 | Art. 6439 | GOST 11109-74 | | M | 1.200 | 1.200 | 1.200 |
| **Products of the leather industry** Leather saddlery smooth or pebbled brown form L | 8617000000 | | GOST 1904-81 | Thickness 1.4-2.5 mm | dm$^2$ | 11.500 | 11.500 | — |
| **Fuels and lubricants** Spindle oil | 0253410101 | AU | GOST 1642-75 | | kg | 6.000 | 6.000 | 6.000 |

| Material | OKP code | Material characteristics | | | Unit of measurement | Rate of application for repair of 100 weapons | | |
|---|---|---|---|---|---|---|---|---|
| | | type. grade | № of standard | variation (dimebsion. № of standard) | | 6P20 | 6P21 | 6P26 |
| Lubricant rifle liquid | 0254530102 | RZh | GOST 9811-61 | | kg | 6.000 | 6.000 | 6.000 |
| **Miscellaneous materials** | | | | | | | | |
| Rivets (grommets) | 9675950000 | ZSP-96 № 25 | OST 17-600-81 | | kg | 0.500 | 0.500 | — |
| Brush, panel KFK | 4833270000 | № 8 | GOST 10597-80 | | pc. | 0.5 | 0.5 | 0.5 |
| Oxygen, gaseous technical Grade | 2114110100 | | GOST 5583-78 | | M³ | 0.200 | 0.200 | 0.200 |
| Contact paper | 0258120100 | | OST 38 0116-76 | | kg | 0.040 | 0.040 | 0.040 |
| Laundry soap solid | 9144110000 | | GOST 790-69 | | kg | 0.100 | 0.100 | 0.100 |
| Seals metal alloy type I | | | GOST 18677-73 | Size 6×10 mm GOST 18677—73 | kg | 0.020 | 0.020 | 0.020 |
| ADIM | | | | | | | | |
| Silk fabrics for screens | 8378070000 | | GOST 4403-77 | | dm² | 4.800 | 4.800 | 4.800 |
| Charcoal cloth (hemp) | | | GOST 12285-77 | | kg | 0.200 | 0.200 | 0.200 |
| Sandpaper 2 740 × 50.S2.24A.12MA | 3985000000 | grit 12 | GOST 5009-82 | | M | 0.200 | 0.200 | 0.200 |
| Sandpaper 2 740 × 50.S2.24A.25MA | 3985000000 | grit 25 | GOST 5009-82 | | M | 0.200 | 0.200 | 0.200 |
| Sanpaper 2 740 × 50.S2.24A.40MA | 39850000 | grit 40 | GOST 5009-82 | | M | 0.200 | 0.200 | 0.200 |

# RATE OF APPLICATION OF SPARE PARTS FOR MEDIUM LEVEL REPAIRS 5.45-mm KALASHNIKOV LIGHT MACHINE GUNS (6P18, 6P19, 6P18N1, 6P19N1)

| Line № | Designation or standard № | OKP code | Suf. | Name | Number used in the weapon, pcs. | Rate of application of spare parts for repair of 100 weapons | |
| --- | --- | --- | --- | --- | --- | --- | --- |
| | | | | | | 6P18 | 6P19 |
| 1 | 6P20.0-15 | 7114130167 | 07 | Auto-sear | 1 | 1 | 1 |
| | or 6P20.0-5 | 7114130154 | 01 | Same | 1 | 1 | 1 |
| 2 | 6P19.Sb 1-10 | | | Sling swivel assembly | 1 | — | 2 |
| 3 | 6P18.Sb 5-3 | 7115240254 | 02 | Same | 1 | 2 | 2 |
| 4 | 6P18.2-7 | | | Windage adjustment screw | 1 | 2 | 2 |
| 5 | 6P20.3-11 | 7114130295 | 00 | Extractor | 1 | 10 | 10 |
| 6 | 6P20.0-19 | 7114130175 | 07 | Grip screw | 1 | 2 | 2 |
| 7 | 6P20.0-27 | 7114130181 | 09 | Trigger axis pin bushing | 1 | 3 | 3 |
| 8 | 6P18.2-9 | | | Grip nut | 1 | 1 | 1 |
| 9 | 6P20.0-16 | 7114130168 | 06 | Same | 1 | 2 | 2 |
| 10 | 6P20.Sb 0-2 | 7114130133 | 06 | Retarder assembly | 1 | 1 | 1 |
| 11 | 6P20.Sb 3-2 | 7114130272 | 07 | Bolt assembly | 1 | 1 | 1 |
| 12 | 6P20.3-4 | 7114130286 | 01 | Bolt body | 1 | 1 | 1 |
| 13 | 6P19.1-52 | 7115240631 | 08 | Stock latch | 1 | 2 | 2 |
| 14 | 6P18.5-2 | 7115240262 | 02 | Butt plate | 1 | — | 1 |
| 15 | 6P 19.0-25 | 7115131045 | 05 | Stock latch hook | 1 | — | 1 |
| 16 | 6P19N.0-28 | | | Stock latch hook (only for 6P19N1) | 1 | 1 | — |
| 17 | 6P18.9-7 | 7115240304 | 09 | Retarder latch | 1 | 1 | 1 |
| 18 | 6P20.0-7 | 7114130156 | 10 | Same | 1 | 1 | 1 |
| 19 | 6P20.0-11 | 7114130161 | 02 | Magazine catch | 1 | 1 | 1 |

| Line № | Designation or standard № | OKP code | Suf. | Name | Number used in the weapon, pcs. | Rate of application of spare parts for repair of 100 weapons 6P18 | Rate of application of spare parts for repair of 100 weapons 6P19 |
|---|---|---|---|---|---|---|---|
| 20 | 6P20.2-3 | 7114130503 | 00 | Rear sight elevation slide latch | 1 | 2 | 2 |
| 21 | 6P18.Sb 5-2 | 7115240253 | 03 | Cleaning kit trapdoor assembly | 1 | 1 | 1 |
| 22 | 6P18.0-1 | 7115240124 | 03 | Receiver cover | 1 | 1 | 1 |
| 23 | 6L20.0-11 | 7114131531 | 03 | Magazine floor plate | 1 | 2 | 2 |
| 24 | 6P20.0-29 | 7114130183 | 07 | Trigger | 1 | 1 | 1 |
|  | or |  |  |  |  |  |  |
| 25 | 6P20.0-8 | 7114130157 | 09 | Same | 1 | 1 | 1 |
|  | 6P20.0-2 | 7114130151 | 04 | Hammer | 1 | 1 | 1 |
| 26 | 6P20.Sb 0-1 | 7114130132 | 07 | Firing mechanism | 1 | 1 | 1 |
| 27 | 6P18.4-4 | 7114120315 | 07 | Recoil spring retainer cap | 1 | 2 | 2 |
| 28 | 6L18.Sb | 7115130001 | 10 | Magazine , extended | 5 | 5 | 5 |
| 29 | 6P20.1-32 | 7114130239 | 08 | Front sight post | 1 | 5 | 5 |
| 30 | 6P18.Sb 4 | 7114130311 | 06 | Recoil mechanism assembly | 1 | 2 | 2 |
| 31 | 6P18.1-40 | 7114110204 | 07 | Upper handguard | 1 | 3 | 3 |
| 32 | 6P18.Sb 1-12 |  |  | Gas tube assembly | 1 | 2 | 2 |
| 33 | 6P18.Sb 4-1 | 7114130312 | 05 | Recoils spring guide | 1 | 1 | 1 |
| 34 | 6P20.0-13 | 7114130163 | 00 | Magazine catch axis pin | 3 | 3 |  |
| 35 | 6P20.0-32 | 7114130187 | 03 | Retarder base | 1 | 1 | 1 |
|  | or |  |  |  |  |  |  |
| 36 | 6P20.0-4 | 7114130153 | 02 | Retarder base | 1 | 1 | 1 |
|  | 6P19.0-26 |  |  | Stock latch hook axis pin | 1 | — | 1 |

| Line № | Designation or standard № | OKP code | Suf. | Name | Number used in the weapon, pcs. | Rate of application of spare parts for repair of 100 weapons | |
|---|---|---|---|---|---|---|---|
| | | | | | | 6P18 | 6P19 |
| 37 | 6P18.9-8 | 7114130169 | 05 | Bipod latch axis pin | 1 | 2 | 2 |
| 38 | 6P20.0-17 | 7114130238 | 09 | Retarder catch axis pin | 1 | 2 | 2 |
| 39 | 6P20.1-31 | | | Front sight base | 1 | 1 | 1 |
| 40 | 6P20.0-25 | 7113130178 | 04 | Firing mechanism axis pin | 5 | 5 | 5 |
| 41 | 6P20.5-11 | 7114130339 | 05 | Trapdoor cover axis pin | 1 | 5 | 5 |
| 42 | 6P18.9-10 | 7114130294 | 01 | Bipod axis pin | 1 | 1 | 1 |
| 43 | 6P20.3-10 | | | Extractor axis pin | 1 | 3 | 3 |
| 44 | 6P19.1-55 | | | Folding stock axis pin | 1 | — | 3 |
| 45 | 6P20.Sb 1-3 | 7114130202 | 10 | Selector lever assembly | 1 | 1 | 1 |
| 46 | 6P18.1-61 or 6P18.1-70 | 7114130151 | 08 | Flash hider / Same | 1 | 1 | 1 |
| 47 | 6P18.Sb 2 | 7115240189 | 05 | Rear sight leaf assembly | 1 | 1 | 1 |
| 48 | 6L20.Sb 0-2 or 6L18.0-1 | 7114131511 / 7114131701 | 07 / 03 | Magazine follower assembly / Magazine follower | 1 | 1 | 1 |
| 49 | 6L18.Sb 0-4 | | | Magazine lock plate spring | 1 | 4 | 4 |
| 50 | 6L18.0-9 | | | Magazine spring | 1 | 1 | 1 |
| 51 | 6L18.0-2 | | | Magaazine lock plate | 1 | 2 | 2 |
| 52 | 6P18.Sb 5 | 7115240251 | 05 | Buttstock assembly (for 6P18 and 6P18N1) | 1 | 2 | 2 |
| 53 | 6P19.Sb 5 | 7115240646 | 06 | Buttstock assembly (for 6P19) | 1 | — | 2 |
| 54 | 6P19H1.Sb 5 | | | Buttstock assembly (for 6P19N1 only) | 1 | — | 2 |

226

| Line № | Designation or standard № | OKP code | Suf. | Name | Number used in the weapon, pcs. | Rate of application of spare parts for repair of 100 weapons | |
|---|---|---|---|---|---|---|---|
| | | | | | | 6P18 | 6P19 |
| 55 | 6P20.0-6 | 7114130155 | 00 | Auto-sear spring | 1 | 2 | 2 |
| 56 | 6P20.0-3 | 7114130152 | 03 | Mainspring | 1 | 2 | 2 |
| 57 | 6P18.4-3 | 7114120314 | 08 | Recoil spring | 1 | 5 | 5 |
| 58 | 6P20.3-7 | 7114130289 | 09 | Extractore spring | 1 | 5 | 5 |
| 59 | 6P20.0-28 | 7114130182 | 08 | Retarder spring | 1 | 3 | 3 |
| 60 | 6P20.0-12 | 7114130162 | 01 | Magazine catch spring | 1 | 2 | 2 |
| 61 | 6P19.0-27 | | | Stock latch hook spring | 1 | — | 2 |
| 62 | 6P18.1-38 | | | Muzzle deveice retainer spring | 1 | 2 | 2 |
| 63 | 6P20.2-4 | 7114130504 | 10 | Rear sight elevation slide latch spring | 1 | 2 | 2 |
| 64 | 6P20.5-10 | 7114130337 | 07 | Trapdoor cover spring | 1 | 2 | 2 |
| 65 | 6P20.5-5 | 7114130335 | 09 | Cleaning kit case retainer spring | 1 | 1 | 1 |
| 66 | 6P20.0-23 | 7114130177 | 05 | Rear sight leaf spring | 1 | 2 | 2 |
| 67 | 6P18.9-11 | 7115240308 | 05 | Bipod spring | 1 | 2 | 2 |
| 68 | 6P19.1-53 | 7115240632 | 07 | Stock latch spring | 1 | 2 | 2 |
| 69 | 6P18.2-8 | 7115240201 | 04 | Windage adjustment tension spring | 1 | — | 1 |
| 70 | 6P20.0-10 | 7114130159 | 07 | Disconnector spring | 1 | 1 | 1 |
| 71 | 6P18.Sb 8 | | | Pistol grip | 1 | 2 | 2 |
| 72 | 6P18.Sb 1-14 | 7115130202 | 03 | Bipod assembly | 2 | 1 | 1 |
| 73 | 6P18.4-5 | 7114120316 | 06 | Forward guide rod for recoil spring | 1 | 1 | 1 |
| 74 | 6P20.3-5 | 7114130287 | 00 | Firing pim | 1 | 2 | 2 |

| Line № | Designation or standard № | OKP code | Suf. | Name | Number used in the weapon, pcs. | Rate of application of spare parts for repair of 100 weapons | |
|---|---|---|---|---|---|---|---|
| | | | | | | 6P18 | 6P19 |
| 75 | 6P20.1-41 | 7111130252 | 00 | Upper handguard retainer spring | 1 | 7 | 7 |
| 76 | 6P18.2-6 | 7115240198 | 04 | Windage adjustment lock knob | 1 | 1 | 1 |
| 77 | 6P18.1-37 | | | Flash hider retainer pin | 1 | 1 | 1 |
| 78 | 6P20.2-2 | 7114130502 | 01 | Rear sight elevation slide | 1 | 2 | 2 |
| 79 | 6P18.Sb 6 | 7115240281 | 10 | Lower handguard assembly | 1 | 3 | 3 |
| 80 | 6P18.2-5 | 7115240197 | 05 | Rear sight blade | 1 | 1 | 1 |
| 81 | 6P18.Sb 1-6 | 7114110167 | 06 | Gas tube latch assembly | 1 | 3 | 3 |
| 82 | 6P18.1-28 | | | Lower handguard retainer latch | 1 | 1 | 1 |
| 83 | 6P20.0-9 | 71HI30158 | 08 | Disconnector | 1 | 1 | 1 |
| 84 | 6P18.2-10 | | | Windage adjustment nut pin | 1 | 2 | 2 |
| 85 | 6P20.3-2 | 7114130283 | 04 | Gas piston | 1 | 1 | 1 |
| 86 | 6P19.1-54 | | | Stock latch pin | 1 | — | 2 |
| 87 | 6P20.3-9 | 7114130293 | 02 | Firing pin retaining pin | 1 | 5 | 5 |
| 88 | 6P20.3-3 | 7114130284 | 03 | Gas piston pin | 1 | 2 | 2 |
| 89 | 6P20.5-4 | 7114130333 | 00 | Sling swivel screw | 2 | 3 | — |
| 90 | 6P20.5-3 | 7114130329 | 07 | Buttstock / butt plate screw | 4 | 5 | 5 |

228

# RATE OF APPLICATION OF MATERIALS FOR MEDIUM LEVEL REPAIRS
## 5.45-mm KALASHNIKOV LIGHT MACHINE GUNS
### (6P18, 6P19, 6P18N1, 6P19N1)

| Material | OKP code | Material characteristics | | | Unit of measurement | Rate of application for repair of 100 weapons | |
|---|---|---|---|---|---|---|---|
| | | type, grade | № of standard | variation (dimebsion, № of standard) | | 6P18 | 6P19 |
| **Rolled ferrous metal** | | | | | | | |
| Steel hot-rolled structural carbon quality bars | 0950100000 | Steel 50 | GOST 1050-74 | Round Ø 50 mm GOST 2590-71 | kg | 0.084 | 0.108 |
| | | Steel 50 | GOST 1050-74 | Same, Ø 6.5 mm | kg | 0.214 | 9.218 |
| | | Steel 50 | GOST 1050-74 | Same, Ø 9.0 mm | kg | 0.342 | 0.342 |
| | | Steel 50 | GOST 1050-74 | Same, Ø 13.0 mm | kg | 3.343 | 0.343 |
| | | Steel 50 | GOST 1050-74 | Same, Ø 23.0 mm | kg | 0.110 | 0.110 |
| | | Steel 50 | GOST 1050-74 | Strip14×25 mm GOST 103-76 | kg | — | 0.105 |
| Total… | | | | | kg | 1.093 | 10.226 |
| **Products further recast** | | | | | | | |
| Steel billet carbon quality calibrated cold drawn | 1141000000 | Steel 50 | GOST 1051-73 | Round Ø 3.0 mm GOST 7417-75 | kg | 0.021 | 0.021 |

229

| Material | OKP code | Material characteristics | | | Unit of measurement | Rate of application for repair of 100 weapons | |
|---|---|---|---|---|---|---|---|
| | | type, grade | № of standard | variation (dimebsion, № of standard) | | 6P18 | 6P19 |
| **Hardware** | | | | | | | |
| Carbon steel spring wire | 1221000000 | Grade 1 | GOST 9389-75 | Ø 0.5 mm GOST 9389-75 | kg | 0.001 | 0.001 |
| | | Grade 1 | GOST 9389-75 | Ø 0.56 mm GOST 9389-75 | kg | 0.003 | 0.003 |
| | | Grade 1 | GOST 9389-75 | Ø 0.6 mm GOST 9389-75 | kg | 0.002 | 0.002 |
| | | Grade 1 | GOST 9389-75 | Ø 0.8 mm GOST 9389-75 | kg | 0.003 | 0.003 |
| | | Grade 1 | GOST 9389-75 | Ø 0.9 mm GOST 9389-75 | kg | — | 0.004 |
| | | Grade 1 | GOST 9389-75 | Ø 1.0 mm GOST 9389-75 | kg | 0.023 | 0.023 |
| | | Grade 1 | GOST 9389-75 | Ø 1.4 mm GOST 9389-75 | kg | 0.008 | 0.008 |
| | | Grade 1 | GOST 9389-75 | Ø 1.5 mm GOST 9389-75 | kg | 0.034 | 0.034 |
| | | Grade 1 | GOST 9389-75 | Ø 1.6 mm GOST 9389-75 | kg | — | 0.010 |
| Total... | | | | | kg | 0.074 | 0.088 |
| Wire made of carbon structural steel | 1221000000 | Steel 50 | GOST 17305-71 | Ø 1.5 mm GOST 17305—71 | kg | 0.001 | 0.001 |
| | | Steel 40 | GOST 17305-71 | Ø 2.5 mm GOST 17305—71 | kg | 0.013 | 0.013 |

| Material | OKP code | Material characteristics | | | Unit of measurement | Rate of application for repair of 100 weapons | |
|---|---|---|---|---|---|---|---|
| | | type, grade | № of standard | variation (dimebsion, № of standard) | | 6P18 | 6P19 |
| | | Steel 40 | GOST 17305-71 | Ø 3.0 mm GOST 17305—71 | kg | — | 0.045 |
| Total... | | | | | kg | 0.014 | 0.059 |
| Steel wire welding | 1211010000 | SV-08 | GOST 2246-70 | Ø 2 mm GOST 2246-70 | kg | 0.300 | 0.300 |
| Tape cold-rolled spring steel | 1231000000 | U8A | GOST 2283-79 | Tape 1.45×14 mm GOST 2283-79 | kg | 0.021 | 0,021 |
| Tape cold-rolled carbon structural steel | 1231000000 | Steel 50 | GOST 2284-79 | Same, 0.45×26 mm GOST 2284-79 | kg | 0.007 | 0.007 |
| | | Steel 50 | GOST 2284-79 | Same, 0.7×20 mm GOST 2284-79 | kg | 0.021 | 0.021 |
| | | Steel 50 | GOST 2284-79 | Same,1×34 mm GOST 2284-79 | kg | 0.043 | 0.043 |
| | | Steel 50 | GOST 2284-79 | Same,1×16 mm GOST 2284-79 | kg | — | 0.011 |
| Total... | | | | | kg | 0.071 | 0.082 |
| Coated metal electrodes for manual metal arc weld-ing and surfacing | 2720000000 | | GOST 9467-75 | GOST 9466-75 | kg | 0.500 | 0.500 |

| Material | OKP code | Material characteristics | | | Unit of measurement | Rate of application for repair of 100 weapons | |
|---|---|---|---|---|---|---|---|
| | | type, grade | № of standard | variation (dimebsion, № of standard) | | 6P18 | 6P19 |
| **Chemical products** | | | | | | | |
| Ammonium carbonate pure | 2621160781 | Ch | GOST 3770-75 | | kg | 0.250 | 0.250 |
| Calcium carbide | 2155310000 | | GOST 1460-81 | | kg | 0.300 | 0.300 |
| Potassium dichromate technical grade | 2146140100 | | GOST 2652-78 | | kg | 0.050 | 0.050 |
| Alcohol-soluble nigrosine | 2463229010 | A | GOST 9307-78 E | | kg | 0.160 | 0.160 |
| Polyvinyl butyral | 2215120301 | PSh | GOST 9439-85 | | kg | 0.640 | 0.640 |
| Paste PHZ (such as GOI) average | 2123241120 | № 3 | TU 6 18 178-80 | | kg | 0.010 | 0.010 |
| Rectified ethyl alcohol technical grade | 9182100000 | | GOST 18300-72 | | kg | 0.015 | 0.015 |
| Formaldehyde resin | | SFZh 309 (VIAM-B) | GOST 20907-75 | | kg | 0.200 | 0.200 |
| **Paint and varnish products** | | | | | | | |
| Primer phosphating | 2313630104 | VL-02 | GOST 12707-77 | | kg | 3.600 | 3.600 |
| Lacquer black | 2311130600 | BT-577 | GOST 5631-79 | | kg | 0.050 | 0.050 |
| Varnish NC-62 black | 2314110102 | | OST 6-10-391-74 | | kg | 0.050 | 0.050 |
| Varnish NC-5119 | 2314113500 | | OST 6-10 392-76 | | kg | 1.000 | 1.000 |

| Material | OKP code | type, grade | № of standard | variation (dimebsion, № of standard) | Unit of measurement | Rate of application for repair of 100 weapons 6P18 | Rate of application for repair of 100 weapons 6P19 |
|---|---|---|---|---|---|---|---|
| Varnish NTs-5119 | 2314114100 | | OST 6 10 392-76 | | kg | 0.500 | 0.500 |
| Solvent | 2319130300 | 646 | GOST 18188-72 | | kg | 3.600 | 3.600 |
| Adhesive phenolpolyvinyl-acetate | 2252110103 | BF 4 | GOST 12172-74 | | kg | 0.100 | 0.100 |
| Solvent Carboniferous technical grade | 2415710130 | 1st Grade A | GOST 1928-79 | | kg | 4.800 | 4.800 |
| **Pulp and Paper products** | | | | | | | |
| Newsprint | 5431112200 | B | GOST 6445-74 E | | kg | 0.200 | 0.200 |
| **Products of the textile industry** | | | | | | | |
| Wiper rags assorted fine | 8181000000 | Art. 625 | TU 63-178 77-82 | | kg | 0.800 | 0.800 |
| Cotton wool, furniture | 8195331110 | Art. 11 | GOST 5679-74 | | kg | 0.100 | 0.100 |
| Bleached household muslin | 8319600000 | Art. 6439 | GOST 11109-74 | | M | 1.200 | 1.200 |
| **Fuel and lubricant materials** | | | | | | | |
| Spindle oil | 0253410101 | AU | GOST 1642-75 | | kg | 6.000 | 6.000 |

233

| Material | OKP code | Material characteristics | | | Unit of measurement | Rate of application for repair of 100 weapons | |
|---|---|---|---|---|---|---|---|
| | | type, grade | № of standard | variation (dimebsion, № of standard) | | 6P18 | 6P19 |
| Lubricant rifle liquid | 0254530102 | RZh | GOST 9811-61 | | kg | 6.000 | 6.000 |
| **Miscellaneous materials** | | | | | | | |
| Brush, panel KFK | 4833270000 | № 8 | GOST 10597-80 | | pc. | 0.500 | 0.500 |
| Oxygen, gaseous technical Grade | 2114110100 | | GOST 5583-78 | | M3 | 0.200 | 0.200 |
| Contact paper | 0258120100 | | OST 38 0116-76 | | kg | 0.040 | 0.040 |
| Laundry soap solid | 9144110000 | | GOST 790-69 | | kg | 0.100 | 0.100 |
| Seals metal alloy type I | | | GOST 18677-73 | Size 6×10 mm GOST 18677—73 | kg | 0.020 | 0.020 |
| ADIM | 8378070000 | | GOST 4403-77 | | dm | 4.800 | 4.800 |
| Silk fabrics for screens | | | GOST 12285-77 | | 2 | 0.200 | 0.200 |
| Charcoal cloth (hemp) | 3985000000 | grit 12 | GOST 5009-82 | | kg | 0.200 | 0.200 |
| Sandpaper 2 740 × 50.S2.24A.12MA | 3985000000 | grit 25 | GOST 5009-82 | | M | 0.200 | 0.200 |
| Sandpaper 2 740 × 50.S2.24A.25MA | 39850000 | grit 40 | GOST 5009-82 | | M | 0.200 | 0.200 |
| Sanpaper 2 740 × 50.S2.24A.40MA | | | | | M | | |

# REGISTRATION LIST OF CHANGES OF CONTENTS

| Changes | Number of sheets (pages) | | | | Total sheets (pages) in document | Document № | Belongs to № of accompanying document | Signature | Date |
|---|---|---|---|---|---|---|---|---|---|
| | modified | replaced | new | removed | | | | | |
| | | | | | | | | | |

# Table of Contents

## 5.45-mm KALASHNIKOV ASSAULT RIFLES AK74, AKS74 AND AKS74U AND 5.45-mm KALASHNIKOV LIGHT MACHINE GUN RPK74 AND RPKS74

Editor *A. M. Alekseeva*
Technical editor *M. V. Fedorova*
Proofreader *E. V. Yavorskaya*

| | |
|---|---|
| Type set 22./04/87, | Publuished 30/09/87, |

Paper size 60×90/16 ; Printed sheets 15; Defined printed sheets 15; Conventional die imprints 15,13; Publishers printed sheets 13,26

| | | |
|---|---|---|
| Ed.№ 5/3808 | Free of charge | Customer 191 |

Military Publishing House, 103160 Moscow, K 160
2nd Printing House of the Military Publishing House
19/065, Leningrad, D 65, Palace of PD, 10

www.ingramcontent.com/pod-product-compliance
Lightning Source LLC
Chambersburg PA
CBHW081433270326

41932CB00019B/3181